CW01214690

MALEBRANCHE'S THEORY *of the* SOUL

MALEBRANCHE'S THEORY *of the* SOUL

A Cartesian Interpretation

TAD M. SCHMALTZ

New York   Oxford
Oxford University Press
1996

Oxford University Press

Oxford   New York
Athens   Auckland   Bangkok   Bogota   Bombay
Buenos Aires   Calcutta   Cape Town   Dar es Salaam
Delhi   Florence   Hong Kong   Istanbul   Karachi
Kuala Lumpur   Madras   Madrid   Melbourne
Mexico City   Nairobi   Paris   Singapore
Taipei   Tokyo   Toronto

and associated companies in

Berlin   Ibadan

Copyright © 1996 by Oxford University Press, Inc.

Published by Oxford University Press, Inc.
198 Madison Avenue, New York, New York 10016

Oxford is a registered trademark of Oxford University Press, Inc.

All rights reserved. No part of this publication may be reproduced,
stored in a retrieval system, or transmitted, in any form or by any means,
electronic, mechanical, photocopying, recording, or otherwise,
without the prior permission of Oxford University Press.

Library of Congress Cataloging-in-Publication Data
Schmaltz, Tad M., 1960–
Malebranche's theory of the soul : a Cartesian interpretation /
Tad M. Schmaltz.
p.   cm.
Includes bibliographical references and index.
ISBN 0-19-510344-0
1. Malebranche, Nicolas, 1638–1715—Contributions in doctrine of
the soul.   2. Soul.   3. Philosophy of mind.   4. Descartes, René,
1596–1650—Influence.   I. Title.
B1898.S68S55   1996
128'.1'092—dc20   95-32041

1 3 5 7 9 8 6 4 2

Printed in the United States of America
on acid-free paper

For my parents

Jeanne Elizabeth and Norman John Schmaltz

PREFACE

This book derives from my interest in philosophical psychology in the Cartesian tradition. It is conventional to approach this area of study, as I have done in the past, by looking primarily at the writings of Descartes. There is good reason for this sort of approach, of course, since the Cartesian tradition has its source in these writings. Yet work informed by such an approach can give the misleading impression that Descartes and his followers adopted essentially the same account of the mind. The historical fact is that some of the later Cartesians, including Malebranche, were quite critical of fundamental elements of Descartes' own account. One reason for focusing here on Malebranche rather than Descartes is to highlight this significant but somewhat overlooked fact.

Yet I also have another reason for focusing on Malebranche rather than on other Cartesians critical of Descartes. Malebranche is distinguished from these critics by his attempt to argue, on Cartesian grounds, that our consciousness of our own soul produces a radically deficient knowledge of its nature. His discussion of this point is admittedly somewhat less prominent than his remarks on other issues (such as the nature of ideas) that have attracted much of the attention of commentators. Moreover, his conclusion that for Cartesians consciousness of the soul can yield only confused knowledge seems oddly out of step with the consensus among Descartes, his loyal followers, and his other Cartesian critics that the perception of the self is clear and distinct. Yet I think this undeniably idiosyncratic conclusion, which Malebranche attempted to defend in different ways on several different fronts, is essentially correct. In fact, I want to claim that this conclusion deepens our understanding of the Cartesian theory of mind by drawing attention to negative and limiting consequences of this theory that Descartes and others have failed to recognize. But I also firmly believe that Malebranche's discussion of the soul is deep and original in its own right, and that for this reason alone it deserves a more careful and detailed consideration than it has recently received.

Work on this book was made possible by a fellowship from the National Endowment for the Humanities, by various grants from the Duke University Research Council, and by a Junior Faculty Research Leave from Duke University. I want to acknowledge as well my debt to Karl Ameriks, Bob Sleigh, and Margaret Wilson for their generous support.

Nicholas Jolley and Owen Flanagan commented helpfully on early versions of parts of the book. Steven Nadler and an anonymous reader for Oxford University Press read the entire penultimate draft of the manuscript and offered sage advice as well as notice of various mistakes. Moreover, there are several improvements in my manuscript that are due to the efforts of Henry Krawitz, my manuscript editor at Oxford University Press. For all its remaining faults, this book is considerably better than it would have been without the assistance I have received.

Sections of chapter 2 include material first published in the *History of Philosophy Quarterly* and the *Philosophical Review*, and major portions of chapters 4 and 6 are based on material first published in the *Journal of the History of Philosophy* and the *British Journal for the History of Philosophy*, respectively. I am grateful to the editors of these journals for their kind permission to reproduce this material here.

On a more personal note, I owe an immense debt to my wife, Louise, for her unfailing love and encouragement. I am grateful also to my daughter, Johanna, for her particular interest in the progress of "the Nick book," as she called it (her younger brother, Sam, on the other hand, was blissfully unaware of its existence). I am happy to report to her here that the book is now finished.

CONTENTS

Introduction 3

PART I. Confused Consciousness of Modifications

1. THE COGITO 15
    1.1 The Cogito, Consciousness, and Sensation 16
        1.1.1 *The Cogito and Consciousness* 16
        1.1.2 *Consciousness and Sensation* 19
    1.2 The Cogito Argument 23
        1.2.1 *The Simple View of Existence* 23
        1.2.2 *General Principles and Substance* 26
        1.2.3 *The Paris Conference* 29
    1.3 The Cogito and the Nature of the Soul 35
        1.3.1 *Déchéance du Cogito* 35
        1.3.2 *Descartes' Response to Gassendi* 36
        1.3.3 *Consciousness and the Subjective View* 40

2. SENSATION 44
    2.1 Sensations and Body 45
        2.1.1 *Malebranche, Augustine, and Descartes* 45
        2.1.2 *Sensations, Occasionalism, and Bodily Qualities* 49
        2.1.3 *Sensation and the Teachings of Nature* 59
    2.2 Two Kinds of Knowledge 63
        2.2.1 *Knowledge of Body through a Clear Idea* 63
        2.2.2 *Knowledge of Soul through Inner Sentiment* 69

  2.3 Two Cartesian Arguments 78
    2.3.1 *Sensible Qualities as Modifications of the Soul* 78
    2.3.2 *Knowledge of Sensation through Experience* 84

3. PURE PERCEPTION 93
  3.1 Pure Understanding and Sentiment 94
    3.1.1 *Pure Understanding and Pure Perception* 94
    3.1.2 *Sentiment and Sensation* 101
  3.2 Idea, Sensation, and Pure Perception 109
    3.2.1 *The Idea of Extension* 109
    3.2.2 *Sensation and Pure Perception* 114

PART II. Clear Demonstrations of Properties

4. SPIRITUALITY 127
  4.1 Malebranche on Spirituality 129
    4.1.1 *Two Views of Consciousness* 129
    4.1.2 *Malebranche's Cartesian Argument* 136
  4.2 The Cartesians and Malebranche's Argument 142
    4.2.1 *Arnauld's Critiques and Malebranche's Argument* 142
    4.2.2 *Cartesian Sources for Malebranche's Argument* 146
  4.3 Descartes and the Real Distinction Argument 149
    4.3.1 *The Sufficiency Thesis and Materialism* 149
    4.3.2 *The Idea of Body and the Unextended Mind* 156

5. IMMORTALITY 163
  5.1 Descartes' Proof of Immortality 164
    5.1.1 *The Possibility of a Proof* 164
    5.1.2 *The Proof in the* Synopsis 165
  5.2 Malebranche's Proof of Immortality 170
    5.2.1 *Animal Souls and Immortality* 171
    5.2.2 *The Proof in the* Recherche 173
    5.2.3 *The Proof in the* Entretiens sur la mort 180
  5.3 Desgabets on the Indefectibility of Substance 184
    5.3.1 *Matter, the Void, and Indefectibility* 184
    5.3.2 *Eternal Truths, Substance, and the Divine Will* 187

6. FREEDOM 192
  6.1 The Nature of the Will 193

   6.1.1 *Bodily Motion and the Will* 193
   6.1.2 *Spiritual Habits, Moral Worth, and the Will* 197
 6.2 The Nature of Freedom 204
   6.2.1 *The Cartesian Proof of Freedom* 204
   6.2.2 *Descartes on Freedom, Indifference, and Divine Power* 207
   6.2.3 *The Cartesians on Mental Causation and Motion* 213
   6.2.4 *Malebranche on Freedom and the Motion of the Will* 217

Notes 235
Bibliography 289
Index 303

MALEBRANCHE'S
THEORY
of the
SOUL

La vie de Caesar n'a poinct plus d'exemple que la nostre pour nous; et emperière, et populaire, c'est tousjours une vie que tous accidents humains regardent. Escoutons y seulement: nous nous disons tout ce de quoy nous avons principalement besoing.

The life of Caesar is no more of an example for us than our own; whether imperial or common, it is always a life subject to all human accidents. Let us only listen: we tell ourselves all we principally need.

Les difficultez et l'obscurité ne s'aperçoivent en chacune science que par ceux qui y ont entrée. Car encore faut il quelque degré d'intelligence à pouvoir remarquer qu'on ignore, et faut pousser à une porte pour sçavoir qu'elle nous est close. D'où naist cette Platonique subtilité, que, ny ceux qui sçavent n'ont à s'enquerir, d'autant qu'ils sçavent, ny ceux qui ne sçavent, d'autant que pour s'enquerir il faut sçavoir de quoy on s'enquiert. Ainsin en cette-cy de se cognoistre soy mesme, ce que chacun se voit si resolu et saisfaict, ce que chacun y pense estre suffisamment entendu, signifie que chacun n'y entend rien du tout....

—Montaigne, "De l'experience," *Essais*

The difficulties and obscurity in each science are perceived only by those who have access to it. For again some degree of intelligence is necessary to be able to notice that one is ignorant, and it is necessary to push against a door to know that it is closed to us. Whence is born this Platonic subtlety, that neither those who know need inquire, since they know, nor those who do not know, since in order to inquire it is necessary to know what one is inquiring about. Thus in this matter of knowing oneself, that each finds himself so resolute and satisfied, that each thinks he understands himself sufficiently, signifies that each understands nothing at all about it....

INTRODUCTION

There is something deeply puzzling about the theory of the soul that emerges from the writings of Nicolas Malebranche (1638–1715). From the time of his first published work, the *Recherche de la Vérité* (1674–75), Malebranche adopted several fundamental tenets of the theory of the soul or mind in Descartes.[1] For instance, a section of this text is devoted to a defense of Descartes' argument for the certainty of our knowledge of our own existence. Moreover, in this and later writings Malebranche endorsed the ontological core of Descartes' dualism, namely, the thesis that the soul (thinking substance) is distinct from the body (extended substance) and also attempted to argue, in a Cartesian manner, for the immortality of the soul and the freedom of the will. Yet in the *Recherche* he concluded—in striking contrast to Descartes' official doctrine that "the nature of the human mind" is "better known than body" (*Second Med.*, AT VII 23/CSM II 16)—that "we do not have a knowledge of the nature of the soul as perfect as that of the nature of body" (RV III-2.7, OCM I 451/LO 238).[2] Such a conclusion is not limited to this text; as we will see, it is present in later discussions by Malebranche not only of philosophical psychology but also of issues in moral theory and theology. What is so puzzling here is how someone as profoundly influenced by Descartes' account of mind as Malebranche apparently was could nonetheless be so firmly committed to this sort of skeptical and seemingly anti-Cartesian conclusion regarding our knowledge of the nature of the soul.

This puzzle has not been central to the renewed interest in Malebranche in the recent English literature, even though a significant portion of the new work focuses on his philosophy of mind and its relation to Cartesianism. What has been emphasized is rather Malebranche's notorious doctrine of "the Vision of all things in God," that is, his claim that ideas are objects of our perceptions that exist in God's mind.[3] It is not wholly surprising that this doctrine is taken to be relevant to the issue of the nature of Malebranche's Cartesianism. The topic of the nature of ideas was after all quite prominent in his debate with his most famous Cartesian adversary, Antoine Arnauld (1612–94), a debate which began significantly enough with a work from Arnauld bearing the title, *Des vraies et des fausses idées*. The recent work on Malebranche's doctrine of the vision in God has advanced our understanding of Malebranche's psychology, moreover, leading to a hightened awareness that when he said that we see all things in God, he meant that we have intellectual perceptions that are intentionally directed toward abstract or general ideas in God's mind.

Yet this understanding of Malebranche's account of ideas fails to touch important elements of his theory of the soul and its relation to Cartesianism. Though the account of ideas does bear on Malebranche's view of intellectual perception, its main point is that ideas exist in God rather than in us. Thus the account itself is related only indirectly to the issue of the nature of our own soul. And while Malebranche's discussion of intellectual perception has strong Cartesian components, it was not Descartes who was the primary inspiration for his view of the ideas that are the objects of this perception. Beginning with the *Recherche*, and throughout his later writings, Malebranche cited Augustine as the authority for his position that such ideas are eternal and immutable features of the divine understanding.[4] He even came to emphasize that this Augustinian position is incompatible with Descartes' own doctrine that God has created the eternal truths.[5]

When Malebranche considered the topic of the nature of the soul more directly he tended to focus on sensations rather than on intellectual perceptions. The authority for his account of sensation, moreover, was Descartes rather than Augustine. Indeed, Malebranche pointed out that since Augustine could not free himself from the prejudice that colors, for instance, are genuine properties of bodies, one must correct his view by taking into account advances that derive from the work of Descartes. In particular, one must apply the argument in Descartes that since bodily modifications are known clearly through the idea of extension, and since colors and other sensible qualities are perceived only in a confused manner, the sensible qualities are only modifications of the soul. Yet Malebranche also urged in the *Recherche* that this Cartesian argument reveals that our clear knowledge of bodily modifications is superior in kind to our confused consciousness of sensible qualities. He himself suggested that it was Augustine who led him to see that ideas are located in God, but Descartes who revealed to him that one can know the nature of the soul only in a radically imperfect manner.[6]

This is not to say that Malebranche took his negative thesis regarding our knowledge of the soul to be unrelated to his account of ideas. He in fact initially presented this thesis as a limiting feature of such an account. Immediately following his defense in the *Recherche* of the doctrine that "we see all things in God," Malebranche cautioned that "we see in God only the things of which we have ideas, and there are things we perceive without ideas, or know only through sentiment." He noted in particular that we do not know our own soul "through its idea—we do not see it in God; we know it only through consciousness, and because of this, our knowledge of it is imperfect" (RV III–2.7, OCM I 451/LO

237). Yet the difference here can be expressed in a manner that does not depend on the contentious ontological thesis that the ideas we perceive exist in God. Malebranche's main point is the epistemic one that our "consciousness" or "inner sentiment" of modifications of the soul such as sensations of colors, sounds, pleasure and pain is confused. He did emphasize with Descartes that such consciousness provides secure access to these modifications, and thus enables us to know the existence of our soul more immediately than the existence of body. Nonetheless, he also insisted contrary to Descartes' own official view that inner sentiment yields a knowledge of the nature of these modifications that is radically inferior to our knowledge of the nature of the modifications of extension.

While Malebranche clearly recognized the controversial nature of his account of ideas, and in the *Recherche* was concerned to respond in detail to opposing accounts, his remarks in this text regarding our knowledge of the soul make only a passing reference to "those who say that there is nothing one knows more than the soul, and those who say that there is nothing they know less" (OCM I 452/LO 238). Yet his own views are linked in a noteworthy manner to the related dispute between Descartes and his critic, Pierre Gassendi, over the thesis of the *Second Meditation* that the nature of mind is better known than the nature of body.[7] Gassendi had charged in his *Fifth Objections* that Descartes cannot claim to have established such a thesis prior to an examination of the internal nature of his mind "by a certain chemical-like labor" (AT VII 267–77/ CSM II 193), to which Descartes responded with some irritation that he can know his sensory thoughts directly without engaging in such labor (*Fifth Rep.*, AT VII 360/CSM II 249).[8] Malebranche proposed in the *Recherche* that his own view "serves to reconcile" dogmatic and skeptical claims concerning our knowledge of the soul, but his emphasis there on the imperfection of such knowledge is more in line with Gassendi's negative remarks. Moreover, just as Gassendi had protested in the *Disquisitio Metaphysica* (a follow-up to his *Fifth Objections*) that it cannot be the case that we know "the total nature of the mind" given that we know only a small portion of its attributes,[9] so Malebranche urged in the *Recherche* that our knowledge of the soul is imperfect since "the consciousness that we have of ourselves shows us only the least part of our being" (OCM I 451/LO 238). Far from forging a middle way, Malebranche seems simply to have sided with Gassendi against Descartes.[10]

To be sure, certain remarks in the *Recherche* are reminiscent of Descartes' claim against Gassendi that we can know our own sensations even without conducting "a chemical-like labor." In his text Malebranche responded to the position that we cannot know sensations since we cannot picture them in the corporeal imagination, for instance, by emphasizing that we can easily discern the differences among these sensations. His conclusion is that "there are some things that not being corporeal, cannot be represented to the mind through corporeal images, such as the soul and its modifications" (RV I.13, OCM I 143–47/LO 61–63). There is more than a little resemblance to Descartes' claim—directed against Gassendi's view that our idea of the human soul is "corporeal, or as if corporeal" (*Fifth Obj.*, AT VII 332/CSM II 230)—that someone who attempts to imagine the mind through a corporeal image "is attempting to imagine a thing not imaginable [since] a true idea of the mind contains only thoughts and its attributes, none of which is corporeal" (*Fifth Rep.*, AT VII 385/CSM II 264). Malebranche therefore cannot be characterized as a Gassendist.

By the same token, he cannot be characterized as an orthodox Cartesian. From the start he departed from the official Cartesian position that mind is better known than body. It is true that he failed in the *Recherche* to draw attention to this departure, focusing instead on the points of contact with the theory of mind in the writings of Descartes and the Cartesians. One commentator has attempted to explain this failure by claiming that Malebranche wanted to present himself in the *Recherche* as a Cartesian, and thus did not complicate matters by breaking openly with Descartes on an issue as fundamental as our knowledge of the soul. On this reading, Malebranche recognized from the beginning his radical differences from Descartes, but did not stress these differences for tactical reasons.[11] A closer inspection of the textual evidence, however, tends to support the different reading suggested by the remark in Ferdinand Alquié's valuable study *Le cartésianisme de Malebranche* that Malebranche "seems to have convinced himself little by little that the essence of the soul is not as easily accessible as Descartes had believed."[12] We will discover that while remarks in the initial edition of the *Recherche* tend to emphasize how much we can know about the soul, alterations in later editions serve to highlight the limitations of such knowledge. To my mind these changes indicate some sort of battle in which those features of Malebranche's theory of the soul that deviate from the official Cartesian line won out over his more orthodox pronouncements.

In any case, not long after the initial publication of the *Recherche* Malebranche acquired the conviction or confidence he needed to express openly his disagreement with Descartes. In the eleventh of the *Éclaircissements* published along with the third (1678) edition of this text, he noted that he found it necessary to defend his view in the earlier work regarding our knowledge of the soul because "the authority of Descartes, who clearly says that the nature of the mind is better known than the nature of any other thing, has so prejudiced some of his disciples" (OCM III 163/LO 633). Malebranche responded to the view of Descartes and his followers by developing points he had broached in the *Recherche*. Furthermore, Malebranche raised considerations not found in his earlier work when he mentioned "the ignorance of most men with regard to their own soul, of its distinction from the body, of its spirituality, of its immortality, and of its other properties" (OCM III 164/LO 633), as well as the fact that "we do not know what the dispositions of the soul consist in that make it readier to act and to represent objects to itself" (OCM III 169/LO 636). He concluded by emphasizing again that he made these additions to what he said in the *Recherche* "only because of the criticism it received from certain Cartesians" (OCM III 171/LO 638).

The Gassendist background to these remarks, as well as the fact that they are directed specifically against Descartes and the Cartesians, may seem to reveal that Malebranche's thesis that we do not know our soul through a clear idea of its nature is a radically anti-Cartesian feature of his system.[13] But there is another perspective—one that informs this study—that focuses on the claim in *Éclaircissement XI* that what the Cartesians themselves must say about various features of the soul actually supports such a thesis.[14] Such a claim indicates that Malebranche took his negative thesis concerning our knowledge of the soul to involve not so much a rejection of Cartesianism as an internal correction of it. This claim therefore serves to illustrate his remark, added to the final (1712) edition of the *Recherche*, that "I owe to Descartes or to his manner of doing philosophy the sentiments that I oppose to his own, and the boldness to criticize him" (RV VI–2.9, OCM II 449/LO 526).[15]

"Le grand Arnauld," for one, did not take kindly to Malebranche's corrections to Descartes' theory of mind. In a 1680 letter in which he reported his largely favorable initial reactions to the *Recherche*, Arnauld nonetheless warned that the position in this text that "we know our soul only by sentiment, and that we do not have an idea of what it is substantially" seems to weaken the belief in the spirituality and the immortality of the soul.[16] In fact, this reservation concerning Malebranche's account of our knowledge of the soul predates his Jansenist worries about the doctrine of grace in Malebranche's *Traité de la Nature et de la Grâce* (1680), worries that led him to reject the account of ideas in the *Recherche*. It is not surprising, then, that in his *Vraies et fausses idées* (1683), Arnauld devoted a section to criticism of Malebranche's doctrine that we do not know the soul through a clear idea of its nature.[17] Malebranche rose to this initial attack in his *Réponse* (1684) to Arnauld (c. 23, OCM VI 160–64), and returned to his negative doctrine concerning our knowledge of the nature of the soul throughout his extended public debate with his Cartesian adversary.[18] The discussion of this topic admittedly is brief in relation to the prolix remarks on both sides concerning the nature of ideas. But this brevity should not cause us to overlook the importance of Malebranche's negative doctrine to his view of what is valuable in the work of Descartes and the Cartesians.

Malebranche's contributions to the Cartesian philosophy of mind can usefully be contrasted with the contributions of two other Cartesians known to him, the Saumur physician Louis de la Forge (1632–66) and the French Benedictine Robert Desgabets (1610–78). La Forge is perhaps the better known, and certainly the more orthodox, of the two. He worked with Descartes' friend and editor, Claude Clerselier, to produce *L'Homme de René Descartes*, which was published in 1664 with La Forge's *Remarques*. Apparently it was a new copy of this edition that roused an intense interest in Cartesianism in the newly ordained Malebranche, who prior to ordination had been a rather uninspired theological student in the Oratory. The work itself, however, does not provide the most complete statement of the Cartesian programme. Descartes announced at the start that he intended to discuss first the body on its own, then the soul on its own, and finally the nature of the union between soul and body (AT XI 119–20/CSM I 99), but he went on to address in detail only the first topic. In his *Traité de l'esprit de l'homme* (1666), La Forge attempted to complete *L'Homme* by presenting an account of the human mind and of its union with body that is faithful to what Descartes had written.[19]

An indication of this fidelity is the title of the second chapter of the *Traité*, "Of the nature of the mind of man, and that it is easier to know than the body," which is simply a paraphrase of the title of the *Second Meditation*. In the chapter proper, La Forge wrote that "my soul, that is to say, this substance that thinks in me, is more easily known than the body, or extended substance, since the most hypothetical doubts cannot make me doubt its existence; and since I discover an infinity of properties of my thought before I can only dream of searching for those of body."[20] Malebranche had a copy of La Forge's text in his library, and there is evidence that he referred to it in writing the *Recherche*.[21] Though in the *Recherche* he chose not to emphasize his rejection of the Cartesian position of the *Traité* that the nature of mind "is easier to know than the body," it is safe to say that he was thinking of La Forge, among others, when he referred in *Éclaircissement XI* to disciples prejudiced by the authority of Descartes.

Malebranche was even more critical of the work of Desgabets, but for different reasons. The immediate occasion for the public encounter between the two was the publication in 1675 of the *Critique de la Recherche de la Vérité*. Written by Simon Foucher, the canon of the Sainte Chapelle of Dijon, who was a skeptical critic of Cartesianism, this work attacked Malebranche's remarks in the volume containing the first three books of the *Recherche*.[22] Desgabets took it upon himself to defend Malebranche in his *Critique de la Critique de la recherche de la vérité*.[23] Malebranche expressed his displeasure with Desgabets' defense in an "Avertissement" added to the second volume of the *Recherche*, in which he wrote that "those who take it upon themselves to defend or to combat others, must read their works with some attention in order to know well their sentiments" (OCM II 500).[24]

This remark is understandable given that Desgabets was concerned to defend against Foucher's objections the position that ideas are modifications of our soul that represent external objects, even though Malebranche himself had rejected such a position in the *Recherche*.[25] Desgabets' acceptance of this view places him on the side of Cartesian critics of Malebranche such as Arnauld, who arguably were more faithful to Descartes' own account of ideas than was Malebranche.[26] Nonetheless, on other issues Desgabets intentionally deviated from the orthodox Cartesian line. Thus he wrote to Malebranche in 1674 that he was concerned to reveal "the faults that have appeared to me in the method of M. Descartes" (OCM XVIII 83). In the same letter Desgabets referred to his unpublished notes on the *Meditations*, the *Supplément à la philosophie de Descartes*, in which he rejected the orthodox Cartesian position that the soul is better known than body on the grounds that our knowledge of thought must involve a knowledge of body since all our thoughts bear an essential connection to motions in the brain.[27] In this work he further disowned the Cartesian project of doubting the senses so as to establish the existence of mind as a thinking thing, arguing that the presence of sensory thought establishes the existence of body as certainly as it establishes the existence of our soul.[28] Though in particular matters Desgabets followed Descartes closely,[29] with respect to issues concerning knowledge of the mind he felt himself free to reject central Cartesian doctrines.

Desgabets was not without admirers in the Cartesian community. The Cartesian natural philosopher Pierre-Sylvain Regis (1632–1707) called him "one of the greatest metaphysicians of our century."[30] As I indicate below, the influence of Desgabets is apparent in Regis' 1690 *Système de philosophie*, and even more so in his 1704 *Usage de la raison et de la foy*.[31] Desgabets' opinions drew a more critical response, however, from other Cartesians. In the 1840s French scholars discovered manuscripts pertaining to a series of conferences that apparently took place in Commercy in 1677, at which the organizer, the French Cardinal de Retz (Jean-François Paul de Gondi), as well as other "disciples of Descartes" presented reservations concerning Desgabets' objections to Descartes.[32] It is evident from these manuscripts that the conferences were based on a number of unpublished writings contributed by Desgabets, including his *Descartes à l'alambic*, a work that reflects the criticisms in the *Supplément* of Descartes' method of doubt as well as of his account of knowledge of the human soul.[33] After his arrival in Commercy in June 1677, the Italian scholar Jean de Corbinelli, a distant cousin and confidant of the cardinal, contributed to these discussions by providing summaries of Desgabets' objections to Descartes. Within a month of his arrival, Corbinelli departed for Paris, apparently in order to participate in a session on these objections that involved various Cartesians, including Malebranche.[34] This Paris conference, which took place in August or September 1677, was devoted in particular on Desgabets' objections to Descartes' cogito argument. We know from the record that we have of the conference that Malebranche provided the responses to Desgabets on behalf of the Cartesians. Malebranche did not always see Desgabets as an opponent of Cartesianism; indeed, there is evidence that he sometimes had Desgabets in mind when characterizing the Cartesian position.[35] Nonetheless, it is clear that with respect to issues involving our knowledge of our own soul, he was a more orthodox Cartesian than was Desgabets.

Malebranche therefore took as his model neither La Forge's modest extension of Descartes' theory of mind, nor Desgabets' radical revision of it. Like Desgabets and unlike La Forge, he was concerned to reject Descartes' views concerning our knowledge of the nature of the soul. And like Desgabets again, he focused on certain difficulties for Descartes that derive from the nature of sensory thought. Unlike Desgabets and like La Forge, however, Malebranche adopted the main elements of Descartes' argument for the existence of the soul. And unlike Desgabets again, he was faithful to Descartes' view that the soul has non-sensory or intellectual thoughts that cannot be correlated with motions in the brain.[36] In Malebranche there is an unprecedented attempt to offer a critique of Descartes' doctrine that mind is better known than body that is internal to Descartes' own system. At times Malebranche's critical remarks are directed more at certain of Descartes' followers, and concern Descartes himself only indirectly. Moreover, some of the views he claimed to take from Descartes differ in various ways from what can be found in Descartes' own writings. Nonetheless,

Malebranche had a unique perspective on Descartes since he was, unlike La Forge, a critic of the Cartesian system who, unlike Desgabets, accepted many of its fundamental doctrines concerning the soul.

Malebranche did of course call for modifications in the official Cartesian view of the soul, and thus can be seen as part of a group of "revisionary" Cartesians that includes Desgabets and Regis. A focus on this aspect of Malebranche is useful, moreover, insofar as it brings to light the somewhat overlooked complexity of later Cartesian discussions of mind. Such a focus can serve to reveal, in particular, that the doctrine that mind is better known than body simply was not sacrosanct among Descartes' followers. It is important not to overlook the fact, however, that Malebranche's rejection of this doctrine differs significantly from the rejection in Desgabets and Regis. I have already alluded to the fact that Malebranche distanced himself from the view in Desgabets, found also in Regis, that we know equally well the *existence* of soul and body. On the other hand, the position common to Desgabets and Regis that we also know equally well the *nature* of soul and body brought them into direct conflict with the claim in Malebranche that the nature of body is better known to us than the nature of the soul. Malebranche's revisionary theory of the soul was therefore attacked both by these more radical critics to his "left," as well as by more conservative critics such as Arnauld to his "right." The fact that the criticism of this theory was so widespread among Cartesians raises some question about its own Cartesian credentials. I am concerned to argue, however, that the critics both left and right failed to come to grips with Malebranche's claim that his theory of the soul has a significant Cartesian basis. There is thus an important ambiguity in the subtitle of this study: the interpretation here of Malebranche's theory presents it as fundamentally Cartesian, and thereby serves to reinforce his own view that he has provided an authoritative interpretation of the account of mind in the writings of Descartes and other Cartesians.

My study of Malebranche's theory of the soul has two main parts. In the first I consider directly Malebranche's thesis that the knowledge of the nature of the modifications of the soul that derives from consciousness or inner sentiment is itself confused. Such a thesis must be balanced against Malebranche's acceptance of the claim, deriving from Descartes' cogito argument, that we have direct access to our thoughts by means of consciousness; I take up his discussion of this claim, as well as his consideration of Descartes' argument, in chapter 1. There I also introduce a reading on which Malebranche held that inner sentiment is restricted to a subjective view of our own modifications that while being immediate and certain, is nonetheless radically inferior to the objective view of bodily modifications that derives from the clear idea of extension. This point about the inferiority of our subjective view of our own modifications is most evident in those passages in which Malebranche emphasized the distinction between confused sensory modifications in us and clear ideas in God. I have urged that his view that clear ideas exist in God is more Augustinian than Cartesian. But I argue in chapter 2 that his account of sensation is beholden to, even while it modifies, the account in Descartes. This chapter indicates as well that Malebranche's defense of the claim that we have only a confused inner sentiment of ourselves is relevant to the development of Descartes' account of sensation in the writings of the Cartesians. Indeed, some of Malebranche's remarks seem to suggest that all of the modifications to which inner sentiment gives access are sensory, a suggestion that is at some odds with his acceptance of Descartes' position that we have intellectual perceptions distinct from our sensations. To remove this difficulty we need an account that explains why Malebranche's discussion of consciousness or inner sentiment focuses so much on the case of sensation, but at the same time shows that this discussion is compatible with his acceptance of intellectual or pure perceptions; I attempt to provide such an account in chapter 3. I conclude that while Malebranche's own view of pure perception and its relation to sensation is not free of difficulty, it nonetheless serves to reinforce his main thesis that we have only a confused consciousness of our own soul.

The structure of the second part of this study derives from Arnauld's objection to Malebranche that since "one can demonstrate nothing about an object of which he does not have a clear and distinct vision," it follows that "if we did not have a clear and distinct vision of the soul, we could demonstrate neither its immortality, nor its spirituality, nor its freedom."[37] In particular, this part focuses on Malebranche's argument that his negative thesis concerning our knowledge of the soul does not preclude the Cartesian project of constructing clear and evident demonstrations of the three properties of the soul mentioned by Arnauld: spirituality, immortality, and freedom. In chapter 4 I consider the evolution in Malebranche's writings resulting in an indirect demonstration of spirituality that proceeds from the premise that the nature of body consists in extension to the conclusion that the substance that thinks cannot be a body. I conclude that while such a demonstration is anticipated more clearly in the writings of certain Cartesians than in Descartes' own works, it nonetheless has some claim to his attention. In chapter 5 I turn to Malebranche's proof of the immortality of the soul, which is more directly connected to the proof of this property in Descartes. A claim running through Malebranche's discussion of both arguments (though one that is more prominent in his discussion of the argument for spirituality) is that Cartesians depend on the clear idea of extension for their knowledge of the nature of the soul. He argued in effect that Cartesians can offer only what the important French scholar, Martial Gueroult, has called a "pseudo-psychologie rationnelle";[38] a psychology that is "pseudo" because it does not derive from a clear idea of thought, but that is "rationnelle" because it does derive from a clear idea of extension. This latter idea does not play a central role in Malebranche's demonstration of the absolute freedom of the will, which following Descartes' own demonstration relies simply on consciousness or inner sentiment. Yet as I indicate in chapter 6, Malebranche insisted that Cartesians know through a clear idea of the soul neither the dispositions of the will that prepare for its action, nor its own power to act freely. As in the case of his discussion of the soul in general, so his discussion of freedom has both a positive and a negative side. I am not concerned here to defend the positive aspects of Malebranche's account of properties of the soul such as freedom; indeed, I argue that his own demonstrations of these properties are in varying degrees problematic. I can only conclude, then, that his rational psychology is to some extent a failure. But what I hold does not fail is Malebranche's negative argument—which is linked to the notion of Cartesian psychology as *pseudo*-rational—that on their own terms Descartes and his followers do not possess a clear objective view of that which constitutes the nature of the substance that thinks.

Part I

Confused Consciousness of Modifications

one

THE COGITO

One would expect that any Cartesian theory of the soul must start from the famous proposition *cogito ergo sum*, which Descartes took to be "the first and most certain of all to occur to anyone who philosophizes in an orderly way" (PP I.7. AT VIII–1 7/CSM I 195). It is therefore surprising that only in the final book of his main text, *Recherche de la Vérité*, did Malebranche offer a relatively brief discussion of the cogito argument. Moreover, whereas Descartes asserted in the *Third Meditation* that his knowledge of his own existence involves a perception of his mind that is the very model of a clear and distinct perception (AT VII 35/CSM II 24), Malebranche emphasized at several points in the *Recherche* that what we know of the nature of our soul through consciousness or inner sentiment is in fact confused and obscure. Thus French commentators have tended to emphasize, with Gueroult, that there is in Malebranche a *déchéance du cogito*.[1]

It cannot be denied that Malebranche held that our knowledge of our own soul is more limited than Descartes himself believed. But this difference is not properly considered apart from his somewhat neglected remarks on the soul that derive from Descartes. Malebranche accepted, with revisions and complications introduced by the work of La Forge, the view of Descartes that consciousness provides direct access to our thoughts, and to our sensory thoughts in particular. Moreover, Malebranche's claim that such thoughts reveal immediately the existence of our soul is best interpreted in light of Descartes' own discussion of the cogito argument. In response to objections raised by Desgabets, Malebranche once even defended the Cartesian position that we can know the existence of our soul without knowing that any body exists. It is evident that his account of our knowledge of our soul has a significant Cartesian component.

It is nonetheless true that when Malebranche mentioned these positive aspects of his account of our knowledge of the existence of the soul, he also often indicated that the nature of the soul is much less clear to us than the nature of body. He eventually came to admit that this negative thesis is incompatible with

Descartes' official doctrine, later defended by Arnauld, that mind is better known than body. Yet Malebranche supported his thesis by an examination of the very features of consciousness that allow Cartesians to conclude that they know with certainty the existence of their own soul.

1.1 The Cogito, Consciousness, and Sensation

1.1.1 The Cogito and Consciousness

(1) The Influence of La Forge. Though the fact that Malebranche considered the cogito argument only toward the end of the *Recherche* is surprising in light of Descartes' writings, it is rather unremarkable given La Forge's remarks in the *Traité*. It is only in the penultimate chapter of this work, after all, that La Forge himself discussed this argument. In this chapter he held, in line with Descartes' own position in the *Discourse*, that the proposition *Je pense donc je suis* is "the first certain conclusion that presents itself to those who seek the truth in order."[2] Moreover, La Forge concluded as Descartes had earlier,[3] that "I am walking, therefore I exist" is not as certain as "I am thinking, therefore I exist," since "I am not as assured that I am walking, when I believe that I am walking, as I am that I think, when I believe that I am thinking."[4] The late placement of the discussion of the cogito argument in the *Traité* in no way indicates a lack of commitment to this argument on La Forge's part.

There is reason to think that the *Traité* provided an important source for the final book of the *Recherche*, which considers the cogito argument.[5] While the *Recherche* itself is more negative than the *Traité*, emphasizing as it does the errors that arise from the various faculties of the soul,[6] it is interesting that in the final section of his text Malebranche sought to mitigate this negative tone by giving an account of "the order we must follow in our studies in order to avoid error." Moreover, he noted in this section that since there is a discussion of this order in "the works of others," "I shall content myself with reviewing them [i.e., the works]" (RV VI–2.6, OCM II 369/LO 480). It seems difficult to resist the conclusion that Malebranche was looking here to his copy of La Forge's *Traité*, and in particular to the chapter of this text on the cogito argument, bearing the title "Of the Principal Source of Our Errors, and of the Means of Evading Them."[7] In the chapter itself La Forge held—following again Descartes' remarks in the *Discourse*—that one must resolve complex problems into various parts in order that 'one may "begin with the most simple and the most easily known."[8] According to La Forge, our investigation of the complex properties of bodies must begin with a consideration of the nature of extension, for in order to know such properties "we have nothing other than [the notion] of extension, and afterwards those of shape and motion."[9] In a similar vein, Malebranche emphasized in the last book of the *Recherche* that "if, to avoid error, we should always preserve evidence in our reasonings, it is clear that we should reason on the basis of ideas of numbers and extension rather than on the confused or complex ideas of physics, morals, mechanics, chemistry, and all the other sciences" (RV VI–2.6, OCM II 373/LO 482).[10]

In light of these similarities, the positive remarks in the *Recherche* concerning the cogito argument take on added significance. Malebranche echoed La Forge's Cartesian position when he affirmed toward the end of this work that "[o]f all our knowledge, the first is of the existence of the soul" (RV VI–2.6, OCM II 369/LO 480). His additional remark that "all our thoughts are incontestable demonstrations" of our existence (OCM II 369/LO 480) moreover, reflects La Forge's emphasis on the case of thought. Malebranche was as firmly committed as La Forge to Descartes' basic position that we can know with certainty that we exist because we can infer our existence from something else that we know with certainty, namely, the fact that we are thinking.

(2) The Consciousness of Thought. Malebranche's acceptance of the premise that we can be certain that we are thinking is explained by his Cartesian account of the nature of thought. The starting point for such an account is his claim in the *Recherche* that

> by the words *thought, manner of thinking,* or *modification of the soul,* I understand generally all those things that cannot be in the soul without the soul perceiving [*apperçoive*] them through the inner sentiment [*intérieur sentiment*] that it has of itself—such as its sensations, imaginings, pure intellections, or simply conceptions, as well as its passions and natural inclinations. (RV III–2.1, OCM I 415/LO 218)

Whereas Malebranche referred here to a perception of thought through "inner sentiment," he spoke elsewhere of our knowledge of the soul through "consciousness" (*conscience*).[11] But nothing seems to hang on this difference in terminology since he identified consciousness and inner sentiment alike with the awareness of thought.[12]

Here again, there is a resemblance to remarks in the *Traité*. La Forge had written that "the nature of thought consists in this consciousness [*conscience*], this testimony, this inner sentiment [*sentiment intérieur*] by which the mind attends [*adverty*] to all that it undergoes [*souffre*], and generally all that passes immediately in it, at the same time that it acts or it suffers."[13] This similarity in terminology confirms the hypothesis that La Forge's text helped to shape Malebranche's position in the *Recherche* that we perceive all our thoughts through consciousness or inner sentiment.

The emphasis on consciousness common to Malebranche and La Forge derives ultimately from Descartes. In the *Second Replies* Descartes defined thought as "all that is in us in such a way that we are immediately conscious [*conscii*] of it. Thus all operations of the will, intellect, imagination, and the senses are thoughts" (AT VII 160/CSM II 113). Later in the *Principles* he spoke in the same way of thought as "all that which, we being conscious [*consciis*], are in us, insofar as the consciousness [*conscientia*] of them is in us. And thus not only to understand, to will, to imagine, but also to sense, is here the same as to think"

(PP I.9, AT VIII–1 7/CSM I 195). Geneviève Rodis-Lewis has argued that the French term "conscience," which is the equivalent of the Latin term 'conscientia' employed in the *Second Replies* and *Principles*, was used prior to Descartes in a moral rather than a psychological sense. This would explain why in Clerselier's French edition the passage from the *Second Replies* says that thought is "all that which is in us such that we have immediate knowledge [*connaissants*] of it" (AT IX–1 124), whereas in the French edition prepared by Claude Picot the passage from the *Principles* says that thought is "all that which is in us in such a way that we perceive [*appercevons*] it immediately by ourselves" (AT IX–2 28).[14] The reference in the French edition of the *Third Replies* to a "pensée, ou perception, ou conscience et connaissance" (AT IX–1 137) may well be the first case of the use of the French "conscience" in a nonmoral sense.[15] It seems to have been Descartes, then, who is the source of the view—adopted later by La Forge and thereafter by Malebranche—that we have a *conscience* of all our thoughts.

Descartes himself was not entirely clear, however, on the nature of our consciousness of thought. At one point he spoke of the soul's consciousness of its own thought as involving the thought "that it is thinking by means of a reflection [*reflexio*]" (*Seventh Rep.*, AT VII 559/CSM II 382), thereby seeming to hold that this consciousness involves a thought distinct from the thought of which the soul is conscious. In another text, though, he noted that the perception of a volition "is really one and the same thing as the volition" (PS I.19, AT XI 343/CSM I 336), thus indicating that at least in some cases the consciousness of a thought can be a feature of that very thought. La Forge opted for a more general form of the latter position when he noted in the *Traité* that he had stated that thought passes *immediately* in us "so that you know that this testimony and this inner sentiment is not different from the action or the passion, and that these are themselves what display [*advertissent*] that which occurs in us; and that you thus do not confuse this inner sentiment with the reflection we sometimes have of our actions, which is not found in all of our thoughts, of which it is only a species."[16]

Malebranche indicated that the inner sentiment or consciousness of a thought can be distinct from that thought when he noted early in the *Recherche* that it is by means of pure understanding that the soul perceives "generally all of its thoughts, when it knows by the reflection [*reflexion*] that it has of itself" (RV I.4, OCM I 66/LO 16). I believe, however, that he also allowed in this text for La Forge's position that the initial inner sentiment of a thought is a feature of that very thought. Thus in Book Three Malebranche equated sensing what takes place in us with the actual sensations of qualities such as pain, heat, and light (RV III–2.7, OCM I 451/LO 237). This position is anticipated by his claim in Book One that "it is the same thing for the soul to receive the manner of being that one calls pain, as it is to perceive or to sense pain, since it cannot receive pain in any other way than by perceiving it" (RV I.1, OCM I 43/LO 3). To have the modification of a pain, this passage implies, is simply to be conscious of that pain. Malebranche thus suggested that the immediate consciousness of sensory modifications is not distinct from the modifications themselves.

This reading indicates one way of understanding the claim that consciousness or inner sentiment reveals with certainty that we are thinking. Malebranche held that we can be certain only of what is accompanied by an "evidence" that is present just in case what is perceived "seem[s] so evidently true" that we cannot deny what we perceive "without sensing an inner pain and the secret reproaches of reason" (RV I.2, OCM I 55/LO 10).[17] He could say that we cannot deny without reproach that we are thinking when we first become aware of a thought through consciousness or inner sentiment on the grounds that this initial awareness is not distinct from that thought. La Forge offered just this position when he claimed that we have certain knowledge of our own thought since we know this thought only *par elle*, through or by means of itself.[18] He concluded from the fact that we know thought in this manner that "the testimony of our consciousness [*conscience*] assures us so certainly and so evidently that we have the faculty of thought, that I would be ridiculed if I would wish to furnish other proofs of this truth than that of our own experience [*expérience*]."[19] I have argued that there is a strong connection between discussions of our knowledge of our soul in the *Traité* and the *Recherche*. My suggestion here is that Malebranche simply assumed the view of La Forge, later adopted by other Cartesians, that the immediate consciousness of a thought must provide direct access to that thought given that this consciousness is simply an aspect of the thought itself.[20]

1.1.2 Consciousness and Sensation

In Book Six of the *Recherche* Malebranche indicated that he perceives with certainty not only that he thinks, but also "what I am thinking of" (RV VI–2.6, OCM II 370/LO 481). He had earlier attempted to illustrate this position by focusing on the case of sensation. Thus, he emphasized in Book One that "a person who burns his hand, for example, distinguishes quite well the pain that he senses from light, color, sound, tastes, odors, pleasures, and from all pains other than he senses.... We therefore know in some manner what we sense immediately, when we see colors, or have some other sensation" (RV I.13, OCM I 144/LO 61). The first edition version of this passage is somewhat stronger, implying that we know "with evidence and certitude what the pain is" (OCM I 144f). The reservation that we know our sensations only "in some manner," which was first added to the third edition (1678) (OCM I 144g), is more in line with Malebranche's official view that we do not know our modifications through a clear idea of the soul. Such a reservation also is linked to the more standard Cartesian position that we often falsely judge that the qualities we sense belong to external objects. Thus Malebranche noted that visionaries err in thinking that "what they see really exists externally because they see it externally." Nonetheless, he emphasized as well that it is certain that "they see what they see" (RV I.14, OCM I 160/LO 69–70). We can be certain that we have the sensations of which we are conscious, on his view, once we restrict ourselves to internal appearances and make no claims about how such appearances relate to the external world.

Descartes anticipated Malebranche's suggestion that we can be certain that we are experiencing a certain sort of sensory thought. In the *Second Meditation* Descartes argued that sensations can be attributed to the "I" that exists since they are simply a form of thought.

> Finally I am the same one who senses, or who observes [*animadverto*] corporeal things as if through the senses; clearly now I see light, hear sound, feel heat. This is false, for I sleep. But certainly I seem to see, to hear, to feel heat. This cannot be false; this is properly what in me is called sensing; and this strictly speaking is nothing other than to think. (AT VII 29/CSM II 19)

Just prior to this passage Descartes suggested that he cannot be certain that he has sensations, since these depend on the body, "and besides I seemed to sense in sleep many things that afterwards I observed [*animadverti*] that I had not sensed" (AT VII 27/CSM II 18). But this can be reconciled with his later remark that he can be certain that he has sensations by means of the distinction between actual sensation, which is caused by the bodily senses, and apparent sensation, which may only appear to be so caused. Descartes' position in effect is that while the supposition of the malicious genius provides reason to doubt that he has actual sensations, it cannot provide reason to doubt that he has an apparent sensation of a certain sort, since such a sensation is not distinct from his thought.

Passages like this support the view that for Descartes and the Cartesians incorrigibility or indubitability is the mark that distinguishes the mental from the physical.[21] But there may be grounds in Descartes for doubting the incorrigibility of our beliefs concerning our own sensory states. He did note at one point in the *Passions of the Soul* that the passions, or perceptions such as sadness that are referred to the soul,[22] "are so close and interior to our soul that it is impossible for the soul to feel them without their being really as the soul feels them" (*PS* I.26, AT XI 348/CSM I 388). Yet a few articles later he asserted that "experience teaches us that those who are most strongly agitated by their passions are not those who know them best" (*PS* I.28, AT XI 349–50/CSM I 339). It may well be the case, as one commentator has claimed, that Descartes was referring here merely to ignorance of proximate bodily causes of the passions.[23] But later in this text Descartes appears to have broached a different sort of ignorance when he mentioned the case of the husband who feels the passion of sorrow at the death of his wife yet at the same time has "a secret joy in his innermost soul" (*PS* II.147, AT XI 441/CSM I 381). He seems in particular to have allowed that the strong passion of the husband could prevent him from seeing clearly that he is feeling a distinct internal emotion of joy.[24] Admittedly, this line of thought concerns passions and internal emotions rather than apparent sensations of objects. Yet the suggestion that we can misclassify states that are interior to our soul seems to undermine the position that we cannot be mistaken about our apparent sensations simply because they are our thoughts.

It is interesting that Malebranche offered a case analogous to the one I have drawn from the *Passions* that indicates more explicitly than Descartes' own remarks that we can misclassify our own sensations. He invoked this case in the course of the discussion early in the *Recherche* of his claim that "a sensation that is agreeable to one person, is also so to all who sense it" (RV I.13, OCM I 151/LO 65).[25] Malebranche mentioned as a counterexample to such a claim that people who had formerly enjoyed eating a certain meat can later come to abhor it, say, because they once found foreign matter mixed in it while eating it. In this case, it seems, the same sensation of the taste of the meat that was once agreeable to these people is now abhorrent to them. Malebranche responded that when these people taste the meat they abhor, they actually have two sensations, the agreeable sensation of the meat and the abhorrent sensation that arises from the vivid imagination of the foreign matter. He then concluded that if they imagine that the sensation of eating the meat is abhorrent, "that is because it is joined and confounded with another that is more disgusting than it itself is agreeable" (OCM I 152/LO 65). Malebranche's view that people can have an agreeable sensation and yet not know it to be agreeable appears to be in some tension with his official position in Book Three of the *Recherche* that our consciousness of the modifications of our soul "does not involve us in error" (RV III–2.7, OCM I 453/LO 239).

There is a distinction in Descartes that sheds some light on this apparent tension. He wrote, in response to Arnauld's request for a clarification of the way in which "that reflection [*reflexio*], in which intellectual memory consists" differs from "the simple reflection [*reflexione*] intrinsic to all thought" (July 1648, AT V 213):

> [T]he first and simple thoughts of an infant (when they feel when some wind distends their intestines, or the pleasure they feel when nourished by sweet blood) I call direct, not reflex [*reflexas*]; however when an adult senses something, and simultaneously perceives that he has not sensed it before, I call this second perception reflection [*reflexionem*], and refer it to the intellect alone, although it is so linked to sensation that they are together and do not seem to be distinguished from each other. (29 July 1648, AT V 221/CSMK 357)

Descartes held, in effect, that consciousness of a direct thought must involve a distinct act of intellectual reflection. But on Arnauld's view such consciousness could be identified with the "simple reflection intrinsic to all thought." On my reading, Malebranche allowed for La Forge's related position that the immediate consciousness of a thought is simply a feature of that thought. I therefore hold that Malebranche could also allow that there is a sort of consciousness of sensation that is not distinct from Descartes' direct sensory thought. Let us call this *direct consciousness*. The consciousness that a particular sensation is of a certain kind, on the other hand, involves the intellectual perception that the sensation is similar to past sensations. Such consciousness can be identified with Descartes' reflex thought. Let us call this *reflective consciousness*.

If Malebranche's thesis that consciousness does not involve error entails that the testimony of reflective consciousness must be incorrigible, then it follows from this thesis that the first person claim that a certain sensation is abhorrent must be correct. This consequence directly contradicts the position in Book One of the *Recherche* that we can mistakenly take an agreeable sensation to be an abhorrent one. If this thesis entails only that the testimony of direct consciousness must be incorrigible, on the other hand, then what follows is merely that we feel the agreeable sensation as it is. Since the sensation itself just is a certain kind of conscious feeling it could be true that we feel this sensation as it is although we fail to characterize properly how we feel. This weaker interpretation of Malebranche's thesis would eliminate the tension in his system that I have indicated.

As I have noted, though, Malebranche claimed in Book Six of the *Recherche* that we cannot err in our perception of the content of our thought, and he asserted in Book One that we can "distinguish quite well" among our sensations. It is difficult to resist the conclusion that the tension in his system is real after all. It is interesting, however, that in the passage from Book Six Malebranche emphasized that only perception independent of memory is immune from doubt (see §1.2.1). It is far from clear that the classification of our sensations does not require memory.

Moreover, it is not evident that the main point of the thesis in Book Three that consciousness never involves error is that the testimony of reflective consciousness is incorrigible. In his discussion of this thesis, Malebranche was concerned to contrast our error-free knowledge of the soul through consciousness with our false "knowledge" of the body through sensation (RV III–2.7, OCM I 453/LO 239). His acceptance of Descartes' position that "sensory perceptions do not show us what really exists in things" (PP II.3, AT VIII–1 41/CSM I 224) explains his claim that knowledge of the body is false. On the other hand, his view that sensations allow us to know what really exists in our soul since the sensations themselves "are but the soul itself in such and such a manner" (RV III–2.1, OCM I 415/LO 218) explains his remark that knowledge of the soul is not false. The distinction between the two kinds of knowledge thus rests on the fact that our sensations reveal directly our own modifications but not those of body. The sort of consciousness essential to sensation as such, though, is direct rather than reflective. Malebranche admittedly suggested at times, with Descartes, that the testimony of our reflective consciousness of our own sensations is incorrigible. His remarks in Book Three, however, serve to emphasize more that we have immediate access to the sensory modifications of our soul by means of direct consciousness.[26]

It is helpful to understand Malebranche's own position in terms of the distinction, which I borrow from Owen Flanagan, among the following three "Cartesian" theses regarding knowledge of thought: *Simple Cartesianism*, where one knows with certainty that one has a thought; *Content Cartesianism*, where one knows indubitably that one has a certain sort of thought with a certain content; and *Process Cartesianism*, where one has indubitable knowledge of the internal mental processes or structures that explain that thought.[27] A central point in the following discussion of Malebranche's account of the will is that he could not have accepted Process Cartesianism (see §6.1.2). While certain passages in the *Recherche* conflict with Content Cartesianism, on the other hand, there are other passages from this work that suggest it. It cannot be said that Malebranche had an entirely consistent view regarding this thesis. But it is worth noting that his remark in Book Six of the *Recherche* that he cannot doubt what he is thinking of, which is so indicative of Content Cartesianism, is in fact something of an aside. Malebranche emphasized in this section that since "what actually exists is actually something," his thoughts provide "incontestable demonstrations" of the existence of his soul (RV VI–2.6, OCM II 370/LO 480). What is important here is his knowledge not that he has a certain kind of thought, but merely that he is thinking. Malebranche's argument for his own existence as a thinking thing thus requires only Simple Cartesianism and not the stronger Content Cartesianism.

1.2 The Cogito Argument

1.2.1 The Simple View of Existence

In the *Recherche* Malebranche argued that his thoughts provide incontestable demonstrations of his existence by appealing to the fact that he perceives the connection between his thought and his existence by means of a simple view (*simple vûë*) rather than by means of reasoning (*raisonnement*). This distinction is important because "when one reasons [*raisonne*] the memory acts, and where there is memory, there may be error, supposing that there is some malicious genius on whom we depend in our thoughts, and who amuses himself in deceiving us." Memory is subject to doubt, in particular, because a deceptive God could join our recollection to false principles, and thus cause us to draw false conclusions (OCM II 370/LO 480–81). According to Malebranche, then, the simple view that he exists because he thinks does not involve the use of memory and therefore is immune to the power of a *mauvais génie*.

This general line of argument is familiar from Descartes. Descartes had emphasized in the *Second Meditation*, after all, that even a *genius malignus* can "never bring it about that I am nothing as long as I think I am something" (AT VII 25/CSM II 17). What is perhaps unfamiliar, however, is Malebranche's distinction between a simple view and reasoning.[28] Such a distinction is related to his more complex distinction in Book One of the *Recherche* among three kinds of perception of the understanding: simple perception (*simple perception*), perceptual judgment (*jugement*),[29] and reasoning (*raisonnement*).[30] On the view in this earlier section, the understanding has a simple perception when it "perceives a simple thing without any relation to anything else whatsoever"; for instance, when it perceives twice two or four. It has a perceptual judgment, on the other hand, when "it perceive the relations between two or more things"; for instance, when it perceives that twice two is equal to four. Finally, the understanding reasons when it "perceives the relations among the relations of things"; for instance, when it perceives that four being less than six, twice two, being equal to four, is less than six (RV I.2, OCM I 49–50/LO 7–8).

In Book Six Malebranche offered as examples of perception by a simple view the perception "by which I know that I am" and the perception that twice two equals four. The first seems to be an instance of a simple perception, since it is the perception of a thought "without any relation to anything else whatsoever."[31] The second example is the very one cited in Book One as an instance of perceptual judgment. Malebranche evidently came to believe that simple perception and perceptual judgment differ in some fundamental way from reasoning, that is, the perception of relations among relations. One important similarity between the first two kinds of perception, I would suggest, is that they involve an immediate grasp: in the case of simple perception, of a simple object; in the case of perceptual judgment, of a relation. In the case of reasoning, on the other hand, the grasp of a relation is mediated by the grasp of another relation.

This difference does not obviously involve memory, the notion of which is so prominent in the discussion in Book Six of the distinction between a simple view and reasoning. An initial suggestion is that Malebranche held that the grasp of relations among relations cannot take place at a single temporal instant, and thus relies on memory of temporally prior stages. But this position runs up against his claim early in the Recherche that just as there are no indivisible atoms, so there are no durationless instants of time (RV I.8, OCM I 104/LO 38–39). Such a claim implies that acts of simple perception and perceptual judgment, as well as acts of reasoning, have temporal duration. A more promising suggestion is that unlike the other two kinds of perception, reasoning cannot be accomplished by means of a single mental act. Malebranche seems to have believed that he cannot perceive a relation$_1$, and by the very same act infer from that relation and a relation$_2$ to a further relation$_3$. The view here is that the inference to relation$_3$ depends on the memory of the distinct act that involves the perception of relation$_1$. While to my knowledge Malebranche never stated this view in so many words, it does help to explain his position that reasoning, as opposed to simple perception and perceptual judgment, requires an act of memory.

The claim toward the end of the Recherche that thoughts serve to demonstrate the existence of the soul suggests that existence is inferred from the presence of thought. A critic might object that such a suggestion commits Malebranche to the view that our perception of our own existence does not take place by means of a single act, and thus is as open to skeptical doubt as any act of reasoning.[32] The best response here, I believe, is that this perception is more akin to perceptual judgment than to an act of reasoning. Malebranche could say that we perceive immediately by a single act the necessary relation between the fact that we think and the fact that we actually exist. On this position, there is no conflict between his suggestion that our perception of our own existence is inferential and his claim that such a perception is a simple view since it involves an immediate grasp.

The distinction between a simple view and reasoning, which is vital to the argument in the Recherche for the existence of the soul, turns out to be remarkably similar to a distinction in Descartes' early Rules for the Direction of the Mind between intuition and deduction. In his text Descartes defined intuition as "the undoubted conception of a pure and attentive mind [that] arises from the light of reason alone" and gave as an example his perception that he exists (*RM III*, AT X 368/CSM I 14). He defined deduction as a series of successive intuitions that involves the derivation of a conclusion "from some other propositions known with certainty" (AT X 370/CSM I 15). The two differ because "we are aware of a movement or a sort of sequence in the former but not in the latter, and also because immediate self-evidence is not required for deduction, as it is for intuition." Descartes went on to note, in anticipation of Malebranche's view that the inference from thought to existence is an instance of a simple view, that propositions immediately deduced from first principles "can be said to be known in one respect through intuition." Just as Malebranche took reasoning to require recollection, moreover, so Descartes emphasized that a deduction "derives its certainty from memory" (AT X 370/CSM I 15).[33] Though the *Rules* was not published prior to the *Recherche*, there is evidence that before 1674 Malebranche had access to Descartes' text in manuscript form.[34] It seems likely that this manuscript was a source for the discussion of the cogito argument toward the end of Malebranche's text.

To be sure, the *Rules* does not anticipate the point in the *Recherche* that any arguments that depend on memory would be vulnerable to the wiles of a powerful deceiver. But this point is quite prominent in one notorious text where Descartes addressed what has come to be known in the recent literature as the problem of the Cartesian Circle. This problem was first broached by the authors of the *Second Objections*, who charged that Descartes' claim in the *Meditations* that he cannot be certain of anything until he achieves knowledge of the existence of a nondeceptive God undermines his argument in the *Second Meditation* for the conclusion that he can be certain that he exists as a thinking thing (AT VII 125/CSM II 89). Descartes responded, "I declared by my express words that I was speaking only of knowledge of those conclusions that memory can recall when we no longer are attending to the very reasons from which we deduced them." He went on to conclude that a person can be certain of his own existence because "he does not deduce existence from thought by means of a syllogism, but recognizes the known thing as if per se by a simple intuition of mind [*simplici mentis intuitu*]" (AT VII 140/CSM II 100).

There is a residue in this passage of the distinction in the *Rules* between immediately evident intuitions and deductions that derive their certainty from memory. New to the *Second Replies* is the claim that without a proof of the existence of a nondeceptive God, arguments that depend on memory are epistemically unreliable. This claim is reminiscent of the comment in the *Recherche* that because reasoning involves memory, it "can always be mistaken if one supposes a deceiving God" (OCM II 371/LO 481). The position in the *Second Replies* that knowledge of the existence of the self is beyond doubt since it derives from a simple intuition that does not rely on memory, moreover, recalls the view in the *Recherche* that the existence of the soul is incontestable since it is perceived by a simple view rather than by reasoning. There is some reason to suspect that the *Second Replies*, as well as the *Rules*, helped to shape Malebranche's account of our knowledge of our own existence.

I have taken Malebranche's claim that we perceive our own existence through a simple view—and thus without the use of memory—to imply that we perceive immediately the connection between our thought and our existence. In light of this claim, it is interesting that in the *Second Replies* Descartes' discussion of the unreliability of memory is followed by the remark that the existence of the self is known by a simple intuition of mind and not deduced from the major premise of a syllogism. This juxtaposition suggests that any argument that involves a deduction from general principles must also rely on memory and thus cannot be trusted prior to the proof of the existence of God. It is far from clear that Descartes himself accepted such a position; he held that his proof for the existence of God in the *Third Meditation* is immune to doubt, for instance, even though he admitted that this proof employs abstract causal principles. Malebranche, however, could be excused if he took the passage from the *Second Replies* to indicate that an argument deducing the existence of the self from general principles cannot be intuitively evident. In any case, he himself suggested that he derives the conclusion that he exists directly from consciousness of his own thought, without the intervention of general principles. Such a view is required, at least, in order to render fully intelligible his claim that he perceives the existence of his own soul by means of a simple view rather than by means of reasoning.

1.2.2 General Principles and Substance

(1) The Role of General Principles. There is an unresolved tension, however, in Malebranche's discussion in the *Recherche* of the existence of the soul. Even though he suggested there that he derives the conclusion that he exists immediately from his awareness that he is thinking, he also emphasized the importance of the general principle, "what actually thinks is actually something" (*ce qui penser actuellement est actuellement quelque chose*) (RV VI–2.6, OCM II 369/ LO 480). It is unclear what role this principle is supposed to play. There is a further complication introduced by his claim in the 1688 *Entretiens sur la Métaphysique* that a different general principle is involved in the argument for his existence. At the outset of this work Malebranche had his spokesman, Theodore, assert, "Nothing has no properties [*l'neant n'a point de properties*]. I think. Hence, I am" (*EM* I, OCM XII 32/D 25). This passage not only strengthens the difficulty in the *Recherche* regarding the function of general principles in the argument for the existence of the self, but also introduces a further difficulty since it seems to conflict with the suggestion in the *Recherche* that if any principle is needed for this argument, it is the principle that what actually exists is actually something.

French commentators who stress the differences between the cogito arguments in Malebranche and Descartes have drawn attention to the passage from the *Entretiens*, though they have paid scant attention to the interpretive difficulties this passage raises. Thus, André Robinet emphasizes the fact that in this passage Malebranche inferred the conclusion, *sum*, not directly from the premise, *cogito*, but rather from the general principal, *l'neant n'a point de properties*. He claims that Malebranche deviated from a more orthodox Cartesian position in taking this metaphysical principle, rather than the cogito, to provide the foundations for metaphysics.[35] One problem with this claim, however, is that the import of the remarks in the *Entretiens* is somewhat unclear given Malebranche's position in the *Recherche* that he perceives his own existence by means of a simple view.

Moreover, it is worth noting that the difficulty in Malebranche concerning the role of general principles, brought to light by his position in the *Recherche*, is similar to a tension in Descartes' own writings. In the passage from the *Second Replies* previously cited, Descartes argued that he does not deduce his existence by means of a syllogism since he does not know the general principle "everything that thinks is or exists" (*illud omne, quod cogitat, est sive existu*) prior to knowing that he exists. Yet he also wrote in the *Principles* that "when I said that this proposition, *ego cogito, ergo sum*, is the first and most certain of all to occur to anyone who philosophizes in an orderly way, I did not deny that one must first know ... that it is impossible that that which thinks does not exist" (PP I.11, AT VIII–1 8/CSM I 196). So Descartes seems to have proposed with Malebranche conflicting views of the role of general principles in the argument for the existence of the self.

The conflict in Descartes is mitigated somewhat by his claim in the *Discourse* that while he can be immediately certain of the proposition *Je pense donc je suis*, further consideration of "what is required of a proposition in order for it to be true and certain" reveals that there is nothing in this particular proposition "to assure me that I am speaking the truth, except that I see very clearly that in order to think it is necessary to be [*pour penser, il faut être*]" (DM IV, AT VI 33/CSM I 127). On the position here, which is perhaps the best Descartes has to offer, the claim that we know first the general principle *pour penser, il faut être* indicates not that we must recognize it in order to be certain that we exist when we think but rather that such a principle is a condition of the possibility of such certainty. Thus, even though we recognize our own existence immediately without the help of this general principle, we need to consider this principle in order to understand how it is that we can be certain that we exist.

At one point Malebranche offered a brief comment on Descartes' cogito argument that brings to mind the remarks in the *Discourse*. In 1699 Malabranche responded to the objection that this argument is viciously circular because "Descartes supposed that he existed before having proved that he existed."[36] The objection, familiar from Leibniz and Kant, is that Descartes' claim that he thinks already assumes that he exists.[37] Malebranche noted in response that Descartes would say that "it is because it is necessary to be in order to think [*il faut être pour penser*] that I can conclude that I am because I think" (*Lettre III*, OCM IX 948). According to Malebranche's response, Descartes' argument presupposes not his existence but rather a general principle that links thought and existence. This response further suggests that Descartes derived the conclusion that he exists not from this general principle but rather from the claim that he thinks. Malebranche's view, which is in line with Descartes' own remarks in the

Discourse, is that the general principle is required for the soundness of the inference from thought to existence even though it is not itself something from which existence is inferred. To be sure, Malebranche did not so much endorse this view as offer it on Descartes' behalf. But it is interesting that he could have appealed to such a view in order to overcome the tension between his claim that his existence follows from the general principle *what actually thinks is actually something* and his position that he perceives by a simple view, and thus immediately, the connection between his thought and his existence.

In his foundational work on Malebranche, Gueroult has argued that this response to Arnauld cannot represent Malebranche's own position since in the *Entretiens* he cited not Descartes' hypothetical principle *il faut être pour penser* but rather the categorical principle *l'neant n'a point de properties*.[38] This sort of argument, however, overlooks Malebranche's appeal in the *Recherche* to the proposition *ce qui actuellement penser est actuellement quelque chose*. Gueroult also has failed to give due weight to the fact that Descartes himself cited a proposition similar to the one mentioned in the *Entretiens* when he wrote in the *Principles* that the conclusion that sensory judgments reveal the existence of mind follows from the proposition, revealed by the natural light, that "there are no affections or qualities of nothing [*nihili nullas esse affectiones sive qualitates*], so that wherever we come upon any, there must necessarily be found a thing or substance whose they are" (*PP* I.11, AT VIII–1 8/CSM I 196).

To be sure, Gueroult is aware of this passage and notes quite correctly that in the *Principles* the proposition is linked to the thesis that mind is better known than body rather than to the cogito argument itself.[39] Yet Descartes indicated that this proposition is, in fact, connected to the cogito argument when he asserted that "it is certain that a thought cannot exist without a thing that is thinking; and in general no act or accident can exist without a substance for it to belong to" (*Third Obj. and Rep.*, AT VII 175–76/CSM II 124). On the view here, it is impossible to think without existing because an act of thought cannot exist without a substance that is the subject of that act. It seems likely that Malebranche believed as well that the principle in the *Recherche* that whatever actually thinks is actually something derives from the principle in the *Entretiens* that nothing has no properties. Descartes' remarks therefore help to link the different general principles that Malebranche invoked in his discussions of the cogito argument in these two works. They also serve to confirm Henri Gouhier's position that "Malebranche was not unfaithful to the spirit of Cartesianism when he commenced his philosophy in saying: 'Nothingness has no properties. I think, therefore I am....'"[40]

(2) Knowledge of Substance. For Malebranche the principle that nothingness has no properties reveals that our thought provides direct access to our substance. He took it to follow from this principle that "no manner of being can subsist without some substance, because the manner of being is only the being or substance itself in a certain way" (*MC* IX, OCM X 105). Since a particular

thought is simply the soul existing in a certain manner, awareness of this thought is itself an awareness of that soul. Malebranche's view thus is in line with Leibniz's claim that knowledge of our own existence is immediate since "nothing comes between the understanding and its object."[41]

The tenet that nothingness has no properties, however, appears to have rather the opposite implication for Descartes. In the *Principles* he held that given this tenet, once we perceive an attribute we can "conclude [*concludimus*] that there is necessarily some existing thing, or substance, to which it can be attributed" (*PP* I.52, AT VIII–1 25/CSM I 210). The presence of substance, it appears, is posited rather than perceived.[42] There appears to be an even stronger endorsement of such a position in Descartes' remark in the *Third Objections and Replies* that "we do not come to know a substance immediately, through being aware of the substance itself; we come to know it only through its being the subject of certain acts" (AT VII 176/CSM II 124). It seems that although Descartes and Malebranche both invoked the principle that nothingness has no properties, they took that principle to have different implications concerning our knowledge of our own substance.

But even here, there is less of a difference than meets the eye. Descartes can be read as denying not that we are immediately aware of substance but that we are aware of substance *devoid of properties*. The claim in the *Third Objections and Replies*, therefore, is that we have no immediate knowledge of substance in the sense that we do not know substance apart from all of its acts. Prior to the remarks in the *Principles* just cited, moreover, Descartes noted that "we cannot become aware of a substance merely through its being an existing thing, since this alone of itself does not have any effect on us" (AT VIII–1 25/CSM I 210). The position here seems to be that we are not aware of a substance possessing no other properties than the property of existence.[43] But this position is consistent with Malebranche's view that we are immediately aware of our own substance when we are aware of one of its modifications. Such a view is not without its difficulties. For instance, Malebranche seems merely to have taken over from Descartes the assumption, challenged most notably by Locke and Kant, that we can be conscious of being the same substance over time.[44] It is perhaps disappointing that Malebranche did not advance beyond Descartes on this point. Nonetheless, he did see more clearly than Descartes himself the implication of the cogito argument that from the presence of our thought we can know immediately the existence of our soul as thinking substance.

1.2.3 The Paris Conference

(1) The Paris Argument. There are further features of Malebranche's account of the cogito argument that are significant in a Cartesian context, but emerge primarily in his remarks at the 1677 Paris conference on the views of the unorthodox Cartesian, Robert Desgabets. This conference concerning "the question of whether all thoughts of the soul depend on the body" began with a consideration of "the famous *je pense, donc je suis* of M. Descartes, that D. Robert

found defective" (OCM XVIII 122). The author of the record of the conference, most likely Corbinelli,[45] attempted to defend Desgabets' position that it is impossible to conceive the *I think* "without seeing there at the same time a property of extension" (OCM XVIII 123). Though initially reluctant to respond to this defense,[46] Malebranche finally agreed to speak in favor of the more standard Cartesian view that one can conceive of the *I think* without taking it to be linked to some property of extension.

The position that one cannot conceive the *I think* on its own is not evident in Desgabets' main published work, the *Critique de la Critique* (1675). In a passage from this text directed against the *Recherche* though somewhat reminiscent of Malebranche's own view, Desgabets wrote that since "modes, states or manners of being of things can neither exist nor be conceived without the substance which is their subject," it follows that "we know the thing itself that thinks."[47] In *Descartes à l'alambic*, however, Desgabets emphasized more that this knowledge of the thing that thinks depends on knowledge of body. At the outset of this work he rejected Descartes' position that we can know the first truth, *Je pense, donc je suis*, even while supposing that we have no body. For Desgabets all our thoughts derive from the senses or the imagination and thus are produced by the motions of the body to which our soul is united.[48] He took it to follow from the fact that our thoughts depend on our body in this way that it is impossible to know Descartes' first truth "if one supposes that one has no body."[49]

Desgabets submitted *Descartes à l'alambic* for discussion at the Commercy conferences. As discussant at those conferences, Cardinal de Retz offered several penetrating objections to the claims in this text.[50] In particular, in response to Desgabets' argument, Retz noted that we can know the nature of our soul as a thinking thing without knowing that our thoughts derive from the soul–body union. Thus, even if it were the case that all our thoughts depend on this union, it would not follow that we must know that there is such a dependence in order to know that our soul exists with a certain nature.[51] The objection here, in other words, is that Desgabets has simply confused knowledge of the nature of our soul with knowledge of the origin of our thoughts.

This objection has considerable force. Desgabets indicated, however, that he would reject the view—which Retz simply assumed—that the nature of the soul consists in thought. Indeed, in *Descartes à l'alambic* Desgabets urged that such a view is "the source of the faults that are found in the metaphysical meditations of Descartes." Desgabets countered there that the nature of the soul is better defined as "the intellectual substance depending on body."[52] No doubt encouraged by Descartes' position in the *Principles* that duration is measured by means of "the most regular motions,"[53] Desgabets argued that duration is "nothing other than local motion."[54] He concluded that one must reject Descartes' official position that duration pertains to all things since "one falls into a great error, if one attributes [duration] to things that do not have movement."[55]

In his *Supplément*, on which *Descartes à l'alambic* was based, Desgabets illustrated his position by pointing out the difference between angelic and human thought. He noted there that while the thoughts of angels and other *esprits purs* are "without discursiveness [*discours*], without succession, without composition or division," the thoughts of the human soul have succession or duration in virtue of the fact that they arise from the successive motions of the human body.[56] Human sensory thought has duration as an essential component and thus is linked by its very nature to body, whereas purely intellectual thought lacks duration and thus is not so linked. For this reason, according to Desgabets, the human soul is best defined not as a thinking thing, but rather as a thinking thing united to a body.

Desgabets' position is not without its difficulties. One obvious problem is that his claim in *Descartes à l'alambic* that the duration of human thought is nothing other than local motion seems to imply the materialist position, which he in fact rejected, that this thought is simply a kind of motion.[57] A different interpretation of this claim is suggested, however, by his remark in the *Supplément* that motion "makes [thoughts] continue more or less for a long time with a dependence so great and yet so sensible that the most speculative people cannot have nothing to do with time."[58] It appears that Desgabets was trying to say not that the duration of our thoughts is identical to the succession of certain motions, but rather that this duration depends essentially on such succession. The *Supplément* takes the dependence to be essential because motion must cause human thought. Elsewhere Desgabets indicated that dependence is also essential because any duration, including the duration of human thought, must be measured by the succession of motion.[59] In any case, he concluded that the fact that our thoughts have duration reveals that they are by their very nature connected to motion. Thus in the *Supplément* Desgabets rejected Descartes' conclusion from the cogito argument that the soul "was known before [body] and more clearly than it" on the grounds that we cannot understand the nature of our thoughts without understanding that they derive from motions in our body.[60]

Desgabets' defender at the Paris conference had just this sort of argument against Descartes in mind when he claimed, pointedly in Malebranche's direction, that since the human soul cannot conceive of its thoughts apart from duration, "one cannot have the idea of the *je pense* of M. Descartes with a perfect abstraction from all properties of extension or of body" (OCM XVIII 123). In particular, one cannot have this idea in abstraction from the property of local motion essential to the duration of thought.[61] Forced to respond, Malebranche did not reject the identification of succession with local motion. Rather, he denied the view of his interlocutor that "duration and succession are the same thing" (OCM XVIII 123), offering instead the view that the duration of a substance is "nothing other than its very existence" (OCM XVIII 124).[62] Malebranche implied that while we cannot conceive the existence of our thought in abstraction from duration, we can conceive its existence in abstraction from succession.

Malebranche's remarks have difficulties of their own. He did not explain, for instance, the sense in which we can conceive the duration of thought in abstraction from succession. Moreover, the distinction between duration and succession is not anticipated in his own writings. Just as Descartes had spoken of "the successive duration that I detect in my own thought,"[63] so in the *Recherche* Malebranche identified the duration of thoughts with their successiveness.[64] It is possible that Malebranche's remarks at the Paris conference were misreported. After all, the record of this conference was not from his own hand. I suspect, however, that the difficulties pertaining to the record can be explained by the fact that he took over the terms introduced by his interlocutor. Such a borrowing might indicate that Malebranche was simply being courteous although it may well be the case that he also found himself unprepared to defend his position in his own terms. The lack of rigor in the scattered remarks in his published writings on the cogito argument would seem to indicate that Malebranche was in fact unprepared.

It is thus tempting, at this point, to dismiss Malebranche's comments at the Paris conference as merely casual and unreflective of any deep view. I recommend resisting that temptation. These comments, as well as the discussion of the cogito argument in his published writings, seem to me to broach profound issues from a Cartesian standpoint. Moreover, I believe that—as in the case of his published writings, so in the case of his Paris comments—these issues are best brought to light by looking to Descartes. Malebranche wanted to hold against Desgabets that we can conceive the duration of our thought in abstraction from the succession of motion. Descartes himself had spoken of abstraction in a similar context when he wrote to a correspondent that "if I said simply that the idea that I have of my soul does not represent it to me as being dependent on the body and identified with it, this would be merely an abstraction." Descartes downplayed the importance of the fact that he can think of the soul in abstraction from body, emphasizing instead that he can think of the soul as excluding body in the sense that "it can exist even though body be excluded from it" (2 May 1644, AT IV 120/CSMK 236). As I argue in chapter 4, Malebranche came to believe that our conception of the soul does not suffice to demonstrate that the soul excludes body in this sense. Nonetheless, at the Paris conference he took the fact that we have a conception of the soul that does not represent it as being dependent on body to refute the claim of Desgabets' representative that "one cannot have an idea of the *je pense* of Descartes with a perfect abstraction from all properties of extension and of body" (OCM XVIII 123).

Malebranche seems merely to have assumed what Desgabets explicitly denied: that we can conceive the duration of thought without conceiving that duration to be dependent on the succession of motion. But here, I think, Malebranche could fall back on Retz's response to Desgabets at the Commercy conferences. The Cardinal insisted that on Descartes' view "there is a *before* and an *after* in spiritual things themselves, founded on the change of the modes to which they are subject."[65] Thus duration can be defined in terms of changes in our thoughts considered simply as modes of a thinking thing. Desgabets of course held that human thoughts are not properly considered simply as modes of a thinking thing. For him a human being is "a compound [*composée*] of body and soul" and human thought "a compound of motion and of the passion or action of the soul."[66] However, Retz urged that we can conceive of the passions or actions of the soul as existing, and thus as having duration, even though we do not consider the motions with which these states are purportedly linked. Desgabets would no doubt want to insist that the duration of thought must be measured by motion, but it is far from clear that the motion itself, rather than the sensory thought of the motion, must provide the standard for measurement. Malebranche could argue, then, that Desgabets has failed to defeat the view that we can conceive that our soul thinks, and thus exists, without conceiving that it depends on some body.[67]

(2) Knowledge of the Existence of Soul and Body. Malebranche's comments at the Paris conference serve to extend his point in Book Three of the *Recherche* that "we know the existence of our soul more distinctly than the existence of our body and of those that surround us" (RV III–2.7, OCM I 451/LO 238). This point is directed against the view of those who assert that "there is nothing that they know less" than the soul in order to support the view of "those who say that nothing is better known than the soul" (OCM I 452/LO 238). The Paris discussion reveals, however, that it can be directed as well against Desgabets' position that we know soul and body equally well, a position that Desgabets himself had offered as a response to Descartes' doctrine that "we know our soul before we know our body."[68]

I have focused on Desgabets' argument that we must know soul and body equally well given that the duration of the soul depends on bodily motion. He offers a different argument, however, in the *Critique de la Critique*: we can be certain that extended substance exists whenever we think of it since it is impossible that "one thinks without thinking of anything."[69] Desgabets concluded that "one knows intuitively the nature of the soul, as also external things when the senses make us think of them."[70]

This sort of argument is in fact connected to an interesting shift in the position of Desgabets' disciple Pierre-Sylvain Regis. In the *Système de philosophie* (1690), Regis adopted Desgabets' view that the human soul is distinct from a purely intellectual mind in virtue of the fact that all of the thoughts of the former derive from the motions of the body to which it is united.[71] Regis also began the metaphysical portion of this work with the claim that he knows his own existence "by a simple and inner knowledge, which precedes all acquired knowledge."[72] Moreover, he defended against Malebranchean objections the thesis that "the soul knows itself better than it knows its body."[73] By contrast, in the later *Usage de la raison* (1704) Regis was silent on the cogito argument, and he there defended against Malebranche the thesis that "we know the soul by the same view that we know body."[74] His final position is that the mere presence of the ideas of thinking and extended substance proves equally the existence of mind and body since the idea of substance must be the idea of something that actually exists in order to be the idea of anything at all.[75] There is thus an evolution in Regis' thought toward the view of Desgabets that knowledge of mind and knowledge of body are on an equal footing.[76]

In the context of these developments in later Cartesian thought, Malebranche's assertion that the existence of the soul is better known than the existence of body is positively reactionary. That is to say, the assertion goes back to the older view of Descartes in the *Second Meditation* that he can know himself "not only much more truly, more certainly, but even much more distinctly and evidently" than body since his judgment that he exists is more certainly true than his judgment that some body exists. Descartes continued that any evidence for the existence of, say, a piece of wax reveals his own own existence with more certainty, since

> if I judge that the wax exists, from the fact that I see it, certainly it follows much more evidently that I myself exist, from the fact that I see it. For it can be that this which I see is not truly wax ... but it obviously cannot be that when I see, or (what I now am not distinguishing) when I think I see, that I, thinking this, am not something. (AT VII 33/CSM II 22)

Earlier I noted that the *Second Meditation* suggests a distinction between actual sensation, which requires the presence of external bodies and sense organs, and apparent sensation, which requires the presence only of sensory thought. In terms of this distinction, the claim in the passage above is that while the mere fact that we have an apparent sensation cannot reveal that we have an actual sensation and thus cannot demonstrate the existence of bodies, it can establish the existence of the soul that has the apparent sensation.

Malebranche himself noted in the first edition of the *Recherche* that though we are not mistaken in believing in properties of extension external to us when we see them, the existence of these properties "is very difficult to prove" (RV I.10, OCM I 122a).[77] In response to Foucher's objection that Malebranche has no good reason to affirm the existence of such properties,[78] Desgabets offered the previously mentioned principle that one cannot think of anything, including body, without thinking of something.[79] Malebranche was reacting to this principle as well as to Foucher's original objection, no doubt, when he wrote in *Éclaircissement* VI that apart from faith there is no argument for the existence of body that is "perfectly demonstrative" in the sense of having "geometric rigor" (OCM III 60/LO 572). His position is not fully aligned with Descartes' own view; indeed, the remark about the lack of a demonstrative argument is directed specifically against Descartes. Nonetheless, Malebranche held with Descartes, and against Desgabets and Regis, that our sensory thoughts themselves do not suffice to establish the existence of body. As we have seen, he held as well, again with Descartes, that such thoughts serve to demonstrate immediately the existence of our soul as a substance that thinks. So while Malebranche's discussion of our knowledge of the existence of our soul is admittedly sketchy, his dispute with Desgabets reveals his firm commitment to Descartes' position that our sensations provide a more secure epistemic access to our soul than they provide to any body.

1.3. The Cogito and the Nature of the Soul

1.3.1 *Déchéance du Cogito*

In Malebranche's writings there is a tendency, which Cartesian critics such as Arnauld took to be perversely paradoxical, to couple positive claims concerning our knowledge of the existence of our soul with more negative remarks concerning our knowledge of its nature. Thus, after concluding in Book Six of the *Recherche* that "it is easy to know the existence of the soul," Malebranche went on to warn that "it is not so easy to know its essence or nature" (RV VI–2.6, OCM II 369/LO 480). He had elaborated on this point earlier in this text when he noted, in a passage that I cited in the Introduction, that while we know the existence of our soul more distinctly than the existence of body, "we do not have a knowledge of the nature of the soul as perfect as that of the nature of body" (RV III–2.7, OCM I 451/LO 238). We can know immediately the existence of our soul since we have direct access to its modifications, but our knowledge of these modifications is not as distinct as our knowledge of the modifications of body.[80]

Malebranche's position clearly involves a *déchéance du cogito*, to use Gueroult's memorable phrase. One of the primary purposes of Descartes' cogito argument was to reveal an idea of the nature of mind that is clear and distinct. Thus when Gassendi objected that we can know that we are without knowing what we are, Descartes responded indignantly in the *Fifth Replies* that "the one cannot be demonstrated without the other" (AT VII 359/CSM II 248). Descartes clearly would not have accepted Malebranche's position that the perception of ourselves that leads us to conclude that we exist is not in fact distinct. The difference here is captured by Gueroult's claim that whereas Descartes took the cogito argument to be based on an *expérience rationnelle*, involving a clear and distinct perception of our nature, Malebranche took it to derive merely from an *expérience vécue*, involving a perception of our nature that is confused and obscure. A *déchéance*, or demotion, of the cogito results from Malebranche's emphasis on the limitations of our knowledge of the nature of our soul.[81]

As I have indicated, Malebranche gave little hint of the radical nature of this demotion in the *Recherche* itself. There is an acknowledgment in *Éclaircissement* XI, however, where he confronted directly the more orthodox Cartesian view on these matters. Indeed, in this writing he referred explicitly to the response to Gassendi in the *Fifth Replies* when criticizing those Cartesians who follow Descartes in saying that one knows

> the nature of a substance more distinctly the more attributes of it one knows. But there is no other thing of which one knows more attributes than of our mind; because as many as one knows in other things, one may count as many in the mind from the fact that it knows them. And thus its nature is better known than that of any other thing. (OCM III 167/LO 635)[82]

Malebranche went on to challenge these Cartesians by asking, "But who does not see that there is quite a difference between knowing through a clear idea and knowing through consciousness?" In what is no doubt an allusion to La Forge's claim that "I find an infinity of properties of my thought, before I can only think of seeking [songer] those of body,"[83] he noted that even if "I would be able to count an infinity of properties in me," it does not follow that "one would know *clearly* the nature of things that one can *count*" (OCM III 167/LO 636).

According to Malebranche, the claim to Gassendi that we know more properties of soul than properties of body confuses the different sorts of knowledge that we have in these two cases. Malebranche held that on the Cartesian view we know the modifications of body through a clear idea of extension, but we know the modifications of our soul only through consciousness or inner sentiment. Along with other Cartesians, Malebranche did allow that this consciousness or inner sentiment provides direct knowledge of the existence of the modifications of our soul. Yet what most caught the eye of Malebranche's contemporaries was his claim that the knowledge of the nature of the soul that derives from consciousness or inner sentiment is itself confused.[84] Malebranche himself took it to follow from this claim that such knowledge is less perfect in kind than the knowledge of the nature of body that Cartesians take to derive from the clear idea of extension. He was concerned here of course to reject Descartes' official doctrine that the nature of the soul is better known than body, but even more Malebranche wanted to stand this doctrine on its head, or rather to set it back on its feet, by arguing that there is for Cartesians a sense in which the nature of body is better known than the nature of the soul. To appreciate the force of this quite radical response to Descartes, we need to consider the response to Gassendi that serves as its target, as well as the refinements to this response that Arnauld introduced in his polemic with Malebranche.

1.3.2 Descartes' Response to Gassendi

(1) The Thesis of the Fifth Replies. As Malebranche noted, Descartes concluded in his remarks to Gassendi that the nature of mind "is the best known of all" (AT VII 360/CSM II 249); as Malebranche also indicated, he was most concerned to defend the more specific thesis of the *Second Meditation* that mind is better known than body.[85] We have seen that Malebranche, in opposition to Desgabets, readily accepted the view in the *Meditations* that we know the existence of our mind with more certainty than we know the existence of any body. But Descartes went on to make the claim, which Malebranche was concerned to dispute, that the nature of mind is better known than the nature of body. In support of this claim, Descartes noted toward the end of the *Second Meditation* that "no reasons can aid the perception either of the wax or of any other body, without all the same better proving the nature of my mind" (AT VII 33/CSM II 22). He explained in the *Fifth Replies* that since knowledge of the various properties of the wax—for example, its whiteness and hardness—carries with it knowledge of the

corresponding properties of the mind—for example, the power to know the whiteness and the hardness—it must be the case that "whatever is known in some other thing, as many also can be counted in the mind, by virtue of which it knows them" (AT VII 360/CSM II 249).

These remarks show only that we know as many properties of mind as properties of body and thus do not yield the conclusion in the *Fifth Replies* that "there is nothing of which so many attributes are known as our mind" (AT VII 360/CSM II 249).[86] However, another premise is broached by the parenthetical remark in the *Second Meditation* that "so many other things are in the mind itself from which the notion of it can be made more distinct that that which emanates to it from body scarcely seems to count" (AT VII 33/CSM II 22). Elsewhere in the *Fifth Replies* Descartes indicated that these "other things" are non-sensory thoughts, knowledge of which does not involve knowledge of any property of body (AT VII 358–59, 385/CSM II 248, 264). According to Descartes, the fact that we know such thoughts shows that we know more properties of mind than properties of body.

The full argument for the conclusion that the nature of mind is better known than the nature of body requires the premise provided in the *Fifth Replies*: nothing is "required for the manifestation of a substance except its various attributes [and] insofar as we know many attributes of a substance, we thereby understand its nature more perfectly" (AT VII 360/CSM II 249). Descartes' acceptance of this premise can be explained in terms of his technical definition in the *Principles* of a clear perception as "that which is present to the attentive mind," and of a distinct perception as that which "as well as being clear . . . is so sharply separated from all other perceptions that it contains in itself only what is clear" (PP I.45, AT VIII–1 22/CSM I 207–8). He apparently held that the more properties of a substance that are present to the attentive mind, the more this mind can separate the notion of that substance from notions of other substances, and thus the more it can render the former notion distinct. This explains his conclusion that it follows from the fact that we clearly perceive more properties of mind than properties of the wax or of any other body that our notion of mind is more distinct than any of our notions of particular bodies.

As I have indicated, Gassendi anticipated Malebranche's own objections to this line of argument. Gassendi complained to Descartes, "[T]hose things which you have deduced about the wax prove only the perception of the existence of the mind, but indeed not the nature of it" (AT VII 275/CSM II 191). Gassendi's main reservation is that it is not true in general that a listing of the observable properties of an object renders the notion of that object more distinct. He illustrated by considering the case of our notion of a particular species of body:

> Surely, of a notion of Wine superior to that of the vulgar that is asked of you, it will not be enough to say: Wine is a liquid thing, pressed from grapes, white or red, sweet, inebriating, etc.; but you will undertake to explore and declare in what manner the internal substance of it, insofar as it is observed to be compounded, [is composed] of spirit, phlegm, tartara, and other parts, mixed together in some quantity and proportion or other. In the same way, when a

notion of yourself superior to that of the vulgar, that is, possessed up till now, is asked for, you without doubt see that it is not enough if you announce to us that you are a thing thinking, doubting, understanding, etc.; but it is incumbent on you to examine yourself by a certain chemical-like labor, so that you can determine and demonstrate to us your internal substance. (*Fifth Obj.*, AT VII 276–77/CSM II 193)

In order to form a distinct notion of the wine, therefore, we must know the inner structure that is causally responsible for observable properties such as whiteness and sweetness. According to Gassendi, Descartes must similarly display the inner structure of mind that provides a causal explanation of observable properties such as thinking and doubting before he can claim to have a notion of mind that is even as distinct as the notions of bodily kinds that are linked to the various empirical sciences.[87]

Descartes' response that our knowledge of the nature of a substance becomes more perfect as we know more of its attributes seems wholly inadequate. As Margaret Wilson has urged, one serious difficulty is that Descartes himself accepted Gassendi's position that a knowledge of particular bodies that is "superior to that of the vulgar" must include a causal explanation of observable properties in terms of inner structures.[88] Descartes wrote in the *Principles*, after all, that "natural effects almost always depend on structures [*organis*] that are so minute that they all escape the senses," so one must "undertake to investigate by means of the observable effects and parts of natural bodies, what kind of insensible particles and causes of them there are" (*PP* IV.203, AT VIII-1 326/ CSM I 288–89). Given that he offered this position in opposition to the view of those who "take their own senses to be the measure of what is known" (*PP* I.201, AT VIII-1 324/CSM I 286), it seems that Descartes cannot allow that we can render our notion of particular bodies more distinct merely by increasing our knowledge of the observable properties of these bodies. His remarks toward the end of the *Principles* therefore appear to conflict with his endorsement earlier in this same text of the doctrine central to the response to Gassendi that "we know a thing or substance the more clearly, the more we observe [*deprehendimus*] in it" (*PP* I.11, AT VIII-1 8/CSM I 196).

Certain remarks in the *Fifth Replies* itself, moreover, seem to be inconsistent with the implication of such a doctrine that knowledge of mind is to be judged by the same standards as knowledge of body. Descartes prefaced his main argument against Gassendi by emphasizing the difference between the two kinds of knowledge. He mocked Gassendi for implying that one must ask

what is the color, odor, and taste of the human mind, or of what salt, sulfur, and mercury is composed; for you wish us to examine it as though it were wine, *by a certain chemical labor*. That is really worthy of you, O Flesh, and of all those who, since they conceive nothing except what is wholly confused, are ignorant of what should be asked of a given thing. (AT VII 359–60/CSM II 248–49)

This suggests that while questions to be answered by chemical labor are appropriate in the case of bodies with inner structures, these questions are inappropriate in the case of mind since the mind has no such structure. This suggestion addresses Gassendi's original objection consistently with the remarks toward the end of the *Principles*, but it seems hopelessly at odds with the main point in the *Fifth Replies* that the same question must be asked with respect to knowledge of mind and body, namely, how many attributes are observed in the substance.

(2) Arnauld's Defense. In his *Vraies et fausses idées*, Arnauld argued that these difficulties can be overcome. Prompted by Malebranche's criticisms, Arnauld held that Descartes is most charitably read as saying in the *Fifth Replies* that we "know the nature of a thing so much more distinctly as we know more attributes of it, provided that we know them clearly."[89] If Arnauld took "clearly" to mean "present to the attentive mind," this revised principle would fail to address Gassendi's objection that a greater awareness of the observable properties of a body does not render our knowledge of the nature of that body more perfect. Prior to this passage, however, Arnauld emphasized that on Descartes' view we know our own sensations "CLEARLY AND DISTINCTLY insofar as we regard them only as sentiments and thoughts."[90] So the suggestion here on Descartes' behalf is that we know the nature of a thing more distinctly insofar as we know more attributes of it, provided we know those attributes distinctly.

This suggestion can accommodate Gassendi's point that chemical labor is required if we are to improve our knowledge of the nature of particular bodies. In the *Principles* Descartes opposed those who identify various sensible qualities with "substantial forms and real qualities" by claiming that such qualities are simply "the various dispositions of the very objects that bring it about that our nerves can move in various ways" (PP IV.198, AT VIII-1 322–23/CSM I 285). Commenting on this passage, Descartes explained to a correspondent that sensible qualities are to be explained only in terms of "certain shapes and motions that cause the sensations we call light, heat, etc." (To Chanut, 26 Feb. 1649, AT V 292/CSMK 369). The dispositions thus are grounded in these shapes and motions, and as the passage from the *Principles* cited above makes clear, the shapes and motions are features of "structures so minute that they escape all the senses." On Descartes' view, the perception of these dispositions can be distinct only insofar as the dispositions themselves are understood entirely in terms of these features. In order for us to know the whiteness and the hardness of the wax in a distinct manner, we must uncover by chemical labor the unobservable structures of bodies. However, Arnauld took Descartes to indicate to Gassendi that we can know the nature of our sensations of whiteness and hardness distinctly simply by considering them as nondispositional properties, namely, as conscious thoughts. We need consider only those properties of which we are conscious and thus need not appeal to an inner structure of mind. According to Arnauld, Descartes' commitment to the claim that no such appeal is required for distinct knowledge of mental properties explains why he took the conclusion that the nature of mind is better known to us than the nature of body to follow simply from the fact we know more properties of mind than properties of body.

Arnauld therefore helps us to see the position in the *Fifth Replies* as internally consistent and as compatible with remarks in the *Principles* that stress the need for explanations of observable bodily qualities in terms of unobservable structures. However, his main concern in the *Vraies et fausses idées* was to undermine Malebranche's claim that what we know of the soul through consciousness or inner sentiment is confused and obscure. Arnauld simply could not understand how Malebranche can say on the one hand that we know with certainty that we are thinking by means of consciousness and on the other that the knowledge we obtain through consciousness is confused. Arnauld emphasized Augustine's view that we know our own faith *"certissima scientia, et clamante conscientia,* through a most certain knowledge and as if by a cry of our consciousness." He went on to note that we know our own thoughts in the same way; thus "what we know through inner sentiment can be as certain for us as the Saint says it is, only because it is clear and evident, for in natural knowledge only clarity and evidence can produce certainty."[91] Descartes himself noted to his critics at one point that in the *Meditations* "I did not doubt that I *had a clear idea of my mind,* inasmuch as I was intimately conscious [*intime conscius*] of it" (*Sixth Rep.*, AT VII 443/CSM II 298). Likewise, for Arnauld it simply follows from the fact that we have direct access to our own thoughts that our knowledge of our nature as a thinking thing is clear and evident.

1.3.3 Consciousness and the Subjective View

(1) The Imperfection of Consciousness. In his *Réponse au Livre de Arnauld* (1684), Malebranche complained that "those who would distinctly conceive my thought would have no trouble discovering [Arnauld's] mistakes and his continual sophisms" (*Réponse,* c. 23, OCM VI 160). He readily conceded to Arnauld, "I know that I am, that I think, that I will, because I sense myself." Thus Augustine is correct to say that "I know myself, *certissima scientia, clamante conscientia*" (OCM VI 161). But he held that even though we know our existence as a thinking thing more certainly than we know the existence of body, our knowledge of the nature of our thoughts is more limited than our knowledge of the nature of bodily modifications. Malebranche followed the official Cartesian line in holding that body is simply extension and "in contemplating the idea of extension, I see that [body] is divisible and mobile, and by consequence that it is capable of all sorts of shapes" (OCM VI 161). Body, therefore, has modifications that anyone can grasp by means of intellectual reflection on the idea of extension. But Malebranche asserted that we know our own modifications through consciousness rather than through an idea to which others have access. Our knowledge of the modifications of our soul is thus radically imperfect because it is restricted to our particular form of consciousness in a manner in which our knowledge of body is not.[92]

One point here is that we do not know all the modifications of which our soul is capable. As I noted in the introduction, Gassendi anticipated this point in his dispute with Descartes. However, Malebranche raised an additional point when he told Arnauld that while "I can think of a circle, when I wish it, and make another think of it by my words," it is not possible to "make the person sense my pleasure, my pain, etc." (OCM VI 160). This remark involves a reworking of an earlier point in the *Recherche* concerning the limitations of our knowledge of sensation. In Book One of this text, Malebranche noted that although it depends on our will to attach words to ideas of objects such as the sky, we cannot attach words in this way to sensations. Thus, "if one asks me, that I explicate to him what is pain, pleasure, color, etc., I could not do what is required through words" (RV I.13, OCM I 145/LO 62). In Book Three he picked up on the claim concerning sensation, stating that since "such sentiments, of pleasure, for example, of pain, of heat, etc. are not attached to terms," it must be the case that "if someone had never seen color, or felt heat, he could not be made to know these sensations by all the definitions that one would give to him" (RV III–2.7, OCM I 452/LO 238). The point here that sensations are not attached to words becomes the somewhat clearer point in the *Réponse* that we cannot at will, simply though the use of words make others know how our sensations feel to us. Moreover, whereas in the *Recherche* Malebranche cited the contrasting example of our attaching words to ideas of material objects, in his remarks to Arnauld he employed the example of our knowledge of a circle, which more directly involves the idea of extension.[93]

Malebranche's point that we cannot know our sensations through definitions is found in other Cartesian texts. There is something of an anticipation, for instance, in Descartes' parenthetical remark in the *Fifth Replies* that a man born blind can know the hardness of a piece of wax without knowing its whiteness (AT VII 360/CSM II 249). This remark is linked to passages in later Cartesian texts that address more directly the issue of the definability of terms for sensations. Thus in the *Art de penser* (1662), which is largely the work of Arnauld, there is the claim that "it is impossible by any convention to bring a blind man to understand what the word for red, for green, for blue means."[94] Likewise in the *Traité de Physique* (1671), the influential Cartesian physicist Jacques Rohault cited the case of the man born blind in a section entitled, "That the sentiment of light or color cannot be described."[95] Malebranche went beyond these Cartesians, however, when he added that the fact that terms for sensations are indefinable reveals that our knowledge of our sensory modifications falls short of the knowledge we have of the modifications of extension.[96]

(2) Subjective and Objective Views. Malebranche's distinction between these two kinds of knowledge can be understood in terms of the more recent distinction in Thomas Nagel between objective and subjective views of the world.[97] According to Nagel a view is subjective to the extent that it is bound up with the way things appear to us from our particular perspective and objective to the extent that it can be detached from such appearances.[98] Malebranche took the fact that we can make others think of various shapes to indicate that we can think of these shapes from a general rational perspective, apart from the peculiarities of the ways they appear to us in sensation. In Nagel's terms, Malebranche

held that we can take a purely objective view of the modifications of extension. He claimed, on the other hand, that we can apprehend our sensations only by means of our consciousness of the way they subjectively appear to us. The position here, once again in Nagel's terms, is that our view of our own sensations is irreducibly subjective.

This point about subjectivity can be linked to Malebranche's remark in Book Three of the *Recherche* that "the knowledge that we have of our soul through consciousness is imperfect, granted, but it is not false" (RV III–2.7, OCM I 453/ LO 239). I previously took the main point of his thesis that consciousness is not false to be that we have immediate access to our sensory modifications by means of direct consciousness. I now propose that Malabranche held that we have such access because the sensations are merely subjective appearances. While we cannot analyze by means of definitions the phenomenal differences between the sensations of red and yellow or the taste of sugar and salt, our consciousness directly acquaints us with these differences.

I understand Malebranche to have suggested to Arnauld, however, that our inability to analyze sensory appearances through definitions reveals that our knowledge of our own modifications through consciousness is less perfect than our knowledge of body through a clear idea. Rational reflection on the idea of extension provides a perspective on bodily modifications that can be detached from the subjective manner in which these modifications appear to us in sensation. In the case of our own sensory modifications, on the other hand, all we have to go on are the appearances themselves; we find ourselves unable to have a more objective view of phenomenal qualia. The same subjective view that provides noninferential access to our sensations also restricts our knowledge of them. On my reading, it was perfectly natural for Malebranche to conclude that the knowledge of our own modifications that we have through consciousness is immediate and certain and at the same time limited and imperfect.[99]

This reading also allows us to appreciate more fully Malebranche's exasperation with Arnauld. Following Descartes, Arnauld asserted that the fact that we know our thoughts with certainty proves that we have clear and evident knowledge of their nature. According to Malebranche, this line of argument involves a glaring non sequitur since it in no way follows from the fact that we know with certainty the existence of our thoughts that we clearly and distinctly know the nature of thought. Indeed, he held that the very feature that renders our thoughts immediately accessible to consciousness likewise renders their nature obscure to us. Arnauld would perhaps insist that the fact that we can have only a subjective view of our thoughts does not show that our knowledge of these thoughts is any more obscure than our knowledge of bodily modifications. Malebranche's full argument for the claim that the subjective features of consciousness are confused and obscure in fact depends on the details (to be considered in the next chapter) of his account of the distinction between knowledge of soul through inner sentiment and knowledge of body through a clear idea. However, his initial remarks to Arnauld at least have the virtue of broaching the possibility that we do not have a clear and distinct knowledge of that with which we are most directly acquainted.

In any case, it was neither perversity nor a relish for paradox that led Malebranche to link the positive claim that knowledge of the existence of the soul and its modifications is certain and the negative claim that knowledge of the nature of the soul is radically imperfect. He took the claims to be two sides of the same Cartesian coin. We can doubt the existence neither of our own modifications nor of the substance they modify since we directly feel the modifications of that substance. Descartes' cogito argument, therefore, is secure. Nonetheless, the radical imperfection of our knowledge of the modifications of our soul derives from the fact that we can only feel these modifications and thus cannot have the sort of view of them that we can have of bodily modifications.

To be sure, Malebranche's argument that we can only feel the modifications of our soul tends to focus on our sensations to the exclusion of our intellectual perceptions. Nicholas Jolley aptly notes that "Malebranche sometimes has difficulty acknowledging that the realm of the psychological is not simply coextensive with that of the sensory."[100] I address this sort of difficulty in chapter 3. In chapter 2, though, I look more closely at Malebranche's own account of sensation. Given his discussion of the cogito, it would not be surprising if his remarks on sensation failed to be Cartesian in any straightforward manner; in fact his account differs in sometimes subtle but nonetheless important ways from the more orthodox view of sensation in the writings of Descartes and some of his followers. However, Malebranche's account also has certain Cartesian features that strengthen his argument for the negative thesis that our knowledge of the nature of the soul is less perfect than our knowledge of the nature of body.

two

SENSATION

Malebranche stressed repeatedly to his Cartesian critics the Augustinian nature of his view that the ideas that represent bodies to us exist in God rather than in our own soul. Nonetheless, he also admitted that there is a confusion in Augustine's own account of our knowledge of the material world that derives from his prejudice that sensible qualities such as colors exist in bodies. One of Descartes' greatest accomplishments, according to Malebranche, was his discovery that body has only those modifications that are clearly contained in the idea of extension. He held that in light of Descartes' accomplishment, Cartesians can see what Augustine could not: these sensible qualities are only modifications of our soul.

This is not to say that Malebranche accepted Descartes' account of sensation without revision. In some cases he set aside features of this account. Malebranche was led by his occasionalism to reject the tenet in the writings of Descartes and some Cartesians that bodily motions cause sensations, and he was critical of the suggestion in certain of these writings that sensations correspond neatly to bodily qualities. In other cases Malebranche supplemented Descartes' account. While he accepted the main elements of Descartes' doctrine that the primary purpose of sensation is to teach us about the needs of our own body, for instance, he also provided an account of the nature of sensory judgment that is uniquely his own.

For our purposes, however, the most important feature of Malebranche's account of sensation is his thesis that we know our own sensory modifications through inner sentiment but not through a clear idea of the soul. I understand this thesis to say that while we have a subjective view of these modifications, we do not have an objective view of them that is similar to the objective view that we have of body through the clear idea of extension. Critics as varied as Arnauld, Desgabets, and Regis protested that Cartesians have as much reason to say that they know their sensations through a clear idea of thought as they have to say that they know bodily modifications through a clear idea of extension. While these critics detected some problems with Malebranche's argument, they failed to grapple with his main contention that our objective view of body is superior in kind to our subjective view of our own sensations.

Malebranche did not take this contention to be wholly external to the Cartesian system. Indeed, he claimed at one point that since Cartesians must appeal to the clear idea of extension in order to show that sensible qualities are modifications of the soul, it must be the case that they do not have access to a clear idea of the nature of the soul. His further argument that the obscurity of sensations follows from the fact that knowledge of them depends on experience, moreover, is linked to the discussion of sensation and the soul–body union in Descartes and later in Desgabets and Regis. Malebranche wrote to Arnauld, "I believe that ... without fundamentally distancing myself from the principles of St. Augustine, or rather, I believed, in following them, I could assert that one sees or that one knows in God even material and corruptible objects" (*TL I*, OCM VI 201). I contend he also held that in following out the account of sensation in Descartes and the Cartesians, which itself must be used to correct Augustine, he could assert that we do not see or know our own soul in God— that is to say, in somewhat more muted terms, that we do not have the same sort of objective view of our soul that God has.

2.1 Sensations and Body

2.1.1 Malebranche, Augustine, and Descartes

It is beyond doubt that Malebranche understood his doctrine of the vision of ideas in God to be simply a version of the Augustinian theory of divine illumination. In his initial discussion of this doctrine in the *Recherche*, for instance, he asserted that Augustine has proven in "an infinity of passages [that] we already see God in this life through the knowledge we have of the eternal truths" (RV III–2.6, OCM I 444/LO 233).[1] When Arnauld charged that this doctrine is dangerously novel, Malebranche retorted that "it is principally [Augustine's] authority which has given me the desire to put forth *the new philosophy of ideas*" (*Réponse*, c. 9, OCM VI 80).[2] He understood himself in particular to follow the central teaching in Augustine that "the eternal Wisdom is the light of all intelligences [*La Sagesse éternelle est la lumière des intelligences*]," and that "it is only by the manifestation of his substance ... that God illumines us internally" (*EM*, Preface, OCM XII 18).[3]

Malebranche noted two differences, though, between his own view and that of Augustine. First, he pointed out in the *Recherche* that where Augustine claimed that we see eternal truths in God, he wanted to say that what we see in God are in fact ideas. According to Malebranche, eternal truths are not real beings but rather mere relations between ideas.[4] The ideas themselves, on the other hand, are real beings that we intellectually perceive when we grasp eternal truths. Strictly speaking, what we see in God are the ideas rather than the truths. Malebranche stressed, however, that since "it might even be said that this was Saint Augustine's meaning," there is reason to think that his view is essentially in accord with Augustine's own position (RV III–2.6, OCM I 443–45/LO 233–34).

Second, Malebranche was aware that Augustine did not say that we see changeable and corruptible bodies in God. Here again Malebranche was inclined, at least initially, to minimize the differences. He told Arnauld that he himself denied that what we see immediately in God are the bodies themselves; "to speak exactly, one sees in God only their essences, which are immutable, necessary and eternal" (TL I, OCM VI 200). Malebranche held that the Augustinian doctrine of illumination, which concerns our knowledge of eternal truths, can also be used to explain our knowledge of the geometrical features of bodies.[5] Thus he stressed that on Augustine's view "it is immediately in the Eternal Wisdom [*Sagesse Eternelle*] that one sees extension, I understand *intelligible* extension, which is the object of the knowledge [*science*] of the geometers" (OCM VI 201).[6] Malebranche concluded that with respect to the view of what we see in God, "there is no difference in the end between [Augustine's] sentiment and mine" (*Réponse*, c. 7, OCM VI 68).

Nonetheless, there are fundamental differences that Malebranche ultimately could not explain away. He indicated these differences when he admitted to Arnauld that Augustine himself could not have accepted the view that we see bodies in God.

> What prevented this holy doctor from speaking as I have done [i.e., from saying that we see all things in God] is that being in the prejudice that colors are in objects . . . as one sees objects only by colors, he believed that it was the object itself that one saw. He could not say then that one saw in God these colors that are not a nature immutable, intelligible, and common to all minds, but sensible and particular modifications of the soul, and according to Saint Augustine, a quality that is spread on the surface of bodies. (*Réponse*, c. 7, OCM VI 68)

According to one commentator, this passage attributes to Augustine the argument that we cannot see colors in God since the colors of bodies change while nothing in God is subject to change.[7] However, the emphasis here is not that colors must be mutable since bodies can change in color but that colors are not immutable and intelligible natures since we cannot understand them, as we understand geometrical properties, through God's intellectual ideas. The Augustinian conclusion that we see colors in objects is tied to the premise that we see these colors as "spread on the surface of bodies." According to Malebranche, Augustine took the senses themselves to reveal that colors are qualities that exist in bodies and thus not simply "sensible and particular modifications of the soul."

As we have seen in §1.3.3 (1), Malebranche himself emphasized that we can know sensations only through consciousness and not through definitions. He therefore agreed with Augustine's purported view that the colors we see are sensible rather than intelligible. As we will discover, Malebranche also allowed that we naturally see colors as qualities spread on the surface of bodies (see

§2.1.3). But what he could not accept was the claim, which he attributed to Augustine, that we see bodies "in themselves" [*en eux-mêmes*] when we see colors.[8] Malebranche interpreted such a claim to mean that we see them "by species that come from them or are received from them," species that are "images that resemble" these bodies.[9] He apparently thought that since no reflective person could believe that bodies at a distance are immediately present to us, this is the only sense in which Augustine could say that we see bodies in themselves. At times Malebranche suggested an objection to the Augustinian account of sensation that stresses the sheer implausibility of the appeal to species. In the *Recherche*, for instance, he devoted a chapter to the refutation of the position, which he attributed to the Peripatetics,[10] that "external objects send species that resemble them" (RV III–2.2, OCM I 418/LO 220–21). The initial objection in this text is that given that there are a multitude of these "little bodies" flying around, they would constantly run into each other and impede each other's progress. There are echoes here of Descartes' ridicule of "all those little images flitting through the air, called 'intentional species' [*espécies intentionnelles*], which so exercise the imagination of the philosophers" (AT VI 85; CSM I 153–54).

It must be admitted that this sort of objection misses its target since the scholastics themselves distinguished intentional species from material images. It must also be said, however, that Descartes had what he took to be a deeper objection to the scholastic account of sensation. He understood the main problem with such an account to be that it is linked to the childhood prejudice that our sensory ideas belong to bodies. Thus he wrote to one correspondent,

> The earliest judgments that we make in our childhood, and later on the influence of traditional philosophy, have accustomed us to attribute to the body many things that belong only to the soul, and to attribute to the soul many things that belong only to the body. So people commonly mingle the two ideas of body and soul when they construct the ideas of real qualities and substantial forms, which I think should be altogether rejected. (22 July 1641, AT III 420/ CSMK 188)

According to Descartes, for instance, the scholastic position that color is a real quality of a body is made possible by the fact that from our earliest years when we saw a color, "we supposed we see a thing positioned outside us, and quite similar to the idea of color that we experienced within us then" (PP I.66, AT VIII–1 32/CSM I 216).

Descartes held that we can eliminate this confusion of colors with bodily qualities once we recognize that

> nothing at all belongs to the definition [*ratio*] of body except that it is a thing with length, breadth, and depth, admitting of various shapes and various motions; that its shapes and motions are only modes that no power could make to exist apart from it; that colors, odors, tastes, and the like are merely sensations existing in my thought, and differing no less from body than pain differs from

the shape and the motion of the weapon that inflicts it. (*Sixth Rep.*, AT VII 440/CSM II 297)

Thus the fundamental difference between the Cartesian and scholastic accounts of sensation does not consist in the fact that the latter requires flying images while the former eschews them. Rather, Descartes took the basic problem with the scholastic account to be its failure to adhere to an intellectual conception of body that is clear and distinct.

In the same way, Malebranche saw as the main weakness of Augustine's account of sensation not his claim that we see bodies "by species that come from them" but his conclusion that "colors are in objects."[11] He told Arnauld at one point that he had learned from Descartes that colors and other sensible qualities are in fact "only modalities of the soul" (*TL I*, OCM VI 201). Malebranche also understood himself to follow Descartes in emphasizing that the prejudice that the qualities exist in bodies derives from a failure to distinguish between soul and body. He noted in the preface to the *Recherche* that

> although one must agree that [Saint Augustine] explained the properties of the soul and the body better than all those who preceded him and who have followed him until our own time, nonetheless, he would have done better not to attribute to the bodies surrounding us all the sensible qualities we perceive by means of them, for in the final analysis these qualities are not clearly contained in the idea that we have of matter. As a result, it can be said with some assurance that the difference between the mind and the body has been known with sufficient clarity for only a few years. (OCM I 20/LO xxvi)

The recently discovered idea of matter to which this passage alludes clearly is that of Descartes. Descartes had argued that matter is simply extension by contrasting the idea of extension and the idea of shape. He noted that while the idea of shape is incomplete because he cannot conceive shape apart from extension, "the idea that I have of a substance with extension and shape is a complete idea, because I can conceive it entirely on its own and deny of it everything else of which I have an idea" (*To Gibieuf*, 19 Jan. 1642, AT III 475/CSMK 202). This line of argument reappears in Malebranche's remark that although we cannot conceive of roundness without extension since roundness is only extension itself existing in a certain way, we can conceive extension apart from anything else; thus this extension "is not a mode of any being, and consequently is itself a being." Malebranche concluded that since matter is a single being and "not composed of several beings—as is man, who is composed of body and mind—matter clearly is nothing other than extension" (RV III–2.8, OCM I 462/LO 244).

Malebranche explained the remark in the preface that sensible qualities "are not clearly contained in the idea we have of matter" when he wrote in Book One of the *Recherche* that since the idea of extension "can represent only successive or permanent relations of distance, that is to say, instances of movements and shapes," it cannot represent "relations of joy, pleasure, pain, heat, taste, color, or any of the other sensible qualities, although these qualities are sensed when a certain change occurs in body" (RV I.10, OCM I 123/LO 49). Later Malebranche emphasized that any account of sensation must rely on a conception of body derived from "pure intellection" rather than from sensation:

> In order thus to judge soundly about light and colors, as well as all the other sensible qualities, one must distinguish with care the sentiment of color from the movement of the optic nerve, and recognize by reason that movements and impulsions are properties of bodies and that hence they can be encountered in the objects and in the organs of our senses; but that light, and the colors we see, are modifications of the soul quite different from the others, and of which also one has quite different ideas. (RV I.12, OCM I 141/LO 59)

The particular argument in this passage is linked to the principle, central to Book One of the *Recherche,* that one must reject "that prejudice common to all men, *That their sensations are in the objects that they sense*" (RV I.16, OCM I 169/LO 75). Malebranche held that this very prejudice was the source of Augustine's projection of color sensations onto bodies.[12] He also emphasized that Descartes provided the means to eradicate such a prejudice when he discovered an intellectual idea of body that entails that there is nothing in bodies that resembles such sensations.

While Malebranche often touted Augustine's doctrine that we see eternal truths in God, Descartes' claim that the idea of extension represents the nature of body was in some respects no less fundamental for him. After all, Malebranche took such a claim to reveal "with sufficient clarity" the distinction between soul and body, a distinction that he admitted Augustine did not see as clearly due to sensory prejudice.[13] Malebranche's debt to Augustine is no doubt profound, but a consideration of the case of sensation provides perhaps the most direct support for Alquié's conclusion that "the Saint Augustine of Malebranche is a Saint Augustine thought according to Descartes, and not a Saint Augustine whose doctrine suffices by itself."[14]

2.1.2 Sensations, Occasionalism, and Bodily Qualities

In remarks to Arnauld, Malebranche drew attention to the contrast between Augustine's position that colors are qualities that we see in bodies and his own view that they are "only modalities of the soul [that] God affects [*touche*] in me on the occasion of the presence of bodies" (TL I, OCM VI 201).[15] While we have seen that Malebranche took his view to have a Cartesian foundation, its relation to the position in Descartes' writings is somewhat more complex than he indicated. I consider two complications. The first concerns Malebranche's claim that sensations arise "on the occasion of" the presence of bodies, and the second concerns his claim that sensible qualities are "only modalities of the soul." Despite his use of occasionalist terminology, it is fairly clear, I think, that Descartes himself was inclined to the view, popular in certain Cartesian circles, that bodily motions are real causes of sensations. Moreover, though Descartes asserted at one point that "colors, odors, tastes and the like are only sensations existing in my thought," his more considered position seems to be that sensible qualities can be identified with dispositions in bodies. These features of Descartes' account of sensation serve to distinguish it from the account in Malebranche, yet they also broach certain difficulties that Malebranche himself sought to avoid. It may well be the case, then, that Malebranche's account of sensation is in some respects more consistent and sophisticated than the account in Descartes.

(1) Sensations and Occasionalism. Leibniz remarked at one point that while Descartes "had given up the game" [*avoir quitté la partie*] when faced with the question of how soul and body interact, some of his disciples—and in particular the author of the *Recherche de la Vérité*—proposed the occasionalist response that "God causes thoughts to arise in our soul on the occasion of motions of matter, and that when our soul, in turn, wishes to move the body, it is God who moves the body for it."[16] This remark is perhaps the source of the standard textbook view that Descartes' followers appealed to God in an ad hoc manner in order to explain the interaction of substances as distinct in nature as mind and body.[17] There is now a growing awareness among English-speaking commentators, however, that such a story involves both historical and philosophical distortion.[18] I want to strengthen this awareness by emphasizing the extent to which some Cartesians attempted to hold on to Descartes' claim that the human body causes the sensory states of the soul to which it is united. Though La Forge followed Descartes in speaking of bodily motions as "occasions" for the soul to have sensations, for instance, he also suggested with Descartes that the motions have some sort of causal efficacy. Cartesians such as Desgabets and Regis dropped the occasionalist terminology altogether and offered the view, which Descartes also encouraged at times, that motions in the brain directly cause sensations. There is evidence that Malebranche came to recognize in Descartes and the Cartesians this straightforwardly nonoccasionalist alternative to his own account of sensation. As the standard account indicates, moreover, he attempted to provide a Cartesian argument against this alternative. Contrary to this account, however, he did not focus on the problem of soul–body interaction but stressed instead the implications of the Cartesian view of the nature of body and bodily motion. The path from Descartes to Malebranche thus is different and somewhat less direct, though to my mind also more interesting, than that suggested by the textbook view of "Cartesian Occasionalism."

Malebranche's copy of Descartes' early work, *L'Homme*, included a preface originally published in the 1662 Latin edition of this text in which Florentius Schuyl wrote that there is an "absolute dependence that creatures have on the Creator, [since] their operations depend entirely on God."[19] Schuyl's occasionalist claim seems at first to reflect Descartes' remarks in the text itself on the nature of sensation. There Descartes interrupted his discussion of the mechanistic functions of the human body to claim that

> when God unites a rational soul to this machine ... he will place its principal seat in the brain, and will make its nature such that the soul will have different

sensations corresponding to the different ways in which the entrances to the pores in the internal surface of the brain are opened by means of the nerves.

He illustrated this position by noting that a certain disturbance in the foot causes a pulling of the "tiny fibers that make up the marrow of the nerves," which in turn causes a movement in the brain "that gives occasion to the soul [*donnera occasion à l'âme*] . . . to have the sentiment of pain" (AT XI 143–44/CSM I 102–3). In subsequent paragraphs he spoke of motions in the brain as "giving occasion" to the soul both to feel the pleasure of titillation (AT XI 144/CSM I 103) and to hear sounds (AT XI 149/H 46).[20] La Forge picked up on these remarks when he wrote in his *Traité*, the companion piece to *L'Homme*, that God is "the author of the union of soul and body, . . . [who causes] all those ideas which we have without the use of our will, on the occasion [*à l'occasion*] of those species that are traced on the gland by some [external] cause."[21] It is not surprising that commentators have taken Descartes and La Forge alike to hold that bodily motions serve as noncasual occasions for the soul to have sensations.[22]

The situation is considerably more complex, however, than these passages suggest. It is significant, for instance, that in *L'Homme* Descartes alternated causal and occasionalist locutions. Thus immediately after remarking that motions "give occasion to" the soul to feel pain, he referred to such motions as the "cause" (*causer*) of pain (AT XI 144/ CSM I 103). He also claimed in this text that motions "make the soul to have" (*fera avoir à l'âme*) the feelings of heat and cold (AT XI 145/H 39) and that small particles of food "can make the soul to sense" (*peuvent faire sentir à l'âme*) various kinds of tastes. It seems, therefore, that Descartes did not take motions to be *noncausal* occasions.[23]

This impression is strengthened by the fact that in a later exchange with Princess Elisabeth the Palatine, Descartes asserted in no uncertain terms that bodily motions cause sensations. In response to queries from Elisabeth regarding soul–body interaction, he wrote that we have a primitive notion of the union of soul and body that is distinct from our notions of the body and of the soul, "on which depends [the notion] of the power [*force*]" that the body has "to act [*agir*] on the soul, in causing [*causant*] sensations and passions" (21 May 1643, AT III 665/CSMK 218). Pressed to explain his position, Descartes told Elisabeth in a second letter that "those things that pertain to the union of the soul and the body [are] known only obscurely through the understanding alone," while they are "known very clearly through the senses." Thus it is, he noted, that those who do not philosophize but use only their senses "do not doubt that . . . the body acts [*agisse*] on the soul" (28 June 1643, AT III 692/CSMK 227). I take this correspondence to indicate that Descartes' most considered position is that we know by sense experience that the human body has a special power to cause sensations in virtue of its union with the soul.[24] La Forge was faithful to the basic point here when he noted in the *Traité* that even though God unites mind and body, "you must nevertheless not say that it is God who does everything, and that the body and the mind do not truly act [*agissent*] on one another:

Because if the body had not had such a motion, the mind would not have had such a thought."[25]

To be sure, La Forge also held that the action of body is merely a "remote and occasional cause" (*cause éloignée et occasionelle*) that "compels the faculty of thought that we have, and that determines it to produce those ideas of which it is the principal and effective cause [*cause principale et effective*]."[26] He was, however, simply paraphrasing Descartes' own account of the origin of sensory ideas in the *Notes on a Certain Programme* (1647). In response to the view of his wayward disciple Henricus Regius (Henri de Roy) that no ideas are innate to mind, Descartes claimed that "nothing is in our ideas that is not innate to mind." He explained that external objects have not literally transmitted sensory ideas to the mind but merely have transmitted something that "gave the mind the occasion [*dedit . . . occasionem*] to form [the ideas], at this time rather than another, by means of a faculty innate to it" (AT VIII–2 359/CSM I 304).[27] Later in this text Descartes distinguished between "the proximate and primary cause" and the "remote and merely accidental cause, which gives occasion [*dat occasionem*] to the primary [cause] to produce its effect at one time rather than another" (AT VIII–2 360/CSM I 305). The position here, as in La Forge's *Traité*, is that motions transmitted to the brain by external objects are remote and accidental (or remote and occasional) causes that give occasion to the proximate and primary (or principal and effective) cause, namely, a mental faculty (not God), to produce sensory thoughts.

Such a position admittedly weakens the suggestion to Elisabeth that the human body acts directly on the soul to which it is united. It need not be inconsistent, though, with the claim that bodily motion is a cause of sensation. The scholastics had earlier taken remote, accidental, or occasional causes to be real causes, albeit ones that are more indirect and less perfect than primary and efficient causes.[28] Likewise, La Forge emphasized that "one must not conclude that the body is not a cause of thoughts that arise in the mind on its occasion."[29] I take him to be reflecting Descartes' view in the *Notes* that bodily motions are real causes that elicit the activity of the mental faculty that produces sensory ideas.[30]

However, in the *Discernement du corps et de l'âme* (1666), which Malebranche admired,[31] the Cartesian Geraud de Cordemoy defended the view that bodily motions are noncausal occasions for the soul to have thoughts.[32] Malebranche himself followed Cordemoy when he used La Forge's term *cause occasionnelle* in a noncausal manner, noting in the *Recherche* that "*natural* causes are not true causes: they are only *occasional* causes, which act only by the power [*force*] and efficacy of the will of God" (RV VI–2.3, OCM II 315/LO 448). Thus Malebranche had a noncausal sort of occasioning in mind when he claimed toward the start of this text that sensation is simply "the understanding perceiving something on the occasion of [*à l'occasion de*] what takes place in the organs of our body" (RV I.1, OCM I 44/LO 3). We must be careful, then, not to allow the common use of occasionalist terminology to obscure real differences between the accounts of the sensory role of bodily motions in Descartes and La Forge, on the one hand, and in Cordemoy and Malebranche, on the other.

A consideration of Desgabets' position helps to bring these differences into relief. Soon after the initial publication of the *Recherche* in May 1674, Desgabets wrote to Malebranche that "the organs of bodies," which are united to our soul in a special manner, are "the true cause [*vraye cause*] of our thoughts" (Sept. 1674, OCM XVIII 87). We are immediately aware of the bodily causation of our thought by means of experience (*expérience*), and thus need not "undertake a consideration of the nature of peripatetic causes to learn [*apprendre*] what one senses" (OCM XVIII 90). In this letter Desgabets rejected Arnauld and Nicole's view in the *Art de penser* (1662), deriving ultimately from Descartes' response to Regius, that motions in the brain serve as the occasions for the formation of ideas by a mental faculty.[33] He therefore was somewhat unorthodox in failing to adhere to Descartes' more qualified account of the action of body on the soul. Yet Desgabets' remarks still served to represent to Malebranche an unambiguous version of the view in Descartes' correspondence with Elisabeth that we know by sensory experience that our body has a power to cause our sensations.[34]

Malebranche did not discuss this nonoccasionalist Cartesian view in the 1674 *Recherche*, which perhaps reveals that he was taken in by the occasionalist terminology in Descartes' *Notes* as well as in the related works of Cartesians such as Arnauld and La Forge. But in the 1678 *Éclaircissement* X he must have been thinking of his letter from Desgabets when he referred to the position of certain "Cartesian gentlemen" that we should "stop at what experience teaches [*l'experience apprend*] us about our senses: we experience [*experimentons*] also that they are the cause [*cause*] of our ideas" (OCM III 144/LO 622).[35] There are even indications that he came to see that Descartes had offered a similar position. In his 1688 *Entretiens sur la Métaphysique*, Malebranche had Ariste say that bodies can act on minds "by a power [*puissance*] that results from their union with minds" and that "experience does not allow us to doubt" that bodies have this power (EM VII, OCM XII 150-51/D 147, 149). These remarks are reminiscent of Descartes' claim to Elisabeth that the notion of the power of the body to act on the soul depends on the union, and that people who use their senses do not doubt that the body acts on the soul. Given that Malebranche himself owned the volume of Clerselier's edition of Descartes' letters that includes the correspondence with Elisabeth,[36] there is reason to think that this resemblance is more than coincidental. Desgabets' remarks may well have brought Malebranche to recognize in his copy of Descartes the nonoccasionalist account of the union presented to Elisabeth. It is clear, in any case, that Malebranche used Ariste to represent the position, offered by Descartes as well as by Desgabets, that we know by experience that our body has a power to cause sensations in virtue of its union with our soul.

In the *Entretiens* Malebranche argued against such a position by invoking recognizably Cartesian doctrines. Thus he had his spokesman, Theodore, emphasize Descartes' view that the nature of body consists in extension. Theodore notes that on such a view bodies can have only "the passive faculty of receiving various shapes and various movements" and thus "cannot possibly act on minds." When Ariste suggests that the human body could have a power to act in virtue of its union with a mind, Theodore responds,

> But that bodies should be able to receive in themselves a certain power, by the efficacy of which they are able to act on mind, it is something I cannot understand. For what would this power be? Would it be a substance or a modality? If a substance: the bodies would not act, but this substance in bodies. If this power is a modality: thus now a mode in bodies that would be neither movement nor shape. (*EM VII*, OCM XII 150–51/D 147)

It is interesting that La Forge offered a similar argument against the claim that the power to cause motion is a mode of body, when he wrote in the *Traité* that a notion of this power is not "included in the concept [of body], the idea of extension, as are the other modes of body."[37] La Forge also urged that the conclusion that bodies lack the power to cause motion need not entail the claim that they lack the power to act on mind, since the body does not literally move the mind.[38] Theodore seems to have the upper hand here, however, since he could point out that La Forge himself derived this conclusion from the doctrine that body is nothing more than extension and that this doctrine itself entails that body cannot act on mind.

In the course of his argument in the *Entretiens*, Theodore also invoked the view that God's will is needed not only to create bodies ex nihilo, but also to sustain them in existence by a continuous creation (see §6.2.4 (1)). Theodore claims that when God sustains a particular body, he must create it with particular relations of distance to other bodies. However, since "it is a contradiction that God should will the existence of [a] chair yet not will that it exist somewhere and, by the efficacy of his volition, not put it there, not create it there," it follows that "no power can transport it where God does not transport it, nor fix and stop it where God does not fix and stop it" (OCM XII 160/D 157). Theodore concludes that bodies cannot have the power to move other bodies, much less the power to act on minds. Here again this argument uses elements found in the *Traité*, in which La Forge claimed that "there is no creature, spiritual or corporeal, that can change [the position of a body] or that of any of its parts in the second instant of its creation if the Creator does not do it himself," since God must sustain a body by creating it in a particular position and since "if he were to put it somewhere else, there is no force that would be capable of moving it from there."[39] La Forge concluded that body cannot have the power to cause motion, though, as we have seen, he also attempted to resist the conclusion that body cannot be the cause of sensation. For Theodore, and thus for Malebranche, on the other hand, the Cartesian account of motion serves to highlight the fact that bodies are merely passive bits of extension that cannot possess the power to act on mind.[40]

As La Forge had earlier, Malebranche took Descartes' remarks in the *Principles* to provide the foundation for the view that God, rather than bodily power, is the cause of motion in the world.¹ Descartes had indeed emphasized in this text that God is "the universal and primary cause, which is the general cause of all motions that are in the world", since he not only created matter and set it in motion but "now conserves all this matter in entirely the same manner and in the same respect in which he first created it" (PP II.36, AT VIII–1 61–62/ CSM I 240). Nonetheless, Descartes himself never denied in this text that bodies can cause motion. Moreover, in his correspondence with Elisabeth, he referred in a relatively straightforward manner to the power (*force*) that "a body has to act on another" (21 May 1643, AT III 667/CSMK 219).[42]

In his *Système* Regis later defended this sort of appeal to the power that bodies have to act on other bodies. He granted there that "God alone is the primary and total cause of all motion in the world"[43] but went on to distinguish between God's willing "directly or *par soy* that bodies in motion are applied successively to different parts of body that can touch them immediately," which is "active" (*Actives*), and his willing "only indirectly, or *par accident*, that the other bodies are applied to bodies in motion," which is "passive" (*Passives*).[44] These remarks are problematic, especially given the attribution of a passive will to God. Regis may well have been aware of the difficulties, since in the later *Usage de la raison* he distinguished instead between God's immediate willing of the total quantity of movement and his mediate willing of the various forms of this movement, which forms are caused immediately by creatures.[45] It is clear, in any case, that he had a continuing desire to make room for the position that bodies have active powers that are involved in the causation of motion. With Desgabets, moreover, Regis wanted to leave room for the view that the motions of the human body are "true secondary causes" (*véritables causes secondes*) of the states of the soul to which it is united.[46] The correspondence with Elisabeth thus indicates certain respects in which Regis, rather than Malebranche or even La Forge, is Descartes' true successor.

Unlike La Forge, however, Malebranche was not concerned to be faithful to Descartes in all respects. Indeed, there is reason to think that his remarks in the *Entretiens* are directed against Descartes' claim to Elisabeth that body has the power to cause sensations. It is perhaps surprising, given the standard textbook account of Occasionalism, that these remarks focus so much on the fact that body, qua passive extension, cannot be the cause of motion. The focus is understandable, though, in light of the account of motion in La Forge's *Traité*. Malebranche simply took features of this account to be inconsistent with an appeal to the bodily power to cause sensations, an appeal that he may not have recognized in La Forge but that he could not have failed to recognize in Desgabets and, later, in Regis. Malebranche thus invoked Cartesian principles in support of an occasionalist account of sensation that was rejected by Cartesians he saw as adhering in an overly credulous manner to Descartes' own views. This argument is similar in structure to the argument that he directed against those disciples so prejudiced by the authority of Descartes that they failed to recognize the implication of the Cartesian position that we do not know the soul through a clear idea of its nature.

(2) *Sensations and Bodily Qualities.*   Malebranche told Arnauld that he learned from Descartes that sensible qualities such as colors, temperatures, and tastes are "only modalities of the soul." While he emphasized that there is nothing in body that resembles these qualities, however, Descartes with other Cartesians stated, in anticipation of the position in Locke's 1690 *Essay concerning Human Understanding*, that secondary qualities can be attributed to bodies. Indeed, in one important but somewhat neglected passage, Malebranche himself admitted that the terms for heat, color, and flavor can signify "such and such a movement of insensible parts" of bodies. Yet he went on to note that when we use the terms in this way, we say "nothing certain" and "nothing distinct" (RV VI–2.2, OCM II 302–3/LO 441–42). This point reveals that there is in Malebranche an interesting alternative to the more standard account of sensible qualities in Descartes and Locke.

Malebranche had some reason to think that his own view of sensible qualities has a basis in Descartes; it was Descartes, after all, who claimed in the passage from the *Sixth Replies* previously quoted that "colors, odors, tastes, and so on, are merely sensations existing in my thought" (AT VII 440/CSM II 297). When arguing in the *Fifth Replies* for the conclusion that we know at least as many attributes of mind as attributes of body (see §1.3.2), however, he referred to the whiteness of wax that corresponds to our sensation of that quality (AT VII 360/CSM II 249). The suggestion is that whiteness is an intrinsic property of the wax, though one that does not resemble our sensation of whiteness. Descartes developed and expanded this suggestion in the *Principles* when he claimed that the terms for light, color, smell, taste, heat, and cold can be applied to "properties in external objects" and in particular to "the various dispositions of the very objects that bring it about that our nerves can move in various ways" and that bring it about ultimately that we have the relevant sensations (*PP* IV.198, AT VIII–1 322–23/CSM I 285).[47] In other passages, moreover, he indicated that these dispositions in external objects are constituted by the shapes and motions of their insensible parts.[48] Descartes' position that terms for sensible qualities can denote bodily properties may seem to conflict with the claim in the *Sixth Replies* that the qualities themselves are "merely sensations," but even in the *Principles* he allowed that qualities such as color and pain are "clearly and distinctly perceived when they are regarded merely as sensations, or thoughts" (*PP* I.68, AT VIII–1 33/CSM II 217). His considered view appears to be that sensible qualities can be regarded either as properties in external objects or as sensations in us. The consequence of such a view is that terms for sensible qualities are simply equivocal.

This is precisely the consequence that the Cartesian Rohault drew in his *Traité de physique* (1671). In Book One of this work he wrote, with particular reference to our terms for heat and cold:

> These two words each have two meanings: For first, by heat and cold, one understands two particular sentiments that are in us, and that resemble in some

manner those which one calls pain and pleasure; such as the sentiments one has when one approaches the fire, or when one touches ice. Secondly, by heat, and by cold, one understands the power that bodies have to cause in us these two sentiments of which I come to speak.[49]

This position of course receives its canonical expression in Locke's *Essay*. Locke emphasized that the ideas of qualities such as colors, sounds, and tastes are distinct from "secondary Qualities," that is, from the powers in bodies "to produce various Sensations in us by their *primary Qualities, i.e.* by the Bulk, Figure, Texture, and Motion of their insensible parts." These secondary qualities, as opposed to their (nonresembling) sensory effects, are "real Qualities in the Subject."[50]

The broadly realist view that terms for sensible qualities can denote real qualities in bodies as well as sensations in us, which Descartes suggested and Locke and Rohault explicitly affirmed, seems at odds with Malebranche's claim that sensible qualities are "only modalities of the soul." Thus, it is somewhat surprising that in the *Recherche* Malebranche drew attention to the fact that "only since Descartes do we respond to these confused and indeterminate questions, whether fire is hot, grass green, sugar sweet, and so on, by distinguishing the equivocation of the sensible terms that express them." In the portion of this passage cited above, Malebranche noted that if by heat, color and taste one means "such and such a movement of insensible parts," then "fire is hot, grass green, sugar sweet" (RV VI–2.2, OCM II 302/LO 441). He here accepted the position, properly attributed to Descartes, that sensible qualities can be understood in terms of the "movement of insensible parts" of a body. Moreover, in this passage Malebranche offered a relatively innocuous reading of the claim that sensible qualities are only modalities of the soul when he noted that "if by heat and other qualities you mean what I feel near the fire, what I see when I see grass, and so forth, then fire is not hot at all, nor is grass green, and so forth, for the heat we feel and the colors we see are only in the soul" (OCM II 302/LO 441). Certainly neither Locke nor Descartes nor Rohault would have demurred to the conclusion that "the heat we feel and the colors we see" are only in us in the sense that they do not resemble anything in bodies. Malebranche's account of sensible qualities thus appears to be less radical than we first supposed.

This appearance is deceptive; Malebranche's account is more than trivially distinct from its Lockean counterpart. One notable difference derives from his occasionalism. While Descartes, Rohault and Locke all spoke of bodily qualities as having the power to cause sensations, Malebranche concluded that these qualities can serve only as noncausal occasions for God to produce the sensations in us. Yet in the same section of the *Recherche* that includes his concessions to the view that sensible qualities can be attributed to bodies, Malebranche indicated a more subtle difference. There he emphasized that people go wrong not only when they "think that what they sense is the same thing that is in the object" but also when "they believe that they have the right to judge the qualities of objects by the sentiments they have of them" (OCM II 302/LO 441). In support of the claim that people have no right to judge the qualities of bodies in this way, Malebranche noted that "different objects can make [*faire*] the same sensation of color. Plaster, bread, sugar, salt, and so on, have the same sensation of color; nevertheless, their whiteness is different if one judges it other than through the senses" (OCM II 303/LO 442). Thus it is that "when one says that flour is white, one says nothing distinct" (OCM II 303/LO 442). One might anticipate that Malebranche would emphasize here that the judgment that flour is white is obscure simply because there is nothing in the flour that resembles our sensation of whiteness. But what he in fact argued in this passage is that it is obscure because the same sensation of whiteness can be linked to objects with very different internal configurations.[51]

As we will discover presently, Malebranche allowed that our natural inclination to judge that sensible qualities exist in bodies is useful insofar as such an inclination contributes to the preservation of our own body; his point in the preceding passage, though, is that we fall into error when we take differences in our sensations to correspond to differences among bodily configurations. Rohault and Locke indicated a possible response when they spoke of sensible qualities as powers to produce certain sensations. Objects with different internal configurations could have the same color, for instance, simply in virtue of being able to produce in us a sensation of that color. Thus Locke did not assume that the powers to which the sensory ideas answer and agree have the same underlying structure; indeed, he required only something in the bodies that provides the basis for sensory discrimination.[52] These ideas, on Locke's view, suffice to indicate powers that correspond to real qualities in bodies even if the only thing the same qualities in different bodies have in common is their power to produce in us a certain kind of sensation.

Malebranche naturally could not accept that bodies have any sort of causal power to produce sensations in us. But he indicated a different objection to the view that human sensations are "constant effects" that "answer and agree to" bodily qualities when he noted in the *Recherche*, in further support of the conclusion that no one is entitled to judge objects by sensations, that "men do not have the same sentiments of the same objects, nor does the same man at different times, or when he senses these same objects by different parts of his body." Malebranche took the great diversity in reactions to tastes and temperatures in particular to reflect differences in the sense organs of different people.[53] It is because people differ in this way that "when we say that this or that thing is cold, sweet, or bitter, it means nothing certain" (RV VI–2.2, OCM II 302–3/ LO 441–42).

In an earlier section of the *Recherche*, Malebranche admitted that it is more difficult to argue that sensations of color vary among different people since these sensations are not linked to obviously variable sensations of pleasure and pain in the way in which sensations of tastes and temperatures are (RV I.13, OCM I 152/LO 65–66).[54] He even allowed that "it never, or almost never, happens that people see white and black other than as we see them." Yet he also added that what people see in these cases "may not seem equally white or black to them." He went on to propose that not everyone has the same sensations of "intermediate" colors (viz. red, yellow, blue, and their combinations) since "one cannot doubt that there is as great a diversity in different people's organs of sight, as there is in those of sound and taste" (OCM I 152/LO 66). While Malebranche granted here that it is "likely" that the same motions in the optic nerve produce the same sensations of color,[55] he nonetheless took it to be rather unlikely that the same objects always bring about in everyone the very same motions in the optic nerve and consequently the very same sensations of color. Thus it must also be the case that when we say that an object has a particular color, we say "nothing certain."

Malebranche of course did not depart entirely from Descartes' view of sensible qualities. He followed Descartes closely, for instance, in rejecting the scholastic view that there are real qualities in bodies that resemble our sensations of them. Whereas Descartes and followers such as Rohault continued to appeal to (nonresembling) bodily correlates of our sensations, Malebranche took such an appeal to be rendered more difficult by the heterogeneity of the physical bases of sensible qualities, as well as by the variability of the effects of bodies on human perceivers. He therefore offered what in the context of Cartesian thought is a surprisingly sophisticated critique of the prejudice that our sensations exist as qualities in objects.[56]

2.1.3 Sensation and the Teachings of Nature

While Malebranche differed with Descartes over the nature of sensible qualities in bodies, his account of the sensory modifications of our soul has a core Cartesian element. Central to this account, in particular, is the claim in the *Sixth Meditation* that the sensations supplied by nature teach us the needs of our own body but not the nature and properties of the material world. Characteristically enough, Malebranche did not merely repeat Descartes' own position but developed it in innovative ways. Unlike Descartes, he considered in some detail the manner in which sensory judgment is linked to the teachings of nature. Nonetheless, he took Descartes' main point that the senses naturally lead us astray to provide the material for an argument for the conclusion that we do not know the soul through a clear idea of its nature.

In Book One of the *Recherche*, which concerns the errors deriving from the faculty of sensation, Malebranche concluded that the "principal thing" he wanted to stress is "that one conceive well that our senses are given to us only for the conservation of our body; that one fortify oneself in this thought; and that to deliver oneself from ignorance, one seek some means other than those that [the senses] provide us" (RV I.20, OCM I 187/LO 85). The ultimate source of this passage is surely Descartes' remark in the *Sixth Meditation* that the purpose of sensation is not to "teach [*docet*] us to conclude anything ... about things located outside us without the intellect examining it first" but instead to teach us "to avoid that which induces a sensation [*sensum*] of pain, and to seek out that which induces sensations of pleasure" (AT VII 82/CSM II 57). Admittedly, Descartes prefaced this remark with the claim that we can conclude that our sensations possess variations "corresponding to" (*respondentes*) variations in bodies "though perhaps not similar to them" (AT VII 81/CSM II 56). Such a claim can be read as anticipating the view in the *Principles* that our sensations correspond neatly to bodily dispositions or qualities. While rejecting this view, Malebranche was nonetheless concerned to promote the central doctrine in the *Sixth Meditation* that the senses often lead us astray when we do not use them primarily to determine what is helpful or harmful to our body.[57]

Malebranche held in the *Recherche* that "the basis for all other errors of our senses" is our confusion of four different elements of sensation. The first two elements involve only the body: "the action of the object" (e.g., the impact of the motions of a burning object on the fibers of our hand), and "the passion of the sense organ" (e.g., the communication of motion from the agitated fibers of the sense organ to our brain). The third element is "the passion, sensation, or perception of the soul" (e.g., feeling heat and pain). Like the first two elements, the third involves a passion, but unlike the first two it pertains to the soul alone. The fourth element is "the judgment the soul makes that what it perceives in the hand is near the fire" (e.g., the judgment that the heat is in the fire and that the pain is in the hand). This element is an act of the will rather than, as in the case of the third element, a perception of the understanding (RV I.10, OCM I 129–30/LO 52–53).

Here again Malebranche was borrowing from Descartes, who distinguished, in the *Sixth Replies*, between three "stages" (*gradus*) of sense: the stimulation of the corporeal sense organ by external objects, the sensations of the soul that are "the immediate effects" of motions in this organ, and the judgments of the will that follow on these sensations (AT VII 436–37/CSM II 294–95). Indeed, it seems that Malebranche's distinction differs from Descartes' only by virtue of the fact that he distinguished bodily elements of sensation—the action of the external object and the passion of the sense organ—that Descartes had combined. While Malebranche followed Descartes in distinguishing judgment from sensation proper, however, his discussion of the role of sensory judgment, and in particular its connection to the doctrine of the teachings of nature, goes beyond anything in Descartes' writings.

In the *Sixth Objections* Descartes' critics attempted to defend the reliability of the senses by pointing out that we can use one sense to correct other senses; we can use the sense of touch, for example, to correct the conclusion deriving from the sense of vision that a stick in water is bent (AT VII 418/CSM II 281–82). Descartes responded that strictly speaking corrective judgments concerning the stick, as opposed to the "mere perception of the color and light reflected from the stick," belong to the intellect rather than to the senses.[58] He noted that he had referred to judgments of this sort as sensory out of deference to the fact that we often assign "judgments about things outside us that we have become accustomed to make from our earliest years" to the senses. Yet he emphasized that while these judgments may seem distinct from rational inferences that we make for the first time on the basis of some new observation, they are in fact made "in the same manner" as these inferences. Descartes cited, in particular, calculations concerning "the size, shape and distance of the stick," which are commonly referred to the senses as they are made "at great speed because of habit," but in fact "can be perceived by reasoning alone" (AT VII 437–38/CSM II 295).[59] His conclusion is that judgments deriving from habits acquired in our youth are as intellectual in nature as our most considered judgments.

Malebranche also asserted in the *Recherche* that "it is given to the senses only to sense and never, properly speaking, to judge." In line with Descartes' position, he went on to claim that the "sensation" of the size, shape, and distance is actually a "compound sensation" (*sensation composé*) that involves a comparison of various sensory features of the object.[1] Malebranche took this comparison to be a *jugement naturel* that accompanies our sensation (RV I.7, OCM I 96–97/LO 34). Whereas Descartes concluded that sensory judgment derives from our intellect, however, Malebranche claimed that a natural judgment is "but a sensation" that "the Author of Nature" excites in us (OCM I 97/LO 34). The remark here that natural judgments are "but sensations" serves to highlight Malebranche's view that they are passive aspects of our sensory experience that depend on God rather than on ourselves.[61] In this respect they differ from our consent to a natural judgment, which for Malebranche is a free judgment that derives from the activity of our will (RV I.14, OCM I 156/LO 68).

Malebranche held that natural judgments are the source of our misguided free judgment that sensible qualities are in bodies. This point is not clear in the *Sixth Replies*, where Descartes focused on often reliable intellectual judgments concerning features of extension. While Malebranche admitted that judgments regarding extension are "not entirely false" since "they include at least this truth, that there are outside us extension, shapes and motions," he was more concerned to emphasize that "the same is not true of those [judgments] concerning light, colors, tastes, odors, and all of the other sensible qualities, for truth is never encountered here" (RV I.10, OCM I 121–22/LO 48).[62] The view suggested in this passage is that our sensations of those sensible qualities that do not resemble anything in bodies always include a false natural judgment. More precisely, Malebranche held that we naturally feel each of these qualities as if they are in bodies, even though the qualities themselves are merely modifications of our soul.

Malebranche noted that we are not responsible for feeling sensible qualities as if in objects, since "all of this occurs in us independently of us, and even in spite of us, as natural judgments" (RV I.11, OCM I 133/LO 55). He also held, however, that we are responsible for our free judgment that the manner in which we feel these qualities by means of natural judgment reveals their true nature. Our natural judgments are unavoidable, but we can refrain from our misguided free judgments by fixing our attention on the fact that God has given us the senses primarily to teach us about the needs of our own body.

Malebranche did not borrow this distinction between natural and free judgment from Descartes' writings. Descartes in fact failed to discuss in any detail the sensory judgments connected to the teachings of nature. As I have indicated, his discussion of the third stage of sense in the *Sixth Replies* does not directly concern those judgments associated with the pursuit of pleasure and the avoidance of pain. There is a complementary incompleteness in Descartes' notion of the teachings of nature. Given his official position that judgment involves a free act of will,[63] it is not clear in which sense the judgments that instruct us derive primarily from "God or nature."[64] Malebranche's remarks thus help to fill out Descartes' own discussion of the teachings of nature.

There is a further complication in Malebranche's account of sensory judgment that is relevant to Descartes' writings. Malebranche distinguished among three different kinds of sensation, each associated with a different kind of natural judgment (RV I.12, OCM I 137–42/LO 57–60). The first kind consists of "strong and vivid sensations," such as pain, tickling sensations, and great heat or cold, "that startle the mind and that arouse it with some force because they are quite agreeable or quite inconvenient to it." The soul "not only judges that [these sensations] are in objects, but it also believes that they are in the members of its body, which it considers as part of itself." The soul thus feels heat and cold as if in the hands of its body as well as in the external objects. In the limiting case of strong sensations such as those of pain and pleasure, the soul feels them as if they are only in its own body and not in external objects.[65]

The second kind of sensation includes "weak and languid sensations," such as sensations of moderate light and colors, that "touch the soul little and that are neither quite agreeable nor quite inconvenient." The soul "does not believe that they belong to it, neither that they are within itself nor in its own body, but only in the objects." The soul therefore sees the colors of relatively distant external objects as if in those objects but not as if in its own body.

Finally, the third kind of sensation includes those sensations intermediate between strong and weak sensations. Sensations of certain qualities can be placed on a continuum between strong and weak with intermediate sensations being at the midpoint. The sensation of the light of a torch, for instance, is stronger the closer the torch is to our body, in which case we are more inclined to feel the light as if in the sense organ as well as in the torch. This sensation is weaker the farther it is from our body, in which case we feel it more as if only in the torch. When the torch is at an intermediate distance, "the soul finds itself puzzled" and "no longer knows what to believe, when it judges only by the senses."

Descartes offered an analogue of the Malebranchean distinction between strong and weak sensations in the *Passions of the Soul*, where he distinguished between "perceptions we refer to objects outside us," such as the light of a torch or the sound of a bell, and "perceptions we refer to our body," such as pain, hunger, and thirst (PS I.23–24, AT XI 346–47).[66] The claim here that we "refer" our perception to an object, moreover, could be read in terms of Malebranche's point that we naturally judge that this perception belongs to the relevant object. Whereas Descartes had offered very little explanation of why we are inclined to refer our perceptions in just this manner, Malebranche emphasized that the difference between strong and weak sensations derives from the fact that the primary purpose of sensation is to aid the conservation of our body. Given this purpose, according to Malebranche, "it is more to our advantage to perceive pain and heat as being in our body than to judge them to be only in the objects causing them" since such a perception motivates us to avoid these objects. Sensations of colors, on the other hand, serve "only to know objects more distinctly, and that is why our senses lead us to attribute them only to objects" (OCM I 142/LO 60). If these different sensations are to instruct us in the proper manner, it cannot be the case that they all are felt in the same way. Malebranche went beyond Descartes when he appealed to the purpose of sensation in order to explain the heterogeneity of our experience of sensible qualities. Even so, it is clear that he was attempting to develop rather than merely to replace the account of sensory judgment and the teachings of nature in Descartes' own writings.

One of Malebranche's most controversial innovations on Descartes' account of sensation concerns his thesis that we do not know our soul through a clear idea of its nature. At several points he argued that the fact that we naturally judge that sensible qualities belong to bodies rather than to our soul reveals that we know the soul itself only through inner sentiment and not through a clear idea. Malebranche also insisted that we cannot determine that we are capable of sensations of these qualities apart from our actual experience of them. For these reasons, he concluded that our knowledge of our own sensory modifications is less perfect than our knowledge of body that derives from a clear idea of extension.

Before I turn to Malebranche's two arguments, however, I must consider the distinction he wanted to draw between the knowledge of body through the clear idea of extension and the knowledge of soul through inner sentiment. Cartesian critics singled out for attack his view that knowledge of body is more perfect than knowledge of the soul. These assaults admittedly undermine some of the points that Malebranche made in defense of such a view. Nonetheless, they fail to touch his central claim that the knowledge that derives from an objective view of the geometrical modifications of body is superior in kind to the knowledge that derives from a subjective view of our own sensory modifications.

2.2 Two Kinds of Knowledge

2.2.1 Knowledge of Body through a Clear Idea

In the *Recherche* Malebranche had noted that "when we perceive something sensible, two things are found in our perception: *sentiment* and *pure idea*" (RV III–2.6, OCM I 445/LO 234). He later expanded on this point in *Éclaircissement* X by distinguishing between knowledge through illumination (*par lumière*) and knowledge through sentiment (*par sentiment*). The mind has knowledge of objects through illumination "when it has a clear idea of them, and when by consulting this idea it can discover all the properties of which these things are capable." It has knowledge through sentiment, on the other hand, "when it finds no clear idea of these things in itself to be consulted, when it is thus unable to discover their properties clearly, and when it knows them only through a confused sentiment, without illumination and without evidence" (OCM III 141–42/LO 621).

Malebranche attempted to differentiate these two kinds of knowledge when he told Arnauld that "in the perception that I have, for example, of a column of marble, there is an idea of extension, which is clear, and a confused sentiment of whiteness that is related to it." The whiteness, which the Cartesians take to be a modification of the soul, is "a confused *sentiment* that one senses, without knowing what it is." On the other hand, the pure or intellectual idea of extension, which Cartesians take to represent the nature of body, is "a clear *idea*, by which one may know matter and the properties of which it is capable" (*Réponse*, c. 13, OCM VI 98). Malebranche went on to indicate another difference between clear ideas and confused sentiments when he noted that extension "is an object common to all minds," as shown by the fact that different people can know the same truths about extension, whereas sensations are modifications that are tied to a particular soul (OCM VI 98–99).[67] This difference is related to the point that we can have an objective view of the modifications of extension but not of our own sensory modifications. I will return to this, but for the moment I want to focus on the claim that the fact that the idea of extension is clear serves to distinguish it from our sensations.

(1) The Clear Idea of Extension. Malebranche indicated to Arnauld that an idea of an object is clear just in case it is capable of revealing all the properties which that object can possess. He noted in the *Recherche* that the idea of extension involved in our perception of body is clear in this sense since it "suffices to inform us of all the properties of which extension is capable" (RV III–2.7, OCM I 450/LO 237). We are to understand this position in terms of the distinction in this text between internal relations among the parts of a body, which are modifications of that body in a strict sense because they are constituted entirely of features of itself, and external relations between a body and other bodies, which are modifications of the former body only in a loose sense because they are not so constituted (RV I.1, OCM I 42/LO 3).[68] Geometrical shapes are the primary example of strict bodily modifications since a body has a certain shape in virtue of internal relations among its parts. One mark of the clarity of the idea of extension for Malebranche is that it allows us to know precisely how the parts of a body must be related in order for it to be modified by the shapes it can possess. Another is that the idea reveals those modifications a body cannot possess. Through this idea we can discover that since all bodily modifications are reducible to the geometrical relations between the parts of the body they modify, "pleasure, pain, heat and all other sensible qualities are not modifications of body" (*Écl.* XI, OCM III 165/LO 634). As Malebranche had emphasized

against Augustine, the very fact that colors in particular are not so reducible to such relations shows that they cannot be "spread on the surface of bodies."

The simplest case of external relations pertaining to body are the relations between the strict modifications of different bodies. Malebranche emphasized that the clarity of the idea of extension is revealed by the fact that "we can compare a square with a triangle, a circle with an ellipse, a square or a triangle with every other square or triangle, and we can thus discover clearly the relations between these shapes" (*Écl. XI*, OCM III 168/LO 636). The idea of extension tells us, on the other hand, that a body cannot stand in the nonquantifiable relation of being hotter or brighter than another body. Thus does Ariste conclude in the *Entretiens* that the idea of extension is clear because it "makes known to us [the] nature [of bodies], their properties, the relations they have or that they can have to one another, in short the truth" (*EM* V, OCM XII 113/D 107).

Malebranche suggested at times that it is not sufficient for the idea of extension to be clear that it reveal the properties of which body is capable. He wrote in *Éclaircissement III*, for instance, that a clear idea is "anything that represents things to the mind in a way so clear that we can discover by simple perception whether such and such modifications belong to them" (OCM III 44/LO 561). He applied this point to the case of the idea of extension in *Éclaircissement XI*, noting that "we discover by a simple view [*simple vûë*], without reasoning [*raisonnement*] and solely through the application of the mind to the idea of extension, that roundness and every other shape is a modification that pertains to body; and that pleasure, pain, heat, and all other sensible qualities are not modifications of it" (OCM III 165/LO 634).[69] This suggests that the idea of extension is clear because it produces a simple view or simple perception of bodily modifications.

The additional requirement that a clear idea yield knowledge through a simple view is problematic given the position in the *Recherche*, so important for the argument in Book Six for the existence of the soul, that a simple view is distinguished from reasoning in virtue of the fact that it involves a nondiscursive grasp of its object. Arnauld indicated the central difficulty here when he challenged Malebranche in the 1683 *Vraies et fausses idées* by asking:

> Did Pythagoras need only to consult the idea of a rectangular triangle, and of a square, to discover, by a simple view, that the square on the base must be equal to the square of the two sides? Did Archimedes need only to consult the idea of the sphere, to discover by a simple view, that the extension of its surface must be four times the area of one of its great circles? Are all the properties of conic sections also discovered by a simple view?[70]

Arnauld concluded in this text that, given Malebranche's view of what is required for an idea to be clear, "we do not have clear ideas of almost anything contained in the most certain sciences, such as algebra, geometry, and arithmetic, for outside of the first principles and the most simple definitions, which are discovered by a simple view [*simple vue*], all the rest is known only through demonstrations, which often consist in a very long sequence of reasonings [*raisonnements*]."[71]

This objection has some force against Malebranche, who had noted in the *Recherche* that sciences such as arithmetic and geometry cannot be certain apart from the knowledge that a nondeceptive God exists since they include *raisonnements* (RV VI–2.6. OCM II 371/LO 481).

In response to Arnauld's criticisms, Malebranche insisted that we know by a simple view the *proprietez generales* of extension, such as divisibility and mobility, as well as the subsequent capacity to have various kinds of shapes. However, he went on to distinguish these properties of body from its more derivative *proprietez particulaires*, which we know "by examining the diverse shapes with which this idea [of extension] furnishes me" (*Réponse*, c. 23, OCM VI 160). This suggests that in order to perceive extension through a clear idea, it is necessary only that one can perceive its general properties by a simple view.

This qualification fails to restore the plausibility of Malebranche's appeal to the simple view of extension, however. The central problem is that his distinction between the perception of a general property and the perception of the particular properties that derive from the general property is unclear, especially so given his remark to Arnauld that the simple view of a general property includes a perception of "what [the property] contains and what it excludes" (OCM VI 160).[72] Moreover, this problematic distinction between the two kinds of perception is not required for the point, common to the *Recherche* and *Éclaircissement* XI, that our idea of body is clear because it suffices to inform us of the modifications of which extension is capable.[73] Malebranche himself may have seen that this is so, for in his 1688 *Entretiens* he dropped the point about simple perception altogether and had Theodore emphasize merely that we see truths and relations pertaining to body "clearly in the idea or archetype of extension" (*EM* III, OCM XII 66–67/D 59). Thus, for Malebranche it is not so much the fact that the idea of extension yields nondiscursive knowledge of general bodily properties that shows that it is clear but the fact that this idea itself yields a priori knowledge of the internal and external relations of which bodies are (and are not) capable.

(2) Knowledge of Bodies. In his *Vraies et fausses idées*, Arnauld directed most of his attention to Malebranche's ontological thesis that the clear idea of extension exists in God. Yet, as we have seen, he also considered the epistemic conclusion in the *Recherche* and *Éclaircissement* XI that the knowledge afforded by the clear idea of extension is more perfect than our knowledge of soul. In the passages from this work considered in §1.3.2 (2), he urged that our knowledge of our own soul is clearer than Malebranche took it to be. Arnauld also made the point there, however, that Malebranche overstated the clarity of our knowledge of body. Thus he claimed that "a peasant's or a child's knowledge of the sun is more imperfect than a philosopher's knowledge of the soul." Moreover, he noted that even philosophers know body only in an imperfect manner, as shown by the fact that "none of the philosophers before Descartes have the same notion of the sun, the stars, fire, water, salt, clouds, rain, snow, hail, wind and so many other works of God, as that philosopher had."[74]

One point here is that not even philosophers can know immediately all the properties bodies can possess. Arnauld attempted to reinforce this point when he criticized Malebranche for confusing a clear idea with a comprehensive idea "that gives us such a complete knowledge of an object that none of its essential attributes, or even of its simple modifications, is hidden from us." Arnauld argued that since it is impossible to determine whether we have such a complete knowledge of body, Malebranche's confusion helps to support the Pyrrhonist conclusion that we cannot know that we possess a clear idea of body.[1] Malebranche left himself open to this sort of criticism when he claimed that a clear idea of an object allows us to know by a simple view all of the modifications of which the object is capable. Nonetheless, at other points he was careful to allow that our knowledge of body is incomplete even though it derives from a clear idea. Thus, in the *Recherche* itself he noted, "What is lacking in our knowledge of extension, shapes, and motions is the shortcoming not of the idea representing it but of our mind considering it" (RV III–2.7, OCM I 450/LO 237).[76] The idea of extension is clear for Malebranche simply because we need only consider it in order to know a priori whether or not body is capable of certain properties. The mere fact that philosophers must learn which properties a body can or cannot possess does not serve to establish that the idea of extension is not clear in this manner.

Another point of Arnauld's claim that "even philosophers know body only in an imperfect manner" may well be that their knowledge of properties of bodies such as the sun and stars is irreducibly empirical and thus cannot derive a priori from the idea of extension. Certainly such a point is explicit elsewhere in the *Vraies et fausses idées*. For instance, Arnauld told Malebranche that there are particular features pertaining to body like the effects of gunpowder and of the heaviness of the air that we would not know "if we had not learned it by experience [*expérience*]."[77] The suggestion in Arnauld is that the philosopher's knowledge of particular bodies must be less clear than their knowledge of their own soul given that the former sort of knowledge depends on *expérience* in this manner. Other Cartesians appealed to the experiential nature of our knowledge of bodies in support of the different conclusion that such knowledge is no better off than our knowledge of our soul. Thus Desgabets wrote in *Critique de la Critique*, published nearly ten years prior to Arnauld's *Vraies et fausses idées*, that just as one knows by experience the sort of thoughts and sentiments that the soul has, "one knows also the properties of bodies only as far as one senses them and studies them."[78] In his *Système* Regis developed this line of thought in response to the Malebranchean objection that "one cannot deduce from the idea of the soul the idea of hunger, of thirst, or of pain." He noted there that one likewise cannot "deduce from the idea of the human body the idea of vital spirits, of animal spirits, and of free movements."[79] Regis indicated that the soul in fact knows what properties particular bodies possess by attending to "what the senses offer to it constantly."[80]

Malebranche adressed the objection that our knowledge of particular bodies does not derive a priori from the clear idea of extension, however, when he told

Arnauld that in claiming that there is a clear idea in our perception of a marble column, "I say clear idea of extension, and not of the marble. Because I know the nature and the properties of extension, but I do not know the internal configuration of the parts of the marble; what makes the marble what it is, and not a brick or lead." (*Réponse*, c. 13, OCM VI 98). When we perceive the marble column through a clear idea of extension, then, we consider it abstractly as a purely geometrical object, a portion of intelligible extension. The clear idea of extension reveals only those possible properties that pertain to the column *so considered*. Such an idea, therefore, does not allow us to know properties of the column that do not derive merely from its nature as an extended thing. This idea does not tell us, for instance, that the column exists or that it actually possesses a certain sort of internal configuration. But the fact that we cannot know these properties through a clear idea provides no counterexample to the thesis that the idea involved in the perception of the column is clear in the sense that it allows us to determine a priori the properties that derive from the nature of this object as an extended thing. Malebranche could complain that his Cartesian critics are rejecting a theory of apples because it does not apply to oranges.

Consider this sort of complaint in light of Regis' remarks concerning our knowledge of features of the human body such as animal spirits and free movements. In his *Réponse à Regis* (1693), directed against Regis' *Systême*, Malebranche failed to address these particular remarks, noting simply that we know extension through a clear idea (*Rép. Regis*, c. 2, OCM XVII-1 297). But it is open to him to point out that the features mentioned by Regis differ from the properties that we can know through the clear idea of extension. According to Malebranche, Regis, and Descartes, animal spirits are the rarefied parts of the blood that travel from the brain to the muscles by means of the nerves, resulting in bodily motion.[81] Malebranche is committed to the view that we can know through a clear idea the various geometrical features of which these parts are capable. He could say, however, that this idea cannot reveal the characteristic effects of the spirits, given that these effects depend on divinely instituted laws of motion.[82] Since for him such laws depend in some way on the divine will, our knowledge of the characteristic effects would differ from our knowledge of truths deriving from a clear idea, truths that "do not depend on a free act of God" (*Écl.* X, OCM III 142/LO 621).[83]

Malebranche's position that the laws of motion rather than clear ideas depend on the divine will reveals the need to qualify his claim to Regis that "the idea of extension is so clear, so intelligible, so fecund in truth, that the Geometers and the physicists derive from it the knowledge that they have of Geometry and of Physics" (*Rép. Regis*, c. 2, OCM XVII-1 297). One commentator has recently attributed to Malebranche the view that physics provides a paradigmatic example of knowledge through a clear idea since "the physicist, recognizing that extended things are movable, can discover *a priori* the general laws concerning motion and its communication."[84] However, Malebranche himself conceded at one point, in a 1687 response to Leibniz's criticisms, that his own account of laws governing collisions may well be incorrect and that, in any case, the truth about collisions "is arbitrary and depends on the volitions of the Creator." He concluded that we must employ *expérience* in order to determine the actual manner in which God regulates motion (OCM XVII–1 45).[85] Such *expérience*, or empirical evidence, is not necessary in the case of our geometrical knowledge, though, since this knowledge can derive a priori from the clear idea of extension. Thus on Malebranche's own view it is geometry, rather than physics, that best illustrates the nature of knowledge through a clear idea.

The point about the geometrical nature of knowledge through the clear idea of extension can be applied to Regis' example of our knowledge of the free movements of the human body. While Malebranche claimed that this idea reveals the motions of which body is capable (e.g., at RV III–2.7, OCM I 450/LO 237), he seems to have been thinking of the purely geometrical understanding of the nature of motion in terms of the change in external relations of distance between the parts of different bodies. On his view the human body is capable of certain free movements not only because it can stand in certain relations of distance to other bodies but also because these movements are linked to certain volitions of the human soul by means of divinely instituted laws governing the union of soul and body.[86] Here again, there seems to be a difference between the features of body that depend on God's will and the features of it that derive solely from the idea of extension. Malebranche could say that only the latter are relevant to his claim that this idea is clear.

Given that Malebranche's claim is restricted in this way, it has force even against critics such as Desgabets and Regis who emphasized the foundational role of the senses in our knowledge of body. In his *Supplément* Desgabets had referred to the fact that mathematicians "reason a priori in drawing out their consequences from one thing to another in virtue of which they see that the consequent is contained in the antecedent, and in this manner they have found the nature of all proportioned shapes imaginable."[87] Regis did not go this far toward Malebranche's position, though he did distinguish our geometrical perception of body from our sensation of it. Thus, he allowed in his *Seconde Réplique* to Malebranche's *Réponse à Regis* that "we sense [*sentons*] properly pleasure or pain, and we perceive [*appercevoir*] properly a triangle or a square; from which it follows that sentiment and perceptions are two very different manners of knowing."[88] In the end, Regis came to accept the Malebranchean position that our perception of geometrical modifications yields a more perfect knowledge of body than do our confused sensations. He also concluded, contrary to Malebranche, that the soul knows itself through perception rather than through confused sentiment. Nonetheless, this conclusion indicates that what is central to Malebranche's dispute with his Cartesian critics is not so much his view that our geometrical knowledge of body is clear, but more his claim that our knowledge of our own soul through inner sentiment is confused.

2.2.2 Knowledge of Soul through Inner Sentiment

Malebranche coupled the positive claim that we know our soul "through consciousness or inner sentiment" with the negative claim that we do not know it "through its idea—we do not see it in God" (RV III–2.7, OCM I 451/LO 237).

The negative claim here is not that there is no such idea in God to be seen. Indeed, Malebranche is committed to the view that God has such an idea. He insisted to a correspondent that God contains "the primordial ideas of all beings created and possible" (14 Jan. 1684, OCM XVIII 281). He applied this point to the material world when he told Regis that God possesses "the idea that is the archetype or exemplar according to which matter has been created" (*Rép. Regis*, c. 2, OCM XVII–1 287). Since the soul is equally a being that has been created by God, God must also possess an archetypal idea of the soul.[89]

In the case of the material world, Malebranche came to emphasize by 1678 that God contains not particular ideas of specific bodies, but only intelligible extension, that is, the general idea of the nature of extension. This account of the idea of body seems to suggest that the divine idea of the soul is a general idea of the nature of thought.[90] It is interesting, however, that Malebranche failed to assert that the idea of the soul is only general or universal as he did in the case of the idea of body. He told Regis as late as 1693, for instance, that a person does not see "the idea of his soul or the archetype of minds" (*Rép. Regis*, c. 2, OCM XVII–1 297). Moreover, in the *Réflexions sur la prémotion physique* (1715), his last published work, Malebranche insisted that God has an idea of the soul that allows him to know that Eve would freely consent in an undetermined manner to the suggestions of the serpent and Adam to the persuasions of Eve (*Pré. phy.*, sec. VIII, OCM XVI 23). Apparently, this divine idea represents not only the general nature of the faculty of free will but also the nature of the specific faculties of Adam and Eve. This consideration involving free will does not reveal that God must also have ideas of particular bodies given Malebranche's view that body can have no sort of volitional faculty. Malebranche thus appears to have reasons peculiar to the case of the soul to say that God possesses ideas of specific souls (see §6.2.4 (3)). In any event, it is clear that he holds that there is something in God that serves as the blueprint for the divine creation of our soul. When Malebranche said that we do not see an idea of our soul in God, therefore, he meant only that we do not have epistemic access to this divine blueprint.[91]

(1) Divine Ideas and Inner Sentiment. The conclusion of the *Recherche* that we do not have any idea of the soul, however, does not seem to follow from the premise that we do not have access to God's idea. Indeed, Malebranche's Cartesian critics protested that we have an idea of our own soul simply in virtue of being aware of our own thoughts or perceptions. Thus Desgabets wrote that "it is inconceivable to me that when one thinks of the soul one does not have in it the thought and the idea which are the same thing."[92] There is an echo of this claim in Regis' later assertion that "I know the thought that is in the subject by perception, or by idea, which are the same thing according to me."[93] Malebranche himself conceded something to this line of objection when he wrote in 1678, subsequent to Desgabets' critique but prior to Regis', that

> the word, *idea*, is equivocal. Sometimes I take it as anything that represents some object to the mind, whether clearly or confusedly. More generally I take

it for anything that is the immediate object of the mind. But I also take it in the more precise and more restricted sense, that is, as anything that represents things to the mind in a way so clear that we can discover by a simple view whether such and such modifications belong to them. For this reason sometimes I have said that we have an idea of the soul, and sometimes I have denied it. (*Écl.* III, OCM III 44/LO 561)

I have acknowledged the difficulties raised by Malebranche's claim here that an idea "in the more precise and more restricted sense" allows for a discovery of modifications "by a simple view." Now I want to focus on his admission in this passage that there is in us an immediate object of thought that serves to represent our soul to ourselves. According to Malebranche, it is the case both that the modifications of the soul are immediate objects since they "cannot be in the soul without the soul perceiving [*apperçoive*] them through the inner sentiment it has of itself" and that these modifications serve to represent the soul to itself since "they are only the soul itself in such or such a manner" (RV III–1.1, OCM I 415/LO 218). Thus, he could say that inner sentiment yields an idea of the soul, though one that cannot be an idea in a precise and restricted sense given that it represents the soul only in a confused manner. This point is perhaps obscured by remarks in the *Recherche*, yet it is clear enough in *Éclaircissement* XI, where Malebranche asserted not that we have no idea of the soul but rather that "we have no *clear idea* of the soul, but only consciousness or inner sentiment of it" (OCM III 163/LO 633).

As we have seen, Arnauld objected that perception through clear ideas is not opposed to perception through inner sentiment. At several points Malebranche attempted to address this sort of objection by citing God's knowledge of our sensations. In 1684 he wrote to Arnauld that

> God knows pain, but he does not sense it. He knows it, since he causes it. He sees clearly in the idea that he has of the soul how it must be modified in order to have such or such a pain; but one may not say that he senses anything of it. To know and to sense, idea and sentiment are thus very different. (*Réponse*, c. 23, OCM VI 162)

He made the same point to Regis nearly ten years later when he noted that "God, who senses neither pain nor color, knows clearly the nature of these sentiments. He knows perfectly how the soul must be modified to sense them" (*Rép. Regis*, c. 2, OCM XVII-1 289).[94] Malebranche's claim that God cannot have sensations was something of a commonplace. What is new is his position that the clear idea of the soul allows God to know how the soul must be modified in order to have its various sensations. In light of the distinction invoked previously between objective and subjective views, Malebranche can be read as affirming that God has an objective view that allows Him to know the aspects of the soul that explain how it can have modifications with certain phenomenological features. In this way God can know these features even though He lacks the subjective view of them afforded by sensation.

Such knowledge is to be contrasted with our inner sentiment of our own sensory modifications. While this sentiment reveals the phenomenological features of these modifications, it cannot tell us how it is that our soul is capable of modifications with just these features. The difference here between sensing and knowing the soul is not merely one of degree; it is not simply a matter of God's viewing more aspects of the soul than we do. The difference is also one of kind; our inner sentiment yields a subjective view of our soul that is of a radically inferior sort than God's objective view of it through a clear idea.[95]

Malebranche's appeal to God's knowledge of our sensations can be contrasted with an apparently similar appeal by George Berkeley, who was influenced early on by Malebranche's writings.[96] In his *Three Dialogues* (1713), Berkeley had Hylas object that Philonous' view that ideas exist in the mind of God has the unpalatable consequence that God himself possesses the idea of pain and thus has the imperfection of suffering pain. Philonous responded by distinguishing between the knowledge of pain and painful sensation.

> That God understands all things, and that He knows among other things what pain is, even every sort of painful sensation, and what it is for His creatures to suffer pain, I make no question. But that God, though He knows and sometimes causes painful sensations in us, can Himself suffer pain, I positively deny.[97]

As spokesman for Berkeley, Philonous thus endorses the Malebranchean position that there is a difference between our sensory awareness and God's intellectual comprehension. Nonetheless, Berkeley himself stopped short of saying that God knows our own sensory states better than we do. He did claim, with Malebranche, that we have no idea of spirit, but he also emphasized, in a passage no doubt directed against Malebranche himself, that "it ought not to be looked on as a defect in a human understanding, that it does not perceive the idea of *spirit*."[98] Berkeley's ultimate view is that even though we have no idea of spirit, we do know its nature by means of notions supplied by reflection.[99] It's a small wonder that he failed to endorse Malebranche's conclusion that our view of our own soul through inner sentiment is radically inferior to God's view of it through its archetype.

Berkeley failed to endorse as well the Malebranchean position that there is in God a nonsensory archetypal idea of body. He suggested instead that if divine ideas are archetypes at all, they are archetypes of our own sensory ideas; the world revealed by divine ideas does not differ in nature from the world we sense.[100] For Malebranche, on the other hand, it was essential to distinguish God's objective view of bodies from our own subjective view of them through sensation. After all, he went out of his way to emphasize that the Augustinian position that the qualities we sense exist in objects is unacceptable in light of Descartes' discovery that our senses fail to reveal the true nature of body. Whereas Berkeley was concerned to deny that "the *true* and *real* nature of things" is hidden from the senses,[101] Malebranche urged that our sensations cannot show us the material world as it really is, the world as God sees it.

In the end, though, Malebranche concluded that we can see the material world as it really is since we have access to God's intellectual idea of body. Thus, he emphasized in the *Recherche* that we can have a view of body that is similar to God's own view:

> [A mind] in some manner knows things as God knows them. In effect this mind may even say that it knows their true relations, and God knows them also; this mind knows them in the perception of God's perfections that represent them, and God knows them also in this way. For finally God does not sense, God does not imagine, God sees in himself, in the intelligible world that He contains, the sensible and material world that He has created. The same is true of a mind that knows the truth; it does not sense, it does not imagine; . . . whoever discovers the truth perceives it only in the intelligible world to which the mind is united, and in which God himself sees it.

Malebranche went on to add that the mind sees truths "only in a way that is very imperfect and therefore different from the way in which God sees them" (RV V.5, OCM II 168–69/LO 364). Even though he admitted that our knowledge of the material world differs from God's in degree, his main point is that there is no difference in kind. When we have an intellectual perception of the internal relations the parts of a body must have to each other in order for that body to have a certain shape, we have the same sort of objective view of body that God has. Malebranche had just this position in mind when he told Arnauld that when he sees that "all lines drawn in a sphere, which pass through the center, are all equal," that which is true for him "is true equally with regard to God himself, and all minds." The view of this truth is not one limited to a particular perspective, but rather is one that is "common to all intelligences" (*Réponse*, c. 13, OCM VI 99). In the case of the sphere, but not in the case of our own sensations, we can take up an objective view that is not limited to sensory appearances.

We need to pause at this point to consider the precise manner in which Malebranche's claim that we have a view of body that is objective in the sense of being "common to all intelligences" is related to his doctrine that the clear idea of extension yields demonstrative knowledge of bodily modifications. On his own terms, the two points cannot be identical.[102] While Malebranche suggested that we can have an objective view of bodily properties, he is committed to holding that some of our knowledge of these properties does not derive a priori from the clear idea of extension. He indicated in *Éclaircissement* X that we judge the existence of bodies "through sentiment" rather than "through a clear idea" (OCM III 142/LO 621), for instance,[103] even though he could not say that our view of bodies in this case is merely subjective. Furthermore, I have noted that on his considered position we cannot know a priori which motions bodies actually possess since these motions depend on laws the derive from God's "arbitrary" will. Nonetheless, Malebranche surely would not deny that the truth that bodies possess such motions is one that is "common to all intelligences."

It is open to Malebranche to say, however, that we can take up an objective view of an object only if we can know clearly how it must be modified in order to be in certain states. In the case of body, we can have objective knowledge of it because the clear idea of extension reveals to us precisely which relations the parts of bodies have stand to each other in order for those bodies to have various shapes and motions. This clear idea makes possible an objective view of body even though not all of the knowledge that we obtain from such a perspective derives directly from the idea. In the case of our soul, however, objective knowledge is not possible for us since we do not know how it must be modified in order to have its sensations. Thus when Arnauld complained that we know clearly by inner experience that sensations are modifications of our soul, Malebranche responded that while he senses pain in himself since it is "very vivid and very sensible," still it is "not intelligible to my regard" (*Réponse*, c. 23, OCM VI 162). In order to have an objective view of our sensations, we need to know not only that they are modifications of our soul, but also what changes in the soul make them possible. According to Malebranche, until we obtain this additional knowledge we cannot claim to see our sensory modifications as we see bodily modifications, namely, from a God's-eye view that reveals them as they are in themselves.

(2) Confused Sensory Relations. In passages from the *Recherche* mentioned in §1.3.3, Malebranche pointed out that while we can provide definitions of bodily modifications, we cannot know by definition our own sensations. He offered a variation on this theme in *Éclaircissement* XI where he argued that we cannot compare our sensations in the same clear manner in which we can compare geometrical shapes. One problem here is that we have access only to our sensory modifications; thus "one cannot compare his mind with other minds in order to discover clearly some relation between them." The central difficulty, however, is that we cannot discern the nature of the relations even between our own sensations.

> One cannot discover clearly the relation between pleasure and pain, heat and color; or, to speak only of manners of being of the same kind, one cannot exactly determine the relation between green and red, yellow and violet, or even between violet and violet. One senses that the one is darker than the other. But one knows with evidence neither by how much nor what it is to be darker and more brilliant.

Malebranche urged that while he undoubtedly senses various colors, flavors, and odors, "I do not know them through a clear idea, since I cannot discover clearly their relations" (OCM III 168/LO 636).[104]

In response to Malebranche's claim that a clear idea of an object must reveal its relations, Arnauld offered the counterexample that "we have very clear ideas of the circle and of the square, of the sphere and of the cube, even though we do not know the relation of the circle to the square or of the sphere to the cube."[105] As far as I know, Malebranche did not directly address this counterexample in his various replies to Arnauld. He did address it in his *Entretiens*, though, when he had Ariste say that even though we do not know the proportion of a circle to a square, "we can approach it to infinity and can see evidently that the difference between a circle and some other shape is smaller than any given amount" (*EM* V, OCM XII 124/D 119). Thus we understand the circle to stand in some sort of geometrical relation to the square, even though we cannot comprehend the exact relation due to the limitations of our minds.

One of the contentions in *Éclaircissement XI*, on the other hand, is that when we consider sensible qualities of different kinds, we cannot even begin to understand the sort of relations they could stand to each other. In a recent article Robert Adams gives expression to this point when he asks, "But is there a unique objectively valid spectrum in which all phenomenal qualia are ordered? Or at any rate a unique phenomenological natural order in which the taste of anise, perhaps, comes between blue and the smell of hydrogen sulfide? Surely not."[106] Adams is concerned to argue against the plausibility of naturalistic explanations of correlations of phenomenal qualia with physical states and does not directly consider Malebranche's claim that we do not clearly know the qualia themselves. Nonetheless, I take his conclusion that "the different sorts of phenomenal qualia are too diverse" to allow for a natural ordering to be in line with Malebranche's own view.[107]

Malebranche admitted that in certain cases we can order sensible qualities of the same kind by correlating the qualities with bodily states. He noted in *Éclaircissement XI*, for instance, that we can determine relations among sounds that are drawn from the numerical relations among vibrations. He also emphasized there, however, that we cannot know the relations among the sounds "compared in themselves, or insofar as they are sensible qualities and modifications of the soul." A musician can discover differences among sounds through the sense of hearing, but these differences will lack the precision of the relations between the vibrations. It follows, according to Malebranche, that "one cannot say that the ear judges through a clear idea, or otherwise than through sentiment" (OCM III 168–69/LO 636).[108]

Arnauld's judgment on this particular passage is harsh: "Nothing is more muddled than that argument."[109] Arnauld made the legitimate point that, given Malebranche's own position that the senses do not judge, he is entitled to say not that the senses judge sounds rather than reason but merely that reason judges sounds "only by the ministry of the senses, which shows that it cannot perceive them by means of clear ideas."[110] Arnauld went on to contend, in typical fashion, that a judgment "by the ministry of the senses" may itself involve a perception through a clear idea. Here he cited explicitly the remark from the first edition of the *Recherche*, considered in §1.1.2, that a person "distinguishes quite well the pain he senses and light, colors, sounds, tastes, odors, pleasure and pain other than the one he senses."[111] It must be said on Arnauld's behalf that the position in this text that we can distinguish the sensations in this way seems to entail that the sensations themselves are not only clear in Descartes' sense of being "present and accessible to the attentive mind," but also distinct in his sense of being "so separated and cut off from all other [perceptions], that it contains in itself nothing other than what is clear" (*PP* I.45, AT VIII–1 22/

CSM I 208). Arnauld therefore had reason to conclude that remarks in the *Recherche* commit Malebranche to Descartes' own conclusion that we see sensations "*clearly and distinctly* when we consider them only as sentiments and thoughts."[112]

Certainly the argument in *Éclaircissement* XI for the unintelligibility of our sensations indicates a shift in emphasis from the point, prominent in the first edition of the *Recherche*, that we can easily distinguish our sensations. We have seen that such a point, which following Flanagan I have called Content Cartesianism, is not fully consistent with other passages from the *Recherche*. However, it is not clear that this point is itself incompatible with the argument in *Éclaircissement* XI. Even if we could determine immediately and precisely the phenomenological differences among our sensations, it would not follow that we have the sort of knowledge of them that Malebranche took to derive from a clear idea. We could immediately perceive these differences in a manner that Descartes would call clear and distinct, and yet be unable to take up an objective view that allows us to see precisely how the sensations are related to each other as modes of thought. Arnauld complained that Malebranche was unfairly requiring here that nonquantitative sensations stand in precise quantitative relations.[113] Although some of Malebranche's remarks are perhaps open to this charge, he need insist only that the relations be "common to all intelligences," that they be comprehensible even to beings that have not sensed the qualities. We have access to the appearances of sounds but not to the objective manner in which they modify the ectoplasm, as it were, of the soul. We thus cannot determine what constitutes the differences between the sounds considered as modifications of the soul. This fact alone reveals that we do not know these sensations through a clear idea.

I have alluded to Adams' argument that phenomenal qualia are irreducibly different from physical states. Drawing on the work of Thomas Nagel, he concludes that materialist attempts to eradicate the mind/body problem "have no intrinsic plausibility."[114] Malebranche could hardly be sympathetic to materialistic solutions to this problem, of course, given his claim against Augustine that sensible qualities "are not clearly contained in the idea we have of matter." However, he recognized that the postulation of the soul to account for qualia does not eliminate one central difficulty. Such a difficulty is indicated by Nagel's remark that the invocation of an immaterial substance "does not explain how [this substance] can be the subject of mental states." Nagel concludes, "The real difficulty is to make sense of the assignment of essentially subjective states to something which belongs to the objective order."[115] As I see it, Malebranche argued in effect that since the assignment of subjective sensory states to the soul does not in the end "make sense" to us, it cannot be the case that we know our soul through a clear idea. Admittedly, most contemporary philosophers who, like Nagel, are critical of eliminative or reductive treatments of consciousness also follow Nagel in rejecting a Cartesian appeal to an immaterial soul of the sort found in Malebranche.[116] But this difference should not blind us to the fact that Malebranche anticipated, as Cartesians like Arnauld did not, the recent position that consciousness of mental states is unintelligible to us from an objective point of view.

This is not to say that Malebranche's point about the limitations imposed by our consciousness of our own sensations is wholly unrelated to themes in other Cartesian texts. I have mentioned the admission by Descartes and other Cartesians that the man born blind could not have knowledge of colors (see §1.3.3 [1]). Moreover, Malebranche's point can be seen as an extension of the Cartesian commonplace that we cannot understand sensible qualities such as colors to be objective features of body. Descartes gave expression to this commonplace when he noted, in a passage cited prominently in Arnauld's *Vraies et fausses idées*, that "we know more evidently, what it is in [a body] that is a shape, than what it is that is a color" (PP I.69, AT VIII-1 34/CSM I 218).[117] I take the difference here to derive from the fact that our knowledge of color is bound up with sensory appearances in a way in which our knowledge of shape is not.[118] For Malebranche, however, the very fact that our knowledge of color is restricted in this way reveals that we cannot conceive this quality to be a feature of our soul. Just as we do not understand what color is in body, so we do not understand what it is in the soul. Berkeley could perhaps be excused for failing to see the difficulties here concerning our knowledge of color since he rejected the position that a subjective view of body differs in kind from an objective view of it. But from Malebranche's perspective the Cartesians have no excuse since they themselves emphasized the inadequacy of the subjective view of body afforded by sensation.

Arnauld did not recognize any difference between the subjective and objective views of the soul, presumably because he thought that, unlike in the case of the body, the subjective view reveals the soul as it really is. It seems that here, as elsewhere, Arnauld had a more orthodox Cartesian sensibility than did Malebranche. Nevertheless, Malebranche offered two arguments for the obscurity of subjective sensory states that broach points made by Descartes and his followers. The first emphasizes that Cartesians need to consult the clear idea of extension in order to see that sensible qualities are modifications of their soul. That they must reason in this indirect manner reveals that they do not have access to a clear idea of the soul. Arnauld protested that this line of argument simply misrepresents the position of Descartes and the Cartesians. Although he did not fail to detect some weaknesses in the argument, Arnauld overlooked the very real connection it bears to Descartes' own discussion of sensation. Further Cartesian features of these remarks are highlighted by a little-known dispute, which Malebranche himself cited, over Desgabets' purported view that the soul is "painted" with the colors it sees.

Malebranche's second argument emphasizes the indispensability of experience for our knowledge of our own sensory states. This argument assumes that since we do not know a priori the sensory modifications of which the soul is capable, it follows that we can know the modifications themselves and thus the soul they modify only in a confused and obscure manner. It is not widely recognized that Descartes conceded much to the obscurity of the modifications in his 1643 correspondence with Princess Elisabeth. Admittedly, he also suggested in this correspondence that the subject of sensations is in some way distinct from the mind considered in itself, a suggestion that was developed in the writings of two of Malebranche's Cartesian critics, Desgabets and Regis. In the end, however, this suggestion does not provide these Cartesians with much of a defense against Malebranche's conclusion that they have no clear idea of the nature of their soul.

2.3 Two Cartesian Arguments

2.3.1 Sensible Qualities as Modifications of the Soul

In passages from the first edition of the *Recherche* that we have considered previously, Malebranche emphasized the positive point that we can easily distinguish our various sensory modifications. In passages added to the second edition (1675), however, he introduced the more negative point that in contrast to the case of modifications of extension, we do not know immediately whether certain sensations are modifications of our soul. Thus, he inserted into Book One the claim that whereas we have a clear idea of extension, as shown by the fact that "everyone agrees that roundness, for instance, is a modification of extension," we do not have a clear idea of the soul since "we do not know through a simple view, but only through reasoning, whether brightness, light, color and the other weak and languid sensations are or are not modifications of our soul" (RV I.12, OCM I 139–40/LO 58).[119] The indication that we know the modifications of extension "through a simple view" is problematic for reasons we have discussed. The main point here, however, is that we do not have an idea of the soul that reveals directly that weak and languid sensations are modifications of it. This is also the point of Malebranche's claim, inserted into the discussion of our knowledge of the soul in Book Three, that there are "certain sensations such as colors and sounds that most people cannot know whether they are or are not modifications of the soul; and there are no shapes that everyone, by the idea that they have of extension, does not recognize to be modifications of bodies" (RV III–2.7, OCM I 452/LO 238).[120]

Malebranche further developed this negative thesis concerning sensory modifications in *Éclaircissement XI*. Here his claims are directed specifically against the Cartesians rather than "most people," as in the *Recherche*. In particular, he stressed in *Éclaircissement XI* that the Cartesians themselves employ the following argument for the conclusion that sensible qualities are modes of the soul: "Heat, pain, color cannot be modifications of extension; because extension is capable only of different shapes and different movements. But there are only two kinds of beings, minds and bodies. Thus pain, heat, color, and all other sensible qualities pertain to mind" (OCM III 165/LO 634).[121] Malebranche concluded that since even the Cartesians must appeal in this manner to the idea of extension, "is it not evident that one has no clear idea of the soul? Otherwise why would one ever bother with this detour?" (OCM III 165/LO 634).[122]

Beyond the focus on the Cartesians, this passage differs from the *Recherche* in citing our knowledge of sensible qualities rather than of sensations. Moreover, in *Éclaircissement* XI Malebranche spoke of sensible qualities in general, whereas in the *Recherche* his claims were for the most part limited to weak and languid sensations. These further differences are, we shall discover, germane to Arnauld's critique.

Another distinctive feature of *Éclaircissement* XI is the appeal, missing entirely from the *Recherche*, to the fact that "one even subjects oneself to ridicule among certain Cartesians, if one says that the soul actually becomes blue, red, yellow; and that it is painted with the colors of the rainbow when [the soul] considers it" (OCM III 166/LO 634). Whereas the Cartesians employ an idea of extension that is clear, as shown by the fact that "everyone agrees on what it contains, and what it excludes," their idea of the soul must be confused since they themselves "constantly dispute whether modifications of color pertain to it" (OCM III 167/LO 635). For Malebranche the curious dispute among the Cartesians over the painted soul serves to confirm that Cartesians have no access to a clear idea of the soul.

(1) Sensations and Sensible Qualities. In his *Vraies et fausses idées*, Arnauld responded to the claim in *Éclaircissement* XI that Cartesians argue in a roundabout way for the conclusion that sensible qualities are modifications of the soul by protesting, "I do not know what Cartesians reason as they are made to reason here, and I have trouble believing that there are any who do." At least, he went on to say, Descartes did not reason in this manner. After citing at length Descartes' defense in the *Principles* of the position that we know our sensations clearly and distinctly as thoughts,[123] Arnauld claimed that any person can see

> through what everyone can recognize in himself, as Descartes did, that no person needs to consult the idea of extension in order to apprehend that the sensations of colors and of pain are modifications of our soul, because no person could have doubted it since they are things of which everyone is internally convinced [*intérieurement convaincu*] by his own experience.

He went on to conclude that "the grand detour that this author has attributed to the Cartesians, for proving that colors and pain are modifications of our soul, is a pure illusion."[124]

For some commentators, Arnauld's claim that Descartes never took "the grand detour" overlooks Descartes' own remark in the *Passions of the Soul* that "because we do not conceive that body can think in any manner, we have reason to believe that all the kinds of thoughts that are in us belong to the soul" (*PS* I.4, AT XI 329/CSM I 329).[125] To my mind a more basic problem is that *Éclaircissement* XI considers the status not of sensations, as Arnauld assumed, but rather of sensible qualities.[126] And while Malebranche did speak in the *Recherche* of our indirect knowledge of sensations, there is some evidence that he had sensible qualities in mind. At one point in this text he noted that most people think of sensations such as odors, tastes, sounds, and colors as "spread [*répan-*

duës] on objects" and as "united to the soul, but not as modifications of it" (RV III–1.1, OCM I 388/LO 201). This passage is most charitably read as saying that the qualities we sense, rather than the sensations themselves, are so united to our soul.[127] In any case, this point is clear in *Éclaircissement XI*, where Malebranche claimed that we imagine that color is "spread [*répanduë*] on the surface of objects, although these objects are distinct from the soul" (OCM III 165/LO 634). Whereas Arnauld attributed to Malebranche the position that Cartesians do not know directly that sensations are modifications of their soul, Malebranche's considered view is rather that they do not know in this manner that the qualities they sense are nothing distinct from these sensations.

Even so, the remarks in *Éclaircissement XI* are somewhat vulnerable to Arnauld's critique. The central difficulty derives from the claim in this text that Cartesians must consult the idea of extension in order to know that pain is a modification of the soul. In Book One of the *Recherche*, Malebranche had characterized pain as among the sensations that are so strong and lively "that the soul can hardly refrain from recognizing that they pertain to it in some manner" (RV I.12, OCM I 139/LO 58). He went on to state, in the passage added to the second edition, that "for vivid sensations such as pleasure and pain, we judge easily that they are in us, because we sense well that they touch us; and that we have no need to know them by their ideas, to know that they pertain to us" (OCM I 140/LO 58). This passage can be read as implying that we can know directly, without recourse to the idea of extension, that the sensation or, better, the sensible quality of pain "pertains to us."

To be sure, matters are complicated somewhat by the claim in the *Recherche* that the soul can know that pain pertains to it only "in some manner." In particular, Malebranche noted there that the soul takes this quality to pertain to itself in the sense that it belongs "to the members of its body, which it considers as a part of itself" (OCM I 139/LO 58). In *Éclaircissement XI*, moreover, he cited the fact that "one imagines that pain is in the body, which occasions one to suffer it" as evidence that "one cannot discover through simple perception" whether this quality "belongs to the soul" (OCM III 164–65/LO 634). However, the Cartesians to whom Malebranche referred in this text assume that "there are only two kinds of beings, minds and bodies." For such Cartesians, the discovery that qualities such as pain pertain to them just is the discovery that they pertain to their soul; that is to say, these qualities are modifications of this substance. The argument is even clearer in the case of other modifications, given Malebranche's own claim that "the sentiments that accompany love and hate, joy and sorrow, are not referred to the objects of the passions. One senses them in the soul, and they are there" (EM V, OCM XII 123/D 117).[128] There is room for Arnauld to complain that on Malebranche's own view, Cartesians do not require the clear idea of extension in order to discern that the qualities they sense in a strong and vivid manner (strong sensible qualities), as well as sentiments that they do not refer to objects, are modifications of their soul.

Malebranche would have done well, then, to limit himself to the claim that

Cartesians cannot know without recourse to the idea of extension that the qualities they sense in a weak and languid manner (weak sensible qualities) are modifications of their soul. Even here Arnauld would perhaps insist that they can know the nature of weak sensible qualities without recourse to this idea when they consider them merely as thoughts. At this point, however, Malebranche could draw on Descartes' remark in the *Passions* that we refer light to a torch and sound to a bell "in such a way that we think that we see the torch itself, and hear the bell" (PS I.23, AT XI 346/CSM I 337). Even Cartesians, it seems, are disposed to refer sensible qualities such as light and sound to external objects rather than to the soul. Malebranche explained this disposition in terms of natural judgments that are inextricably linked to our sensation of these qualities. While these judgments are necessary for the preservation of our body, they prevent us from seeing immediately that the sensible qualities that we refer only to external objects are in fact merely sensations in us. Malebranche's best argument, as I see it, is that Cartesians must take the detour of consulting the idea of extension because their natural judgments block any more direct route to the conclusion that weak sensible qualities are modifications of their soul.

Descartes did not anticipate the Malebranchean notion of natural judgment and therefore failed to offer this particular argument. However, he did anticipate the point that there is a feature of our sensations that lead us to attribute them to extramental objects. I have in mind his notorious claim in the *Third Meditation* that sensory ideas of "light and colors, sounds, smells, tastes, heat and cold and the other tactile qualities" are perhaps "materially false" in the sense that "they represent what is not a thing as if a thing" (AT VII 43/CSM II 30). When Arnauld protested in his *Fourth Objections* that the admission of material falsity is inconsistent with the official position in the *Meditations* that ideas apart from judgments cannot be false (AT VII 206/CSM II 145),[129] Descartes insisted that he is entitled to hold that the sensory ideas themselves are false in the sense that they provide "matter for error" (*materiam erroris*) (*Fourth Rep.*, AT VII 232/ CSM II 163). His emphasis here is on the somewhat obscure point that these ideas would provide matter for error if they represented privations, given that they are "as if images of things" (*tanquam rerum imagines*) (*Third Med.*, AT VII 37/CSM II 25). However, Descartes also held that we have from early on taken all such ideas to be images of real qualities that can exist apart from mind. While he did not stress the point, it seems that he must allow that one way sensory ideas provide matter for error is in leading us to conceive as (at least potentially) mind-independent features of sensible qualities that are in fact wholly mind-dependent.[130]

What is striking, in the context of a discussion of the remarks in *Éclaircissement XI*, is Descartes' view that materially false sensations do not lead us to conceive certain perceived aspects of sensible qualities as they are, that is, as inseparable from mind. Given such a view, Descartes could hardly have endorsed Arnauld's position that mere inner experience can reveal the true nature of these qualities. Indeed, he reminisced at one point that he became convinced that "colors, odors, tastes, and so on [are] merely certain sensations existing in my thought" only when he considered that "nothing whatever belongs to the concept of body except the fact that it has length, breadth and depth and is capable of various shapes and motions" (*Sixth Rep.*, AT VII 440/CSM II 297). There seems to be considerable force, then, to Malebranche's point that the Cartesians themselves consult the idea of extension in order to discern that those sensible qualities that they naturally refer to external bodies are in fact modifications of their soul.

(2) *The Painted Soul.* Malebranche attempted to bolster his argument against the Cartesians by citing the dispute among them over the position that the soul "is painted with the colors of the rainbow when looking at it" (OCM III 166/ LO 634). There is little doubt that he was referring here to the discussion at the Commercy conferences of Desgabets' view of sensible qualities. In one work that provided the basis for this discussion, Desgabets expressed his admiration for Descartes' discovery that sensible qualities "are uniquely in us, because they are the very perceptions of our soul," taking this discovery to show that "it is the soul itself that is white or black, hot or cold, of a low or sharp tone."[131] During the course of the conferences, moreover, Desgabets asserted that, given Descartes' view of sensible qualities, "it follows that the soul itself and all its faculties, etc., are the proper object of the senses."[132] In response, Cardinal de Retz took issue with the claim that "the soul is the object of the senses" by poking fun at "the green souls [*âmes vertes*], of which the Reverend Father has spoken to us from time to time."[133] The joke caught on not only with Retz's good friend Mme de Sévigné, who referred in several letters written around the time of the Commercy conferences to green and other colored souls,[134] but also with others.[135] Retz's original remarks were no doubt also the source of the claim, in *Éclaircissement* XI, that the person who says that the soul becomes the colors of the rainbow "renders himself ridiculous among some Cartesians" (OCM III 166/LO 634).

Malebranche indicated that he himself accepts this purportedly ridiculous view when he noted in this text that the Cartesians can be made to see by reasoning, though not by a clear idea of the soul, that the soul is actually green or red (OCM III 166/LO 635).[136] He did not defend this position in that work; in particular, he did not respond to the suggestion of the Cartesians that it is just silly to say that the soul sees colors by looking at itself. However, he returned to the position in a 1690 letter to the Oratorian A. Ville in which he noted that "your soul is green, or has a modification of green that you see when you are in the middle of a meadow, your eyes open" (Dec. 1690, OCM XIX 564). This implies that saying the soul is green is simply saying the soul has a modification of green that it sees. On the reading of his account of consciousness in chapter 1, moreover, Malebranche need not hold that the soul sees the modification by means of a reflective act that has this modification as its object. Rather, it is open to him to hold that the immediate consciousness of that modification is a feature of the modification itself. Such a position is in fact quite close to

Desgabets' view, offered at the Commercy conferences, that "all thought is known through itself [*par elle-même*], that is to say by way of sentiment and of intuitive knowledge without reflection."[137] For both Desgabets and Malebranche, it seems, the soul is green in the sense that it has a sensation of greenness of which it is immediately aware.[138] Cartesian critics would be hard pressed to deny that the soul is green in this sense.

At this point it may appear that not much is at issue in the dispute among Cartesians over the painted soul. Certainly this was the view of Arnauld, who noted in response to Malebranche that all Cartesians can agree that sensible qualities are modifications of the soul and not of extension. The only remaining question for Arnauld is whether the terms for qualities such as colors are properly used to talk about bodies. He concluded that such a question is easily answered, since

> the intention of the author of nature is that our soul attach them and apply them [to objects] in some way, in order to distinguish them more easily one from another. That suffices to authorize the usage, according to which it would be bodies that one calls *green* or *yellow*, and not our soul.[139]

Malebranche would be hard pressed to deny this conclusion, it seems, since on his own view God gave us color sensations for just the reason Arnauld indicated.

But Malebranche took Cartesians who ridicule the notion of the painted soul to resist more than a certain use of terms. As he indicated in *Éclaircissement XI*, they are also resisting the position that the soul "formally" possesses the colors it senses.[140] According to Descartes, properties exist formally in an object when they are in the object in a way that is "such as we perceive them" (*Second Rep.*, AT VII 161/CSM II 114). What is at issue among the Cartesians, then, is the more than verbal matter of whether the soul actually has the colors that it perceives as spread on the surface of bodies. It may be suggested that the Cartesians could admit that the soul formally becomes the colors it sees in the sense that these colors exist in the soul in some subjective manner. But the initial Cartesian reaction to the hypothesis of the painted soul itself illustrates how difficult it is to conceive of colors as merely subjective effects. Desgabets' critics simply assumed that when he said that the soul possesses colors, he meant that it has some nonsubjective feature that is spread on its surface.

Malebranche must grant Arnauld's point that Cartesians can agree that colors are modifications of the soul. He was concerned to argue, however, that they can come to this agreement only by consulting the idea of extension. Thus, in his 1690 letter Malebranche challenged Ville, who was a Cartesian, to prove to someone "that his soul is green, or that the color that he sees is a modality of his mind" without recourse to "the clear and luminous idea of matter, in which one discovers clearly that it is capable only of different relations of distance." He told his fellow Oratorian that the only way such a proof could be possible is if "you have a clear idea of the soul, in which you discover what you are, and the modalities of which you are capable" (OCM XIX 564–65). For Malebranche,

I take it, the fact that Cartesians themselves are confused about what exists in the soul when it senses colors reveals that they do not discover these features of the soul through a clear idea of its nature.

This line of argument is perhaps more suited to the case of weak sensible qualities, such as colors, than it is to the case of strong sensible qualities, such as pain. After all, it does not seem as ridiculous to say that the soul has the pain it feels as it does to say that the soul has the colors it sees. There is some reason to think that the subjectivity of pain is more immediately apparent than the subjectivity of colors. But then I have suggested that the main argument in *Éclaircissement XI* that Cartesians do not know directly that sensible qualities are modifications of the soul is best limited to weak sensible qualities. It should be said, however, that this argument for the obscurity of the soul is itself restricted for the most part to *Éclaircissement XI* and the related additions to the *Recherche*. Malebranche in fact relied more heavily on a different argument for the claim that Cartesians do not know sensory modifications through a clear idea of the soul, one that applies to strong (and intermediate) as well as to weak sensible qualities.

2.3.2 Knowledge of Sensation through Experience

(1) Experience and Idea. In the same later addition to the *Recherche* in which he emphasized that most people do not know whether or not certain sensations are modifications of the soul, Malebranche also introduced the point that whereas the soul "knows that extension is capable of an infinite number of shapes by the idea it has of extension," it "knows that it is capable of a given sensation not through the view [*par la vûë*] it has of itself in consulting its idea, but only through experience [*par expérience*]" (RV III–2.7, OCM I 452/LO 238). Descartes himself had spoken of the soul as knowing its own states through *expérience*.[141] What is new to the passage from the *Recherche* is the point that we do not know these states, and our own sensations in particular, by means of an idea. In support of this point, Malebranche later wrote in *Éclaircissement XI*, "If we sensed neither pleasure nor pain we could not know if the soul is or is not capable of sensing it. If a man had never eaten a melon, seen red or blue, had he consulted well this alleged idea of his soul, he never would discover whether [his soul] is or is not capable of such sentiments or of such modifications." In the case of extension, on the other hand, "one sees without pain and by a simple view what it contains and what it excludes" (OCM III 164/LO 634).

Once again, it must be admitted that the claim that we know the modifications of which extension is capable through a simple view and not through reasoning is problematic. But the central contention in this passage is not that our knowledge of extension is nondiscursive; it is rather that such knowledge derives a priori from the intellectual idea of extension. The fact that we know that our soul is capable of weak sensations of pain as well as strong sensations of colors only through experience shows that such knowledge does not derive a priori from an intellectual idea of the soul. So it is the distinction between derivation from an intellectual idea and derivation from experience, and not the one between a simple view and reasoning, that is most important for Malebranche's argument.

This distinction between idea and experience relates to the further distinction in the *Entretiens* between what is intelligible and what is merely sensible. Malebranche had Theodore say in this text that

> if my substance were intelligible through itself or in itself, . . . certainly I could contemplate in me that I am capable of being touched by such and such sensations that I have never met with, and of which I may perhaps never have any knowledge. I would not have needed a concert to know what the sweetness of harmony is, and although I had never tasted a certain fruit, I would have been able, I do not say to sense, but to know with evidence the nature of the sentiment that it excites in me. (*EM III*, OCM XII 67/D 61)

The argument here is not confined to the *Entretiens*; in several other texts Malebranche appealed to the fact that we sense but do not know our own modifications in support of the conclusion that we do not have a clear idea of the nature of our soul.[142]

Let us suppose, contrary to Malebranche's first argument, that we can determine merely by introspection that all sensible qualities—strong, weak, or intermediate—are modifications of the soul. According to his second argument, it still would not be the case that the soul is intelligible to us. We can sense in ourselves the sweetness of a concert or the taste of a fruit; we know the subjective features of these sensations through experience. It could be said, moreover, that we can know subsequent to the experience of these particular sensations that our soul is disposed to have certain feelings in certain circumstances. We do not know in an objective manner, however, the nondispositional features of our soul that serve to ground these dispositions. Theodore points to this very distinction between subjective experience and objective knowledge when he concludes in the *Entretiens* that sensations are something "that I sense keenly without knowing them but that God knows clearly without sensing them" (OCM XII 67/D 61).

Malebranche's position that the subjective features of our sensations are merely sensible is somewhat reminiscent of the recent view that we can know qualia only by means of experience. Whereas one proponent of this view argues that sensory introspection increases our knowledge because it provides the only possible access to phenomenal information,[143] though, Malebranche emphasized the limitations of such introspection. He simply assumed that there is an objective, God's-eye view of the soul that renders fully intelligible how the soul can possess its particular sensory modifications.[144] Malebranche took the fact that we can know our sensations only through experience, however, to show that such a view is not available to us. He concluded that since the idea of extension affords us an objective view of body that captures the nature of its modifications, it follows that our knowledge of soul is less perfect than our knowledge of body.

In *Éclaircissement XI* Malebranche did not claim that Cartesians in particular are committed to the position that we can know our sensations only by experience. His argument here is thus less explicitly Cartesian than the argument in this text that stresses the indirectness of the knowledge that sensible qualities are modifications of the soul. But it is significant that in the passage from the *Fifth Replies* that concludes that the nature of mind is "best known of all," which Malebranche cited in *Éclaircissement* XI, Descartes used examples—which Malebranche failed to mention—that suggest the importance of experience for knowledge of sensation.[145] Descartes noted in particular that when the mind knows that the wax is white, hard, disposed to melt, and so on, it knows at the same time that "it has the power of knowing [*vim cognoscendi*] the whiteness of the wax, another that it has the power of knowing the hardness of it; another that it has the power of knowing that it can change in hardness or liquefy, etc." There is no indication here that the mind can know that it has these powers apart from its actual experience of the various sensible qualities of the wax. Indeed, as I noted in §1.3.3 (1), Descartes appealed in this text to the fact that "one born blind" would not in fact have the power to know the whiteness of the wax (AT VII 360/CSM II 249). These remarks thus confirm Alquié's claim that "the analyses by which Descartes establishes that we have an idea of the soul, and those by which Malebranche proves that we do not have this idea, are often identical."[146]

Even so, Descartes failed to endorse Malebranche's conclusion that the nature of the soul is obscure.[147] In the course of his correspondence with Elisabeth, however, Descartes did affirm the intellectual obscurity of our sensations. I have mentioned his claim in this correspondence that our sense experience reveals that the body can act on the soul. He also held there that while we know the soul clearly through the intellect, we know the sensations that derive from such bodily action clearly only through the senses and not through the intellect. This sort of epistemic distinction is linked to the view that the nature of the soul must be distinguished at a basic ontological level from the nature of the union of soul and body. Malebranche rejected this sort of distinction, though, and there is some reason to think that Descartes himself abandoned it. When shorn of such an ontological distinction, however, Descartes' remarks to Elisabeth leave us with the position that the sensory modifications of the soul are intellectually obscure.

(2) The Correspondence with Elisabeth. In her initial letter to Descartes sent in May 1643, Elisabeth asked Descartes to explain how an immaterial mind "can determine the spirits of the body to make voluntary actions" given that all "determination of movement" comes about by impulse (*pulsion*), which in turn presupposes that the cause of the determination is in actual contact with the body that is moved and thus is extended (AT III 661). Descartes wrote in reply that same month that there are "two things in the human soul, on which depend all the knowledge that we can have of its nature, the one of which is that it thinks, the other, that it is united to body, that it can act and be acted upon along with it" (21 May 1643, AT III 664/CSMK 217–18). He conceded that he

had said "as if nothing" (*quasi rien*) about our knowledge of the union[148] but went on to claim that our notion of this union is one of the "primitive notions, which are as the originals, on the pattern of which we form all our other acts of knowledge [*connoissances*]." Beyond general notions such as those of being, number, and duration, "which pertain to all that we can conceive," there are only three such notions.

> [W]e have, for the body in particular, only the notion of extension, from which follows the notions of shape and motion; as regards the soul alone [*l'ame seule*], we have only that of thought, in which are comprised the conceptions of the intellect and the inclinations of the will. Finally, for the soul and body together, we have only that of their union, on which depends that of the power [*force*] that the soul has to move the body, and the body to act [*agir*] on the soul, in causing [*causant*] sensations and passions. (AT III 665/CSMK 218)

Descartes held that when Elisabeth attempts to understand the action of soul on body in terms of impulse and contact, she is using the notion of body to explain something that can be understood only in terms of the notion of the soul–body union.

In a second letter Elisabeth focused more on the relation between the notions of soul and soul–body union when she asked Descartes to explain why the soul, "being able to subsist without the body, and having nothing in common with it, is ruled such [by the body]" (June 1643, AT III 684). Descartes responded by attempting to make clearer the difference between knowledge of the soul and knowledge of the union. He noted first that the soul conceives itself only "through pure understanding" (*par entendement pur*). This claim is linked to his official position that the faculty of pure understanding, in contrast to the faculties of sensation and imagination, employs the mind alone.[149] Descartes simply assumed that pure understanding can discover features that pertain to itself alone. However, he continued by telling Elisabeth that "those things that pertain to the union of the soul and the body [are] known very obscurely through the understanding alone," while they are "known very clearly through the senses" (28 June 1643, AT III 691–92/CSMK 227).

One point seems to be that pure understanding cannot discover *that* there is a soul–body union; we can know only by means of sense experience that our soul is actually united to a particular body. This point is suggested by Descartes' remark to Elisabeth that those who do not philosophize but use only their senses "do not doubt *that* the soul moves the body, and *that* the body acts [*agisse*] on the soul" (emphasis mine; AT III 692/CSMK 228). However, his claim that "those things that pertain to the union" are known obscurely by pure understanding indicates that he wanted to make a stronger point. I think he wanted to emphasize that mere intellectual reflection cannot reveal *what* there is to the soul–body union; such reflection cannot reveal, in particular, which particular sensory states derive from this union. This view of the intellectual obscurity of sensation explains Descartes' remark in this letter that while "metaphysical thoughts, which exercise the pure understanding, serve to render the notion of the soul familiar to us," it is only in the absence of such thought that "one is taught to conceive the union of the soul and the body" (AT III 692/CSMK 227). Pure understanding can reveal which thoughts the soul can have apart from the body, but the senses alone allow us to know clearly which thoughts arise in virtue of the soul's union with the body.

Descartes' view that sensory thoughts are "known very clearly through the senses" was suggested by the examples he used in the *Fifth Replies*. What is striking, though, is his claim to Elisabeth that these thoughts are "known very obscurely through the understanding alone." Such a claim in effect concedes Malebranche's point that our sensations are not intelligible to us. But Malebranche's point entails that the nature of the soul is unintelligible to us as well. Sensations are simply modifications of the soul, the soul itself existing in a certain manner. To say that the sensations are unintelligible, then, is just to say that the soul is unintelligible, at least with respect to its sensory manner of existence. Descartes' remarks to Elisabeth therefore appear to support Malebranche's conclusion that Cartesians do not have a clear idea of the nature of the soul.

One way to avoid this conclusion is to deny that sensations pertain to the nature of the soul. Such a position seems, in fact, to be indicated by Descartes' claim to Elisabeth that the notion of the union is on a par with the notions of extension and thought. For Descartes the latter notions represent a "principal attribute" that "constitutes the nature and essence" of a substance; bodily substance in the case of the notion of extension and mental substance in the case of the notion of thought. But then it seems that the notion of the union represents a principal attribute that constitutes the nature of a third substance, the human being. The sensations that derive from the union therefore could be attributed to this third substance rather than to the soul itself.

To be sure, Descartes never claimed explicitly, either in the correspondence with Elisabeth or elsewhere, that the human being is a substance. Prior to his exchange with Elisabeth, however, he had attempted to accommodate the view that it is a unified individual in its own right. Thus he proposed to Arnauld toward the start of 1641 that though mind and body are complete substances when considered on their own since they are "things subsisting per se," still they "are incomplete substances when they are referred to the man that they compose" (*Fourth Rep.*, AT VII 222/CSM II 157). Continuing this line of thought, he wrote to Regius at the end of that same year that one can say that the human soul and body "are incomplete substances; and from the fact that they are incomplete, it follows that what they compose is an ens per se" (Dec. 1641, AT III 460/CSMK 200).[150] It could well be that Descartes was attempting to further develop the claim that the human soul and body compose an *ens per se* when he suggested in his remarks to Elisabeth that the notion of the union represents a nature distinct from the natures represented by the notions of mind and body. Such a suggestion certainly seems to be in line with the view, which John Cottingham has dubbed "Cartesian Trialism,"[151] that the union constitutes a third sort of created substance distinct from mind and body. In any case, it is clear that in his correspondence with Elisabeth Descartes held that there is some sort of basic ontological distinction between the union and the soul that underwrites his epistemic distinction there between the intellectually obscure knowledge of the union, on the one hand, and the intellectually clear knowledge of the soul, on the other.

In his *Traité* La Forge mentioned the view of "other disciples of Descartes" that "the alliance between the mind and the body is made by means of a certain mode that they call a union, which serves as the bond or cement that joins these two substances." Such disciples thus are similar to other philosophers who "conceive that matter and form are united by means of a union that is different from the one and the other." La Forge concluded, in some tension with the remarks to Elisabeth, that the position that the union is something distinct from mind and body "is no less contrary to M. Descartes than to the truth."[152] Malebranche followed La Forge in rejecting this alternative to a more standard Cartesian dualism. In the preface to the *Recherche*, he urged that the view that the two parts of the union "are but one and the same substance" is an aberration due to original sin (OCM I 11/LO xx). In the work itself he warned that even though soul and body are united,

> each substance remains what it is, and as the soul is not capable of extension and of movements, so the body is not capable of sensation and of inclinations. The only alliance of mind and body that is known to us consists in a natural and mutual correspondence of the thoughts of the soul with the traces of the brain, and of the emotions of the soul with the movements of the animal spirits. (RV II–1.5, OCM I 215/LO 102)

Malebranche held that sensations and inclinations are modifications of a mental substance that is distinct from body, just as extension and movements are modifications of a bodily substance distinct from the soul. The soul–body union is not itself a substance but a mere conjunction of distinct substances.

Clearly, this sort of dualistic view is present in Descartes. In the *Principles*, in a section no doubt composed prior to his correspondence with Elisabeth,[153] he wrote that there are "no more than two ultimate classes of things: one is [the class of] intellectual thinking things, that is pertaining to mind or to thinking substance; the other is [the class of] material things, or that which pertains to extended substance, that is to body" (*PP* I.48, AT VIII–1 23/CSM I 208). On the position here, surely, sensory thoughts are modifications of mind or thinking substance.[154] Though Descartes' later proposal that sensations pertain to a third sort of nature can be defended to some extent,[155] it seems difficult for him to hold that they are modifications of something other than thought, the principal attribute of the soul. This difficulty may well explain why Descartes responded to Regius in the 1647 *Notes* that while certain substances are simple entities with a single attribute, "that however in which we consider extension and thought at the same time is composite: namely a man, consisting of a soul and a body" (AT VIII–2 351/CSM I 299). There is no longer any suggestion that the man is a substance with its own attribute. Descartes appears to have settled on the view, then, that the sensations of the man pertain to the nature of the soul rather than to the nature of the union.

Arnauld himself embraced such a dualistic view. He remarked to Malebranche, after all, that on Descartes' view "we see sensible qualities clearly when we consider them only as modifications of our mind."[156] This remark, of course, overlooks the suggestion in the correspondence with Elisabeth that sensations pertain to the soul–body union rather than to the soul itself. It overlooks as well Descartes' distinction between the "very clear" knowledge of sensations "through the senses" and the "very obscure" knowledge of them "through pure understanding." Malebranche can be read as concluding, in terms of this epistemic distinction, that while the senses reveal clearly the phenomenological aspects of sensations, pure understanding reveals only obscurely the features of the soul that constitute such sensations. Thus even though the ontological aspects of the view presented to Elisabeth deviate from Malebranche's account of the nature of sensation, the epistemic aspects of this view provide some support for his conclusion regarding our knowledge of the soul. Arnauld simply failed to come to grips with the fact that this conclusion has a Cartesian basis.

(3) Desgabets and Regis. In order to follow out Malebranche's argument for the obscurity of the sensory modifications of the soul, I want to consider the case of those Cartesians who, unlike Arnauld, picked up on Descartes' suggestion to Elisabeth that the subject of sensations is in some way distinct from the soul or mind considered in itself. In §1.2.3 (1) I noted the view of Desgabets that the thoughts of *esprits purs* differ in nature from the thoughts of the human soul. He emphasized this view in his 1674 letter to Malebranche, in which he took issue with Malebranche's claim that the soul–body union "was not determined by the nature or essence of a thing; which gives an idea of the soul strongly related to that which we have of an Angel." Desgabets responded that the angel in fact has "a nature more contrary to that of the soul than simply distinguished" (OCM XVIII 84). Whereas the angel is "through its essence above bodies" (OCM XVIII 84), the soul is "a thinking substance, but thinking in a certain manner, which is that the thoughts are modes naturally required to be united with corporeal movements" (OCM XVIII 85). Desgabets made clear in his unpublished writings that while the essence of pure minds such as those of angels consists in having thoughts that are causally independent of the body, the essence of the human soul consists in having thoughts that derive from the action of the human body.[157] Citing the scholastic maxim *Nihil est in intellectu quod non prius fuerit in sensu*, he emphasized that all states of the soul are by nature dependent on the body to which that soul is united.[158] There is some sort of ontological distinction here between the pure mind of the angel, which is entirely separate from body, and the human soul, which is essentially united to some body.

While Desgabets made clear that the pure mind is a substance rather than a modification, however, he did not consider in any detail the precise status of the human soul. Regis, Desgabets' admirer, took matters further. As I have indicated, he followed Desgabets when he claimed in his *Système* that all the thoughts of the human soul depend on the movements of the body to which it is united (see §1.2.3 [2]). In line with Desgabets' own position, moreover, Regis distinguished in this text between this soul (*l'âme*) and "the mind [*esprit*] considered in itself and according to its absolute being, according to which it is a substance that thinks."[159] He went beyond Desgabets, though, when he noted in the *Système* that the man (*l'homme*) that is "a mind and a body united together" is not a substance but "a modal being, because the union of mind and body that constitutes its nature, is a true mode." The properties of the man depend on the union in the same way that "all the properties of a triangle depend on what is an extension limited by three sides."[160]

Here we have an alternative to the view, suggested by the trialistic language of the correspondence with Elisabeth, that sensations belong to an entity of a basic kind distinct from mind and body. According to Regis, sensations belong to a member of a species of mind, the soul, which is formed by means of the soul–body union.[161] The position, in terms that Regis no doubt borrowed from Descartes, is that there is a modal distinction between the soul and the mind since the soul cannot exist apart from the mind, whereas the mind can exist even while lacking the sort of dependence on body that is essential to the soul.[162] This distinction between soul and mind is not so strong as to require that the human soul and the human body compose an individual that has a single nature represented by its own primitive notion. It thus allows for the more dualistic view, indicated in the writings of Desgabets and Regis alike, that all created substances are either minds or bodies.[163]

Regis urged that his distinction is strong enough, however, to provide a response to the Malebranchean position that body is better known than soul. In a section of the *Système* considered in §2.2.1 (2), he granted Malebranche that "one cannot deduce as immediately from the idea of thought hunger, thirst, pain, etc. as one deduces from the idea of extension shape, movement, and repose, etc." However, he went on to note that these sensations "are not so much properties of thought, which is the essential attribute of mind, as they are the consequences [*de suites*] of the union of mind and body, which is the formal reason of the soul." To be fair, according to Regis, Malebranche must compare knowledge of the soul to knowledge of the human body, and knowledge of extension to knowledge of mind.[164]

I have mentioned the Malebranchean rejoinder that we do know the modifications of the human body through a clear idea of extension when we consider these modifications in a purely geometrical manner. He could point out as well that we do not have a corresponding knowledge of the modifications of the soul that derives from a clear idea of its nature. After all, Regis himself admitted, in line with the view expressed in the correspondence with Elisabeth, that the soul is "not intelligible by its nature." To be sure, Regis went on to claim that the soul can "be known through things that are intelligible by themselves" and, in particular, through "the mind considered in itself."[165] Given his position that all modifications of the soul derive from the union with the body, though, it is not clear what the consideration of the nature of mind as it is in itself, apart from its union with body, could add to our knowledge of these modifications.[166] It seems difficult for Regis to deny Malebranche's conclusion that the modifications of our soul are not themselves intelligible.

One might object that these considerations fail to reveal that Cartesians in general are committed to Malebranche's conclusion. Regis' own position is compromised by his acceptance of Desgabets' claim that all the thoughts of the soul derive from its union with the body. Desgabets and Regis both have difficulty allowing that we have a knowledge of our modifications that derives from a consideration of the "mind considered in itself" rather than from a consideration of the soul insofar as it is united to body. Descartes had no such difficulty, since he told Elisabeth explicitly that we have pure intellectual thoughts distinct from our sensations that we know through a notion of "the soul alone." Malebranche himself was sympathetic to the admission here of nonsensory thoughts, insisting as he did in the *Recherche* and elsewhere that the soul has pure perceptions (*perceptions pures*) that derive from its union with God rather than, as in the case of its sensations, from its union with the body. On his own view, then, the fact that our sensory modifications are obscure to us cannot itself establish the obscurity of all our modifications. Malebranche must further argue that we do not know even our nonsensory or intellectual modifications through a clear idea of the soul. His attempt to provide such an argument is complicated, however, by difficulties concerning his account of pure perceptions and of the relations they bear to ideas in God, on the one hand, and to sensations in us, on the other. In the next chapter we will consider Malebranche's particular account and its attendant difficulties.

three

PURE PERCEPTION

In the preface to the *Recherche*, Malebranche drew attention to the Augustinian view that the human mind (*l'esprit de l'homme*) is situated between the bodies below it and God above it. For Malebranche this intermediate status is reflected in the mind's dependence in both directions. Through its union with a particular body, the mind has sensations and passions that strengthen its interest in the material world. Because such an interest often leads it astray, Malebranche stated that this union "debases man and is today the main cause of all his errors and miseries." Yet the mind also is united to God in an intimate and essential manner. The union with God "raises the mind above all things. Through it, the mind receives its life, its light, and its entire felicity" (OCM I 9/LO xix).

This account of the two unions is germane to Malebranche's Cartesian view of our knowledge of body. Sensations deriving from the union with body encourage us to make false judgments about the material world; intellectual or pure perceptions deriving from the union with God, and in particular from the clear idea of extension, allow us to see this world as it really is. Malebranche's Cartesianism is qualified by his rejection of Descartes' innatism in favor of the doctrine that the idea of extension exists in God rather than in us. Nonetheless, Malebranche accepted the Cartesian point that knowledge of body must be grounded in a clear and distinct intellectual perception of the nature of extension.

This point, however, seems to create difficulties for Malebranche's thesis that we do not have a clear idea of the nature of the soul. In particular, the admission of clear and distinct pure perceptions conflicts with his conclusion in several texts that our inner sentiment reveals only confused and obscure modifications. Malebranche at first overlooked this conflict, due mainly to the fact that he focused more on the conclusion that clear ideas exist in God than on the claim that they correspond to pure perceptions in us. Moreover, when he did consider pure perceptions in his later writings, he tended to minimize their difference from sensations, emphasizing that both kinds of perceptions derive from divine ideas. Even so, I argue that he was committed at a fairly deep level to two basic positions: the first, the recognizably Cartesian position that intellectual rather than sensory perception reveals the nature of body, and the second, his own distinctive position that the perceptions of the soul are only obscure modifications.

Any adequate interpretation of Malebranche's account of pure perception must address each of these aspects of his thought. I contend that we can do justice to both aspects by bearing in mind that pure perceptions are for Malebranche Janus-faced. On one side, these perceptions have features that are only subjectively accessible; in this respect they are akin to sensations. Unlike sensations, however, pure perceptions have another side to them since they have an objective content that is constituted by infinite divine ideas rather than by their own phenomenological features. Malebranche's discussion of pure perception certainly is not without its difficulties. Nonetheless, his mature writings suggest the consistent position that while we can clearly know the content of pure perceptions, we can have only a confused inner sentiment of the perceptions themselves as thoughts.

3.1 Pure Understanding and Sentiment

3.1.1 Pure Understanding and Pure Perception

(1) The Cartesian Distinction. Toward the start of the *Recherche*, Malebranche indicated that he was assuming the "customary" position that the mind has two principal faculties, understanding and will. The understanding is simply the passive faculty "of receiving various ideas, that is, of perceiving various things" (RV I.1, OCM I 41/LO 2). Taken in this broad sense, the understanding is responsible even for sensation and imagination, since "the *senses* and the *imagination* are only the understanding, perceiving objects through the organs of the body" (OCM I 43/LO 3). Understanding in this broad sense is to be distinguished from "pure understanding," which Malebranche defined as "the mind's faculty of knowing external objects without forming corporeal images of them in the brain" (RV III–1.1, OCM I 381/LO 198). Through this faculty the mind perceives not only "spiritual things, universals, common notions" but also "material things, extension with its properties; for only pure understanding can perceive a perfect circle, a perfect square, a shape of a thousand sides, and similar things." These perceptions Malebranche called "*pure intellections,* or *pure perceptions,*" on account of the fact that the mind does not require the body to have them (RV I.4, OCM I 66/LO 16–17).

Malebranche's reference to "a shape of a thousand sides" recalls the famous discussion in the *Sixth Meditation* of the chiliagon. In order to illustrate the difference between imagination and "pure intellect" (*pura intellectionis*), Descartes noted in this text that while we can intellectually understand the properties of a chiliagon, or thousand-sided figure, we cannot picture it in a way that clearly distinguishes it from a myriagon or any other polygon of many sides. He suggested that this difference is due to the fact that when the mind

> understands, it turns to itself [*se ad seipsam . . . convertat*] in some manner, and inspects [*respicatque*] some of the ideas that are in itself; when however it imagines, it turns to the body, and views [*intueatur*] something in [the body] conforming to the idea, either understood by itself or perceived by the senses. (AT VII 73/CSM II 51)

It is true that Descartes went on to warn that this account of the distinction is "only a probability." However, he provided a less guarded endorsement of it when he told Gassendi that "understanding [*intelligendi*] and imagination do not differ merely as greater or lesser, but as two modes of operation wholly distinct [since] in understanding the mind uses itself alone, but in fact in imagination contemplates [*contemplatur*] a corporeal form" (*Fifth Rep.*, AT VII 385/CSM II 264).[1]

The concept that in imagination the mind "contemplates" or "turns to" bodily images is admittedly somewhat odd. Descartes in fact had a persisting tendency to speak of the mind as sensing or imagining by considering something in the brain.[2] We have seen that Malebranche himself referred to the mind as sensing or imagining objects "through the organs of the body," though at one point he was careful to warn that the soul cannot literally perceive anything in the brain "since it cannot discover the particles composing its brain, that itself where it is said to make its principal residence" (RV IV.11, OCM II 100/LO 320). For Malebranche the claim that we perceive through the sense organs indicates primarily that states of sensation and imagination are correlated with states in the brain.

Desgabets and Regis accepted as well that there is such a correlation. Because they denied that the soul has any faculty independent of sensation and imagination, however, they concluded that all the thoughts of the soul are correlated with states of the body to which it is united. Thus, Desgabets criticized Descartes for failing to see that "we have our purest intellections through the senses, and that the pretended pure understanding, distinguished from the senses, is imaginary."[3] Regis offered a similar criticism of the "hypothesis of the modern philosophers" that the soul has a faculty of pure understanding, noting that "the soul can act as soul only depending on body, and pure understanding does not depend on it, by supposition."[4] As we will discover, Malebranche was not always careful to distance himself from the position that the soul has only sensory thoughts. However, it is clear, at least in the *Recherche*, that he wanted to leave room for a mental faculty of pure understanding that is distinct from mental faculties that depend on the body. In this respect he is closer than some of his Cartesian critics to Descartes' own views.

Malebranche indicated another difference between pure understanding and the faculties of sensation and imagination when he wrote in the preface to the *Recherche* that "the relation that minds have to God is natural, necessary, and absolutely indispensable; but the relation that our mind has to our body, although natural to our mind, is neither absolutely necessary nor indispensable" (OCM 10/LO xx). Pure understanding, which derives from the union with God, thus is essential to mind, whereas the faculties of sensation and imagination, which derive from the union with body, are rather contingent features of it. Descartes himself had claimed in the *Sixth Meditation* that the power of imagination is distinct from the power of understanding in virtue of the fact that "it is not required for me myself, that is for the essence of my mind; for even if it would be absent from me, I would without doubt remain the same that I now am" (AT VII 73/CSM II 51). Later in this text he affirmed that the faculties of sensation and imagination are alike in this respect since "I can clearly and distinctly understand myself as a whole without these faculties" (AT VII 78/CSM II 54). The suggestion here is that only the faculty of pure understanding belongs to the essence of mind, or the mind "considered as a whole."[5] Such a suggestion helps to explain why Descartes was so concerned in the correspondence with Elisabeth to distinguish knowledge of "the soul alone" from knowledge of the soul as united to a body (see §2.3.2 [2]). As I have noted, Malebranche could not accept the particular account of the distinction in that correspondence. Nonetheless he could and did accept Descartes' underlying point that since pure intellect is essential to mind, it is distinct from sensory faculties, which are not so essential.

(2) The Critique of Cartesian Innateness. Malebranche's account of pure understanding is not wholly Cartesian. His reference to a union with God bespeaks his allegiance to a version of the Augustinian doctrine of divine illumination. Citing Augustine's own claim that the mind is not a light to itself,[6] Malebranche insisted that the ideas that are present to us in intellectual perception exist in God rather than in ourselves. Descartes held in the *Sixth Meditation*, by contrast, that the mind engages in pure understanding by "turning to itself" and "inspecting" ideas found within. This position recalls his more general view that the mind must at first "lay aside all our preconceived opinions" that derive from the senses and "give our attention in an orderly way to the notions that we have within us" (PP I.75, AT VIII-1 38/CSM I 221). Descartes would not deny God plays a role in our knowledge of such notions; indeed, he held that God not only implanted the notions in us, but also created the truths that these notions reflect.[7] Nonetheless, for him the notions themselves are features not of God's mind but of our own.

In the *Recherche* Malebranche devoted a chapter to the critique of the view that "all ideas are innate or created with us" (RV III–2.4, OCM I 429/LO 226). He objected that innatists are committed to the implausible position that the mind has an infinite storehouse of ideas, since they must hold that "it has as many infinite numbers of ideas as there are different shapes." He went on to say that even if it is granted that the mind has such a store, still there is the problem of how the mind can select the proper idea. The soul cannot know when to select the sensory idea of the sun, for instance, since it "does not perceive the movement that the sun produces in the fundus of the eyes and in the brain" (OCM I 430–31/LO 227).

These remarks admittedly do not provide the most effective argument against Cartesian innatism. An initial difficulty is that Malebranche was not clear on the scope of the doctrine he was attacking. While he tended to focus on geometrical ideas, thus suggesting that the doctrine is restricted to the intellect, his example of the idea of the sun indicates that doctrine extends even to sensations. A more serious problem is that Descartes himself did not hold that the mind has an innate store of preformed ideas. It is true that he spoke of ideas that "I can as if [*tanquam*] bring forth from the storehouse [*thesauro*] of my mind" (*Fifth Med.*, AT VII 67/CSM II 46), yet the *tanquam* is significant here, given that Descartes indicated elsewhere that innate ideas are not always actually present in the mind. As we saw in §2.1.2 (2), he asserted in the *Notes* that sensory ideas are innate merely in the sense that the mind has an innate faculty that forms them "on the occasion of" the presence of bodily motions. In the same work he distinguished these innate sensory ideas, which are also adventitious in the sense that they are correlated with motions in the brain, from intellectual ideas that are innate in the sense that they come "solely from the power of thinking in me."[8] According to Descartes, these latter ideas are innate

> in the same sense as that in which we say that generosity is "innate" in certain families, or that certain diseases such as gout or stones are innate in others; it is not so much that the babies of such families suffer from these diseases in the mother's womb, but simply that they are born with a certain "faculty" or tendency to contract them. (*Notes*, AT VIII–2 358/CSM I 304)

He concluded that innate intellectual ideas "always exist within us potentially [*potentia*], for to exist in some faculty is not to exist actually, but merely potentially" (AT VIII–1 361/CSM I 305). La Forge later cited just this passage in support of the position that ideas *nées avec l'esprit* are "contained in the mind only in power [*puissance*], and not in act."[9] In order to have an innate idea of a triangle, then, the mind need not have a store filled with infinitely many ideas of particular triangles. It requires only an intellectual faculty or power that enables it to know the properties triangles can possess.[10]

While Malebranche did consider in the *Recherche* the thesis that the mind has the power (*puissance*) to produce ideas (RV III–2.3, OCM I 422/LO 222), he linked such a thesis explicitly to the Cartesians only later in *Éclaircissement* X. In a passage considered in §2.1.2 (1), he cited the view of certain "Cartesian gentlemen [that] the soul thinks because of its nature [and that] God gave it the faculty of thinking and it needs nothing more." Malebranche agreed that "our soul is what it is by its nature and necessarily perceives what affects it" but insisted that "God alone can act on it. He alone can enlighten it, touch it, modify it by the efficacy of his ideas" (OCM III 144/LO 622).[11] Here Malebranche was simply extending his occasionalism to the case of mind. Just as bodies cannot move or shape themselves, so the mind "cannot move itself, it cannot enlighten itself—it is God who works all that there is of a physical nature [*de physic*] in minds as well as in bodies" (OCM III 145/LO 623).[12] Malebranche need not deny that there are features of mind that prepare it to have certain thoughts; indeed, he referred at one point to dispositions in the soul that "render it more ready to act and to represent objects to itself" (*Écl.* XI, OCM III 169/LO 636).[13] Yet he insisted that neither habitual dispositions nor anything else in the soul can cause intellectual perceptions. For him the power to cause these perceptions can reside only external to the soul, in God. There is much to be said for Alquié's conclusion that Malebranche's doctrine of the vision in God is simply "un innéisme transposé et comme extériorisé."[14]

It is important not to overemphasize the Cartesianism of this doctrine; after all, Malebranche took the doctrine of the vision in God to derive more from Augustine than from Descartes.[15] Yet just as Descartes emphasized that "the notions that we have within us" are a source of knowledge that we cannot obtain through the senses, so Malebranche held that the soul's union with God allows it to perceive intellectual truths that it cannot perceive through its union with the body. On the issue of the possibility of purely intellectual knowledge, Malebranche is once again closer to Descartes than is his Cartesian critic, Regis. It is true that in the *Système* Regis had spoken of the idea of extension as "née avec l'âme,"[16] but such talk seems to contradict the central position in this text that all our thoughts depend on motions in the sense organs.[17] Perhaps in response to this difficulty, Regis noted later in his *Usage de la raison* that when he said that the idea of extension is innate to the soul, he meant only that "man cannot be man without sensing or imagining, and he can neither sense nor imagine without having the idea of extended substance." He insisted that the position that the idea of extension is innate since it is always at least implicitly present in sense experience in no way compromises his view, borrowed from Desgabets, that all ideas derive from the senses.[18] Regis thus retained the innatist language but rejected the doctrine, central to Descartes' own innatist view, that intellectual knowledge has a source distinct from the senses. While Malebranche rejected the language, on the other hand, he retained this central doctrine.

One commentator has proposed that Malebranche's critique of the Cartesians in *Éclaircissement* X suggests a total rejection of faculties, including the mental faculty of pure understanding; on this proposal Malebranche's view is more radical than I have allowed.[19] It is significant, however, that his critique of Cartesian innatism focuses only on causally active faculties. Moreover, Malebranche provided a way of speaking of different passive faculties in the soul when he noted in one text that since "understanding and will are not different from the soul itself," the understanding is simply the soul itself insofar as it perceives, and the will the soul itself insofar as it desires its happiness (*Écl.* II, OCM III 40/LO 560).[20] The claim that the understanding is distinct from the will thus could reduce to the claim that perceptions are modifications of the soul that differ in kind from its desires and other volitions.[21] Along similar lines, Malebranche could hold that the faculty of pure understanding is simply the soul itself insofar as it has intellectual perceptions, and sensory faculties the soul itself insofar as it has sensory or imaginative perceptions. This suggests that the distinction between the faculties of understanding in a broad sense would reduce to the distinction between the corresponding perceptions. Malebranche admittedly did not always emphasize or rigorously adhere to the distinction between these two species of perception. Nonetheless, I want to argue that such a distinction, and thus the distinction between the faculties of sense and pure understanding, is deeply rooted in his system.

(3) Pure Perceptions and Efficacious Ideas. From the start, Malebranche made clear that sensations are distinct from purely intellectual ideas. He wrote in the *Recherche*,

> When we perceive something sensible, there is found in our perception, *sentiment* and pure *idea*. The sentiment is a modification of our soul, and it is God who causes it in us; and he can cause [this modification] in us although he does not have it because he sees in the idea that he has of our soul that it is capable of it. As for the idea that is joined with the sentiment, it is in God, and we see it because it pleases him to reveal it to us; and God joins the sensation with the idea when objects are present so that we believe it to be thus, and have all the sentiments and the passions that we should have in relation to them. (RV III–2.6, OCM I 445/LO 234)

What is not so clear in this passage, though, is that the perception of an intellectual or pure idea involves a nonsensory feature of our soul. The emphasis is on the fact that such an idea exists in God rather than in us. It is true that Malebranche referred to the fact that we "see" the pure idea, but he did not indicate clearly that we see it by means of a modification of our soul that differs in kind from our sensations. His presentation of the doctrine of the vision in God in the *Recherche* is oddly detached from the claim in the same text that the soul is capable of pure intellections or pure perceptions.

This oddity reveals that Malebranche is vulnerable to Leibniz's objection that even if it were the case that we see ideas in God, "it would nevertheless be necessary that we also have our own ideas, that is, . . . affections or modifications of our mind corresponding to that very thing we perceived in God."[22] Later I will attempt to explain why Malebranche failed to emphasize that the soul has pure perceptions that differ from its sensations. For the moment, though, I want to focus on developments in his thought that serve to strengthen the distinction between sensation and pure perception. In the preface to the *Recherche*, as we have seen, Malebranche had distinguished the soul's union with God from its union with the body. Fourteen years later, in the *Entretiens sur la Métaphysique*, he attempted to explicate the difference between these two kinds of union by appealing to the nature of the general laws by which God acts. First there are the laws of the soul–body union, "the modalities of which are reciprocally occasional causes of their changes. It is through these laws that I have the power to speak, to walk, to sense, to imagine, and the rest; and that objects have the power to touch me and to move me through my organs." These laws differ from those governing "the union of the soul with God, with the intelligible substance of universal Reason, laws for which our attention is the occasional cause. It is by the establishment of these laws that mind has the power to think of what it wills, and to discover the truth" (*EM XIII*, OCM XII 319/D 321). These remarks indicate one way in which sensations and pure perceptions may be distinguished. Sensations are correlated with motions in the sense organs by means of the laws of soul–body union, whereas pure perceptions are correlated with acts of attention, and ultimately linked to pure ideas in God, by means of the laws of the soul's union with universal Reason.

This account of pure perception does little to accommodate the view, found in the first edition of the *Recherche*, that the soul has a pure perception of "all its thoughts, when it knows them through the reflection it makes on itself" (RV I.4, OCM I 66/LO 16). According to such a view, the soul's reflections on its own thoughts count as pure perceptions even though they are not correlated with pure ideas in God.[23] Talk of a pure understanding of thought, however, seems to be a Cartesian holdover that conflicts with the doctrine in the *Recherche* that we know our modifications through a confused sentiment rather than through an idea.[24] This may explain why Malebranche in later writings tended to restrict pure perceptions to those states of the soul that are linked to ideas in virtue of the laws of the union with God.[25]

In any event, the nomological account of pure perceptions suggested in the *Entretiens* prepares the way for the doctrine of efficacious ideas that, as Robinet has shown, Malebranche offered seriously only after 1695.[26] The occasion for this doctrine was provided by Regis' remark in the *Système* that the "modern philosopher who teaches that we see bodies in God" offers no intelligible account of the union between God and the soul.[27] Regis concluded there that we can dispense with the union with God in favor of the position that we see bodies "by means of ideas that are in us, and that depend on the bodies that they represent."[28] Malebranche responded that this union is easily explained in terms of a special sort of divine power that is itself indispensable. "[I]t is only the intelligible reality of sovereign Reason that can act on minds and communicate to them some intellectual comprehension [*intelligence*] of the truth" (*Rép. Regis*, c. 2, OCM II 295). Soon after this response to Regis, he emphasized that divine ideas alone have the efficacy required to produce our intellectual grasp of the truth.[29] Drawing on Robinet's work, Alquié has claimed that this emphasis on the efficacy of ideas marks a shift in Malebranche's thought from a "vision dans Dieu" to a "vision par Dieu."[30] Malebranche had encouraged the view that ideas are inert objects that we see in God when he spoke in the first edition (1674) of the *Recherche* of an idea as "the immediate' of the mind, or "the object closest to the mind, when it perceives something" (RV III–2.1, OCM I 414a). The shift to a view of ideas as the veh object' icles for God's causation of our perceptions is indicated by the rider that he added to this passage in the last edition (1712): "that is to say, what touches and modifies the mind with the perception that it has of an object" (OCM I 414/LO 217).

While this new emphasis on the efficacy of ideas is not without its difficulties,[31] it helps to bring to the fore the question of how the soul changes when it apprehends pure ideas in God. In the *Recherche* Malebranche did little to explain the precise manner in which pure perceptions that the soul has through pure understanding are related to ideas in God. The introduction of the doctrine of efficacious ideas provided him the opportunity to say that pure perceptions bear a special causal relation to these ideas. In a 1699 response to Arnauld, for instance, Malebranche wrote that the divine archetype or idea of extension "affects" (*affecte*) minds with pure perceptions "in consequence of the general laws of the union of minds with sovereign Reason" (*Lettre III*, OCM VIII 959). To be sure, his position is complicated by the claim in this text that the same idea affects minds with sensible perceptions "in consequence of the natural laws of the union of the soul and the body" (OCM VIII 959). Thus the mere fact that pure perceptions are caused by ideas in God does not distinguish these perceptions from sensations. Nonetheless, Malebranche indicated that only clear and distinct pure perceptions are caused in accord with the laws of the soul's union with God. These perceptions thus differ from confused and obscure sensations that are linked to bodily states by means of the laws of the soul–body union.

Obviously there is more to be said about the precise manner in which pure perceptions are to be distinguished from sensations. For now it suffices to note simply that Malebranche was committed to this sort of distinction, affirming to the end that the sensory perceptions of the soul are tied to the body in a way in which its pure perceptions are not. He of course rejected Descartes' particular account of how the soul acquires knowledge apart from the body. Unlike Desgabets and Regis, however, Malebranche remained Cartesian to the extent of holding that the soul can acquire such knowledge.

3.1.2 Sentiment and Sensation

Malebranche's acceptance of the Cartesian distinction between sense and intellect seems to be compromised by other elements of his system. For instance, Malebranche had a tendency to defend his doctrine of the vision in God by appealing to the fact that the soul can find in itself only obscure sentiments. Thus passages in certain of his works seem to "sensualize" pure perceptions. In other passages, some of which are found in these same texts, Malebranche had a contrasting tendency to claim that even sensations are caused by efficacious ideas in God. These passages seem to "intellectualize" sensations. In both cases it appears that Malebranche rejected any firm distinction between intellectual and sensory perceptions. Without suggesting that Malebranche was always careful or rigorous, though, I want to argue that the position in his later writings is on the whole consistent with his commitment to the Cartesian distinction between sense and intellect.

(1) Sentiments and the Vision in God. In the *Recherche* Malebranche defended the doctrine of the vision in God by responding to the view, which he later attributed to Arnauld,[32] that the soul sees objects by means of ideas in itself. He objected that such a view is unacceptable because it contravenes the Augustinian

dictum that the soul is not a light itself, that God alone can enlighten it (RV III–2.5, OCM I 434/LO 229). In *Éclaircissement* X Malebranche cited this same dictum in response to the position that the soul contains intelligible extension in itself (OCM III 150–51/LO 626). In this text he cited in addition the Cartesian doctrine that "pleasure, pain, taste, heat, color, all our sensations and all our passions, are modifications of our soul." Malebranche noted that we cannot compare these sensations in the same manner in which we can compare various shapes, concluding, "What relation is there between these intelligible shapes, which are very clear ideas, and the soul's modifications, which are only confused sentiments?" (OCM III 150/LO 625). This implies that the soul cannot be a light to itself because it can possess only sensations that are confused modifications of itself.

This suggestion is further underscored in later works. In his 1684 response to Arnauld's *Vraies et fausses idées*, for instance, Malebranche claimed that the modalities of the soul "are only sentiments, which represent to the soul nothing different from itself" (*Réponse*, c. 5, OCM VI 50). Likewise in the 1688 *Entretiens* he announced through his spokesman, Theodore, that souls cannot see the light in themselves since "they can find in themselves only sentiments often very lively, but always obscure and confused, that is modalities full of darkness" (*EM III*, OCM XII 65/D 59).

It is somewhat paradoxical that Malebranche appealed to the premise that the soul has only confused and obscure sentiments in order to support the conclusion that it is enlightened by God's ideas. Insofar as the soul is illuminated by the divine light, at least some of its modifications must be enlightened. But the consequence that some of the soul's modifications are enlightened conflicts with the original premise that its modifications are full of darkness. Martial Gueroult seems to have a point when he takes Malebranche's argument for the vision in God to commit him to saying simultaneously that the soul is and is not enlightened by divine ideas.[33]

We can state the problem here in terms of Malebranche's account of pure perception. As we have seen, he came to hold that we can apprehend the truth by means of pure perceptions that are distinct from sensations in virtue of the fact that they are related in a special way to ideas in God. There is an anticipation of this position in the claim in the *Entretiens* that the soul "must consult not the senses and their respective modalities, which are sheer darkness, but Reason, which enlightens us by its divine Ideas" (*EM III*, OCM XII 82/D 75). It is the indication here that pure perceptions are modalities of the soul that are not engulfed in darkness that seems directly to contradict the remark just cited from this same work that the soul can find in itself only modalities full of darkness.

There is a fairly straightforward solution to this problem. In the preface to the *Meditations* Descartes distinguished between an idea "taken materially, as an operation of the intellect," and that same idea "taken objectively, as the thing represented by that operation" (AT VII 8/CSM II 7). In an analogous manner, Malebranche could distinguish between a pure perception considered as a mere modification, on the one hand, and that same perception considered as related to the object present to it, on the other.[34] Considered apart from any relation to ideas, a pure perception is merely a sentiment, a subjective modification of the soul. Though Malebranche sometimes took the terms "sensation" (*sensation*) and "sentiment" (*sentimen*) to be interchangeable,[35] he indicated a broader sense of the latter term when he wrote in the *Recherche* that the soul perceives through inner sentiment not only its sensations and imaginations but also its "pure intellections" (RV III–2.1, OCM I 415/LO 218). When pure intellections or perceptions are considered solely with respect to those features revealed by inner sentiment, they can be characterized with sensations as "only sentiments."

Unlike other sensations, however, a pure perception is more than a mere sentiment. Since it has an idea in God present to it as its immediate object, it includes—in a manner that admittedly needs to be explicated—a nonsubjective element. In virtue of this relation to a divine idea, a pure perception allows the soul to see the truth in an objective manner. Malebranche could say, then, that while pure perceptions do not have their own light, they reflect the light from clear ideas in God. Such a position is in line with Malebranche's own remark that even though the mind is not a *lumen illuminans*, or illuminating light, it is a *lumen illuminatum*, or illuminated light.[36]

When Malebranche was considering the doctrine that ideas exist in God rather than in us, he tended to emphasize that all our modifications are merely confused sentiments. This would explain why he was not always careful to distinguish the soul's pure perceptions from its sensations. Even so, Malebranche's account of the two unions suggests that he wanted to draw some sort of epistemic distinction between the soul's modifications. Such an account encourages the position that the soul is a *lumen illuminatum* with respect to its pure perceptions but not with respect to its sensations. Whereas sensations are utterly dark, since they are tied to bodily states by means of the laws of the soul–body union, pure perceptions provide light, since they are connected to clear ideas by means of the laws of the soul's union with God. Something akin to this position must be behind the exhortation in the *Entretiens* to turn away from the senses and to seek out those enlightened perceptions that do not depend on the body. Malebranche's claim, in this same work, that all the soul's modalities are confused sentiments therefore need not be inconsistent with the Cartesian position that the soul has a faculty of pure understanding that is epistemically superior to its sensory faculties.

(2) *Sensations and Efficacious Ideas.* We have considered the view in the *Entretiens* that sensations are distinct from pure perceptions in virtue of the fact that they derive from the soul's union with the body rather than from its union with God. However, this same text appears to offer the incompatible position that even sensations derive from the union with God. Malebranche had Theodore say at one point, for instance, that "it is the intelligible substance of Reason that acts on our mind by its all-powerful efficacy, and that touches it and modifies it with color, with taste, with pain, by what there is in it [i.e., in the intel-

ligible substance of Reason] that represents bodies" (*EM* V, OCM XII 116/D 111).

In later writings Malebranche reinforced the link between sensation and Reason by appealing to the doctrine of efficacious ideas. In the course of a long addition to the fifth edition (1695) of the *Conversations chrétiennes*, for example, he noted, again through the character Theodore:

> When the idea of extension affects or modifies the mind with a pure perception, then the mind simply conceives this extension. But when the idea of extension touches the mind more vividly and affects it with a sensible perception, then the mind sees or senses extension. The mind sees it when this perception is a sentiment of color; and it senses or perceives it even more vividly, when the perception by which intelligible extension modifies it is a pain: Because color, pain and all the other sentiments are only sensible perceptions produced in intelligences by intelligible ideas. (*C III*, OCM IV 75–76)[37]

The point here that even sensations derive from efficacious ideas is further strengthened by the remark, added to the fourth edition (1711) in the *Entretiens*, that there is "uniquely and only one idea of a hand that affects us diversely, that acts on our soul, and that modifies it with color, heat, pain, etc." (*EM* V, OCM XII 116/D 111).

The remark from the *Entretiens* is particularly problematic. In this work Malebranche had Theodore conclude on the basis of the fact that our sensations derive from the intelligible idea of extension that the sensations themselves make this idea sensible, and thereby "show us the relations in which consist the truths of Geometry and Physics" (*EM* V, OCM XII 116/D 111). Yet he also had Theodore emphasize that "color, pain, taste, and all the other sentiments of the soul, have nothing in common with the extension that we sense joined with [*jointe avec*] them" (OCM XII 115/D 109), a point that is in line with Ariste's earlier claim that "it is not our senses, but Reason joined to our senses that enlightens us, and discloses the truth to us" (OCM XII 112/D 107). The *Entretiens* therefore appears to waver between the view that sensations derive from the idea of extension and thus reveal its nature, on the one hand, and the view that these modifications are merely joined with this idea and therefore reveal nothing of its nature, on the other.

One might object that when Theodore claims that sensations themselves are modifications deriving from the idea of extension that show us "the relations in which consist the truths of Geometry and Physics," he is merely playing devil's advocate in order to elicit from Ariste the claim that our judgments concerning the nature and properties of bodies must be guided by the idea of extension rather than by our sensations. This explains how Theodore could later commend Ariste for saying that "it is not the case that our eyes were given us to discover exact truths in Geometry and Physics" but instead were given "for the convenience and conservation of life" (OCM XII 119/D 115). Yet the section in the *Entretiens* containing Theodore's more positive remarks on sensation is entitled "The Use of the Senses in the Sciences" (OCM XII 109/D 105). This title implies that Theodore is not simply spurring discussion when he insists that the senses play some constructive role in our knowledge of the truth. There is reason to think that he is speaking for himself, then, when he tells Ariste that sensations are useful since "they awaken our attention, and they thereby lead us indirectly [*indirectement*] to an intellectual comprehension [*intelligence*] of the truth" (OCM XII 118/D 113).

It does not seem to me a promising strategy, therefore, to explain away all of the positive remarks on sensation in the *Entretiens*. A better approach is to emphasize Theodore's claim that sensations lead us only *indirectement* to the truth. I take the point to be that the sensory modifications prompt in us an *intelligence* of the nature of extension by means of pure perception. This position can be understood in terms of Theodore's comment early in the *Entretiens* that "intelligible extension becomes visible and represents some body in particular only through color, since it is only from the diversity of colors that we judge the difference in the objects we see" (EM I, OCM XII 46/D 39).[38] Differences in color draw our attention to the boundaries of the colored objects, which boundaries we understand in turn through pure perception. The fact that sensations of color can lead to an intellectual perception of the nature of various shapes reveals that the sensations themselves derive from the efficacious idea of extension.

This view that sensations can play an instrumental role in our comprehension of extension softens somewhat the position, encouraged by other passages from the *Entretiens*, that the senses have no cognitive value. Yet while some of Theodore's remarks seem to suggest that sensations themselves display the nature of extension,[39] the fuller context of these remarks shows that this is not his position. It is with his encouragement and approval, after all, that Ariste affirms: "It is not pain or color through itself that teaches me the relations bodies have among themselves. I can discover these relations only in the idea of extension that represents them" (OCM XII 117/D 111). Sensations may help us to see the light by means of pure perception, but apart from pure perception they are merely dark and obscure modalities.[40]

On the whole, then, the remarks in the *Entretiens* are consistent with the Cartesian position that it is the intellect, not the senses, that teaches us the truth about the nature of body. I believe that such a position is largely consistent as well with the late addition to the *Conversations chrétiennes*. An initial point here is that this addition retains the view that sensations are tied to the body by means of the soul–body union. Such a view is prominent, for instance, in the following explanation of the claim in the added passage that sentiments are produced by intelligible ideas:

> It is a necessity to say that in the instant that we open our eyes in the middle of a field, God in consequence of the laws of the union of the soul and the body, and in following always exactly the rules of Optics and of Geometry, touches, by the idea of extension that he contains, our mind with this variety of colors, by which we judge the actual existence and the diversity of objects; of their size, of their situation, of their movement and their repose. All of this

teaches us in an instant, and without any application on our part, the infinite relations that our body has with all those that surround us. (OCM IV 76)

Elsewhere in the *Conversations*, moreover, Malebranche had Theodore distinguish the soul's union with the body from its union with God (e.g., in C VII, OCM IV 163). In neither this text nor the *Entretiens* is the union with body clearly displaced by the union with God.

There is admittedly a complication that derives from the claim above that we can judge "in an instant, without any application on our part," features of body such as size, situation, and movement. In the *Sixth Replies* Descartes distinguished the determination of these features from mere sensations in order to draw attention to the fact that it is the intellect that makes this determination. In the *Recherche*, on the other hand, Malebranche emphasized that these features are determined by means of a *jugement naturel* that is "but a sensation" (RV I.7, OCM I 96–97/LO 34).[41] He remarked later that this judgment is one that God forms in us "according to the laws of the union of the soul and body" (RV I.9, OCM I 119/LO 46).[42] So it seems that sensations deriving from the soul–body union can themselves teach us the truth about extension. It is difficult to see how there could be any absolute epistemic distinction between the soul's union with the body and its union with God.[43]

In the *Recherche*, however, Malebranche warned that we should rely on the testimony of the senses in general, and of vision in particular, "not in order to judge concerning the truth of things in themselves, but only to discover the relation that they have to the conservation of our body" (RV I.6, OCM I 79/LO 25). In the case of shapes, for instance, vision alone cannot reveal the precise difference between a circle or square and a ellipse or parallelogram and cannot even determine whether or not a particular line is straight (RV I.7, OCM I 95/LO 33–34). The "look" of shapes and lines therefore cannot itself yield determinate geometrical knowledge.

In the *Entretiens* Ariste puts a somewhat more positive spin on this account of vision when he notes, with Theodore's blessing: "The testimony of my eyes often approaches the truth. This sense can help the mind to discover it. It does not wholly disguise its object. In rendering me attentive, it leads me to intellectual comprehension [*intelligence*]" (EM V, OCM XII 119/D 115). Rough sensory discrimination of shapes approaches the truth and thus can lead to an *intelligence* of the nature of these shapes. But the claim that such discrimination only approaches the truth underscores the fact that it does not itself involve *intelligence*. As Theodore emphasizes later with respect to the sensory determination of size, shape, situation, and movement, "the senses are not given us to discover the truth, or the exact relations that objects have among themselves, but to conserve our body" (EM XII, OCM XII 280–81/D 281).

There is a similar ambivalence in Malebranche's account of imagination. In the *Recherche* he devoted a chapter to extolling the usefulness of the imagination for the discovery of geometrical truths,[44] yet he also noted that "the ideas of the senses and of the imagination are distinct only by the conformity that they have with the ideas of pure intellection" (RV III–2.3, OCM I 425–26/LO 224). Later, in the *Entretiens*, Malebranche developed the qualification by focusing on the case of imagination in particular. There he had Theodore prompt Ariste by introducing the view that "in geometry the imagination forms such clear and distinct images of shapes that you cannot deny that it is by means of them that we learn this science" (*EM* V, OCM XII 125/D 119). Ariste gives the response Theodore seeks:

> I cannot image a square, for example, that I do not conceive at the same time. And it appears evident to me that the image of the square that I form is exact and regular only to the extent that it conforms precisely [*répond juste*] to the intelligible idea that I have of the square, that is to say, of a space terminated by four exactly straight lines, entirely equal, and that being joined at their extremities, make perfectly right angles. But it is of such a square that I am certain that the square on the diagonal is double the square of the two sides.... But one can know nothing of this confused and irregular image traced in the brain by the course of [animal] spirits. Thus the Geometers derive their knowledge not from the confused images in their imaginations, but uniquely from the clear ideas of Reason. (OCM XII 125–26/D 121)[45]

This passage appropriates the old Platonic argument that sensory particulars are too imprecise and irregular to account for knowledge of the Forms. Just as Plato seems to have allowed for the senses to play some sort of role in this knowledge,[46] however, so Ariste claims that the rough images that pertain to the imagination "can indeed hold [the Geometers'] attention, in giving, so to speak, body to their ideas" (OCM XII 126/D 121). Similarly, in the *Conversations* Malebranche blew both hot and cold on the imagination, having Theodore speak of knowledge (*science*) that "consists in a purely intellectual view, in which the imagination has a hand only indirectly" (*C* VII, OCM IV 163). Imagination plays some role in geometrical knowledge and therefore must be linked to intellectual ideas. Yet this role is only indirect or instrumental; properly speaking, knowledge of these ideas belongs to the intellect and not to the imagination.

We are now in a position to understand the remark in the *Conversations* that when the soul has a sensible perception, it "sees, or senses extension." Accompanying the soul's sensations of various colors are natural judgments regarding the boundaries of objects. These rough judgments can make the mind attentive to differences among various shapes, and thus bear the mark of the idea of extension. Malebranche no doubt was thinking of this more positive contribution of sensory judgment when he emphasized, in his later works, that even our sensations are caused by efficacious ideas. Although this new emphasis tends to complicate the distinction between the soul's two unions, it need not eliminate it entirely. Malebranche continued to insist in the *Entretiens* and the *Conversations* alike that the mind can know intelligible extension only when it considers it in a purely intellectual manner. Sensations that derive from the soul–

body union bear a causal relation to divine ideas, but they lack the sort of direct cognitive relation that is characteristic of pure perceptions that derive from the soul's union with God.

We have seen that Malebranche's remark that all modifications of the soul are "only sentiments" allows for the view that pure perceptions are distinct from sensations. Pure perceptions are only sentiments when considered in themselves, but they are set apart from sensations in virtue of the fact that they have ideas as their objects. The claim in the later addition to the *Recherche* that an idea is an immediate object in the sense that it "touches and modifies the mind with the perception that it has of an object" (RV III–2.1, OCM I 414/LO 217) does suggest that an idea is an immediate object present to the mind in perception just in case it causes the perception of the mind. Such a suggestion seems to undermine the distinction between sensation and pure perception that I have attributed to Malebranche, given his later position that ideas cause even sensations.[47] Moreover, Malebranche himself was not always careful to distinguish the manner in which these two kinds of perceptions are related to the idea of extension. Nonetheless, some sort of distinction is indicated by the central contrast in the *Entretiens* between sensing, where the soul contemplates its own modifications, and knowing, where it contemplates external ideas.[48] This suggests that even though the divine idea of extension causes sensations, the soul continues to be directed inward, toward features of itself. On the other hand, this idea causes pure perceptions in a manner that directs the soul outward, toward the idea.

My talk here of the soul's being "directed outward" toward the idea of extension rather than "inward" toward itself is admittedly metaphorical, and talk of pure perceptions bearing a "direct cognitive relation" to this idea is rather vague. There is an obvious need to bring Malebranche's position into sharper focus. A good place to start is with his assertion of the infinity of the idea of extension. One point connected to Descartes' famous discussion of the piece of wax in the *Meditations* is that the unlimited intellectual idea of extension is distinct from our limited sensory ideas of it. Malebranche also insisted, however, that this intellectual idea cannot be identified with any of our finite perceptions. I take this distinction between idea and perception to indicate both a similarity and a difference between sensation and pure perception. The difference is broached by Malebranche's remark that while sensations are "nothing but modes of the mind," pure perceptions are "superficial to the soul." I believe that this distinction is best understood in terms of the difference between the content of sensation, which is constituted by features internal to a particular soul, and the content of pure perception, which is constituted by an external idea common to all souls. On the other hand, there is a similarity revealed by Malebranche's claim that clear ideas must be distinct from confused modifications. Pure perceptions yield an objective view of body in virtue of their relation to a clear idea, but they must in a way be as confused as sensations since they are, along with sensations, subjective modifications of the soul.

3.2 Idea, Sensation, and Pure Perception

3.2.1 The Idea of Extension

(1) Sensory and Intellectual Ideas of Extension. In the *Second Meditation* Descartes was concerned to respond to the position that we can grasp the nature of body in general, and of a piece of wax in particular, by means of the senses. He argued initially that the determinate features of the wax that he apprehends through the senses—its taste, smell, color, size, and shape—cannot be essential to it since these features change even while the wax remains. The nature of this wax thus consists only in being a determinable entity, "nothing other than something extended, flexible, mutable." Yet Descartes also noted that even though he can imagine some of the changes in shape that the wax can undergo, still "I would not judge correctly what the wax is, unless I also take this [wax] to admit more varieties of being extended than I ever would encompass [*complexus*] by means of imagination." The conclusion is that the nature of the wax as infinitely (or, as Descartes preferred to say, indefinitely) determinable is something that is perceived not by means of the sensory faculties but rather "by the mind alone" (*sola mente percipere*), that is to say, by pure intellect (AT VII 30–31/CSM II 20–21).

Malebranche drew attention to the fact that the senses afford an overly restricted view of the body. He warned early in the *Recherche*, for instance, that "our vision is limited; but it must not limit its object. The idea it gives us of extension has very narrow limits; but it does not follow from this that extension is so limited" (RV I.6, OCM I 80/LO 26). It is clear that this narrow and limited idea of extension is not the intellectual idea in God but rather the sensory idea in us. Malebranche's main point is that this sensory idea is relative to a particular perspective. Thus, he went on to emphasize that different people sometimes do not have the same sensory idea of the same object "since not everyone's eyes are disposed in the same manner," and that the same person does not always have the same idea when seeing the object through different eyes or from different perspectives (OCM I 87/LO 29). Because the senses yield a view that is tied to a particular bodily perspective, they cannot reveal bodies as they really are, apart from any particular perspective. Malebranche later emphasized this deficiency in the *Entretiens* when he had Theodore tell Ariste that to confuse the nature of extension with the sensation of it "is to take the absolute for the relative, that is to judge what things are in themselves by the relation that they have to you" (*EM II*, OCM XII 61, D 55).

Malebranche also made the point, more directly related to Descartes' remarks in the *Second Meditation*, that the intellectual idea of extension outruns any sensory idea we may have of it. This point is again broached in the *Entretiens*, where Theodore distinguishes between the soul's conception of a circle "with indeterminate limits with regard to size but with all points equidistant from some given point and all in the same plane" and its vision of a circular patch of color with determinate limits (*EM I*, OCM XII 46/D 39). There are not only two different kinds of thoughts here, conception and sensation, but also two different kinds of ideas, the intellectual idea of an indeterminate circle and the sensory idea of a determinate circle. When Ariste later suggests that the former idea is not distinct from the latter, Theodore responds that without the idea of the indeterminate circle, "you could think of a certain circle, but never of the circle. You could perceive a certain equality of radii but never a general equality of indeterminate radii. The reason is that no finite and determinate idea can ever represent anything infinite and indeterminate" (*EM II*, OCM XII 58/ D 51, 53). Descartes had argued that the sensory idea of determinate features of the piece of wax cannot represent the indefinitely determinable nature of this object. Theodore's related position is that the sensation of a particular circular patch of color cannot represent the infinity of forms a circle can take. More generally, the sensory idea of extension that is tied to a particular distribution of colors cannot represent the infinity of properties of which extension is capable. There is the need for a distinct nonsensory idea of extension that, as Theodore notes, is "inexhaustible" and thus can "represent the place of a hundred thousand worlds, and again at each instant a hundred thousand times more" (*EM I*, OCM XII 44/D 37).

Passages from the *Entretiens* that suggest this distinction between the two ideas admittedly seem to conflict with Theodore's claim, in the same text, that "there are not two different kinds of extension, nor two kinds of ideas that represent them" (*EM II*, OCM XII 60/D 55). This claim, however, occurs in the context of an argument against the view that "the idea of extension that affects you with a sensation is of another nature, or has more reality than that which you think of, without receiving any sensible impression of it" (OCM XII 61/D 55). When Theodore denies that there are two different ideas of extension, he is taking an idea to be the external cause of the sensations of the soul. A sensory "idea" of extension, however, need not be conceived as something external to the soul. Just as the sensory idea of a particular circle could be identified with the sensible perception of a circular patch of color, so this sensory idea of extension could be identified with the sensible perception of a certain distribution of colors. Thus understood, these sensory ideas could be no more distinct from the soul than the perceptions of color with which they are identified. Malebranche often spoke as if the only idea of extension is the one in God. Nonetheless, the distinction in the *Entretiens* between the two ideas of the circle is best accommodated by the view that there is a limited sensory idea of extension internal to the soul that is distinct from the unlimited intellectual idea of extension external to it.[49]

The discussion of the wax example in the *Second Meditation* commits Descartes to the position that the sensory idea of extension is limited and therefore distinct from the unlimited intellectual idea.[50] But, as Arnauld never tired of pointing out, Descartes himself rejected the position that this intellectual idea is external to the soul. Such a position, which is essential to Malebranche's doctrine of the vision of ideas in God, was in fact a rather popular target of his Cartesian critics. In response to these critics, Malebranche pointed out that there are several ways in which to distinguish ideas from our own modifications. He mentioned a number of these in a late addition to the *Recherche* where he contrasted ideas that are "immutable," "universal and general to all intelligences," "eternal and necessary," "very clear and very luminous," and "efficacious" with modifications of the soul that are "changing," "particular," "contingent," and "obscure and shadowy" (RV IV.11, OCM II 103/LO 322–23).[51] For the moment I want to focus on one contrast not mentioned explicitly in this passage but linked to Descartes' remarks concerning the wax, namely, Malebranche's contrast between the unlimited and infinite idea of extension and our limited and finite perceptions of it.

(2) Finite Perceptions and the Infinite Idea of Extension. There is some dispute over whether Malebranche believed from the start that ideas in general are infinite.[52] It is beyond doubt, however, that he held in his later works that the intellectual idea of extension has this particular property. In his 1693 reply to Regis, for instance, Malebranche urged that this idea must be infinite since it "is such that we are certain that we would never exhaust or that we would never find the end of it" (*Rép. Regis*, c. 2, OCM XVII–1 283–84). He had emphasized the related point that the nature of extension is inexhaustible in the *Recherche*, where he noted that "a simple piece of wax is capable of an infinite, or rather of an infinitely infinite number of different modifications" (RV III–1.1, OCM I 384/LO 199). Here there is an obvious connection to Descartes' conclusion in the *Second Meditation* that the nature of the piece of wax is unlimited in virtue of the fact that this object is capable of countless changes.

What cannot be found in Descartes, however, is the additional argument, in Malebranche's response to Regis, that the inexhaustible idea of extension must be distinct from our mind: "[O]ur mind is finite, and the idea of extension is infinite. Thus, this idea cannot be a modification of our mind" (OCM XVII–1 283). Regis had indicated the more standard Cartesian position that the idea of the infinite is identical to a finite perception.[53] In a text by Arnauld published in 1694, the last year of his life, there is a response to Malebranche that urges that a simple distinction supports Regis' original position.

> [I]t is not true that a modality of our soul, which is finite, cannot represent an infinite thing; and it is true, on the contrary, that however finite our perceptions may be, there are some which must pass for infinite in this sense, that they represent the infinite. This is what M. Regis has correctly maintained to you, and what he meant by these terms, that they are finite *in essendo*, and infinite *in repræsentando*. You are not happy with this distinction. So much the worse for you.[54]

In a reply published after Arnauld's death, Malebranche insisted that this distinction does not undermine his argument, insofar as only that which is infinite *in essendo* can be infinite *in repræsentando*:

> [S]ince [the modalities of the soul] are finite modalities, we cannot find the infinite there, since nothingness is not visible, and one cannot perceive in the

soul what is not there. Similarly, from the fact that I perceive in the circle an infinity of equal diameters, or rather, from the fact that there are equal diameters therein *in repræsentando*, I must conclude that they are really there *in essendo*. For, in effect, a circle contains the reality of an infinity of diameters. In order, then, for a reality to be present to the mind, for it to affect the mind, for the mind to perceive or receive it, it necessarily must really be there. (*Lettre III*, OCM IX 954)[55]

Because the soul is finite, it cannot perceive at one and the same time infinitely many circles. By the same token, none of the soul's perceptions can reveal the infinity of properties of which extension is capable. Given the principle that properties can be contained in the soul only if the soul actually perceives them, it follows that the unperceived properties of extension cannot exist in the soul even *in repræsentando*; "one cannot perceive in the soul what is not there." The idea of extension that represents the unperceived properties cannot itself be found in the soul.[56] Thus does Theodore assert in the *Entretiens*, with specific reference to the idea of extension: "Say to yourself, my mind cannot comprehend this vast idea. It cannot take its measure. Hence, the idea goes infinitely beyond my mind. And since it goes beyond it, it is clearly not its modification" (*EM I*, OCM XII 43/D 35).

This line of argument is not wholly unrelated to the discussion in the *Second Meditation* where Descartes suggested that the unlimited idea of the piece of wax cannot be identified with any of the limited perceptions of sense and imagination. Malebranche could be read as arguing, along similar lines, that an unlimited idea of an extended thing cannot be identified even with our limited intellectual perceptions. Indeed, he stressed in the *Recherche* that the piece of wax is capable of an infinite number of modifications "that no mind can comprehend" (RV III–1.1, OCM I 384/LO 199). On his view, then, we can no more completely comprehend the nature of the wax through our intellect than we can through our sensory faculties.

There is a possible response to Malebranche that draws on the Cartesian doctrine of innateness. Descartes told Regius that innate ideas always exist in our intellect not actually but "potentially," in the faculty or power that we have to form this idea.[57] Earlier he drew on this sort of distinction in response to a critic's suggestion that all those who have an innate idea of God must know immediately that he exists. In an open letter to this critic, Descartes wrote that

> all things, the cognition of which is said to be placed in us by nature, are not thereby expressly known by us; but only are such that without any sense experience, we can know them from the powers of our own intelligence [*ex proprii ingenii viribus, cognoscere possimus*]. Of which sort are all the truths of Geometry, not only the most obvious, but even the others, however abstruse they may seem.

Descartes concluded that it would be "silly" to infer "from the fact that all Geometrical truths are in the same way innate in us" that "there is no one in the world who does not know [*nesciat*] Euclid's elements" (May 1643, AT VIII–

2 166–67/CSMK 222). Geometrical truths concerning extension that we do not now know are nonetheless present to us in the sense that we have an inborn power to know them. The implication here is that the unlimited idea of extension is to be identified not with any limited intellectual perception but with the intellectual power that is the source of our ability to increase our knowledge of extension indefinitely.

This appeal to an intellectual power of the soul is, of course, incompatible with Malebranche's occasionalism, but it is interesting that Descartes' open letter in effect concedes Malebranche's point that no occurrent intellectual perception can reveal everything that is contained in the geometrical idea of extension.[58] This concession highlights an ambiguity in Descartes' claim that he can "draw out from an innate idea something that was implicitly contained in it but that I did not at first notice in it" (*To Mersenne*, 23 June 1641, AT III 383/CSMK 184). Descartes suggested at times that he actually perceives what is "implicitly contained" in this idea. At one point, for instance, he defended the cogito argument by noting that even though he may not have "reflective knowledge" (*scientia reflexa*) of thought and existence, he still has "that internal cognition [*cognitione illa interna*], which always precedes reflection, and which concerning thought and existence is thus innate in all men" (*Sixth Rep.*, AT VII 422/CSM II 285). He therefore can be read as saying that he perceives the implicit elements of an innate idea by means of internal cognition even though he does not have reflective knowledge of these elements. Yet a very different reading is indicated by the claim in his open letter that geometrical truths are innate to us merely in the sense that we "can know them from the powers of our intelligence." There is no indication here that we are in any way aware of the truths that derive from the innate idea of extension. On the first reading we perceive (even if nonreflectively) everything contained in this innate idea, whereas on the second we are aware of only a portion of the information encoded in an intellectual faculty or power.[59]

There appears to be a related ambiguity in the *Recherche*. In the course of arguing for the doctrine of the vision in God, Malebranche noted that the fact that we can direct our attention to different particular objects at different times shows that at any one time "all beings are present to our mind," although only "in a general and a confused fashion." The point seems to be that we actually do perceive all beings, albeit confusedly.[60] Nonetheless, Malebranche went on to note in the next paragraph that the mind can know abstract and general truths "only through the presence of him who can enlighten the mind in an infinity of different ways" (RV III–2.6, OCM I 441/LO 232). The suggestion is that all truths are present to the mind merely in the sense that God can produce there the knowledge of them. I find a development of this suggestion in Malebranche's later writings, where he came to emphasize that divine ideas are efficacious and, in particular, that the divine idea of extension produces finite and limited pure perceptions in accord with the laws governing the soul's union with God. The law-governed action of this idea allows us to move in a proof from a pure perception of certain properties of a triangle, for instance, to a pure perception of other of its properties.[61] The nature of the object of our pure perceptions of a triangle—the representational content, as it were, of these perceptions[62]—is fully revealed not by the perceptions themselves but by the external idea of triangularity (an aspect of the external idea of extension) that is their causal source.

In his mature writings, of course, Malebranche emphasized that divine ideas cause our sensations as well. This extension of the doctrine of efficacious ideas to the realm of sensation raises the question of precisely how sensations are related to pure perceptions. There actually are two questions here, both of which I have touched on already. First, given that divine ideas cause sensations and pure perceptions alike, what sense can be made of Malebranche's claim that the latter are epistemically superior to the former? Second, given that there is such a fundamental difference, what sense can be made of his claim that both pure perceptions and sensations are merely confused modifications of the soul? More complete answers to these questions will provide a clearer perspective from which to determine why Malebranche thought our pure perception of extension is epistemically superior to our inner sentiment of the pure perception itself.

3.2.2 Sensation and Pure Perception

(1) The New Distinction. In the first edition of the *Recherche*, Malebranche attempted to explain the nature of the mental faculty of the understanding by distinguishing between two kinds of "ideas of the soul."

> The first represent to us something external to us, such as a square, a triangle, etc. and the second represent to us only that which passes within us, such as our sensations, pain, pleasure, etc. For one will see in the following that these last ideas are nothing other than a manner of being of the mind; and it is for this that I call them *modifications* of the mind. (RV I.1, OCM I 42b)

This was one of the passages that led his first critic, Simon Foucher, to interpret Malebranche as saying that ideas that represent external objects are simply modifications of the mind.[63] Malebranche responded that he had devoted a section of the *Recherche* to showing that pure ideas exist in God rather than our soul, adding tartly, "When one Critiques a Book, it seems to me that it is necessary at least to have read it" (OCM II 496).[64] As I have noted, though, Malebranche's distinction between sensation and pure idea begs the question of just what it is in the soul that corresponds to the idea in God. Arnauld raised this very question when he objected to Malebranche that the perception of a square is as much a modification of the soul as the perception of color.[65] Partly in response to this sort of objection, no doubt, Malebranche replaced the passage above from the *Recherche* with the following:

> One can say that the perceptions that the soul has of ideas are of two kinds. The first, which one calls pure perceptions are, so to speak, superficial to the soul: they do not penetrate it and do not sensibly modify it. The second, which one calls sensible, penetrate it more or less vividly. Such are pain and pleasure,

light and colors, tastes, odors, and so on. For it will be seen later on that sensations are nothing but manners of being of the soul, and it is for this reason that I call them *modifications* of the mind. (OCM I 42/LO 2)

The earlier distinction between two kinds of ideas, external representative ideas and internal sensory modifications, is replaced by the less confusing distinction between two kinds of perceptual states of the soul, namely, pure perceptions and sensations.

One might anticipate that Malebranche would distinguish pure perceptions that correspond to ideas in God from sensations that do not so correspond. In the revised passage, however, he spoke of both as "perceptions that the soul has of ideas." This language is explained by the fact that Malebranche added this passage to the fifth edition (1700) of the *Recherche*, after he had introduced the doctrine of efficacious ideas. According to that doctrine, sensations and pure perceptions alike are "of ideas" in the sense that they produced in the soul by ideas or, more accurately, by the intelligible idea of extension.

Even so, the addition to the *Recherche* highlights one important difference between the two kinds of perceptions produced by efficacious ideas: sensations "penetrate" the soul "more or less vividly," whereas pure perceptions "do not penetrate it and do not sensibly modify it." For Malebranche sensations form a continuum bounded on the one end by "strong and vivid sensations," like pain and pleasure, that "arouse the mind" and on the other by "weak and languid sensations," like color, that "touch the soul little" (RV I.12, OCM I 137–42/LO 57–60).[66] Pure perceptions are not on this continuum since they do not penetrate the soul in a sensible manner.

Passages from some of Malebranche's mature writings suggest that the difference between sensation and pure perception is one of degree rather than kind. In the 1695 addition to the *Conversations chrétiennes*, for example, Malebranche said the idea of extension "touches the soul more vividly" when it produces a sensation than when it produces a pure perception (C III, OCM IV 75).[67] Here, as elsewhere, the doctrine of efficacious ideas creates difficulties for the Cartesian distinction between sense and intellect. I must emphasize once again, however, that this distinction need not be precluded by such a doctrine. Indeed, we have seen that even in those texts in which Malebranche spoke of sensations and pure perceptions alike as effects of the idea of extension, he continued to emphasize that the former are produced in accord with the laws of the soul–body union whereas the latter are produced in accord with the laws of the soul's union with God. He thus allowed that sensations and pure perceptions are related to the idea of extension in fundamentally different ways. But he also indicated in the addition to the *Recherche* that there is an important difference between the way in which these two kinds of modifications are related to the soul. His main point there is that while sensations are more or less vivid effects that "penetrate" the soul, pure perceptions do not sensibly penetrate the soul at all and thus are merely "superficial" to it.

In the opening section of the *Recherche*, Malebranche attempted to illustrate this point by drawing on a related distinction between the external shape of a body and the internal configuration of its parts.[68] Both the external shape and the internal configuration are modifications of that body; nevertheless, the external shape is superficial to the body and the internal configuration essential to it. A piece of wax, for instance, does not alter greatly when it changes from being round to being square, but it undergoes a considerable change when it changes into fire and smoke due to an alteration in its internal configuration. Likewise, according to Malebranche, the soul does not change considerably when it takes on a pure perception of a square after having had a pure perception of a circle, but it alters greatly when it senses pain after having sensed pleasure (RV I.1, OCM I 41–45/LO 2–4).

Malebranche himself warned that "it must not be imagined that this comparison is exact" (OCM I 45/LO 45). There is in fact a crucial disanalogy between internal configuration and sensation. A body changes from one sort of object (wax) into another (fire and smoke) due to a change in internal configuration, but the mind does not change into another sort of object when it takes on a new sensation. This disanalogy is more damaging than Malebranche allowed, since the fact that a body changes into something else due to a change in its internal configuration explains why this configuration is important to that body. The comparison to internal configuration cannot itself capture the sense in which sensation is more significant to the soul than pure perception.

Malebranche most likely was after the point that sensations, as opposed to pure perceptions, directly concern the well-being of the body to which the soul is united. He emphasized later in the *Recherche*, for instance, that it is for the benefit of the human composite that the soul "is more occupied with a simple prick than with the most elevated speculations" (RV I.18, OCM I 177/LO 80). Yet there seems to be more to the distinction between sensation and pure perception. His contrast in this same section of the *Recherche* between "the attention and the application of the mind to the clear and distinct ideas that we have of objects" (OCM I 176/LO 79), on the one hand, and its attention "to the confused ideas of the senses, which touch it greatly" (OCM I 178/LO 80), on the other, points to a distinction between intellectual attention to clear ideas without and sensory attention to confused ideas within.[69] Such a distinction suggests that pure perceptions are "superficial to the soul" not only because they do not concern the preservation of the body, but also because they involve attention to external ideas.

I believe that this further sense of superficiality is usefully understood in terms of another analogy that Malebranche introduced toward the start of the *Recherche*. I have in mind his comparison there of the difference between perception and inclination to the difference between shape and motion. Both external shape and internal configuration are modifications in a strict sense, or what could be called internal modifications of a body, since both depend simply on the relation between the parts of that body. Motion, by contrast, is not modification in this strict sense but is instead merely an external modification since a body can be in motion only relative to some external body (RV I.1, OCM I 42–43/LO 2–3).[70]

Malebranche's claim that sensations are "nothing but modes of the soul" suggests that they are internal modifications. Indeed, in the *Recherche* he explicitly compared bodily shape to sensations that "have no relation to anything external" (OCM I 42/LO 3). Although he implied in this text (but did not actually say) that pure perceptions have no relation to anything external,[71] on his mature view they do bear an essential intentional relation to an idea in God. A pure perception of a circle, for instance, is intentionally "of" a circle in virtue of its relation to the external idea of a circle, which itself is included in the external idea of extension. This perception could not have the representational content that it has apart from such a relation. Thus it seems that Malebranche could have said, what he did not in fact say, that pure perceptions are superficial to the soul because they are merely external modifications of it.

As we have seen, Malebranche came to think that sensations as well as pure perceptions are "of" ideas in the sense that they bear an essential causal relation to the idea of extension in God. However, in the case of sensation the content is constituted by the "more or less vivid" impression that the idea makes on the soul. The content of the sensation of color differs from the content of the sensation of pain in virtue of the fact that the features of these sensations that we apprehend from a subjective view are different. In this sense the content of sensation is merely subjective. On the other hand, the content of pure perceptions is constituted by something other than the phenomenological features of the perceptions. The content of the pure perception of a circle differs from the content of the pure perception of a square in virtue of the fact that the nature of a circle differs objectively from the nature of a square. There is a sense, then, in which the content of pure perception is objective. While the remarks toward the start of the *Recherche* do not themselves draw attention to this sort of distinction between subjective and objective content, I believe that such a distinction helps us to get to the bottom of Malebranche's account of the difference between sensation and pure perception.

(2) Subjective and Objective Content. In the opening section of the *Recherche* Malebranche noted that sensations "penetrate the soul more or less vividly" and that they are "nothing but modes of the mind," but he said little about the connection between these two properties. There is a clue as to the nature of this connection, though, that is provided by his remark to Arnauld that he cannot make others think of sensations simply by means of words (*Réponse*, c. 23, OCM VI 160). I infer from this remark that we can have only a subjective view of the phenomenal features of the sensations (see §§1.3.3 [2] and 2.2.2). It is these internal phenomenal features that penetrate the soul more or less: more when the soul feels the features as belonging to itself, as in the case of the sensation of pain, less when it feels them as belonging only to external objects, as in the case of the sensation of color. The claim that the content of sensation is con-

stituted by such internal features supports Malebranche's conclusion that the sensation itself is an internal modification, that is to say, in the language of the *Recherche*, "nothing but a mode of the mind."

Malebranche told Arnauld that in contrast to the case of sensation, he can make someone think of geometrical shapes by using definitions. Based on the reading defended in previous chapters, his position is that we can have an objective view of these shapes, and of the modifications of extension in general, that clearly reveals their nature. A major contention in this chapter is that Malebranche adopted the Cartesian line that it is the intellect, rather than the senses, that apprehends the nature of extension. This contention, together with the earlier reading, yields an interpretation on which Malebranche held that pure perception, but not sensation, affords an objective view of this nature.

This account of pure perception is linked to Malebranche's doctrine of the infinity of ideas. We can intellectually perceive only some of the modifications that pertain to a particular geometrical shape, say, a circle. The intelligible idea of circularity, which represents all of the infinite modifications of which a circle is capable, thus cannot be identified with any feature of our finite perceptions. Such an idea is instead, as Malebranche was wont to say, "common to all intelligences."[72] In this respect the idea is akin to Descartes' immutable geometrical natures, which according to him "are not caused [*efficta*] by me and do not depend on my mind" (*Fifth Med.*, AT VII 64/CSM II 45).[73] Since Descartes held that there are innate intellectual powers that correspond to the external immutable natures, however, it is open to him to claim that something internal to the soul determines the content of the perceptions of these natures. On the other hand, Malebranche's occasionalism allows for only the external idea to determine such content. Early on Malebranche tended to suggest that the idea determines the content simply in virtue of the fact that it is the object present to the soul in perception. In his later writings, however, the tenet that we perceive ideas in God becomes a metaphor to be unpacked in nomological terms. As I see it, Malebranche came to hold in particular that the divine idea or archetype of extension is the object present in pure perception in the sense that it causally determines this sort of perception in a manner that reflects the necessary geometrical structure of the material world. The causal activity of this external idea, which is governed by the laws of the soul's union with God, explains why the soul must intellectually conceive extension in a particular manner.[74]

To be sure, there is also the claim in Malebranche's later writings that God causes sensations in accord with laws of the soul's union with body that include "the rules of Optics and Geometry."[75] Once again, the gap between sensation and pure perception seems to have closed. In the case of sensation, though, content is not revealed by these laws since it is constituted only by inner phenomenological features. While these features have a certain pragmatic value, they do not themselves provide any direct insight into the essence of body. When the soul senses, then, it is conscious only of the contingent and subjective features of its own experience. In the case of pure perception, on the other hand, the laws of the soul's union with God reveal the content since they reflect the nature of the idea of extension. When the soul has a pure perception, it has a consciousness that conforms to the necessary and objective structure of reality.

This difference between the laws governing the soul's two unions helps uncover some deep features of the contrast between definable geometrical shapes and indefinable sensations. Malebranche noted in the *Recherche* that in order to bring it about that someone has certain sensations, "it is necessary that I impress on his sense organs the movements to which nature has attached these sensations." He explained that since the sensation of color, for instance, is attached by the laws of the union with body to a motion in the optic nerve rather than to a motion in the ear, we cannot use words to make someone have that sensation (RV I.13, OCM I 145–46/LO 62). The implication here is that sensations are indefinable simply because we cannot by an act of will connect sensations to the motions associated with words. Malebranche pointed out later in this text, however, that the fact that we cannot define sensations shows not only that they cannot be attached to words but also that they cannot be known othrough ideas (RV III–2.7, OCM I 452/LO 238). Even if we could use words to bring about a certain sensation by means of the laws of the union with body, we still could not appeal to the nature of these laws in order to explicate the content of these sensations. It would remain the case that, as Malebranche told Arnauld, the sensation "is not intelligible to my regard" (OCM VI 160).

The claim that we can make others think of geometrical shapes by means of definitions is tied most directly to the claim in the *Entretiens* that the laws of the union with God serve to link the pure perceptions to acts of attention that derive from the will (*EM XIII*, OCM XII 319/D 321). The definability of these shapes indicates that the pure perceptions of the shapes are attached to acts of will rather than, as in the case of sensations, to certain motions in the body. Here again, however, there seems to be a deeper point. According to Malebranche, the content of pure perception is something that is "intelligible to my regard" since it has a necessary and universal structure in virtue of the fact that it is constituted by the divine idea of extension. Whereas the laws of the union with body do not reveal the content of sensation, the laws of the union with God serve to define the content of pure perception.

On the deepest level, then, the difference between sensation and pure perception can be explicated in terms of the difference between subjective and objective content. The representational content of sensation is determined from within by phenomenal features that we can know only from a subjective view. The case of sensation thus provides the most direct illustration of Malebranche's claim to Arnauld that the soul's perceptions "are representative only of themselves" (*Réponse*, c. 10, OCM VI 86).[76] Pure perceptions by contrast allow the soul to know the nature of objects distinct from itself since they have a content with a structure imposed from without by the infinite, universal, and necessary idea of extension. This content is not limited to the subjective features of our experience but is something that we can consider from a wholly objective view.

At this point we are in a position to consider Gueroult's complaint that

Malebranche is caught up in the paradox that "the soul is so much the more penetrated by the light of the Idea when its contact with [the Idea] is more superficial, that is to say that it is so much the less penetrated."[77] Gueroult's talk of the soul being more or less penetrated by an idea reflects the suggestion in Malebranche's later writings that pure perception differs from sensation only in degree. But Malebranche's best position, that is, the position most consistent with his Cartesian distinction between intellect and sense, is that pure perceptions are superficial to the soul because they do not sensibly penetrate it at all. I take Malebranche's position to be that the content of pure perception is constituted by an external idea rather than by the soul's internal subjective features. On this account, the idea of extension could be said to intelligibly penetrate the soul by producing pure perceptions that conform to the nature of extension itself. Gueroult's "paradox" thus overlooks the difference between the sensible penetration of the soul, which the divine idea brings about by means of sensations with subjective content, and the intelligible penetration of it, which this idea brings about by means of pure perceptions with objective content.

(3) The Inner Sentiment of Pure Perception. In his 1684 response to Arnauld, Malebranche stressed the difference between "*knowing [connoître]* numbers and their properties, extension, Geometrical shapes and their relations" and "*sensing [sentir]* pleasure, pain, heat, color, and even the inner perceptions that one has of objects" (*Réponse*, c. 6, OCM VI 55). Here there is not only the standard Cartesian distinction between sense and intellect but also the novel claim that one can only sense the "inner perceptions that one has of objects," that is, the intellectual perceptions that yield knowledge of number and extension. Malebranche noted in the *Recherche* that the soul can have an inner sentiment of its own sensations and pure perceptions because "these things are within the soul, or rather because they are only the soul itself in such or such a manner" (RV III–2.1, OCM I 415/LO 218). In his comment on this passage, responding to Arnauld, he emphasized that since he only senses his pure perceptions, he cannot be said to know them through an idea: "I know [*connois*] a square through an idea; but it is only through inner sentiment of my perception that I am informed [*sçai*] that I know it. To *know*, there must be ideas different from modifications of the mind. But there is no need of [an idea] to *sense* what passes in oneself" (*Réponse*, c. 5, OCM VI 54). In contrast to the sensation of a color, the pure perception of the square yields knowledge through an idea that clearly represents the nature of the square. But the pure perception is nonetheless similar to the sensation given that we are aware of both only through a confused inner sentiment.

Even so, the case of pure perception seems to provide a counterexample to Malebranche's claim to Arnauld that perceptions "represent nothing to the soul distinct from itself" (*Réponse*, c. 5, OCM VI 50). It is through pure perception, after all, that the soul knows the nature of extension. Malebranche addressed this sort of objection in a 1699 response to Arnauld, where he distinguished between representing (*représenter*) and perceiving (*appercevoir*). He admitted that "it is through the perceptions that the objects are perceived" but insisted that finite perceptions cannot themselves represent the infinitely many properties of which these objects are capable. Such features must be represented rather by infinite ideas "that are necessarily preliminary to [*préalables*] perceptions that one has of them" (*Lettre III*, OCM IX 923).[78] Read in terms of the doctrine of efficacious ideas that Malebranche had firmly in hand by this time, the claim that ideas are preliminary to perceptions of objects indicates that the ideas cause perceptions that conform to them and thus also to the objects for which these ideas serve as archetypes. According to Malebranche, strictly speaking it is the efficacious archetypes and not the conforming perceptual effects that represent the objects.

Malebranche went on to admit, however, that a pure perception can be said to represent since it bears a relation to itself as well as to an external idea. Drawing no doubt on Arnauld's own claim in the *Vraies et fausses idées* that "our thought or perception is essentially reflexive upon itself,"[79] he wrote:

> It is true that when one has a perception of a square, one perceives through reflection that one has this perception. Thus one may say that the perception that one has of a square is representative. But it is representative only of itself; and this through *consciousness* or inner sentiment, and not through a *clear idea*. It is the case that the soul not being separated from itself must sense what passes in it, or be informed about [*sçavoir*] what it perceives. But as it is the case that to sense is not to know clearly, this inner sentiment that it has of its perception does not teach it clearly what this perception is. (*Lettre III*, OCM IX 923)

In §1.1.2, I understood Malebranche to hold that the soul has immediate access to its sensations by means of direct consciousness. The claim in this passage that the perception of a square represents itself through reflection highlights the fact that the soul has a similar sort of access to its pure perceptions. As in the case of sensation, however, what the soul knows of pure perception through consciousness or inner sentiment "does not teach it clearly what this perception is." We are aware of sensations and pure perceptions as subjective appearances, but are incapable of a more objective view of the way in which these perceptions modify our own substance. Speaking of the perception of the idea of a square, Malebranche explained to Regis, "I sense well that it is me that perceives this idea; but my inner sentiment does not teach me how it is necessary that the soul be modified so that I can have the intellectual perception or sensible perception of color, to know or see such a shape" (*Rép. Regis*, c. 2, OCM XVII–1 289).

Malebranche must admit a sense in which we can clearly know our pure perceptions. In deriving the properties of the hypotenuse of a triangle from the properties of its sides, after all, we learn how the pure perception of the hypotenuse is linked to the pure perception of the sides. In terms of Malebranche's mature view, we come to understand the connection between these pure perceptions that is reflected in the laws of the union with God. But such an understanding concerns only the objective content of the pure perceptions that is constituted by external ideas. What we cannot comprehend is the inner subjective features of these perceptions. While inner sentiment reveals immediately what it is like for us to have pure perceptions, it does not show us how we are capable of such subjective experiences. Another way of expressing this point, which derives from Alquié, is to say that reflection provides access to the mind as the subject of pure perception but does not clearly display the mind as the substance modified by these perceptions.[80] Such a translation is in fact encouraged by Malebranche's own remarks. In the *Meditation Chrétiennes*, for instance, he admitted that he knows that he is a thinking thing that is capable of knowing clearly the relations among bodies, but he emphasized that he cannot know "this substance that I sense in me capable of knowing the truth" since "I am only dark to myself, my substance appears to me unintelligible" (*MC* IX, OCM X 101–2).

Malebranche was not saying here that no intelligible account of the nature of the soul as substance is possible. He held, after all, that there is an idea or archetype in God that clearly reveals the nature of thinking substance. Also, his point was not that we cannot know each and every one of the modifications that the soul can possess. Indeed, he noted in the *Recherche* that "even if [the mind] knew the capacity of the soul as it knows that of matter," it would still be the case that "it cannot comprehend all the various modifications that the mighty hand of God can produce in the soul." Just so, the fact that the nature of matter or extended substance is intelligible to the mind does not prevent it from being the case that this mind "cannot exhaust or comprehend all the shapes of which matter is capable" (*RV* III–1.1, OCM I 385/LO 200).

When Malebranche said that the nature of the thinking substance is unintelligible, he meant that its modifications are not intelligible to us in the way in which the modifications of extended substance are. Our pure perceptions of matter may be limited, but they nonetheless conform to the necessary and objective order determined by the idea of extension: thus it is that these perceptions yield clear knowledge of the necessary relations that hold among various geometrical shapes. In the case of sensation, though, inner sentiment yields only a subjective view of phenomenal features that bear no clear objective relation to each other. What Malebranche said about sounds also applies to all other sensations: they cannot be clearly known when they are "compared in themselves, or insofar as they are sensible qualities and modifications of the soul" (*Écl.* XI, OCM III 168/LO 636).

To be sure, inner sentiment extends to pure perceptions with contents that can be compared in a clear and objective manner. Given this complication in the case of pure perception, it is understandable that Malebranche focused on the case of sensation when arguing that inner sentiment is confused. Even when he acknowledged that our soul has clear intellectual modifications distinct from its confused sensory ones, however, Malebranche continued to stress that we do not know the soul through a clear idea of its nature. On his view, we no more know how the soul must be modified in order to have pure perceptions that have a clear objective content than we know how it must be modified in order to have sensations with a confused subjective content. In constructing an account of pure perceptions "insofar as they are modifications of the soul," all we have to go on are the appearances that we discover through inner sentiment. Malebranche therefore can say quite generally that the science of the soul is "only an experimental science, which results from the reflection that one makes on what passes within oneself" (*Mor.* I.5, OCM XI 67).

The claim that the science of the soul is *only* experimental is significant here. Malebranche indicated in his mature writings, at least, that the science of the material world is in part experimental. He came to recognize, for instance, that our knowledge of those bodily properties resulting from the laws of motion depends on *expérience* (see §2.2.1 [2]). Yet he also believed that our experimental knowledge of body is backed by an account of its objective geometrical modifications that derives a priori from a clear idea of extension. Thanks to Euclidean geometry, we can know how the parts of extended substance must be related in order for it to have such modifications. Malebranche held, conversely, that our experimental knowledge of the soul has no similar backing. He was drawing attention to the fact that reflection on the nature of thought alone does not yield any deductive science of the soul's ectoplasm or whatever objective feature it is that explains how the soul could have perceptions that appear to it in a certain way from a subjective view.[81]

From Malebranche's perspective, then, the Cartesian dictum that our intellectual perceptions are clear and distinct is ambiguous. Descartes' himself distinguished between the objective or representative reality of perceptions, and their formal reality as modes of mind.[82] While Malebranche rejected Descartes' view that the objective reality of our perceptions is constituted by something internal to our mind, he need not deny the epistemic point that we have a clear and distinct knowledge of the content of our pure perceptions. He held with Descartes, after all, that through our intellect we have access to a clear and distinct idea of extension. Malebranche did not see, however, that the Cartesians provided any reason to think that we have a clear and distinct knowledge of what Descartes called the formal reality of these perceptions. Malebranche's defense in *Éclaircissement XI* of the thesis that we have no clear idea of the soul's modifications in fact culminates in his demand that Cartesian critics "make me recognize this clear idea that I have not been able to find in me, whatever effort I have made to discover it" (OCM III 171/LO 638). On his view, of course, one could never find a clear idea of the soul in oneself. Had the Cartesians provided the requested deductive science of the soul's modifications, Malebranche would have concluded that they have pure perceptions that derive from a clear idea of the soul that exists external to their own soul, in God.[83] However, the force of his challenge does not depend on his ontological thesis that clear ideas are external to the soul. Malebranche's main point is the epistemic one that inner sentiment cannot yield a clear objective view of the manner in which pure perceptions modify the soul, given that this sentiment is restricted to a subjective view of these perceptions.

Gueroult has spoken of a conflict between an Augustinian side of Malebranche's theory of mind and a second, more Cartesian side.

> The mind, on the one hand, must be conceived as a created substance deprived of all light of its own, as a pure affectivity that receives from God its light and its objects of knowledge; on the other hand, it must be conceived as a faculty of knowing, as endowed with an intellect, a pure understanding that indeed belongs to it and obeys its will.[84]

Drawing on this remark, Nicholas Jolley has concluded that "the pulls of Descartes and Augustine generate a certain tension in [Malebranche's] model of mind."[85] On my reading, there is no such tension in Malebranche. His Augustinian thesis that the soul has no light of its own is supported most directly by his position that the soul cannot know in an objective manner the aspects of its sensations that it apprehends from a subjective view. Malebranche did not himself believe that such a position involves a pull away from Descartes; indeed, he took it to be linked to the Cartesian distinction between confused sensory effects and distinctly known bodily modifications. Malebranche's thesis that the soul is endowed with a faculty of pure understanding, on the other hand, derives from his Cartesian view that our intellect has access to an idea of extension that yields a clear objective view of such bodily properties. Malebranche was not an orthodox Cartesian, of course; he rejected Descartes' innatism, after all, in order to make room for a doctrine of the vision in God that he took to be distinctively Augustinian. Nevertheless, the tenet that we can have only a subjective view of the modifications of our soul serves to link Malebranche's non-Augustinian account of sensation to an account of pure perception in his writings that is in certain respects profoundly Cartesian.

Part II

Clear Demonstrations of Properties

four

SPIRITUALITY

Though Malebranche claimed in the *Recherche* that the consciousness or inner sentiment of the soul does not yield a clear view of its nature, he also noted that such consciousness as we do have "suffices to demonstrate its immortality, spirituality, freedom, and several other attributes of which it is necessary that we be informed" (RV III–2.7, OCM 453/LO 239). We have previously considered Malebranche's negative claim that we have only a confused inner sentiment of the passing modifications of our own soul. Now we will turn to his attempt to reconcile such a negative claim to his more positive view that we can demonstrate that our soul has the definitive properties of spirituality, immortality, and freedom.

I focus in this chapter on the attempt at reconciliation as it concerns the demonstration of "spirituality," which is arguably the most plausible of his three demonstrations. An initial difficulty with this demonstration is that Malebranche did not explain in any detail the nature of the property of spirituality. Furetière's *Dictionnaire universel* (1701), however, defines the term "spirituel" as "being that which is not body." In light of this definition, it is somewhat surprising that Malebranche implied that the property of spirituality is distinct from the property of differing from body when he referred in one passage to "the ignorance of most men" with respect both to the soul's "distinction from the body" and to "its spirituality" (*Écl.* XI, OCM III 164/LO 633). For deep reasons that will become clear later, he was not concerned to emphasize the distinction between these two properties. Nonetheless, one could save such a distinction by interpreting his claim that the soul is spiritual to mean that it is a substance that differs in nature from body, and thus is neither body itself nor a modification of body. The property of being spiritual would thereby differ from the property of being distinct from bodily substance since an argument for the latter property would require the further claim that body is not a modification of the soul but a substance that differs in nature from it.

There is some question whether the claim that one can demonstrate that the soul is spiritual, even in the restricted sense just indicated, is consistent with Malebranche's negative thesis that we do not have a clear idea of the nature of the soul. This sort of question did not fail to occur to the ever-sharp Arnauld. In a passage mentioned in the Introduction, he told Malebranche that "if we did not have a clear and distinct vision of the soul, we could demonstrate neither its immortality, nor its spirituality, nor its freedom."[1] Given the truth of this conditional, Malebranche's admission that we can demonstrate that the soul has these properties commits him to the conclusion that we have a clear and distinct knowledge of its nature. Arnauld objected that Malebranche cannot have it both ways; he cannot reject the Cartesian position that we have a clear and distinct idea of the soul and also retain the Cartesian view that we can have certain knowledge that the soul has particular properties, specifically the property of spirituality.

It must be granted Arnauld that passages from the *Recherche* encourage the view that consciousness or inner sentiment is clear enough to establish on its own the spirituality of the soul. In later writings, though, Malebranche stressed that consciousness cannot reveal directly that the soul has such a property. In an important passage from *Éclaircissement XI*, he claimed that the Cartesians themselves can prove that the soul is spiritual only by appealing to the premise, which is entailed by the clear idea of extension, that thought cannot be a mode of body. Malebranche concluded that since they are committed to arguing for spirituality in this indirect manner, it cannot be the case that inner sentiment affords them a clear knowledge of the nature of the soul.

Arnauld had broached profound difficulties with Descartes' own account of our knowledge of the nature of mind but later attempted to defend such an account against Malebranche's critical remarks. While Arnauld detected real problems with these remarks, though, he failed to come to grips with Malebranche's central charge that Cartesians have only an indirect knowledge of the soul's spirituality. This charge cannot be rejected out of hand since there are analogues of Malebranche's indirect argument in the writings of certain Cartesians. There is reason to doubt that Descartes himself relied on this sort of argument to establish the spirituality of the soul. In fact, his discussion in the *Meditations* suggests that, short of a divine guarantee, the cogito argument provides all that is needed to show that the nature of the soul does not include the bodily property of extension. Nonetheless, certain portions of this discussion render him vulnerable to Malebranche's claim that Cartesians cannot discern spirituality in the nature of the soul alone. The discussion itself thus prepares the way for Malebranche's conclusion that the claim that the nature of body consists in extension, and not the result of the cogito argument that the nature of the soul consists in thought, must bear the weight of the Cartesian argument for the spirituality of the soul.

4.1 Malebranche on Spirituality

4.1.1 Two Views of Consciousness

At several points in the *Recherche* Malebranche suggested that consciousness or inner sentiment suffices to block the view, which he took to be represented most vividly in the work of Michel de Montaigne, that the soul is material. The critique of materialism in Malebranche's text confronts difficulties, however, that are similar to those that bedevil Descartes' own response to the skeptical objections of Gassendi. This resemblance is more than a little ironic, given Malebranche's rejection in *Éclaircissement XI* of Descartes' claim against Gassendi that the nature of mind is better known than the nature of any other thing (see §1.3). While Malebranche's remarks in the *Recherche* are perhaps not formally inconsistent with this rejection, there is in his writings at least a marked shift in emphasis. Early on he stressed that consciousness does not reveal the soul to be material and did little to distance himself from the stronger dogmatic view that inner sentiment reveals the soul to be spiritual. In his later writings, however, he rejected such a dogmatic view in favor of the skeptical position that consciousness or inner sentiment cannot itself establish that extension is not part of the soul's nature.

(1) The Critique of Montaigne. In Book Three of the *Recherche* Malebranche noted his desire to forge a middle way between "the different sentiments of those who say that there is nothing that one knows better than the soul, and of those who are assured that there is nothing that they know less" (RV III–2.7, OCM I 452/LO 238).[2] In the fourth edition (1678) he added a footnote referring the reader to *Éclaircissement XI* for an indication of the nature of these opposing positions. While this text makes clear that those disciples of Descartes prejudiced by his authority offer the dogmatic view that the soul is known best, it does not reveal a source for the skeptical view that the soul is known least. In the *Recherche* itself, however, Malebranche had mentioned Montaigne as an influential proponent of such a skeptical view, devoting an entire chapter to Montaigne's masterwork, the *Essais*, in which he commented sourly that its author pretended "to pass for a Pyrrhonist" since "it was necessary in his time, to pass for a clever and tasteful man, to doubt everything" (RV II–3.5, OCM I 367/LO 189).[3] For Malebranche this Pyrrhonistic pretense serves to indicate not that Montaigne is clever and tasteful but that he is "the most ignorant of all men, not only in what concerns the nature of the soul, but also in every other thing" (OCM I 367/LO 189).[4]

In this section Malebranche noted that skeptics are afflicted with an illness that leads them "to speak in a decisive manner on the most uncertain and the least probable things" (OCM I 367–68/LO 189).[5] In the case of Montaigne, this illness results in his tendency to "confuse mind with matter." Such a tendency explains why Montaigne "relates the most extravagant opinions of the Philosophers on the nature of the soul without despising them, and even with an air that makes it rather known that he approves those opinions most opposed to reason" (OCM I 368/LO 189). Malebranche was thinking here of Montaigne's numerous citations in the most famous chapter of the *Essais*, the "Apologie de Raimond Sebond," of materialist remarks concerning the soul in the writings of classical Greek and Roman authors. For Malebranche it was typical of Montaigne to defend materialism in this section not by arguing for it directly but by using a pleasing display of erudition in order to incline others to his own view.[6]

One could well dispute this reading of Montaigne as a committed materialist.[7] Moreover, even if Malebranche did establish that the *Essais* attempts to support a materialist account of the soul merely by citing ancient opinions, that result would hardly suffice to undermine the account itself. Malebranche offered a more direct argument against materialism in Book Six of the *Recherche*, however, after presenting his proof of the existence of the soul. He wrote there that one can overcome difficulties in knowing the essence or nature of the soul by attending carefully to what inner sentiment teaches.

> If one doubts, if one wills, if one reasons, it is necessary only to believe that the soul is a thing that doubts, wills, and reasons, and nothing more, provided one has not experienced other qualities in it; for one knows the soul only through the inner sentiment one has of it. It is not necessary to take one's soul for one's body, or for blood, or for animal spirits, or for fire, or for an infinity of other things for which Philosophers have taken it. It is necessary to believe of the soul only what one would not know how to avoid believing of it, and what one is fully convinced of through the inner sentiment one has of oneself, for otherwise one would be mistaken. (RV VI–2.6, OCM II 369–70/LO 480)

The fact that inner sentiment reveals only that the soul has various thoughts, and thus cannot show it to be identical to bodily elements, serves here as a bulwark against the materialism of "the Philosophers" that Montaigne purportedly related in such an attractive manner.

It must be admitted that the response to materialism in this passage is somewhat weak since the claim there is not that materialism is false but only that inner sentiment does not reveal it to be true. Nonetheless, Malebranche seems to have offered a stronger response in a section of the *Recherche* that concerns the mind as it is "in itself and without any relation to the body" (RV III–1.1, OCM I 379/LO 197).

> But as I am certain that no one has any knowledge of his soul except through thought, or through the inner sentiment of all that takes place in his mind, I am assured also that if someone wishes to consider the nature of his soul, he need consult only this inner sentiment, which continually represents to him what he is, and he should not fancy contrary to his own consciousness that the soul is an invisible fire, a subtle air, a harmony or some other similar thing. (OCM I 389/LO 202)[8]

The claim here that one "need consult only inner sentiment" in order to know the nature of the soul, together with the claim that a materialist account of the soul is "contrary to consciousness," appear to indicate that Malebranche took consciousness or inner sentiment itself to show that the soul is spiritual. Such an appearance is reinforced by the remark in the *Recherche*, cited at the start of this chapter, that consciousness "suffices to demonstrate" the spirituality of the soul.

To be sure, there is a reading of these passages on which they imply only the weak response to materialism indicated earlier. Thus, Malebranche's claim that we "need consult only inner sentiment" in order to know the nature of the soul perhaps says no more than the immediately preceding claim that such sentiment reveals what "takes place in the mind."[9] Likewise, the comment that the materialist account of the soul is "contrary to consciousness" could be read as simply repeating the weak point that such consciousness does not show the soul to be identical to any material element. Finally, the remark the consciousness "suffices" for the demonstration of spirituality could be interpreted as saying only that such consciousness provides all the information *with respect to the soul* that such a demonstration requires. On this interpretation, the remark is compatible with Malebranche's mature position, to be considered presently, that such a demonstration also depends on the account of the nature of body dictated by the clear idea of extension.[10]

The possibility of such an interpretation of these passages from the first edition of the *Recherche* may well explain why Malebranche decided not to excise them from later editions. However, the reading strains against the early remarks themselves. The evidence from the first edition simply does not support the thesis that Malebranche from the start ruled out the dogmatic position that consciousness alone refutes materialism. Indeed, the indication is that he had not thought through the difference between the weak claim that consciousness does not reveal the soul to be material and the strong claim that it reveals the soul to be spiritual. His initial reply to the materialism of Montaigne thus suffers from an important ambiguity.

Interestingly enough, there is a similar ambiguity in some of the remarks that Descartes directed against the objections of Gassendi, an admirer of Montaigne. The exchange between Descartes and Gassendi concerns a central passage from the *Second Meditation* that anticipates Malebranche's point in the *Recherche* that it is contrary to consciousness to conclude that "the soul is an invisible fire, a subtle air, a harmony, or some other similar thing" (RV III–1.1, OCM I 389/LO 202). In his text Descartes had noted that given the doubts he raised earlier concerning the existence of body, he must assume that "I am not some thin air that permeates the limbs, not wind, not fire, not air, not breath, nor whatever I imagine [*fingo*] to myself; for these things are supposed to be nothing" (AT VII 27/CSM II 18). He went on to broach a materialist challenge to this assumption when he asked: "May it not perhaps be the case that these themselves [*viz.*, the imagined bodily elements], which I suppose to be nothing, because they are not known to me, nevertheless in truth of fact do not differ from that me which I know?" In what is, as we will discover, a significant concession to the materialist, Descartes admitted, "I do not know, and now do not dispute this thing; only about those things that are known to me can I make a judgment." Yet he also emphasized in this passage that his notion of himself as a thinking thing "does not depend [*pendere*] on those things the existence of which I do not yet know; therefore not any of the things I invent [*effingo*] by imagination" (AT VII 27–28/CSM II 18–19).

Gassendi conceded that the mind is a thinking thing but objected to Descartes that "it remains for you to prove the power of thinking to be something far beyond the nature of body, so that neither a vapor nor any other agile, pure and rarefied body can be disposed in such a way that would make it capable of thought" (*Fifth Obj.*, AT VII 262/CSM II 183). He observed that far from proving this, Descartes explicitly conceded in the *Second Meditation* that he does not know that his own mind is in fact distinct from the bodily elements depicted in the imagination. So how can it be the case, Gassendi asked Descartes, that "you assume that you are none of these things? *I know, you say, that I exist; however knowledge of this thing taken strictly cannot depend on that of which I am unaware.* Let this be so; but remember that you have not yet made certain that you are not air, or a vapor, or something else of this sort" (AT VII 265/CSM II 185). According to Gassendi, then, Descartes went wrong in conflating the weak claim that he does not know his mind to depend on body, which is consistent with his concession to the materialist, with the strong claim that he knows that his mind does not depend on body, which is not consistent with this concession.

In the *Fifth Replies* Descartes protested to Gassendi that in the context of the discussion in the *Second Meditation*, "I need not admit that this thinking substance was some body that is agile, pure, rarefied, etc., since I had no reason that persuaded me of this." He objected in general that it is unfair of Gassendi to demand "that I prove to be false what I refused to admit for no other reason than that it was unknown to me" (AT VII 355/CSM II 245–46). Indeed, he charged that it is Gassendi who must explain why, "while you have little or no rational basis for proving that the mind is not distinct from the body, you nonetheless assume this" (AT VII 357/CSM II 247).

The suggestion here that Gassendi is a materialist is no more plausible than Malebranche's similar suggestion with respect to Montaigne.[11] Nevertheless, Descartes' remarks to this point at least have the virtue of being restricted to the weak claim that he does not know his mind to be identical to a body. His argument is simply that such a claim allows him to refrain from granting any materialist hypothesis concerning his mind. Descartes complicated matters, though, when he attempted to illustrate the injustice of Gassendi's demands: "It is as if, when I said that I now live in Holland, you were to deny that this be believed, unless I prove that I am not also in China or some other part of the world, on the grounds that it is perhaps possible through divine power that the same body should exist in two different places" (AT VII 355/CSM II 246). The innocent position here is that Descartes' conclusion that he is a thinking thing would hold even if it were the case that he also is a body, just as the conclusion that he lives in Holland could be true even if it were supernaturally possible for him to be in two different places at once. What is not so innocent, though, is his suggestion that being a thinking thing is as distinct from being a body as being in Holland is from being in China. Descartes apparently assumed that after he has established that he is a mind, the only question left to him is whether he can also be a body. He missed entirely the force of Gassendi's objection that for all Descartes knows, his mind may just be identical to a body. Descartes' analogy provides reason to think that he was capable of sliding from the weak claim that he does not know that his mind is a body to the strong claim that he knows that his mind is not a body.

Descartes perhaps was anticipating his conclusion in the *Sixth Meditation* that the thinking thing is distinct from body. Given this conclusion, being a thinking thing and being a body would be as different as being in Holland and being in China. Nonetheless, I later cite evidence that Descartes understood his discussion in the *Second Meditation* to underwrite some form of the strong claim that the mind is not simply a body. I take this evidence to reveal that there is in fact a precedent in Descartes for Malebranche's failure in the *Recherche* to distinguish the thesis that consciousness does not reveal the soul to be material from the dogmatic position that materialism is directly refuted by consciousness. Malebranche, of course, was deeply committed to the thesis by his acceptance of Cartesian dualism. Yet his later writings reflect a skeptical turn in his thought that issues in one of the most striking features of his theory of the soul, namely, his rejection of the dogmatic refutation of materialism.

(2) *The Skeptical Turn.* As we have seen, Malebranche claimed confidently in the 1674 *Recherche* that the knowledge of our soul that we have through consciousness "suffices to demonstrate its immortality, spirituality, liberty, and some other attributes of which it is necessary that we be informed." By stark contrast, in the 1678 *Éclaircissement XI* he drew the attention of his Cartesian critics to "the ignorance of most men with regard to their soul, of its distinction from the body, of its spirituality, of its immortality, and of its other properties," which ignorance of the soul, he held, "suffices to prove evidently that they do not have a clear and distinct idea of it" (OCM III 164/LO 633). Malebranche concluded that there is in fact "some difficulty" in recognizing that mind differs from body and that "it is necessary to reason in order to conclude that the one is not the other" (OCM III 171/LO 638).[12] So whereas Malebranche spoke in his early writings as if materialism is easily refuted, he later emphasized the difficulty of such a refutation in order to bolster his doctrine that we do not have a clear idea of the soul.

One could argue that such a doctrine is in fact consistent with the strong view that consciousness provides all that is needed to prove the spirituality of the soul. The main argument for the doctrine in the first edition of the *Recherche* is that consciousness does not reveal all the properties of which the soul is capable. The claim that consciousness establishes that the soul has the property of spirituality, however, need not require that it can reveal all of the properties of the soul. Consciousness would need to reveal only that the soul has one property that does not belong to body. It is perhaps understandable that Malebranche was not initially worried by the dogmatic position that consciousness alone suffices to demonstrate the spirituality of the soul.

What requires explanation, then, is why Malebranche later became concerned to deny such a position. There are two possible explanations that occur to me, the first of which, though indicated explicitly by Malebranche himself, is somewhat problematic, and the second of which, though suggested by him only obliquely, is more satisfying. The first explanation is tied to Malebranche's remark to Regis in 1693 that the soul

> senses only that it is, and it is evident that it can sense only what is in itself. It sees itself and knows itself if you will, but exclusively through inner sentiment; a confused sentiment that discovers to it neither what it is nor what is the nature of any of its modalities. This sentiment does not reveal to it that it is not extended, still less that color, that the whiteness, for example, that it sees in this paper, is really only a modification of its own substance. This sentiment is thus only shadowy [ténébres] in this regard. (Rép. Regis, c. 2, OCM XVII–1 298)

Here the claim that inner sentiment does not reveal that the soul lacks extension is yoked with the first of the two Cartesians arguments for the obscurity of sensation considered previously, namely, the argument that inner sentiment does not reveal sensible qualities such as colors to be modifications of the soul. As I pointed out in §2.3.1, Malebranche did not offer this argument in the first edition of the *Recherche*. He added it to the second edition, however, and developed it further in *Éclaircissement XI*. My hypothesis is that after Malebranche came to see that inner sentiment does not prevent the confusion of sensible qualities with bodily modifications, he found it increasingly difficult to believe that this sentiment could prevent the confusion of the soul itself with extended substance. On this hypothesis, Malebranche's suggestion in his response to Regis above is that since inner sentiment is so confused with respect to the sensory modifications of the soul, it surely cannot clearly reveal on its own that the soul has the property of spirituality.

We will discover that what Malebranche had to say about knowledge of the soul's spirituality is strongly analogous to what he had to say about knowledge of sensible qualities (see §4.1.2). Even so, his argument that the inner sentiment of sensible qualities is confused does not appear to close off the possibility that consciousness directly reveals that the soul is spiritual. We have seen, after all, that this argument applies more directly to weak sensible qualities such as colors than it does to strong sensible qualities such as pain. Malebranche even allowed that there are sentiments such as love and hate that we do not refer at all to objects, but only to the soul (see §2.3.1 [1]). He therefore left himself open to the objection that inner sentiment can reveal that the soul is spiritual, just as it can reveal that certain qualities or sentiments belong to the soul.

There is another explanation for Malebranche's rejection of the dogmatic refutation of materialism, however, that can be derived from his claim to Regis that inner sentiment does not reveal to the soul "the nature of its modalities." Such a claim is linked to the point in the first edition of the *Recherche* that we cannot know our modifications, and in particular our sensory modifications, by means of definitions. In §1.3.3 (2) I have taken this position to be that while consciousness provides access to the subjective phenomenal features of our sensations, it does not yield a clear objective view of the manner in which these sensations modify the soul. I have argued in §2.3.2 (1), moreover, that the second argument for the obscurity of sensation in *Éclaircissement XI*, namely, the argument that we can know our sensations only through experience, reflects this position. This second argument, unlike the first, is not restricted to a particular sort of quality or sentiment. Further, the implication of this argument that the experience of the soul through inner sentiment is limited to a subjective view is in some tension with the claim that we are directly conscious of the fact that our soul is spiritual. I suspect that as Malebranche developed the view that inner sentiment is restricted in this way, he became convinced that consciousness by itself does not allow us to know in an objective manner any feature of the soul, including its spirituality.[13]

In any case, I suggest that by 1678 Malebranche had rejected the dogmatic view that consciousness shows directly that the soul can lack extension. There is a passage from the 1688 *Entretiens*, to be sure, that seems to conflict with such a suggestion. Toward the start of this work, Malebranche had Theodore remark, in the course of offering an argument for the spirituality of the soul: "I can perceive my thought, my desire, my sadness, without thinking of extension, and even when I suppose that there is no extension. Thus all these things are not modifications of extension, but modifications of a substance that thinks, that senses, that desires, and that is quite different from extension" (*EMI*, OCM XII 34/D 27). At first glance the view in this passage seems to be that the conclusion that a substance that thinks can lack extension follows simply from the premise that we can perceive our thoughts even while supposing that there is no extension. It thus appears to be open to the objection, which is a variant of Gassendi's objection to Descartes, that the mere fact that we can conceive of thinking substance without conceiving of it as extended does not entail that thinking substance is not essentially an extended thing.

Notice, however, that Theodore claims only that his various thoughts differ from the modifications of extension and that the subject of these thoughts is not simply extension itself. This claim seems to leave open the possibility that the substance that has conscious thoughts also is an extended thing. Moreover, after having concluded a few paragraphs earlier that he exists as a thinking thing, Theodore fails to dismiss a materialist challenge similar to the one Descartes had offered in the *Second Meditation*: "But what am I, the I that thinks, at the time that I think? Am I a body, a mind, a man? I do not as yet know any of this." This implies that consciousness does not establish immediately that thinking substance is not simply a body. Indeed, Theodore went on to argue for the difference between mind and body by appealing not to consciousness but to the fact that "extension and matter are but one and the same substance" (OCM

XII 34/D 27). His main argument is that the mind cannot be material since extended substance cannot have thoughts as modifications.[14] Despite the appearances, then, Theodore does not attempt to derive the spirituality of the soul directly from his consciousness of thought. Rather, he takes a more indirect route that appeals to the fact that body cannot think.

Such an indirect route admittedly is not clearly indicated by Malebranche's claim in the first edition of the *Recherche* that consciousness suffices to demonstrate the spirituality of the soul. In the last edition of this text, though, he qualified such a claim by inserting the remark that we can avoid confusing the soul with the body "through reason" since "the idea that we have of body reveals to us that the modalities of which it is capable are quite different from those we sense" (RV III–2.7, OCM I 453/LO 239).[15] The conclusion that the soul is spiritual is carried over from the first edition, but what is new is the implication that such a conclusion is established, not directly by consciousness, but only indirectly by means of an examination of "the idea we have of body." The "we" here evidently refers to the Cartesians, and in *Éclaircissement XI*, first published over three decades earlier than the last edition of the *Recherche*, Malebranche charged that the Cartesians themselves feel compelled to distinguish the soul from matter in this indirect way. This charge might not seem particularly significant, especially since Malebranche was willing to concede the central Cartesian point that the soul is spiritual. Moreover, he accepted the Cartesian account of bodily substance and even defended it against the objections of one critic by emphasizing that it provides what is needed for the refutation of materialism. Nonetheless, Malebranche took the very fact that Cartesians depend on this account for such a refutation to provide further confirmation of his negative thesis that the consciousness that we have of our own soul is confused.

4.1.2 Malebranche's Cartesian Argument

(1) The Critique of the Cartesians. Malebranche offered *Éclaircissement XI* as a response to those Cartesians so prejudiced by Descartes' authority that they assert that they know their soul through a clear idea of its nature. An initial point in this text, which we already have considered in some detail, is that the Cartesians themselves must appeal to the clear idea of extension in order to establish that sensible qualities such as pain, heat, and color are modifications of the soul. The argument, according to Malebranche, is that since these qualities cannot be modifications of extension and since "there are only two kinds of beings, spirits and bodies," it must be the case that the qualities belong to the spirit or soul. Malebranche concluded that Cartesians who offer this argument must not have access to a clear idea of the soul; otherwise "why would [they] ever bother with this detour?" (OCM III 165/LO 634).

Toward the end of this text, Malebranche made the related point that "we" (surely continuing to refer to Cartesians) must consult the clear idea of extension in order to establish that sensible qualities are modes of a substance that differs in nature from body. He wrote that "there is some difficulty in knowing the difference" between soul and body and that this difference

> is not discovered by a simple view, and reason is necessary to conclude that the one is not the other. It is necessary to consult with care the idea of extension, and to know that extension is not a manner of being of bodies, but body itself, since it is represented to us as a substantial thing, and as the principle of all that we conceive clearly in bodies; and thus that since the modes of which the body is capable have no relation [*rapport*] to any sensible qualities, it is necessary that the subject of these qualities, or rather the being of which these qualities are modes, is very different from body. It is necessary to produce such reasons in order to avoid confusing the soul with the body. But if one had a clear idea of the soul, as one does of the body, certainly one would not be obliged to take all these detours in order to distinguish them. (OCM III 171/LO 638)

The positive point here is that Cartesians offer a definitive argument for the conclusion that the soul is a substance that differs from body, one that appeals to the fact that modes of body "have no relation to any sensible qualities." Malebranche elaborated on this argument when he noted earlier in *Éclaircissement XI* that since all bodily modes are simply modes of extension, they can be understood completely in terms of relations of distance between the parts of extension. Sensible qualities, on the other hand, cannot be understood in the same way. Malebranche allowed that one could understand, say, various sounds in terms of relations of distance by correlating them with the motion of air particles; however, he emphasized that the sounds are not *in themselves* explicable in terms of relations of distance, as are the shapes and motions of the particles (OCM III 168/LO 636). This difference reveals that the sensible qualities bear no relation to modes of body.

Malebranche's Cartesian argument seems to overlook the sensations of qualities such as shape and motion that he had considered in some detail in Book One of the *Recherche*.[16] It may be objected that since these qualities can themselves be understood in terms of relations of distance, the argument in *Éclaircissement XI* does not establish that bodily modes lack any relation to sensible qualities. Malebranche, of course, must concede that the nature of the qualities of shape and motion can be understood in this way. However, I have taken him to hold that the visual (as opposed to the pure) perception of a certain shape, for instance, is simply the perception of a bounded patch of color (see §3.2.2 [2]). The corollary of this position is that the sensory perception of shape is inseparable from the sensation of color. On my reading, then, he could argue that the geometrical qualities as sensed (rather than as understood through pure perception) bear no relation to bodily modifications.

At this point, though, one could challenge the assumption that color sensations, or thoughts in general, cannot belong to body. Gassendi had charged Descartes with a failure to show that body cannot be disposed in a manner that makes it capable of thought. Likewise, it may seem as if the Cartesians to whom Malebranche referred (including himself) have not shown that the parts of an extended thing cannot be related in a manner that makes that thing capable of having sensations such as those of color. Leibniz raised such an objection in his 1715 *Entretien de Philarète et d'Ariste*, a companion piece to Malebranche's own *Entretiens* between Ariste and Theodore.[17] In his text, Leibniz had Philarète address Ariste's claim, taken over from Theodore, that "thoughts are not relations of distance because we cannot measure thoughts." Philarète notes that "a follower of Epicurus would say that this is due to our lack of knowledge of them, and that if we knew the corpuscles that form thought and the motions that are necessary for this, we would see that thoughts are measurable and are the workings of some very subtle machines." Likewise, Philarète continues, although colors may not seem to consist in something measurable, it could turn out that the qualities themselves, "in the end, reduce to something measurable, material, and mechanical," given that "the reason for such qualities in objects" may be "found in certain configurations and movements."[18]

Malebranche could well object that the fact that "qualities in objects" can be reduced to configurations and motions does not itself show that the *sensations* of the qualities can be so reduced.[19] Indeed, his Cartesian doctrine that sensible qualities cannot be in bodies seems to preclude the latter reduction. Even today materialists who accept that the sensuous aspects of qualities such as colors do not literally exist in bodies face the difficulty of explaining where, or in what way, these aspects do exist. For Malebranche, however, it was only natural that the qualities with such aspects be, to borrow Michael Ayers' colorful phrase, "kicked upstairs" into the mind.[20]

One specific reason for kicking the sensible qualities upstairs is broached by Malebranche's rhetorical question in the *Recherche* of whether one can "conceive that matter shaped in a given way, such as a square, round, or oval, be pain, pleasure, heat, cold, odor, sound, etc." (RV VI–2.7, OCM II 391/LO 493).[21] Since sensible qualities possess sensuous aspects that we can know only from a subjective view, and since these aspects cannot be reduced to bodily features such as shapes, which we can know in a purely objective manner, serious thought reveals that the qualities cannot be identified with such features. Malebranche's view that the qualities must exist upstairs, in an incorporeal substance, is somewhat out of style, yet his assumption that the sensuous aspects of our sensations are irreducible to objective bodily features continues to have its attractions. In particular, such an assumption seems to underlie the recent argument that reductive and eliminative forms of materialism fail to account for the subjective qualitative aspects of conscious experience.[22]

So far we have focused on Malebranche's positive Cartesian claim that since sensible qualities cannot be reduced to bodily modifications, the subject of these qualities must differ in nature from body. His main point in *Éclaircissement XI* with respect to such a claim, however, is a negative one. As in the case of his earlier discussion in this text of the argument for the conclusion that sensible qualities are modes of the soul, Malebranche emphasized that the fact that Cartesians must compare sensible qualities to modes of extended substance shows that they lack access to a clear idea of the soul. Just as the Cartesians appeal to the clear idea of extension in order to establish that sensible qualities belong to the soul, so they appeal to such an idea in order to show that the soul is a spiritual substance. In both cases, Malebranche argued, they take an indirect route to the conclusion that certain properties belong to the soul because they do not have access to a more direct route that involves only a consideration of the clear idea of the nature of the soul.

Despite this similarity, the two arguments that Malebranche attributed to the Cartesians are importantly different. The first argument appeals to the idea of extension in order to establish that *sensible qualities* belong to the *soul*. This argument simply assumes as a premise that soul and body are distinct kinds of substances.[23] The argument toward the end of *Éclaircissement* XI, however, appeals to the idea of extension in order to establish that the *subject* of sensible qualities differs from *body*. The argument is that since the idea of extension entails that these qualities cannot be modifications of material substance, the soul that they do modify must be an immaterial substance.

We are now in a position to understand why Malebranche did not stress the distinction between the property of being spiritual and the property of being distinct from body. On his view, Cartesians can know that the soul is a spiritual substance, one that differs in nature from body, only by coming to see through the clear idea of extension that body cannot think and thus must be a substance distinct from the soul. For Malebranche, then, there can be no knowledge of the soul's spirituality that is prior to or independent of the knowledge of its distinction from material substance.

Malebranche is in the end committed to a very traditional sort of Cartesian dualism. Such a commitment is reflected in his claim in the *Recherche* that "the essence of the mind consists only in thought, just as the essence of matter consists only in extension" (RV III–1.1, OCM I 381/LO 198). What is less traditional, yet nonetheless an important feature of his system, is the view in *Éclaircissement* XI that what bears the load in the Cartesian demonstration of mind–body distinctness is not the thesis concerning the essence of mind, but rather the thesis concerning the essence of matter.

(2) The Controversy with La Ville. Malebranche's emphasis on the Cartesian account of the essence of matter is relevant to the second main controversy in his career (the first being his controversy with Foucher and Desgabets in 1675–78). The adversary here was the Jesuit Louis le Valois, who in 1680, under the assumed name of Louis de la Ville, published his *Sentimens de M. Des Cartes touchant l'essence et les proprietez du corps*. In this work the author singled out "the author of the *Recherche de la Vérité* [as] manifestly Cartesian in several things, but particularly on the point of the essence of matter."[24] La Ville took the crucial Cartesian point to be that extension and its modifications cannot exist apart from corporeal substance. He argued that such a point conflicts with the Catholic doctrine of the Eucharist and in particular with the determination of the Council of Trent that the accidents of the bread and wine remain while their substance is converted into the substance of Christ's body and blood.[25] La

Ville therefore charged that Malebranche and other Cartesians who adopt Descartes' account of matter give aid and comfort to the Protestant enemies of the Catholic Church.[26]

This charge may now seem rather abstruse, focused as it is on the metaphysics of the Eucharist. However, it was in its time politically potent; this sort of charge, in fact, provided the impetus for the proscription of Cartesianism in France in the second half of the seventeenth century.[27] It is thus understandable that in his official response to the *Sentimens*, the *Défense... Contre M. de la Ville* (1682), Malebranche did not revisit specific claims regarding the Eucharist.[28] Rather, he attempted to change the subject by arguing that La Ville's own rejection of Descartes' account of matter has theologically dangerous consequences regarding the nature of the soul. One specific point he made is that this rejection precludes the only certain argument there is for the spirituality of our soul. Malebranche claimed that it is evident that the soul cannot be material if matter is identified with extension since extension "can neither reason, nor will, nor even sense." Drawing on the argument that he had outlined four years earlier in *Éclaircissement* XI, Malebranche explained to La Ville that since extension is capable only of shapes and movements, it cannot be the subject of thoughts such as reason, volition, and sensation, which have an element that goes beyond objective relations of distance. He concluded that those who accept the Cartesian account of body can be certain that "what is in us that thinks is necessarily a substance distinguished from our body" (OCM XVII-1 521).

This line of argument was not available to La Ville, who denied that the essence of matter consists in extension. It seemed to Malebranche, however, that there is no other intelligible way to refute the view of "the Libertines" who contend that "*this something* in which consists the essence of body, is capable of thought, and that the substance that thinks is the same as that which is extended" (OCM XVII-1 522).[29] These libertines argue that it is "experience" that "teaches us that the body is capable of sensing, of thinking, of reasoning." Faced with the Cartesian claim that reason refutes such experience, moreover, they simply fall back on the following skeptical response: "The essences of beings being unknown to us, we cannot discover through reason that of which they are capable. Thus reason wills that one consult experience, and experience confounds the soul with the body and teaches us that it is capable of thought" (OCM XVII-1 522-23).[30] Here there is the same naïve dependence on experience, the same coupling of skepticism and materialism, that Malebranche had earlier seen in Montaigne's *Essais*. The critique of La Ville thus returns us to the rejection in the *Recherche* of the view in Montaigne that Malebranche had taken to be dangerous to religion.

Given the skeptical turn in Malebranche's thought, however, this critique could not return us to precisely the same point. I have urged that in his early remarks in the *Recherche* Malebranche was not careful to preclude the view that mere consciousness reveals that the soul is spiritual. By the time of his response to La Ville, though, he had accepted that no such direct refutation of materialism is available. Indeed, this acceptance seems to be crucial for his argument against La Ville. If consciousness could directly refute materialism, there would be no need to examine the nature of body in order to establish that the soul is spiritual. Malebranche's defense of the Cartesian account of body thus would be unnecessary. Since the direct route from consciousness is obstructed, however, the only other path to the refutation of materialism is by way of the proof that body cannot think. La Ville cannot offer such a proof, according to Malebranche, given the skeptical upshot of his position that the essence of body consists in being an unknown something that has extension. The conclusion in the *Défense* is that La Ville's argument against the Cartesian identification of matter with extension blocks the only completely certain route to the conclusion that the soul, the substance that thinks, is spiritual.

This criticism of La Ville takes on added significance in light of Locke's notorious suggestion in his *Essay concerning Human Understanding* (1690) that we cannot deny that "God can, if he pleases, superadd to Matter a Faculty of Thinking [since] we know not wherein Thinking consists, nor to what sort of Substances the Almighty has been pleased to give that power."[31] While the focus here is on our lack of knowledge of the faculty of thought, Locke also had emphasized earlier in this text that since we do not know "how the solid parts of Body are united, or cohere together to make Extension," the nature of "the union and cohesion of its parts" is "as incomprehensible as the manner of Thinking, and how it is performed."[32] In a later defense of his suggestion in the *Essay*, moreover, he pointed out that if we deny that matter can think simply on the grounds that there is no conceivable connection between thought and extension, "we must deny even the consistency and being of matter itself; since every particle of it having some bulk, has its parts connected by ways inconceivable to us."[33] The very inconceivability of matter thus renders it impossible for us to perceive a contradiction in the thesis that God can superadd thought to matter. Locke concluded that since his suggestion in the *Essay* was simply that we can see no contradiction in such thesis, and since "I know nobody, before Des Cartes, that ever pretended to show that there was any contradiction in it," the suggestion itself "makes me opposite only to the Cartesians."[34]

What is most significant about Locke's argument against the Cartesians, for our purposes, is its dependence on the rejection of their doctrine that the nature of matter is conceivable to us.[35] His position is that the burden of the Cartesian argument for spirituality rests ultimately on the premise that the nature of body is such that body cannot think. This is precisely where Malebranche had placed the burden of the argument in his response to La Ville. While there is some doubt as to whether Malebranche himself knew of Locke's suggestion in the *Essay*,[36] it is clear that he would have taken such a suggestion to confirm his point against La Ville that those who reject Cartesianism on the grounds that the essence of matter consists in being an "unknown something" that is extended cannot refute the claim that the soul is material.

Malebranche, of course, was concerned to defend the certainty of the Cartesian belief in the soul's spirituality against the Lockean sort of skepticism that he saw first in Montaigne in the 1674 *Recherche*, and later in La Ville in the

1682 *Défense*. However, at the chronological midpoint between these two works, in the 1678 *Éclaircissement XI*, Malebranche's defense of the Cartesians took on a more critical edge. There he appealed to the Cartesian argument for the spirituality of the soul in order to illustrate the difference between the clear idea of body and the confused consciousness of the soul. The idea of body as extended substance must be clear since Cartesians can derive directly from this idea the conclusion that body cannot think. The consciousness of the soul must be confused, on the other hand, since not even Cartesians can derive directly from such consciousness the conclusion that the soul is a spiritual substance. On Malebranche's mature view, then, a consideration of the Cartesian argument for the spirituality of the soul provides sufficient reason to reject the unduly influential doctrine of Descartes that the nature of mind is better known than the nature of body.

4.2 The Cartesians and Malebranche's Argument

4.2.1 Arnauld's Critiques and Malebranche's Argument

By the time of the publication of *Éclaircissement XI*, Arnauld had long since offered in the *Fourth Objections*, first published with the *Meditations* in 1641, his own criticisms of Descartes' discussion of the nature of the mind. In this text Arnauld argued in particular that it does not follow from Descartes' claim that he is unaware that anything else pertains to his nature except thought that nothing else does in fact pertain to it. According to Arnauld, while this claim does entail that "I can obtain some notion of myself without a notion of body," it does not establish that this notion of mind "is complete and adequate, while it excludes body from my essence" (AT VII 201/CSM II 141).

Arnauld's main objection was that Descartes' perception that his nature consists in thought allows for the possibility that body is somehow included in his nature. He suggested the position, offered as a skeptical possibility by Gassendi and as the truth by the materialist Thomas Hobbes, that mind is merely a species of body (AT VII 200–201/CSM II 141).[37] If Hobbes were correct, then the fact that Descartes can consider mind apart from body could not show that the essence of mind does not include body; this fact could reveal only his ignorance of the necessary connection between mind and body.

Arnauld illustrated this point by noting that someone ignorant of the Pythagorean Theorem can form a notion of a right triangle without attributing to that triangle the property (call it the Pythagorean property) of having a hypotenuse the square of which is equal to the sum of the squares of the other two sides. Nonetheless, it does not follow from the fact that the notion can be obtained in this way that the Pythagorean property does not belong to the essence of that triangle. Just so, Arnauld asserted, it does not follow from the fact that he can obtain a notion of his nature without attributing body to it that body does not belong to his nature. It may be that the property of having a body is somehow included in his essence in the same way that the Pythagorean property is included in the essence of a right triangle.

Descartes responded that Arnauld's analogy does not hold up for several reasons, one of which is that the right triangle could not be distinctly understood if the Pythagorean property were denied it, whereas mind can be distinctly understood as a complete thing, that is, as a substance, even though nothing bodily be attributed to it (*Fourth Rep.*, AT VII 225/CSM II 159).[38] As we will discover, the dogmatic position that mind can be distinctly understood as a complete thing apart from body seems to provide little in the way of an argument against more subtle forms of materialism. However, Arnauld's heart was not in his defense of materialism, so he was easily swayed by Descartes' response. He later told Descartes, "What you wrote concerning the distinction between the mind and the body seems to me very clear, evident, and divinely inspired."[39]

It is not surprising that Arnauld later responded on Descartes' behalf to Malebranche's remarks in *Éclaircissement XI*. In a section of his *Vraies et fausses idées* Arnauld singled out as especially pernicious Malebranche's prejudice that we do not know through a clear idea what we know through consciousness.[40] Against such a prejudice, Arnauld cited Augustine's conclusion that we know "through a most certain knowledge" (*certissima scientia*) what we know "by the cry of consciousness" (*clamante conscientia*).[41] Arnauld took such a conclusion to be confirmed by our knowledge of the existence of our soul, which we know through consciousness but also with certainty. Since Malebranche cannot deny the certainty of such knowledge, according to Arnauld, even he must admit that what we know through consciousness can also be known through a clear idea.[42]

Arnauld simply equated knowing with certainty the properties of the soul with knowing these properties through a clear idea of the soul, suggesting that Malebranche himself had equated the two. However, this is a misreading of Malebranche, as demonstrated by his discussion of the Cartesian argument for the difference between soul and body. While Malebranche allowed that the conclusion of this argument that the soul differs from body is known with certainty, he also insisted that this conclusion is not known directly by means of a clear idea of the soul.

The reading of Malebranche in the *Vraies et fausses idées* is further skewed by Arnauld's acceptance of the general principle that we have a clear idea of an object if we can demonstrate that any property belongs to it.[43] This principle led Arnauld to conclude that since Malebranche claimed that we do not have a clear idea of the soul, he is committed to holding that we cannot demonstrate the spirituality of the soul. Malebranche responded by denying that he is so committed; indeed, he drew Arnauld's attention to his own demonstration of the spirituality and immateriality of the soul.

> All the modifications of which extension is capable consist only in diverse shapes, or if one wishes, in shapes and in movements. Thought, desire, pain are therefore not modifications of extension. Now I sense that I think, that I will, that I desire, that I suffer. Thus my soul, although it can exist, is not at all a

modality of my body, or of the extension of which it is composed. Thus my soul is not at all material. (OCM VI 163)

Malebranche argued toward the end of *Éclaircissement* XI that since this sort of demonstration does not rely solely on an examination of the nature of the soul as a thinking thing, it does not derive from a clear idea of the soul. For Malebranche, then, Arnauld's assertion that Cartesians can demonstrate the spirituality of the soul does not suffice to show that they have access to a clear idea of the soul. It is necessary to show further that they can demonstrate that the soul has this property simply by examining the nature of thought.

Arnauld did confront the claim in *Éclaircissement* XI that we have no clear idea of soul because we cannot establish by a simple view that the soul differs from body. He objected that Malebranche's discussion of clear ideas trades on a double standard. When Malebranche wanted to deny that we have a clear idea of the soul, he employed a stringent condition for access to such an idea, requiring that we can know all properties of the soul by simple intuition, without recourse to discursive reasoning. When he claimed that we have a clear idea of extension, however, he had to require a weaker condition for access; even he must admit, said Arnauld, that Archimedes and Pythagoras employed a clear idea of extension when they discovered by reason certain geometrical theorems. Thus Arnauld charged that Malebranche "has two weights and two measures, when, in order to have more in the way of support for the position that we do not have a clear idea of our soul, he decides to claim that one sees, through a clear idea, only what one discovers by simple view, without the need of reasoning."[44]

It is true that Malebranche suggested the sort of stringent condition for access to a clear idea of the soul that Arnauld mentioned. Toward the end of *Éclaircissement* XI, after all, he wrote that the Cartesians must have no clear idea of soul since they can see that soul differs from body only through reasoning and not through a simple view. As I noted previously, this appeal to the distinction between a simple view and reasoning is particularly inappropriate given Malebranche's use of such a distinction in his discussion of the cogito argument in Book Six of the *Recherche*. In this section he made the point that unlike our knowledge of the existence of our soul, which occurs through a *simple vûë*, our knowledge of geometry is subject to radical doubt because it is discursive and thus involves *raisonnement* (RV VI–2.6, OCM II 371/LO 481).[45] Since Malebranche himself held that geometrical knowledge derives from a clear idea of extension, he cannot take the mere fact that Cartesians can know that the soul is distinct from body only through reasoning to show that they do not have access to a clear idea of the soul.

In *Éclaircissement* XI, however, Malebranche emphasized not only that Cartesians must use reason to establish the difference between soul and body but also that they must "consult with care the idea of extension." Moreover, in the demonstration that he presented to Arnauld there is no mention of the fact that knowledge of the immateriality of the soul requires reason. What is central, rather, is that such knowledge is indirect since it depends on a determination of "the modifications of which extension is capable." Thus, while Malebranche suggested at times that knowledge rooted in a clear idea of the soul must be intuitive rather than discursive, his more considered position is that such knowledge must derive directly from an examination of the nature of soul.

Such a position allows Malebranche to escape the charge of applying a double standard. After all, he explicitly affirmed that the idea of extension is clear in the sense that it alone allows us to discover a priori truths concerning the sort of properties body can possess. The fact that we cannot derive psychological theorems in the way in which we can derive geometrical theorems from Euclidean axioms and definitions reveals that we have access to a clear idea of extension but not to a clear idea of soul. Arnauld failed to consider this more modest, though still rather substantial, condition for access to a clear idea. He therefore failed to address Malebranche's claim that it must not be the case that Cartesians know spirituality through a clear idea of soul since they cannot know that the soul is spiritual simply by examining the nature of the soul. It follows directly from such a claim that their knowledge of the nature of the soul is radically inferior to their knowledge of the nature of body.

One might object on Arnauld's behalf that even Malebranche's modest condition for access to a clear idea of the soul is too stringent. Remarks in *Éclaircissement XI* appear to indicate that in order to know the soul through a clear idea of its nature, we must know a priori that it differs from body without consulting the clear idea of body; but it seems implausible to hold that we can demonstrate that two objects differ without consulting ideas of both objects. So wasn't Arnauld on to something after all when he claimed that Malebranche stacked the deck in favor of the position that we do not have access to a clear idea of the soul?

Malebranche provided material for a response when he noted in *Éclaircissement XI* that although we never have taken a square for a circle because we have clear ideas of both shapes, the fact that we can confuse the soul with a body shows that we do not have clear idea of soul as we have a clear idea of body (OCM III 171/LO 638). In order to discern that a square is not a circle, it is of course necessary to consider properties of both shapes. Malebranche's point, however, is that we can know a priori simply by examining the nature of the square that this shape differs from a shape possessing certain essential properties of the circle (just as we can know a priori simply by examining the nature of the circle that that shape differs from a shape possessing certain essential properties of the square). So the claim that we do not know the difference between soul and body through a clear idea of the soul amounts to the claim that we do not know directly, simply by examining its nature, that the soul differs from a substance possessing the essential bodily property of extension. Malebranche concluded that it is evident that Cartesians do not have this sort of direct knowledge since they can establish that their soul differs from body only indirectly by means of an appeal to the fact that the nature of extension is such that body differs from a substance that possesses (sensory) thought.

Arnauld claimed to know of no Cartesian who ever felt the need to offer the indirect argument in *Éclaircissement* XI for the conclusion that sensible qualities are modifications of the soul.[46] However, he did not address the question of whether Cartesians must offer the indirect argument provided in this text for the conclusion that the soul differs from body. I suspect that Arnauld did not feel the need to address it because he took the mere fact that Cartesians can demonstrate the spirituality of the soul to establish that they have a clear idea of its nature. Once one takes seriously Malebranche's distinction between direct and indirect arguments for the soul's spirituality, though, such a question gains in importance. There are actually two questions here that we need to consider: whether the indirect argument for spirituality outlined in *Éclaircissement* XI in fact derives from the Cartesians and whether Cartesians are restricted to such an argument by features of their own system. It turns out that the writings of Cartesians such as Desgabets and La Forge, more than the writings of Descartes himself, provide an answer to the historical question of the source for Malebranche's argument. The answer to the conceptual question regarding the constraints imposed by the Cartesian system, on the other hand, turns on Descartes' discussion of the main argument in the *Meditations* for the real distinction between mind and body.

4.2.2 Cartesian Sources for Malebranche's Argument

Malebranche alluded at the start of *Éclaircissement* XI to disciples "prejudiced" by the authority of Descartes (OCM III 163/LO 633), but he did not indicate which particular disciples he had in mind. It is unlikely that he was thinking here of his major Cartesian critics, Arnauld and Regis; Malebranche engaged them only after the initial publication of the set of *Éclaircissements*. A possible clue as to the identity of the disciples is provided, though, by the reference later in Malebranche's text to the dispute among the Cartesians over the thesis that the soul "is painted with the colors of the rainbow when looking at it" (OCM III 166/LO 634). As I have suggested in §2.3.1 (2), this reference is to the discussion at the Commercy conferences of Desgabets' account of sensible qualities. There is thus some reason to suspect that when Malebranche claimed that Cartesians offer an indirect argument for the difference between soul and body, he had in mind either Desgabets or his Cartesian opponents.[47]

I have found no evidence from the record of the Commercy conferences that Desgabets' critics endorsed this sort of indirect argument. However, in his *Descartes à l'alambic*, which he submitted for discussion at the conferences, Desgabets himself claimed, at one point, that prior to Descartes' discovery that sensible qualities such as "color, light, sound, taste, odor" are "uniquely in us," "no one knew the difference that there is between spiritual and corporeal things."[48] Such a claim is anticipated in Desgabets' 1674 letter to Malebranche, in which he noted that "since Mr. Descartes has shown us the true nature of sensible qualities, one has proofs so natural and so clear for the distinction between the body and the soul" (OCM XVIII 86). There is to be sure no explicit reference here to the idea of extension, but in his unpublished *Supplément à la philosophie de Descartes*, Desgabets held that it was the "grand discovery of M. Descartes" that "there is nothing external to us, in the whole of the corporeal world, other than matter extended in length, breadth and width."[49] When he asserted later in this text that "the doctrine of the nature of sensible qualities is the fundamental proof of the distinction between the soul and the body," it is clear that he took the proof, as well as the underlying doctrine, to rest on the discovery that the essence of body consists in extension.[50] It is admittedly uncertain whether Malebranche saw this unpublished manuscript. Nonetheless, even in *Descartes à l'alambic*, which Malebranche most likely did see, Desgabets emphasized that apart from Descartes' discovery concerning sensible qualities, "one cannot reunite physics with mathematics."[51] It is rather easy to extract from Desgabets' writings the argument in *Éclaircissement* XI that appeals to the idea of extension in order to show that sensible qualities cannot belong to body and thus that the soul that is the subject of these qualities must differ from body.

There is ample circumstantial evidence, then, that Desgabets' writings provided one source for Malebranche's indirect Cartesian argument for the soul's spirituality. I find it difficult to believe, however, that these writings provided the primary source for the discussion of this argument in *Éclaircissement* XI. My main difficulty derives from the fact that in this text Malebranche appealed to the argument primarily in order to refute those Cartesians prejudiced by Descartes' doctrine in the *Fifth Replies* that "the nature of the mind is better known than that of any other thing" (OCM III 163/LO 633). In his discussion of the *Recherche* in the *Critique de la Critique*, however, Desgabets argued not that soul is better known than body but that soul and body are known equally well.[52] Moreover, we have seen in §1.2.3 (1) that at the 1677 Paris conference Malebranche himself defended the official Cartesian position against Desgabets' objection that "one cannot have an idea of the *I think* of Mr. Descartes, with a perfect abstraction from all properties of extension or of body" (OCM XVIII 123). It therefore seems to me incredible that Malebranche could have taken Desgabets to be one of the Cartesians under the spell of Descartes.

I do not mean to suggest that Malebranche could not have understood Desgabets' discussion of the difference between mind and body to yield a standard Cartesian argument; indeed, I think it likely that he interpreted this discussion in just such a manner. My point is that he could not have held that this argument is standard simply on the grounds that Desgabets offered it. There remains the question, then, of why Malebranche took such an argument to be standard in the first place. The answer, I think, is that he found the argument in the writings of La Forge, who compared to Desgabets, was a rather straitlaced Cartesian. In the *Traité de l'esprit de l'homme* (1666), which Malebranche himself owned,[53] La Forge broached the indirect Cartesian argument in the course of defending the thesis "that all that thinks is immaterial" against the objection that since the same object can possess very different sensible qualities, it is possible that thought and extension belong to the same subject. He noted initially that those who "have more or less of a knowledge of the true Physics, and who have renounced all Scholastic Beings, and all the qualities that one falsely attributes to the objects of our senses" realize that objects in fact possess only the "size, shape, situation, and movement of their parts" that allow them to excite (*exciter*) various sentiments or sensible qualities in us. La Forge concluded that

> whatever diversity there is between these qualities, or rather between the sentiments that are in us, we find however such a relation [*rapport*] in their causes, that is to say, in those aspects of the objects that excite them, that one is obliged to recognize that all that there is in them is only the results [*des suittes*] and the dependencies of extension and of its properties. There is thus no comparison between the manner in which these qualities are opposed one to the other and the opposition or the diversity that is found between thought and extension, which is such that one would not know how to conceive one greater.[54]

The reference here to *qualitez sensibles* and to the lack of a *rapport* between these qualities and properties deriving from the nature of extension is reminiscent of the remarks in *Éclaircissement XI*. Just as La Forge held that the recognition of the fact that everything in body is "the results and dependencies of extension" allows us to see that the thing that thinks cannot be extended, moreover, so Malebranche emphasized that Cartesians consult the idea of extension in order to see that the subject of sensible qualities differs from body. It is not difficult to believe that Malebranche discovered his indirect Cartesian argument in La Forge as well as in Desgabets. In any event, the hypothesis that he found this argument in the writings of Cartesians as different as these two thinkers helps to explain why he simply assumed that the argument itself is acceptable to any Cartesian and, in particular, to any Cartesian beholden to Descartes' doctrine that mind is better known than body.

It may seem that I have overlooked the obvious possibility that Malebranche found his indirect argument in Descartes. After all, Desgabets and La Forge cited Descartes as the main source for their own account of sensible qualities. There is indeed the argument in Descartes that since the nature of body consists in extension, it cannot be the case that sensible qualities such as light, color, and odor belong to body.[55] It is, however, rather difficult to find in his writings an appeal to this result concerning the nature of body in support of the conclusion that the subject of sensible qualities differs from body.[56] To my knowledge there is nothing in these writings as straightforward as Desgabets' claim in his letter to Malebranche that the discovery of the nature of sensible qualities provides "proofs so natural and so clear for the distinction between the soul and the body." Malebranche's remarks toward the end of *Éclaircissement XI* thus seem to be directed more against the Cartesians than against Descartes himself.

While Descartes' failure to stress an argument from the nature of sensible qualities to the difference between soul and body is perhaps surprising, it is also understandable given that he took the case of sensations deriving from the soul–body union to provide a barrier to an understanding of such a difference. Thus he wrote in the *Fourth Replies* that our sensory experience of our union with the body "does result in our not being aware of the real distinction between mind and body unless we attentively meditate on the subject" (AT VII 229/CSM II 160). He also admitted in a letter to Elisabeth that he had not previously discussed the soul's union with the body in any detail because that would have compromised his principal aim of proving soul–body distinctness (21 May 1643, AT III 664–65/CSMK 218). The claim is somewhat stronger in a follow-up letter to Elisabeth, in which Descartes wrote that

> it does not seem that the human mind is capable of conceiving well, and at the same time, the distinction between the soul and the body and their union; because it is necessary for that to conceive them as a single thing, and at the same time to conceive them as two, which is contrary to itself [*se contrarie*]. (28 June 1643, AT III 693/CSMK 227)

I have indicated that the suggestion in the correspondence with Elisabeth that sensations pertain to the nature of the soul–body union rather than to the nature of the soul itself does not represent Descartes' most dominant position (see §2.3.2 [2]). Nonetheless, Descartes tended not to focus on sensations and sensible qualities when he considered the issue of the difference between soul and body. At least this is so, as we will discover, in the case of his argument in the *Sixth Meditation* for the conclusion that his mind is "really distinct from body, and can exist without it" (AT VII 78/CSM II 54).

For this reason alone, the discussion toward the end of *Éclaircissement XI* of the Cartesian argument for spirituality cannot apply as directly to this *Sixth Meditation* argument as it does to the writings of Desgabets and La Forge. Nevertheless, Malebranche's discussion does suggest two points against Descartes that warrant closer examination: First, that Descartes must concede that he cannot discern spirituality in the nature of the soul alone, and second, that it simply follows from this concession that his knowledge of the nature of body is superior in kind to his knowledge of the nature of the soul. Since Arnauld did not undertake to respond to these points on Descartes' behalf, we must ourselves attempt to address them by turning to the account in the *Meditations* of the real distinction between mind and body.

4.3 Descartes and the Real Distinction Argument

4.3.1 The Sufficiency Thesis and Materialism

(1) The Sufficiency Thesis. Descartes interrupted work on his responses to critics of the *Meditations* to write to his editor and friend, Marin Mersenne, that "after having come to know the nature of our soul by the steps I used, and having thus recognized that it is a spiritual substance—because I see that all the attributes that belong to spiritual substance belong to it—one does not have to be a great philosopher to conclude as I did that it is not corporeal" (22 July 1641, AT III 396/CSMK 186–87). I suggested at the outset of this chapter that

we can take Malebranche's claim that the soul is spiritual to indicate that it is a substance that differs in nature from body. It will become clear that Descartes understood the soul to be a spiritual substance in the subtly different sense that it is a substance that can exist apart from body. Nonetheless, Descartes could agree with the position, which I have offered on Malebranche's behalf, that the spirituality of the soul differs from, though is related to, its distinction from body. In particular, Descartes could say that in order to establish that the soul is distinct from body, and thus incorporeal, one must show not only that the soul is a substance that can exist apart from body but also that body is a substance that can exist apart from the soul. We will see that the latter conclusion is relatively uncontroversial; this fact serves to explain Descartes' comment to Mersenne that one does not have to be a great philosopher to see that a spiritual substance is also incorporeal.

I have made the point that the difference between the property of being spiritual and the property of being distinct from body was of little importance to Malebranche since he held that knowledge of the soul's spirituality depends on knowledge that the body is a substance distinct from the subject of sensory thought. Descartes suggested that knowledge of spirituality does not depend on a consideration of bodily substance, however, when he told Mersenne that he can come to such knowledge by "the steps I used" to know the nature of the soul. The steps to which he referred clearly are those he used in the *Second Meditation* to arrive at the conclusion that he clearly and distinctly perceives himself to be "precisely only a thinking thing" (*præcise tantum res cogitans*) (AT VII 27/CSM II 18). I will argue that Descartes' official doctrine in the *Meditations*, which sits well with his remarks to Mersenne, is that such a conclusion provides all that is needed for the clear and distinct perception that his mind can exist apart from body and, in particular, from the bodily attribute of extension.[57] I call this doctrine the "Sufficiency Thesis" since, according to it, the understanding of the nature of his mind provided in the *Second Meditation* so suffices for such a clear and distinct perception.

Another way of expressing the Sufficiency Thesis that is more in line with Descartes' own remarks is to say that the understanding of the nature of mind suffices for the distinct perception that this nature "excludes" extension. Descartes explained to Arnauld that the *Second Meditation* establishes that mind excludes body in the sense that "mind can be understood as a subsisting thing even though absolutely nothing bodily be attributed to it" (*Fourth Rep.*, AT VII 226/CSM II 159). To say that the nature of mind excludes body, then, is to say that one need not attribute any bodily property, especially extension, to the mind in order to have a distinct perception of it as a subsisting thing, that is to say, a substance. Descartes restated this position when he wrote in a 1644 letter to Denis Mesland that he distinctly understands his mind to exclude body since the idea of this mind "represents it to me as a substance which can exist even though everything bodily be excluded from it" (2 May 1644, AT IV 120/CSMK 236). According to this passage, the distinct perception that the nature of a particular mind excludes body is simply the distinct perception that that mind can exist as a substance even though it lacks bodily properties such as extension.[58]

Descartes did not say explicitly that an examination of a clear and distinct idea of mind suffices for the distinct perception that this nature excludes body, and one might object that he would, in fact, have demurred to such a thesis. In a passage from the *Second Replies* that Arnauld cited against Malebranche, after all, Descartes had claimed that we cannot clearly understand one thing to be distinct from another "unless the idea of each thing is clear and distinct" (AT VII 133/CSM II 95). It appears to follow from this claim that we must examine the clear and distinct idea of the nature of body, as well as the clear and distinct idea of the nature of mind, in order to distinctly perceive that the nature of mind excludes body.

Notice, however, that the *Second Replies* passage concerns the understanding of the *reciprocal* exclusion of the natures of mind and body. For Descartes' view of what is required for the unidirectional exclusion of body from the nature of mind, we need to consider the main argument in the *Sixth Meditation* for the real distinction between mind and body (which I call the Real Distinction Argument). He drew on the result in the *Second Meditation* that "absolutely nothing else belongs to my nature or essence except that I am a thinking thing" and concluded that "on the one hand I have a clear and distinct idea of myself, insofar as I am only a thinking thing, not extended, and on the other hand a distinct idea of body, insofar as it is an extended thing, not thinking, it is certain that I am really distinct from my body, and can exist without it" (AT VII 78/CSM II 54). The wording of this argument clearly suggests that Descartes' premise that he has a clear and distinct idea of his mind as a thinking, unextended thing can be established independently of his premise that he has a clear and distinct idea of his body as an extended, nonthinking thing. The Real Distinction Argument thus implies that in order to establish that the nature of mind excludes extension, one need not recognize the implication that the nature of body excludes thought.

Some support for this reading of Descartes' argument is provided by his remark in a 1642 letter to Guillaume Gibieuf that

> the idea I have of an extended and shaped substance is complete because I can conceive it all by itself, and deny of it everything else of which I have ideas. Now it is, it seems to me, quite clear that the idea I have of a substance that thinks is complete in this way, and that I have no other idea that precedes it in my mind, and that it is so joined to it that I cannot conceive them well while denying one of the other; for if there were such an idea in me I would necessarily know it. (19 Jan. 1642, AT III 475–76/CSMK 202)

We can determine from this that a substance that thinks is complete on its own, even though extension be denied it, simply by considering the idea of such a substance. Of course, we must give some attention to the idea of extension in order to determine that the idea of thinking substance does not require it in order to be complete, but the important point is that to establish this conclusion regarding the idea of the soul, we need not recognize that the idea of extension is complete in the sense that it can be conceived by itself. So the claim that the idea of mind suffices to show that the nature of mind excludes extension indicates not that no examination of the nature of extension is required to establish such a conclusion but merely that no examination of the fact that the idea of extension is complete on its own is so required.

It is clear from the context of the Real Distinction Argument that when Descartes spoke of his nature as a thinking thing, he focused primarily on intellectual thought. Thus subsequent to his presentation of this argument in the *Sixth Meditation*, he made the point that "I can clearly and distinctly understand myself as a whole" without "faculties for certain special modes of thinking, namely the faculties of imagining and sensing" (AT VII 78/CSM II 54). Since he took the argument itself to concern only what belongs to his nature, or to himself "understood as a whole," his remarks are restricted to the purely intellectual faculties of mind. Such a restriction thus serves to set the Real Distinction Argument apart from Malebranche's Cartesian argument in *Éclaircissement XI*, which emphasizes sensible qualities or sensations. As Margaret Wilson has observed, moreover, Descartes' emphasis on intellectual thought is not a feature of the Cartesian dualism cited in contemporary discussions; indeed, such discussions tend to take sensation to provide the best case for such dualism.[59] With respect to the focus on sensation, these discussions are farther removed from the Real Distinction Argument, which they often cite, than they are from remarks in *Éclaircissement XI*, which they invariably overlook.

It is true that Malebranche's Cartesian argument need not be restricted to sensory states. Indeed, Malebranche expressed this argument in a manner that does not so restrict it when he had Theodore claim at the start of the *Entretiens* that bodily properties "consist only in relations of distance; and it is evident that relations are not perceptions, reasonings, pleasures, desires; in a word, thoughts" (EM I, OCM XII 32–33/D 25). Even so, Malebranche's procedure differs fundamentally from Descartes'. Malebranche argued in effect that bodily states cannot possess the phenomenal features that are most evident in the case of sensation but are present in all thought. By contrast, what underlies Descartes' official argument for mind–body distinctness is not the view that mental states have such features but the position that the faculty of pure intellect does not depend on the body in the way in which sensory faculties do. Thus, while Malebranche's argument attempts to show only that the soul differs in nature from body and not that the soul can exist apart from body, Descartes' argument draws this stronger conclusion about separate existence.

For my purposes, however, there is a more important difference between Malebranche and Descartes that is linked to the fact that the Real Distinction Argument assumes the Sufficiency Thesis. In light of this fact, Descartes' argument provides a counterexample to Malebranche's claim in *Éclaircissement XI* that the Cartesians themselves rely on the premise that extension is "the principle of all that we clearly conceive in bodies" to establish that the soul is not simply a body. Descartes' argument, in fact, requires that reflection on the nature of mind can yield a clear and distinct idea of a thinking, unextended thing. This implies that such reflection can serve to reveal some difference from body, at least insofar as body is essentially extended. Thus, the Real Distinction Argument conflicts with the view in Malebranche that no Cartesian ever attempted to establish any difference between soul and body merely by means of a consideration of the nature of the soul. This conflict is especially ironic given the fact that in the first edition of the *Recherche* Malebranche endorsed the account of the distinction between soul and body in the *Sixth Meditation* (RV I.10, OCM I 123/LO 49). He failed to realize, or if he did realize he failed to mention, that this account is not wholly consonant with the tone of those remarks from his mature works that reflect the skeptical turn in his thought.

(2) The Concession to Materialism. While Malebranche's indirect Cartesian argument differs importantly from the featured argument for mind–body distinctness in the *Meditations*, however, it has some claim to Descartes' attention. The fact that it has such a claim is revealed, ironically again, by Arnauld's own critical remarks in the *Fourth Objections*. As we have seen, Arnauld urged against Descartes that the result that one can conceive of a right triangle without knowing that the Pythagorean property belongs to it reveals that one can conceive mind apart from body even though the nature of mind includes body in some nonevident manner. Of course, Descartes responded, to Arnauld's complete satisfaction, that the triangle example is not similar since mind can be distinctly conceived as a complete thing apart from body, but one could further defend the applicability of Arnauld's example by noting that Descartes' claim that mind can be so conceived is just what is in question. Those who contend, with Hobbes, that mind is merely a species of body will not concede that mind can be conceived in this way. For them any conception of mind that does not include extension will, due to this very lack of inclusion, be as incomplete as the conception of a right triangle apart from its Pythagorean property. Descartes told Arnauld that mind can be conceived to be a complete thing apart from body "because it is in reality distinct" (AT VII 229/CSM II 161). A reasonable Hobbesian retort would be that mind cannot be so conceived because it is not in reality distinct from body. To answer this sort of retort, Descartes cannot simply assert that the idea of his nature in the *Second Meditation* presents his mind as a complete thing that can exist without body or extension.[60] This returns us to the Malebranchean position that an examination of the nature of the soul cannot reveal directly that this nature excludes extension.

Descartes at one point did address the radical Hobbesian view that thoughts are reducible to motion, and so are themselves modifications of extension.[61] Such a view was offered up in a rather garbled form by the authors of the *Sixth Objections* when they protested that Descartes cannot claim that he thinks since he has not demonstrated that "no corporeal motion can be what you call thought" (AT VII 413/CSM II 278). While Descartes simply ignored the eliminativist view here that he does not think, he paused over the different reductionist suggestion that his thought is simply a kind of motion. He noted that since there is a kind of "affinity or connection" between shape and motion, in virtue of the fact that both presuppose extension, we can conceive a thing that has shape and motion to be one "in virtue of a unity of nature," that is, in virtue of being a single substance. Because there is no such affinity between thought and motion, on the other hand, we can conceive a thing that has thought and motion to be one "only in respect of unity of composition," that is, in respect of being composed of two distinct substances (*Sixth Rep.*, AT VII 422–25/CSM II 285–87). Malebranche would be hard pressed to deny the lack of affinity between thoughts and modifications of extension. Indeed, his indirect Cartesian argument assumes it is evident that the modes of which extended substance are capable "have no relation to" sensory thoughts. Malebranche therefore followed Descartes in rejecting out of hand the Hobbesian identification of thought with motion.

Arnauld took Malebranche's rejection of this Hobbesian identification to presuppose a clear knowledge of the nature of thought,[62] but on Malebranche's view, it cannot be the case that we possess such knowledge given that consciousness or inner sentiment is incapable of refuting the more sophisticated materialist position that the subject of thought is extended. Gassendi drew on such a position when he protested to Descartes that the power of thought may depend in some unknown manner on the organization of the body. The fact that thought cannot be straightforwardly identified with extension does not seem to rule out the possibility that the same body that has the property of extension also has the power of thought. Malebranche allowed that inner sentiment precludes the straightforward identification, but he came to hold that it cannot itself rule out the more subtle materialist possibility.

Descartes cannot simply dismiss Malebranche's position that mere consciousness is incapable of ruling out this possibility. We have seen, after all, that he conceded in the *Second Meditation* that the fact that he knows that he thinks without knowing that any body exists does not show that he is not a body. This concession is strengthened by Descartes' introduction later in the *Meditations* of the "supposition" that he has no persuasive reason to believe that his nature as a thinking thing is distinct from the nature of a corporeal thing (*Fourth Med.*, AT VII 59/CSM II 41). Descartes therefore suggested that the result in the *Second Meditation* that he is conscious of himself as a thinking thing cannot provide the sort of reason needed here. He did allow, in the earlier meditation, that his notion of himself as a thinking thing "does not depend on" his notion of body, yet if it were, in fact, the case that his mind is identical to a certain body, then a notion of his mind that does not depend on body could not reveal that mind can be a complete thing apart from body.

It may be significant, however, that the materialist challenge in the *Second Meditation* is restricted to the claim that certain bodily elements "in truth of fact" (*in rei veritate*) do not differ from mind (AT VII 27/CSM II 18). In the Preface to the *Meditations*, Descartes cited the objection that the point in the *Discourse* (1637) that the human mind does not perceive itself to be something other than a thinking thing does not entail the conclusion that "its nature or essence consists only in that, that it is a thinking thing, where the word *only* [*tantum*] excludes everything else that also could be said to belong to the nature of the soul."[63] Descartes attempted to dodge this objection by noting that in the earlier work he did not intend to indicate "exclusion in the order corresponding to the very truth of things (with which I certainly was not concerned at that time) but merely in the order corresponding to my perception" (AT VII 8/CSM II 7). While it is difficult to read this distinction back into *Discourse*, it seems fair enough for Descartes to insist that it be read forward into the *Second Meditation*. The materialist challenge in this latter text could be interpreted as being restricted to the claim that mind excludes body "in the order corresponding to the very truth of things" and thus as allowing for the conclusion that mind excludes body "in the order corresponding to perception."

That Descartes did interpret the challenge in this manner is further confirmed by his claim to Arnauld that he could have concluded in the *Second Meditation* that his mind can subsist without bodily attributes except for his "hyperbolical doubt" of the claim that "things are such as we perceive them." Descartes went on to say that it is because of such doubt that "everything that I wrote about God and truth in the third, fourth and fifth Meditations contributes to the conclusion of the real distinction between mind and body, which I finally perfected in the sixth Meditation" (*Fourth Rep.*, AT VII 226/CSM II 159). On this view, the materialist can raise only the hyperbolic objection that the clear and distinct perception in the *Second Meditation* that the nature of mind excludes body does not correspond to the order corresponding to reality.

There is one important text, however, in which Descartes himself allowed for a further materialist objection. In the *Disquisitio Metaphysica* (1644) Gassendi had protested that the term *only* (*tantum*) in the claim in the *Second Meditation* that mind is "precisely only a thinking thing" implies an exclusion from mind of anything bodily.[64] It is interesting that in his response to Gassendi in a 1646 letter to Clerselier, later included in the 1647 French edition of the *Meditations*, Descartes did not repeat his distinction between exclusion in truth and exclusion in perception. Rather, he emphasized that *only* does not indicate "an entire exclusion or negation, but only an abstraction from material things; for I said that, notwithstanding this, one is not sure that there is nothing in the soul that is corporeal, even though one does not recognize there anything [corporeal]" (AT IX-1 215/CSM II 276). He had explained this distinction between exclusion and abstraction in the 1644 letter to Mesland mentioned previously, in which he wrote that an idea of his soul that "does not represent it to me as dependent on a body and identified with it" is "merely an abstraction" that does not provide a sound argument for the distinction between soul and body, whereas an idea which "represents it to me as a substance that can exist even though everything bodily be excluded from it" does establish this distinction (AT IV 120/CSMK 236). Given this position, it follows from Descartes claim to Clerselier that his account of his mind in the *Second Meditation* merely abstracts from body that such an account does not itself yield the distinct perception that this mind is a substance "that can exist even though everything bodily be excluded from it."

One way to deny that Descartes was committed to such a consequence is to hold that his distinction between abstraction and exclusion comes to the same as his distinction between exclusion in the order corresponding to perception and exclusion in the order corresponding to truth. On this interpretation, the claim to Mesland that an abstracted idea of his soul provides no sound argument for the distinction between this soul and body allows that such an idea establishes the exclusion of body from the soul *in perception*, precluding only that it establishes the exclusion of body from the soul *in reality*. While such an interpretation perhaps allows Descartes to avoid a difficult problem, it cannot stand up to the texts. In the letter to Mesland, Descartes discussed the distinction between abstraction and exclusion in terms of what the idea of his soul represents to him, thus indicating that this sort of distinction pertains merely to the order corresponding to perception. He was even more explicit on this point in his earlier letter to Gibieuf, where he emphasized that he can determine the difference between abstraction and exclusion simply by means of a consideration of his own thought (AT III 474/CSMK 201). So Descartes' final response to Gassendi ultimately does undermine the position that the account of his mind in the *Second Meditation* suffices for the distinct perception that the nature of this mind excludes extension; that is to say, it undermines the Sufficiency Thesis.

Descartes was himself untroubled by his concession to the materialist in the *Second Meditation* because he took his Real Distinction Argument to establish that his mind is distinct from his body.[65] But since the premise of this argument concerning the nature of his mind relies on the Sufficiency Thesis, the concession that undermines this thesis undermines such a premise as well. This concession, when interpreted in light of the remarks to Clerselier, commits Descartes to the view that his knowledge that the nature of his mind consists in thought cannot suffice for the distinct perception that extension is excluded, even merely in perception, by this nature. Such a concession thus forces him to admit that this knowledge cannot itself establish that his mind is not an extended thing. Given Malebranche's position that one who knows an object through a clear idea of its nature must be able to know, merely by considering this nature, the properties the object can and cannot possess, this admission itself entails that Descartes does not know his mind through a clear idea of its nature.

4.3.2 The Idea of Body and the Unextended Mind

Let us assume that Descartes' concession to the materialist in the *Second Meditation* commits him to the rejection of the Sufficiency Thesis and so to the rejection of the claim in the Real Distinction Argument that the idea of his mind suffices for the distinct perception of himself as a thinking, unextended substance. The second point that Malebranche suggested is that it follows from such a rejection that the nature of mind is not intellectually clear to Descartes in the way in which the nature of body is. Relevant to such a point is Descartes' own claim in the Real Distinction Argument that his idea of body suffices for the distinct perception that the nature of body excludes thought. The position here is that some body can be conceived to exist as a substance that has extension but not thought. I have urged that Descartes failed to respond adequately to the materialist objection that no mind can be conceived to exist with thought but without extension, yet the claim that some body can be conceived to exist without thought is less controversial[66] since even the materialist would concede that a stone, for example, can be conceived to exist even while lacking this property.[67]

Descartes asserted at times, however, that a consideration of the nature of extension reveals not only that some body could lack thought, but also that no body can think. He told Arnauld in the *Fourth Replies*, for instance, that "when I examine the nature of body, I find nothing in it which is redolent of thought" (AT VII 227/CSM II 160). This remark assumes the view in the *Fifth Meditation* that properties of material objects are "thoroughly known and perspicuous" (*plane nota et perspecta sunt*) when considered simply in terms of extension. Descartes held there that such properties can be understood entirely in terms of the parts of extension, and in particular of the "sizes, shapes, positions, and local motions" of those parts (AT VII 63/CSM II 44). Moreover, this text suggests that it is evident which properties are subject to this sort of understanding. I take the claim to Arnauld to indicate that an examination of this nature allows one to determine a priori that thought cannot be understood in this way. On the view in this text, the nature of extension is so transparent that one can discern, simply by means of a consideration of it, that thought cannot be a mode of body. The claim to Arnauld thus resembles Malebranche's position in *Éclaircissement XI* that it is obvious from an examination of the nature of extension that "extension precisely as such cannot think" (OCM III 165/LO 634).[68]

Descartes appealed to the transparency of the nature of body in a previously examined passage from the *Sixth Replies* that also is relevant to the remarks in Malebranche's text. In this passage Descartes wrote that

> I observed that nothing pertained to the concept [*rationem*] of body except only that it is a thing with length, breadth and depth, admitting of various shapes and various motions; . . . that colors, odors, tastes, and the like are only sensations [*sensus*] existing in my thought, and differing no less from body, than pain differs from the shape and motion of the weapon inflicting the pain. (AT VII 440/CSM II 297)

The position that the concept of body as an extended thing reveals the sort of qualities bodies can possess recalls the doctrine, invoked in Malebranche's indirect Cartesian argument, that extension is "the principle of all that we conceive clearly in bodies" (OCM III 171/LO 638). To be sure, the passage from the *Sixth Replies* focuses more on the fact that bodies cannot possess qualities that resemble sensations than on the fact that bodies cannot possess the sensations themselves. Given the Cartesian identification of these qualities with the relevant sensations, though, it seems a short step from the claim that bodies cannot possess the qualities to the conclusion of Malebranche's argument that bodies cannot possess the sensations or anything else that includes consciousness or thought. I take Descartes' observations to provide the material for an argument for the conclusion that body cannot think that relies primarily on an appeal to the nature of extension.

Descartes admittedly indicated at one point that the Real Distinction Argument yields a very different way of deriving this conclusion. He wrote in the *Second Replies* that one could say, on the basis of this argument, that "all that can think is a mind, or is called a mind; but since mind and body are distinguished in reality, no body is a mind; therefore no body can think" (AT VII 132/ CSM II 95). On Malebranche's indirect Cartesian argument, the claim that body cannot think is established prior to the claim that mind and body are distinct substances. On the argument suggested by Descartes, however, the claim that body cannot think depends on the claim that mind and body are distinct substances. According to the Real Distinction Argument, moreover, the latter claim derives in part from the Sufficiency Thesis.

As our previous discussion indicates, one problem with the argument outlined in the *Second Replies* is that it requires a thesis that is in some tension with the concession to the materialist in the *Second Meditation*. However, Malebranche emphasized that this sort of argument is unnecessary in the first place. He asserted in *Éclaircissement XI* that with respect to the question of what does and does not pertain to body, "one can answer easily, promptly, boldly by the mere consideration of the idea representing it" (OCM III 165/LO 634). Arnauld properly noted the implausibility of the suggestion here that every geometrical feature of body can be known without the aid of discursive argument. As the context of this passage indicates, though, Malebranche's main concern was to argue that the mere fact that all bodily properties derive from the nature of extension reveals that no body can think. He held, in line with the account of body in the *Fifth Meditation*, that such properties transparently presuppose extension, and he believed, in line with Descartes' remarks to Arnauld, that thought contains something that does not presuppose extension in this way. Malebranche concluded, as Descartes did not, that we do not need to know clearly the feature of thought that fails to presuppose extension in order to establish that body cannot think, since our clear knowledge of the way in which modes of body presuppose extension suffices to establish this conclusion.

At times Descartes offered an argument for the difference between mind and body that seems to be similar to the argument that Malebranche endorsed in *Éclaircissement XI*. Descartes responded to Hobbes' claim that body is the subject of thought, for instance, by noting that all "corporeal acts" (e.g., size, shape, and motion) must be conceived in terms of extension while all "acts of thought" (e.g., understanding, willing, imagining, and sensing) must be conceived in terms of "thought, or perception, or consciousness [*conscientiæ*]." He concluded that acts of thought "have no affinity to corporeal acts, and thought, which is the common concept [*ratio communis*] under which they fall, differs in kind from extension, which is the common concept of the others" (*Third Obj. and Rep.*, AT VII 176/CSM II 124). Whereas the Real Distinction Argument takes the conception of mind as the subject of intellectual thought to reveal that mind can lack extension, the argument in the response to Hobbes emphasizes rather Malebranche's point that body cannot be the subject of thought given that all modes that involve consciousness differ in kind from modes of extension.

Yet there is no hint in Descartes' response to Hobbes of Malebranche's conclusion in *Éclaircissement XI* that knowledge of body is better off than knowledge of the soul. Indeed, Descartes indicated in his response that there is a certain symmetry that holds between the two kinds of knowledge. He held that a comparison between thought and extension reveals that body cannot be the subject of acts of thought, but he also noted that such a comparison reveals as well that mind cannot be the subject of corporeal acts.[69]

Malebranche himself argued that a comparison between the modes of thought and extension is needed to see that the soul is spiritual because this property cannot be discerned in the nature of the soul. However, at one point in *Éclaircissement XI* he ridiculed the position that such a comparison is needed to determine which properties pertain to body. He asked whether since the Cartesian philosopher can see clearly "in the very idea of extension that roundness is a modification of it," it would not be "extravagant" for this philosopher to argue for the conclusion that roundness is such a mode in the following manner: "There are two kinds of beings, minds and bodies. Roundness is not a manner of being of mind. Thus it is a mode of body" (OCM III 165/LO 634). Malebranche's point, I take it, is that the argument is extravagant because its second premise is plausible only in light of the fact that roundness is a mode of extension. Since this fact establishes immediately that roundness is a mode of bodily substance, given the Cartesian notion of this substance, the appeal to the fact that this shape is not a mode of a being that differs from body is simply idle.

It is difficult for Descartes to resist the claim that such an appeal is idle, given his position in the *Sixth Meditation*, deriving from the account of body in the *Fifth Meditation*, that one can know that bodies possess those properties which "regarded generally, are comprehended in the object of pure mathematics" (AT VII 80/CSM II 55). The view here that an examination of extension allows one to determine directly which properties pertain to body recalls Malebranche's claim that body is known through a clear idea of extension. But the result of our discussion in the previous section was that the concession to the materialist in the *Second Meditation* implies that the mind is not known through a clear idea of its nature. This result, together with Descartes' account of our knowledge of bodily properties, yields Malebranche's conclusion that knowledge of the nature of body is superior in kind to knowledge of the nature of the soul.

In light of this conclusion, it seems that the best way for Descartes to demonstrate that the mind is not a body is to appeal to the nature of body as an extended thing. Some of his remarks concerning his concession to the materialist entail that mere reflection on the nature of mind cannot provide what is needed to refute the view that the notion of an unextended thinking thing is an instance of abstraction rather than exclusion. However, these remarks leave open the possibility that reflection on the fact that the nature of body consists in extension could show that this notion is in fact an instance of exclusion. By claiming that thought cannot be a mode of body, on the grounds that it has features that can in no way be "comprehended in the object of pure mathematics," Descartes could hold, even in the face of his concession, that the nature of mind as a thinking thing excludes extension.

I previously addressed the objection that Descartes cannot accept the thesis that an examination of the clear and distinct idea of mind suffices to establish that the nature of mind excludes extension, since it is necessary to examine a clear and distinct idea of extension in order to establish this exclusion. I understood his procedure in the Real Distinction Argument to reveal that he in effect rejected the necessity of such an examination. At this point one might raise the related objection that Descartes cannot accept the Malebranchean proposal that an examination of a clear idea of extension suffices to establish that the nature of body excludes thought, since he held that it is necessary to examine a clear and distinct idea of thought in order to establish that exclusion. For how, on Descartes' own view, could one demonstrate that body cannot think if one did not have a distinct understanding of what thought is?

The response is that Descartes himself provided an analogue of the Malebranchean proposal. In the remarks from the *Sixth Replies* previously cited, he argued that the fact that the nature of body consists in extension reveals that sensible qualities such as colors, tastes and odors do not belong to body. But he also wrote, in a passage from the *Third Meditation* considered in §2.3.1 (1), that these same qualities "are known by me only in a very confused and obscure way, so that I also do not know whether they are true or false, that is, whether the ideas that I have of them are ideas of real things, or not of things" (AT VII 43/ CSM II 30). While this passage is not entirely straightforward, one point it seems to make is that we cannot know, simply by examining the nature of these qualities, whether or not they are real qualities of bodies. Even though Descartes indicated that the ideas of these qualities are confused and obscure in this sense, however, he held in the *Sixth Replies*, in line with the doctrine of the *Meditations*, that the clear and distinct idea of extension reveals that the qualities themselves cannot belong to body. Malebranche could argue, along similar lines, that even though we do not have a clear idea of the nature of thought—as shown by the fact that we cannot determine merely by examining this nature whether or not it excludes extension—we can know by examining the clear idea of extension that body cannot think, from which it simply follows that the nature of the soul excludes extension. Given his remarks on sensible qualities, Descartes could not reject Malebranche's indirect argument for exclusion merely on the grounds that any demonstration of the claim that a certain property cannot belong to body must appeal to a clear and distinct idea of that property. Moreover, Descartes' concession to the materialist reveals that this indirect argument is superior, for reasons internal to his own system, to the argument that he actually did offer in the *Sixth Meditation*.

This result suggests a new understanding of Descartes' contribution to the modern account of mind. Descartes himself held that his most distinctive contribution was his derivation of the difference between soul and body from the result that the soul is a thinking thing. Thus, when a correspondent noted that Augustine had anticipated the famous argument, "I think therefore I am" (*Je pense, donc je suis*), Descartes pointed out that he went beyond Augustine in using such an argument to establish that "this *I*, which thinks, is *an immaterial substance*, and that it has nothing corporeal" (*To Colvius*, 14 Nov. 1640, AT III 247/CSMK 159). Malebranche offered a refreshingly different view, however, when he noted in the preface to the *Recherche* that even though Augustine explained the soul better than his predecessors, still "the difference between mind and body has been known with sufficient clarity for only a few years," and in particular only after Descartes' discovery that sensible qualities are not clearly contained in the idea of matter (OCM I 20/LO xxv–xxvi). From Malebranche's perspective what gave rise to Cartesian dualism was the discovery that the nature of matter consists in extension.

To be sure, the identification of matter with extension was not universally received among the Cartesians; La Ville noted that "Father Maignan, M. de Cordemoy and a few others" took exception to it.[70] The fact that Cordemoy took exception does not help strengthen Malebranche's claim in the *Recherche* that his account of the distinction between soul and body is anticipated in Cordemoy's *Discernement* as well as in Descartes' *Meditations* (RV I.10, OCM I 123/LO 49). The identification of matter with extension, however, is arguably more central to Cartesian dualism than the doctrine that the nature of the soul consists in thought. Even radical Cartesians such as Desgabets and Regis, who rejected Descartes' claim that the *I* is only a thinking thing (see §2.3.2 [3]), nonetheless emphasized that the soul cannot be material given that body is simply extension.[71] Moreover, it is telling that in the eighteenth century materialists were concerned to replace the old concept of inert extension with a new concept of essentially active matter.[72] This development provides further reason to conclude that it was the conception of body in purely geometrical terms, more than the conception of the soul in terms of thought, that underwrote the Cartesian conclusion that the soul is an immaterial substance.

This history of Cartesian dualism thus serves to highlight what Gueroult has called the "paradox" of Malebranche's psychology; namely, the paradox that matter understood as extension is "conceived at the same time as heterogeneous from mind and as the unique instrument of its distinct knowledge."[73] Malebranche in effect took the Cartesian proof of spirituality to reveal that this paradox, far from being idiosyncratic to his system, is a deep feature of Cartesian psychology. For him the fact that Cartesians must use the idea of extension as the unique instrument for distinct knowledge of the soul's spirituality confirms that their consciousness fails to yield a clear objective view of the properties of the soul.

Malebranche thus would have to take issue with Kant's famous remark, in the section on the "Paralogisms of Pure Reason" in his *Critique of Pure Reason*, that the 'I think' is "the sole text of rational psychology, and from it the whole of its teaching is to be developed."[74] Kant reasoned that since such a psychology is rational, it must abstract from all empirical elements of thought and thus must be left with a bare *I*, the unconditioned subject of thought. Malebranche would say that in the particular case of the demonstration of the spirituality of the soul, Cartesians cannot appeal to the "I think" alone. Since their consciousness of the soul is confused, according to him, they must in fact appeal to the clear idea of body as extension in order to establish that the soul is a spiritual substance. Insofar as Kant's critique of rational psychology rests on the charge that a consideration of the bare *I* cannot yield determinate conclusions regarding the nature of the soul, it to a great extent does not apply to Cartesian rational psychology, and more specifically to the Cartesian demonstration of spirituality, as Malebranche understood it.

This is not to say that such a demonstration is itself fundamentally sound. Indeed, one main weakness of Cartesian dualism seems to be something that Malebranche took to be its real strength, namely, its dependence on a conception of matter in terms of extension alone. It was arguably the inadequacy of the account of the natural world bound to such a conception, more than anything else, that brought about the downfall of Cartesianism. Yet it is not at all evident that we now possess an alternative conception of matter that yields a transparent explanation of consciousness. While the positive aspects of Malebranche's dualism are perhaps outmoded, his negative claim that we lack a clear understanding of the subjective aspects of our mental life still has some force.

In the passage from the *Recherche* cited at the outset of this chapter, Malebranche mentioned freedom and immortality, along with spirituality, as attributes of the soul that consciousness or inner sentiment "suffices to demonstrate" (RV III–2.7, OCM I 453/LO 239). One commentator has claimed that while Malebranche's indirect proof of the soul's immateriality is novel, his treatment of freedom and immortality is "perfunctory" with much of it being "borrowed without noteworthy modification from Descartes."[75] In chapter 6 I argue that while this claim is plausible in the case of Malebranche's proof of freedom, it certainly cannot hold for his account of the nature of freedom and of the will. The argument that Malebranche's treatment of immortality is merely derivative is somewhat stronger since such a treatment borrows heavily from Descartes. As I indicate in the next chapter, though, even here Malebranche differed from Descartes not only in attempting to offer a fully demonstrative proof of immortality, but also in emphasizing the importance to such a proof of a consideration of the nature of body. These features of Malebranche's discussion, I believe, involve modifications in Descartes' position that are noteworthy in light of the development of the Cartesian argument for immortality in the work of Desgabets.

five

IMMORTALITY

In the *Recherche* Malebranche praised Descartes as one "who has demonstrated in a very simple and very evident manner ... the immortality of the soul" (RV IV.6, OCM II 57/LO 294). While Malebranche's proof of the soul's immortality deviates from Descartes' more than this remark may suggest, it is nonetheless true that Descartes' writings provided the main source for Malebranche's discussion of immortality. Any account of this discussion, therefore, must begin with Descartes.

There are, however, reasons to question the accuracy of Malebranche's claim that Descartes has offered a simple and evident demonstration of the immortality of the soul. An initial complication is that Descartes himself concluded that reason cannot establish that the soul is in fact immortal, on the grounds that God can annihilate any created substance by means of his "absolute power." He did attempt in the *Synopsis* to the *Meditations* to sketch an argument for the conclusion that the soul cannot be annihilated "by natural means," yet this argument is neither simple nor evident since it depends on complex and somewhat problematic claims regarding mental indivisibility and substantial indestructibility.

Malebranche attempted to modify and strengthen the account of immortality in Descartes. He inherited from Descartes the basic position that humans are distinguished from other animals in virtue of the fact that they have an immortal soul. Moreover, he retained Descartes' emphasis on the indivisibility of the human soul and the indestructibility of substance. However, he went beyond Descartes in two important ways. First, Malebranche emphasized that we need the idea of body to establish that our soul is an indivisible substance and, second, he held that we can demonstrate by reason that the soul is in fact immortal once we recognize the nature of the divine attributes. As is to be expected given the general thrust of his critique of the Cartesian theory of mind, Malebranche attempted to shore up Descartes' argument in both cases by invoking something other than a clear idea of the soul.

What is perhaps unexpected is that Malebranche's thesis that Cartesians know body more clearly than they know their own soul is not itself clearly reflected in his remarks on substantial indestructibility. Interestingly enough, the case of body is quite prominent in the account of the indestructibility or indefectibility of substance in the work of Malebranche's critic, Desgabets. Desgabets urged that this indefectibility is most evident for Descartes in the case of matter since the latter held that the annihilation of matter is impossible even though still, in some sense, within the scope of God's absolute power. I believe that a consideration of this unorthodox but still rather insightful interpretation of Descartes helps us to follow out Malebranche's critique of Descartes' doctrine that mind is better known than body.

5.1 Descartes' Proof of Immortality

5.1.1 The Possibility of a Proof

In 1630 Descartes announced to Mersenne his intention to complete a "little treatise on Metaphysics," the purpose of which was "principally to prove the existence of God and of our souls when they are separate from the body, from which their immortality follows" (25 Nov. 1630, AT I 182/CSMK 29). The issue of immortality is broached again in the letter to the Faculty of Theology at the Sorbonne, prefixed to the *Meditations*, in which Descartes claimed to follow the instruction of the Lateran Council in refuting those who hold that, "as far as human reasoning goes, there are persuasive grounds for holding that the soul dies along with the body" (AT VII 3/CSM II 4).[1] The subtitle of the first edition (1641) of the *Meditations*, "in which is demonstrated the existence of God and the immortality of the soul," goes further. It promises not only the argument that human reason fails to establish that the soul dies with the body, but also a demonstrative proof of the conclusion that the soul is immortal.

There are reasons to think that Descartes himself was not the author of the subtitle to the first edition of the *Meditations* since he had explicitly warned in the text itself that he does not supply a completely demonstrative argument for the immortality of the soul.[2] In the *Synopsis*, for instance, he noted that the *Meditations* establishes only the premise that the soul differs in nature from body, and that subsequent premises that "depend on the whole of physics" are required to fill out the argument for immortality (AT VII 13/CSM II 10). Descartes even admitted to his critics that there is a sense in which reason cannot conclusively establish the soul's immortality. In the *Second Objections*, collected by Mersenne, the point is made that the *Meditations* does not seem to provide the foundation for a proof of immortality insofar as "it does not seem to follow from the fact that mind is distinct from body that it is incorruptible or immortal. What if its nature were limited by the duration of the life of the body, and God had endowed it with just so much strength and existence as to ensure that it came to an end with the death of the body? (CSM II 91). In response, Descartes conceded that he cannot simply through the use of reason eliminate the possibility that his critics are offering. Drawing on the scholastic notion of God's "absolute power" to do what is naturally impossible,[3] he wrote:

> [I]f your question concerns the absolute power of God, and you are asking whether he may have decreed that human souls cease to exist precisely when the bodies which are joined to them are destroyed, then it is for God alone to give the answer.... I do not take it upon myself to try to use the power of reason to settle any of those matter which depend on the free will of God. (Second Rep., AT VII 154/CSM II 109)

Descartes was even more explicit in a 1640 letter to Mersenne in which he remarked that "I could not prove that God could not annihilate the soul, but only that it is by nature entirely distinct from the body, and consequently that it is not bound by nature to die with it. This is all . . . that I had any intention of proving" (24 Dec. 1640, AT IV 266/CSMK 163). Descartes had, in fact, announced to Mersenne in 1630 his intention to prove the existence of our soul in separation from the body, but he in effect admitted to his correspondent ten years later that reason alone can prove only that soul and body are by nature distinct. It is not surprising, then, that Descartes changed the subtitle of the second edition (1642) of the *Meditations*, having it promise a demonstration only of "the distinction between the human soul and the body."

Even so, Descartes emphasized in his 1640 letter to Mersenne that the proof that the soul is distinct from body, and thus not bound by nature to die with it, "is all that is required as a foundation for religion" (AT IV 266/CSMK 163). Likewise, in his response to the *Second Objections* he made the point that since "we do not have any convincing evidence to suggest that any substance can perish," we are entitled "to conclude that the mind, insofar as it can be known by natural philosophy, is immortal" (AT VII 153–54/CSMK 109). Indeed, in the *Synopsis* Descartes held out the possibility of an even firmer foundation for the belief in immortality. He suggested that there would be a demonstrative proof of the immortality of the mind "insofar as it can be known by natural philosophy" (that is, apart from any consideration of God's "absolute power") if two premises could be established: the first, that all substances created by God, including "body taken in general" (*corpus in genere sumptum*), are "by their nature incorruptible, and cannot ever cease to exist, unless they are reduced to nothingness by God's denying his concurrence to them"; and the second, that the human mind, in contrast to the human body, is a "pure substance" (*pura substantia*) that does not lose its identity due to changes in its accidents. From these premises, according to Descartes, it follows that "the mind is by its nature immortal" (AT VII 14/CSM II 10). As we will discover, though, neither of these premises is completely clear, and each raises important difficulties for Descartes.

5.1.2 The Proof in the *Synopsis*

(1) Substance, Divine Power, and Body. The first premise in the *Synopsis* is related in a complex and not entirely satisfactory manner to Descartes' account

of substance. In the *Principles* Descartes emphasized that the term substance does not apply "univocally, as they say in the Schools" to God and creatures.[4] God is a substance in the sense of being "a thing that exists in such a way as to depend on no other thing for its existence." Descartes further claimed that nothing else can be a substance in this same sense, a conclusion that is explained by his argument elsewhere that everything other than God depends on God not only for its initial creation, but also for its continued existence.[5] He also noted, however, that creatures can be said to be substances in a derivative sense just in case they are "things that need only the concurrence of God in order to exist" (*PP* I.51, AT VIII–1 24/CSM I 210).

In the French edition of the *Principles*, the passage states more precisely that created substances require "only the ordinary concourse [*concours ordinaire*] of God in order to exist" (AT IX–2 47). On Descartes' view, God acts through His ordinary concourse just when He preserves the world in a manner that is in accord with natural laws. Since God's ordinary concourse suffices for the continued existence of a created substance, however, it follows that substance cannot be destroyed by natural means. Thus the passage from the French edition is in line with the earlier claim in the *Synopsis* that all created substances are "by nature incorruptible."

Unfortunately, this claim seems to conflict with Descartes' own account of body. In the *Principles* he held that "each and every part" of corporeal substance is itself a substance since it is "really distinct from the other parts of the same substance" in the sense that God has "the power of separating them, or of conserving one without the other" (*PP* I.60, AT VIII–1 28–29/CSM I 213). However, Descartes also suggested that at least some of these separable parts of matter can be destroyed by natural means. In a letter to Mesland written soon after the initial publication of the *Principles*, he noted that when the human body is considered as "a body in general" (*un corps en general*), or as "a determinate part of matter," it must be concluded that once there is any change in the particles that compose it, that body is "no longer the same, or *idem numero*" (9 Feb. 1645, AT IV 166/CSMK 242–43).[6] It seems difficult for Descartes to deny that the destruction of this body can be brought about by natural means, especially given his emphasis in the *Synopsis* on the fact that the human body is "easily destroyed" since it "is something else solely from the fact that the shape of some of its parts are changed" (AT VII 14/CSM II 10). Thus even though the human body qua determinate part of matter must be a created substance, on Descartes' view, this body requires more than God's ordinary concourse in order to be impervious to destruction.

It might be thought that Descartes' remarks concerning divine power provide a way around this difficulty. In the *Sixth Meditation* he made the point that substances are distinct if they can be made to exist separately at least by divine power, and that "it does not matter by what power it is that they are made to exist separately" (AT VII 78/CSM II 54). Descartes drew on this point in the *Sixth Replies* in order to respond to the claim that scholastic real accidents are not substances because they "can be separated from their subjects not naturally, but only through divine power."

> [T]o occur naturally is nothing other than to occur though the ordinary power of God, which in no way differs from His extraordinary power, positing nothing else in reality; thus it is that if everything that can naturally exist without a subject is a substance, whatever can exist without a subject through the power of God, however extraordinary, also must be said to be a substance. (AT VII 435/CSM II 293)

Something is a created substance, then, even when it can be made to exist without a subject only through God's extraordinary power. It seems that Descartes could say, along similar lines, that a substance is incorruptible even when it can continue to exist only through this sort of power.

Although Descartes held that the distinction between God's ordinary and extraordinary power is irrelevant to the question of whether something is a created substance, he could not deny that it is relevant with respect to the question of whether something is incorruptible. In the *Second Replies* he asserted that even though God can annihilate the human soul by means of His "absolute power," this soul must be immortal insofar as it can be known by natural philosophy. In light of his distinction in the *Sixth Replies*, this remark is most naturally taken to say that whereas God can annihilate the human soul by means of his extraordinary power, He cannot annihilate it by means of His ordinary power. Thus, on Descartes' own terms a created substance could not be "by nature incorruptible" if it could be annihilated when God exercises only His ordinary power.

It has been suggested that when Descartes claimed in the *Synopsis* that "body taken in general is a substance" (AT VII 14/CSM II 10), he was referring to body as a whole, or indefinite extension, rather than to individual material parts.[7] Although Descartes spoke at times of the realm of extension as a single substance,[8] it is unclear that he had such a realm in mind in the *Synopsis*. Jean Laporte has drawn attention to the fact that Descartes referred in this text to body *in genere*, rather than *in globo*. His conclusion is that Descartes was thinking of particular portions of extension considered merely as such, rather than of extension in its entirety.[9] This conclusion seems to be confirmed by the fact that Descartes referred in the *Principles* to the space within a particular vessel as "extension taken in general" (*extensionem in genere sumptum*) (PP II.18, AT VIII-1 50/CSM I 230). Moreover, when he spoke of "body in general" in his letter to Mesland, he meant not the extended world as a whole, but only a determinate part of it. There are textual grounds for taking the remarks in the *Synopsis* to imply that even the substantial parts of extension cannot perish by natural means.

The letter to Mesland admittedly does not provide the best defense of this implicit position. Descartes made the point there that the human body qua determinate piece of matter depends essentially on a certain organization of particular particles, and it seems clear that since it is so dependent such a body can easily perish by natural means. There may be other ways of defending the claim in the *Synopsis* that body taken in general is incorruptible,[10] though it must be said that Descartes himself was not concerned to provide such a defense. His discussion in this text simply does not emphasize that bodily and mental substances are equally incorruptible by nature. The argument there for immortality focuses rather on the differences between the human body and the human mind.

(2) Human Bodies and Human Minds. The *Synopsis* concludes that while the human body is "easily destroyed," the human mind is "by its nature immortal." The result concerning the human body derives from the fact that this body is distinguished from other bodies in virtue of its being "constituted out of a particular configuration of members and of other similar accidents." Because it is constituted in this way, the human body "is something else from the fact alone that the shape of certain of its parts is changed" (AT VII 14/CSM II 10). To see the sort of change involved here, we need to turn to the discussion of the human body in the letter to Mesland cited above. There Descartes distinguished the body of a man as determinate part of matter from the body as "the whole of that matter that is united to the soul of that man." We have considered his conclusion that the human body qua determinate part of matter cannot survive a change in its quantity. He went on to tell Mesland that the human body qua matter united to a soul can survive such a change "while it remains joined and substantially united to the same soul," and that it can remain so joined and united "while it has in itself all the dispositions required to preserve that union" (AT IV 166/CSMK 243). The change that causes this body to become something else is that change which eliminates the dispositions required for it to be joined to the human soul.[11] The human body is "easily destroyed" because this sort of change is easily brought about by natural means.

The contrasting result in the *Synopsis* that the human mind is "by its nature immortal" derives from the fact that this mind is a "pure substance" that in no way is constituted by its accidents. Thus, even if all the accidents of the mind change so that it has completely different acts of will, sensation, or pure understanding, "the same mind would not on that account become another" (AT VII 14/CSM II 10). This contention that the mind survives such a change is prefaced by the claim earlier in the *Synopsis* that "we cannot understand a mind except as being indivisible" since "we cannot conceive of half a mind" (AT VII 13/CSM II 9). Because the human mind is indivisible, it is a pure substance, according to this view, and because it is such a substance, it is immortal by its very nature.

Consider first the tenet that the mind is indivisible. The remarks concerning this tenet in the *Synopsis* allude to a second argument for mind–body distinctness in the *Sixth Meditation* (following the Real Distinction Argument), which has as its conclusion that "there is a great difference between mind and body, in that while body is by its nature always divisible, mind is however completely indivisible." In support of the latter part of this conclusion, Descartes noted, "[W]hen I consider this [mind], or myself insofar as I am merely a thinking thing, I can distinguish within myself no parts, but understand myself to be a thing entirely one and complete." He went on to admit that the soul has various faculties, such as those of willing, sensing, and understanding, but held that "these cannot be said to be parts of [the mind], since it is one and the same mind that wills, that senses, that understands" (AT VII 85–86/CSM II 59). The mere fact that mental faculties are not parts cannot suffice to show that the subject of these faculties is indivisible, given Descartes' view that a divisible body has a two-dimensional surface "that is merely a mode and hence cannot be a part of a body" (*Sixth Rep.*, AT VII 433/CSM II 292). What carries the weight of the argument for indivisibility, then, is his claim that he cannot conceive his mind to be divisible.

Descartes' conclusion that his mind is in fact indivisible does not seem to follow from the premise that he cannot conceive it to be divisible, but I think that he was relying on something akin to the Sufficiency Thesis. Recall that in the Real Distinction Argument Descartes simply assumed that his distinct conception of his nature as a thinking thing suffices to show that this nature excludes extension. Likewise, he held that his distinct conception of his mind as an indivisible subject of thought suffices to show that this mind is an indivisible substance. In fact, such a conception could serve to ground Descartes' claim in the Real Distinction Argument that he has a clear and distinct idea of his mind as a thinking, unextended thing. Given Descartes' view that what is extended must be divisible, it simply follows from the fact that he can distinctly conceive his mind to be indivisible that he can distinctly conceive it to lack extension.[12] In any event, it clearly was Descartes' view that we can distinctly conceive that the mind is an indivisible substance merely by means of a consideration of the nature of mind as a thinking thing.

As in the case of the Real Distinction Argument, there are complications for the argument for mental indivisibility that derive from the concession to the materialist in the *Second Meditation* (cf. §4.3.1 [2]). Descartes admitted at this point in the *Meditations* that he cannot rule out the possibility that the subject of his thought is extended. If this subject were in fact extended, then Descartes' conception of his mind as an indivisible substance could not be distinct. Such a conception would have to be redescribed, perhaps as the conception of a mode of a substance that is itself extended, and thus also divisible. Descartes' concession that the mind does not immediately reveal to itself that it is unextended thus undermines his claim that the mind can know immediately that it is an indivisible substance.

In the *Synopsis* Descartes appealed to the result that the mind is an indivisible substance in order to establish that it is immortal by nature. He attempted to forge the connection between indivisibility and immortality by appealing to the notion of a "pure substance." Here he contrasted pure substances with substances, such as the human body, that depend for their identity on the arrangement of their constituent parts. Given that the mind is an indivisible substance, it must also be a pure substance since it has no constituent parts on which its identity could depend. The next step, then, is to show that a pure substance is immortal by nature, that is to say, that it cannot be destroyed by natural means. Descartes noted, without much argument, that since the mind is a pure substance, it cannot cease to exist due to a change in its accidents. But he seems to have assumed the doctrine, which has its classical source in

Cicero, that the natural destruction of an object can involve only the disruption of the parts of that object.[13] Since a change in accidents cannot bring about this sort of disruption in the human mind, as it can in the human body, the human mind is immortal by nature, as the human body is not. The impossibility of the natural destruction of the soul admittedly does not establish that it has what Jeanne Russier has called the *immortalité de fait*. For Descartes it is always possible that the soul is not, in fact, immortal since God can annihilate it by means of his absolute power. Nonetheless, he clearly did take this sort of impossibility to establish that the soul has what Russier has called the *immortalité de nature*.[14] Descartes held that even though there can be no proof from reason for the actual immortality of the soul, still the philosopher can establish that it is naturally immortal.

One could wish for a more explicit defense of the claim, central to the argument for the natural immortality of the soul, that natural destruction can involve only the disruption of parts. But even if one grants Descartes that the soul cannot be destroyed by natural means and also sets aside his view that absolutely speaking God can annihilate the soul, there is still the question of whether he has provided all that is needed to establish the Christian doctrine of personal immortality. The central difficulty, in light of Locke's discussion of personal identity, is that Descartes failed to consider how psychological continuity bears on the issue of immortality. Even prior to the publication of Locke's *Essay* in 1690, Leibniz had complained that "the immortality of the soul, as established by Descartes, is useless and could not console us in any way" because, for all Descartes has said, the soul "might be immortal in fact, but it might pass through a thousand changes without remembering what it once was." If the soul will, in fact, pass through these changes, then the consequence that it does not perish "is completely useless to morality, for it upsets all reward and punishment."[15]

Malebranche did no better than Descartes in considering the importance for immortality of a personal identity rooted in memory. However, his argument for immortality has the virtue of recognizing, as Descartes' argument does not, that consciousness cannot reveal directly that the soul is an indivisible substance. Moreover, Malebranche advanced the Cartesian account of immortality by exploring two points bequeathed by Descartes: that "body taken in general" must be incorruptible and that there can be no demonstrative proof of immortality given that God can annihilate the soul by his absolute power. While Malebranche's remarks concerning these points are unsatisfactory in certain respects, they nonetheless serve to highlight issues that Descartes had considered in a somewhat perfunctory manner but that are significant in the context of the writings of Desgabets.

5.2 Malebranche's Proof of Immortality

In the *Recherche* Malebranche emphasized the need for the general rule that "we should reason only about things of which we have clear ideas" (RV VI–2.1,

OCM II 296/LO 437), claiming that through the use of this rule, among others, Descartes "discovered all those great and fruitful truths by which we can be instructed in his works" (OCM II 299/LO 439).[16] In order to illustrate the importance of such a rule, Malebranche cited two particular truths that Descartes had discovered: that the soul or, more precisely, thinking substance is immortal (RV VI–2.7, OCM II 387–89/LO 491–92) and that animals are mere machines since they do not have a soul in this precise sense (OCM II 389–96/LO 492–96). For Malebranche's contemporaries, the doctrine of the beast–machine was distinctively Cartesian; one Jesuit critic went so far as to say that "with the doctrine, it is impossible not to be a Cartesian, and without it, it is impossible to be one. It is the very spirit and sap ... of pure Cartesianism."[17] Malebranche himself admitted that this doctrine was not anticipated in Augustine, who was blinded by the prejudice that animals have souls.[18] On his view, then, Augustine's position must be corrected not only by Descartes' discovery that sensible qualities do not exist in bodies (see §2.1.1), but also by Descartes' claim that animals do not have spiritual souls. Malebranche followed Descartes rather than Augustine, moreover, in taking the doctrine that animals are mere machines to complement the belief in immortality. It is thus natural that we begin the discussion of Malebranche's Cartesian account of immortality by considering his distinctively Cartesian rejection of animal souls. After such a consideration, we can turn to the particular proof of immortality that he offered initially in the *Recherche*, and later, with some important additions, in the *Entretiens sur la mort*.

5.2.1 Animal Souls and Immortality

In line with the earlier view in his unpublished *L'Homme*, Descartes proposed in his *Discourse* that the body of an animal be regarded "as a machine that, having been made by the hand of God, is incomparably better ordered, and contains in itself far more remarkable movements than any machine that could be invented by man" (*DM* V, AT VI 56/CSM I 139).[19] He went out of his way to note in this work the fact that humans can use language in a rational manner shows that it is "morally impossible" (*moralement impossible*) that they are mere machines that lack rational souls (AT VI 56–59/CSM I 140–41),[20] but this proviso failed to placate critics of the Cartesian doctrine of the *bête–machine*. Thus the Belgian theologian Libert de Froimont noted to a correspondent that the mechanistic explanation of animals in the recently published *Discourse* "perhaps opens the way to the atheist, so that similar causes are assigned to the operations of the rational soul; ... It is not proper that such excellent operations be given such humble causes" (*Fromondus to Plempius*, 13 Sept. 1637, AT I 403).[21] The Jesuit Ignace-Gaston Pardies later picked up on this suggestion; in his popular *Discours de la connoissance des bestes* (1672), he wrote that "if ... one admits that all the operations of the beasts can occur without a soul, and through the machine of the body alone; one would come ... to say also, that all the operations of humans can occur through a similar disposition of the machine of their body."[22] By the time of the publication of the *Recherche* in 1674, then, it was already a stock objection that the Cartesian rejection of the animal soul places one on a slippery slope that ends in the rejection of the immaterial human soul.[23]

In the *Recherche* itself Malebranche had ridiculed Montaigne's claim that there is no great difference between humans and other animals (RV II–3.5, OCM I 368–69/LO 189–90).[24] Later in this text he cited Descartes' remarks in *L'Homme* in support of the conclusion that "all the parts of animals are merely mechanical, and that they can move themselves without a soul through the impression of objects, and through their particular constitution" (RV IV.11, OCM II 106/LO 324).[1] At times Malebranche granted his Peripatetic critics that animals have souls in the sense that they have "a corporeal thing diffused throughout the whole body, which gives it movement and life."[26] He also noted, however, that since few of these critics were willing to admit that animals have in addition "a spiritual and indivisible soul,"[27] the main difference between Peripatetics and Cartesians "is not that the former believe that the beasts have souls and the latter do not believe it; but only that the former believe that animals are capable of sensing, of pain, of pleasure, of seeing colors, of having generally all the sensations and all of the passions that we have; and that the Cartesians believe the contrary" (RV VI–2.7, OCM II 390/LO 492–93). Though the position here is indebted to Descartes' own remarks, the reasoning differs from Descartes' in a characteristic manner. As we have seen, Descartes took intellectual thought to reveal most clearly the difference between soul and body. It was thus natural for him to stress the implausibility of the belief that animals possess rational thought.[28] According to Malebranche, on the other hand, sensations provide the clearest case for soul–body distinctness. This explains the view in the *Recherche* that the Peripatetic account of animals must be rejected since we cannot "conceive that matter shaped in a given way, such as a square, round, or oval, be pain, pleasure, heat, color, odor, sound, etc." (OCM II 391/LO 493).[29]

I have mentioned the Peripatetic objection that the Cartesian account of the beast–machine undermines the doctrine that humans have an immaterial soul. Descartes urged in the *Discourse*, however, that "when we know how much beasts differ from us, we understand much better the arguments that prove that our soul is of a nature entirely independent of the body," and thus "are naturally led to conclude that it is immortal" (DM V, AT VI 59–60/CSM I 141). He later wrote to a correspondent that those who hold that animals have "some thought such as we experience in ourselves, but of a very much less perfect kind" are in fact committed to the implausible position that even oysters and sponges "have an immortal soul like us" since such a soul cannot be attributed to some animals without being attributed to all of them (*To Newcastle*, 23 Nov. 1646, AT IV 576/CSMK 304). The natural conclusion that human souls are immortal thus serves here to undermine the attribution of even imperfect thoughts to nonhuman animals.

Rohault argued against animal souls from the other direction when he claimed in his 1671 *Entretiens sur la philosophie* that "the opinion of those who attribute a soul that thinks [to animals] is very dangerous, in that it furnishes the libertines the means to elude the principal proof that we have of the immortality of the rational soul."[30] Malebranche owned a copy of this text,[31] which may explain the presence of a similar line of argument in his 1682 response to the Jesuit La Ville. Though La Ville's *Sentimens* does not address the Cartesian account of animals, Malebranche took this work to assume the Peripatetic view "that the beasts have souls, and that these souls are more noble than the body that they animate" (*Déf. La Ville*, OCM XVII–1 513). This description seems at first to conflict with his earlier remark in the *Recherche* that even the Peripatetics grant that animals do not have a spiritual soul, but I suspect that he understood his critics to hold that the animal soul is an entity which, while not spiritual, is nonetheless a substance more noble than an inanimate body. One who holds that such a substance can be annihilated, however, must conclude that "although the soul of man is a substance distinct from its body, it can be annihilated when the body is destroyed." Such a critic thus "cannot demonstrate by reason that the soul of man is immortal" (OCM XVII–1 516).[32] Malebranche concluded that it is the Cartesians, not their critics, who are in the best position to carry out the directive of the Lateran Council to "give clear and incontestable proofs that the soul is immortal and distinguished from the body" (OCM XVII–1 527).

Malebranche's remark to La Ville that Cartesians can show that the soul "is a substance distinct from body, and by consequence immortal" (OCM XVII–1 520) appears to indicate that the immortality of the soul follows directly from its immateriality. Such an appearance is strengthened by the related claim in the *Recherche* that the fact that the soul differs in nature from body "suffices to demonstrate that the soul is immortal, and that it cannot perish even should the body be annihilated" (RV IV.2, OCM II 22/LO 273). However, Malebranche's discussion of immortality raises two complications regarding the link between the soul's immateriality and its immortality. The first is broached by his comment in the *Recherche*, following the claim just cited, that the proof of immortality depends on the premise that no substance can be annihilated by "the ordinary forces of nature" (OCM II 23/LO 273). Malebranche's full defense of such a premise appeals to his own view that matter is not subject to natural destruction. The second complication is indicated by his admission in a late work, the *Entretiens sur la mort*, that absolutely speaking it is within God's power to annihilate any substance, including the soul. This admission makes it difficult for Malebranche to say that the fact that the soul is immaterial suffices to show that it is immortal. In contrast to Descartes, though, he attempted to argue that the admission itself does not preclude a fully demonstrative proof of the actual (as opposed to merely natural) immortality of the soul.

5.2.2 The Proof in the *Recherche*

The discussion of immortality in Book Four of the *Recherche* makes two points: first, that since our soul is indivisible, and thus distinct from body, it "is not annihilated, even supposing that death should annihilate our bodies" (RV IV.2,

OCM II 23/LO 273); and, second, that since "nothing can be annihilated by the ordinary forces of nature," it must be the case that even bodies "cannot be annihilated" (OCM II 23–24/LO 273). While Malebranche's official position is that the fact that the soul is indivisible suffices to demonstrate that it is immortal, there are reasons internal to his system to hold that such a demonstration must rely on the premise that body is in some sense indestructible.

(1) Mind and Indivisibility. Malebranche's discussion of immortality has as its moral that people often cannot discover the truth simply because "they are incapable of paying moderately serious attention to it" (OCM II 22/LO 272). Is that much attention necessary, Malebranche asked, "in order to see that a thought is neither round nor square, that extension is capable only of different shapes and motion, and what thinks and what is extended are two completely opposite beings?" Yet, according to Malebranche, the mere fact that soul and body are opposite beings, "suffices to demonstrate that the soul is immortal, and that it cannot perish even should the body be annihilated" (OCM II 22/LO 273).

In order to confirm that mind and body are "opposite beings," Malebranche drew attention to the fact that though bodily parts are divisible, the thoughts of the mind are not. "By a straight line one can cut a square into two triangles, two parallelograms, or two trapeziums; but by what line can one conceive a pleasure, a pain, or a desire to be cut, and what shape would result from this division? Certainly I do not believe that the imagination is so full of false ideas to be satisfied with this" (OCM II 24/LO 274). This argument seems at first merely to repeat Descartes' argument that "we cannot understand a body except as being divisible, while by contrast we cannot understand a mind except as being indivisible" (*Synopsis*, AT VII 13/CSM II 9), yet there is one crucial difference. As we have seen, Descartes suggested in the *Sixth Meditation*, in line with the Sufficiency Thesis, that a consideration of mind as a thinking thing reveals directly that the mind is an indivisible substance. Whereas Malebranche was not always careful to preclude a direct proof of the immateriality of the soul through consciousness, he made clear from the start that there is no direct insight into soul's indivisibility. The argument for indivisibility in the first edition of the *Recherche* begins with the premise that body cannot be the subject of thought since body is simply extension and since extension "is capable only of different shapes and motion, and not of thought and reasoning." If this subject lacks extension, then it must be the case that "it will not be divisible, and if it is not divisible, it must be agreed that in this sense it will not be corruptible" (OCM II 24/LO 274). For Malebranche, then, the argument for the indivisibility of the soul, as well as for its indestructibility, presupposes an argument for its immateriality that is indirect in the sense that it relies on a consideration of the nature of body as an extended thing.

It is easy to focus on the fact that Malebranche and Descartes both concluded that the mind is an indivisible and immaterial substance and thus to overlook any differences between them concerning their arguments for this conclusion. Yet the differences are certainly important with respect to Malebranche's thesis that we have access to a clear idea of body but not to a clear idea of the soul. This thesis helps to explain why Malebranche ended his discussion of immortality in the *Recherche* by emphasizing that we need to consider "the clear and distinct idea of extension in order to recognize that extension cannot be related to thought" (OCM II 25/LO 274).[33] When Arnauld later objected that the proof of immortality presupposes a clear idea of the soul, moreover, he responded that "the idea that one has of body suffices to demonstrate that the soul is immortal" (*Réponse*, c. 23, OCM VI 160). Malebranche himself took the clear idea of extension to bear the weight of his argument for the indivisibility, and subsequent immortality, of the soul.

There is some question, however, of Malebranche's own view of the connection between the indivisibility of the soul, on the one hand, and its immortality, on the other. He indicated a rather direct connection when he claimed in Book Four of the *Recherche* that the fact that the soul lacks extension "suffices to demonstrate" that it is immortal. His argument depends on the view that "since thought is not a modification of extension, our soul is not annihilated, even supposing that death should annihilate our bodies" (OCM II 23/LO 273). In support of such a view, he noted that even though the annihilation of a substance entails the annihilation of its modes, it cannot entail the annihilation of a substance distinct from it. This point seems to show only that the annihilation of the body *need not* bring about the annihilation of the soul, but Malebranche urged that the point establishes the stronger conclusion that the body's annihilation *cannot* bring about the soul's annihilation since a substance has its existence apart from another and thus "cannot be reduced to nothing by the annihilation of the other" (OCM II 23/LO 273). He explained to Arnauld that two different substances "subsist in themselves" and thus that "the annihilation of the one can contribute nothing to the annihilation of the other" (*Réponse*, c. 23, OCM VI 163). The claim that substances "subsist in themselves" serves to distinguish them from modes, which subsist in something else that serves as their subject. Malebranche told La Ville that because the roundness of a body is a mode that is "only a relation of equality in the distance between the parts that circumscribe [*terminent*] this body," it can be destroyed when the relation between the parts changes. Modes such as roundness, therefore, can be destroyed when there is a change in the subject in which they subsist; "what is round can become square." Since a substance subsists in itself, however, there is no underlying subject that could be changed when it is destroyed.

Malebranche simply assumed that natural destruction must involve a change in a subject and thus concluded to La Ville that "no substance can be annihilated by the ordinary forces of nature" (*Déf. La Ville*, AT XVII–1 521). Read in light of his Occasionalism, Malebranche's position is that substance cannot be annihilated when God conserves the world by completely determining its states in a manner that accords with general laws of nature. This position must, of course, be distinguished from the view in the French edition of the *Principles* that "the ordinary concourse" of God suffices for the continued existence of substance, given that Descartes (along with Cartesians as varied as La Forge and Regis) took such a concourse to allow for a real causal contribution on the part of creatures (see §2.1.2 [1]).[34] However, Malebranche followed Descartes in holding that the mere fact that the soul is a substance reveals that it is impervious to natural destruction.

This argument implies that even bodily substances cannot be destroyed by natural means. There is thus some question whether the argument itself is compatible with the fact that particular material entities are subject to destruction. I shall indicate presently that Malebranche addressed this question more directly than did Descartes, but for the moment I want to comment briefly on a question broached by a different sort of comparison between soul and body. Malebranche noted in the *Recherche* that just as the human body is changed into something completely different after death, so our soul "will have thoughts and sensations very different from those that it has during this life" (RV IV.2, OCM II 25/LO 274). This analogy is unsettling insofar as it raises the possibility that the human soul turns into something completely different after death. One might wonder, in particular, whether there could be a break in the continuity of the thoughts of the soul that is so radical that it brings about the existence of a new person. If such a break were possible, then the fact that the soul is indestructible could no more secure personal survival than the fact that body is indestructible could secure the survival of the human body.[35]

I have mentioned that Malebranche, along with Descartes, failed to address this sort of worry (see §1.2.2 [2]). One could perhaps rule out total psychological discontinuity, however, by appealing to Malebranche's position that consciousness of a thought involves consciousness of the substance that has that thought. Whatever changes death brings about in the thoughts of a soul, its postmortem thoughts must be continuous with those which it had prior to death at least to the extent that both sorts of thoughts involve a consciousness of the same particular substance. The necessity of such continuity would be of small comfort to Leibniz, who held that just punishment or reward in an afterlife would not be possible if the soul could not "remember what it once was," yet this sort of continuity seems to be the most that Malebranche can extract directly from the result that the soul cannot be destroyed by the ordinary forces of nature.[36]

(2) Body and Annihilation. In the *Synopsis* Descartes mentioned in passing that "body taken in general" cannot perish but emphasized that the human body, as opposed to the human soul, is "easily destroyed." He offered no explanation of how the destruction of the human body is compatible with the indestructibility of "body in general." In his discussion of immortality in the *Recherche*, however, Malebranche attempted to provide such an explanation. Though he claimed there that the human soul would not be annihilated even if its body could be, he went on to stress that "we are wrong in imagining that the body is annihilated when it is destroyed." Malebranche granted that what was once the flesh of the human body can be corrupted by being changed into "earth, vapor, or whatever you wish"; indeed, he held that there are "certain laws in nature, according to

which bodies successively change their forms." He also insisted, however, that "the substance of what is . . . flesh cannot perish" since there can be "no law in nature for the annihilation of any being" (RV IV.2, OCM II 23–24/LO 273–74).

Somewhat later in the *Recherche* Malebranche admitted that the view that there can be no law for the annihilation of body seems absurd to those who "judge according to what they sense, and not according to what they conceive." Such people claim to see directly that "wood thrown into fire ceases to be what it is" and thus "judge that the greatest part of the wood ceases to be" (RV IV.11, OCM II 91–92/LO 316). Malebranche held that one can resist this rash sensory judgment by using reason to discern that "by the ordinary force of nature what exists cannot be reduced to nothing, just as what does not exist cannot begin to be" (OCM II 92/LO 316). He allowed toward the beginning of the *Recherche* that "matter can be said to receive a considerable change when it loses the configuration proper to the parts of the wax in order to receive those which are proper to fire and smoke, when the wax is changed into fire and into smoke" (RV I.1, OCM I 44/LO 4).[37] Thus wax can be destroyed, and smoke and fire created, by means of a change in the internal configurations, or what Malebranche referred to later in the *Recherche* as the "forms" of particular bodies. What cannot be created or destroyed, however, is the "substance" of these particular bodies, which as the passage from the start of this text indicates, is the matter that constitutes them.

Given the claim in the *Recherche* that "the idea that we have of extension suffices to inform us of all the properties of which extension is capable" (RV III–2.7, OCM I 450/LO 237), it would seem most natural for Malebranche to appeal to such an idea in order to establish the indestructibility of matter. In the *Recherche* itself, however, his defense of the indestructibility of matter invokes, not the idea of extension, but the nature of divine activity. In the section of this text on immortality, for instance, he noted briefly that while God can allow natural laws that dictate the succession of different forms in bodies, since such a succession "produces the beauty of the Universe, and thus admiration for its Author," He cannot allow for a natural law that dictates the annihilation of any being or substance "because nothingness is neither beautiful nor good, and because the Author of nature loves His work" (RV IV.2, OCM II 24/LO 273–74).[38] Later in the *Recherche*, moreover, Malebranche introduced the additional consideration that the annihilation of substance is incompatible with the fact that "the power that gives being to all things is not subject to change" (RV IV.11, OCM II 92/LO 316).[39]

It cannot be said that these appeals to the nature of God's power are free of difficulty. Malebranche's suggestion that God cannot allow for natural laws that detract from the beauty of the universe runs up against his official view that God's wisdom requires that He act in accord with the simplest but most fruitful set of natural laws, even when these laws have evil consequences.[40] To argue against the annihilation of substance, he cannot simply appeal to the fact that God loves His work; further, he must show that no law that entails the annihilation of substance can be among the best set of laws. Moreover, he needs to defend the claim that the change involved in the divine act of annihilation is inconsistent with divine immutability. Malebranche himself allowed at one point in the *Recherche*, after all, that God causes a moving body to come to rest by ceasing to will its motion (RV VI–2.9, OCM II 427–31/LO 514–17).[41] On his own view, then, not all cessation of divine volition need involve a change that is ruled out by divine immutability.

While there are gaps in the defense in the *Recherche* of the view that matter is indestructible, the view itself addresses certain difficulties deriving from Descartes' account of substance. In the *Second Replies* Descartes had stipulated that a substance is anything in which a property resides as in a subject (AT VII 161/ CSM II 114). Thus he spoke of particular material objects, such as hands and clothes, as substances.[42] Because these objects can be destroyed by natural means, however, it seems that the conception of substance in the *Second Replies* must be distinguished from the conception in the *Synopsis*, according to which "absolutely all substances [are] by their nature incorruptible" since they depend only on God's concurrence (AT VII 14/CSM II 10). The mere fact that Descartes offered two different conceptions of substance is not problematic; one could hold, after all, that the term *substance* is merely equivocal. Yet while Descartes claimed in the *Principles* that this term does not apply univocally to God and creatures, he also suggested there that it applies univocally to creatures.[43] What he needed, but did not provide, is a single conception that explains the sense in which both destructible bodies and indestructible "body in general" are created substances.

Malebranche himself claimed, in line with the stipulation in the *Second Replies*, that whatever is not a mode but rather the subject of modes must be a substance.[44] He no doubt had such a claim in mind when he wrote toward the end of his life that material objects such as "Paris, Rome, cubes, spheres, . . . would all be substances of that infinite substance and all of the same attribute, that is to say all extended and of the same nature, all substances but of a greater or lesser size" (*To Mairan*, 12 June 1714, OCM XIX 886).[45] While he admitted in the *Recherche* that particular material objects can themselves be destroyed through a natural change in forms, he also held there that the "substance of" these objects, that is to say, their matter, cannot be annihilated.[46] Indeed, I think that Malebranche held that particular bodies can be called substances because, unlike their modes, there is an element of them that is permanent. On my interpretation, then, he took the upshot of the cogito argument that the soul exists as a thinking substance to show that the soul also has a permanent element.

The fact that Malebranche's discussion of the indestructibility of substance draws so much on the case of matter suggests an argument for immortality that involves a comparison of the soul to material substance. Indeed, he did offer such an argument in the *Entretiens sur la mort* when he wrote that just as body can be changed without "the least atom of its substance" being "returned to nothingness, [so] it is the same with our soul. Its substance is naturally immortal" (*E. mort* II, OCM XIII 368). This passage, however, must be balanced against Malebranche's persistent claim that the argument for immortality goes through even if one gives in to sensory prejudice and believes that bodies can be annihilated.[47] His most dominant view seems to be that this argument does not depend essentially on the premise that matter is indestructible.

It is difficult to dispute the claim in the *Recherche* that no appeal to the indestructibility of matter is needed to show that an indivisible soul "is not susceptible to the same changes as our bodies" (RV IV.2, OCM II 24/LO 274). What seems more questionable on Malebranche's own terms, though, is the suggestion in this text that no such appeal is required to conclude that the indivisible soul is indestructible and thus immortal. I have urged that his argument that the soul could not be annihilated even if the body could be depends on the premise that substance cannot be annihilated "by the ordinary forces of nature." Surely any complete Malebranchean defense of this premise must include a response to the claim, rooted in sensory prejudice, that a piece of wood, for instance, is annihilated when it is thrown into the fire. In the end, it seems, Malebranche must establish that matter is indestructible in order to secure the result that the soul cannot be annihilated.

A more important reason for the indispensability of a consideration of matter, at least for our purposes, is indicated by Gueroult's comment that for Malebranche "it is precisely because the soul does not by itself furnish us a rational knowledge, clear and distinct, of its being, that we are obliged to turn ... toward the source of all rational knowledge for us: extension."[48] Such a position implies that our rational knowledge of soul's indestructibility, as well as of its indivisibility, must be grounded in the clear idea of matter.[49] Malebranche himself noted at one point that while we know that the soul is an indivisible substance, this knowledge does not allow us to understand the nature of the faculties of this substance since we "know nothing of [the faculties] through clear ideas" (*Pré. phy.*, sec. VIII, OCM XVI 28–29). Because we cannot know mental faculties through a clear idea of the soul, our only recourse is to conceive of them on analogy with the faculties revealed by the clear idea of extension. Thus, Malebranche claimed at the start of the *Recherche* that the faculty that matter has for receiving different shapes provides the template for our conception of the mental faculty of the understanding, just as the faculty that matter has for being moved provides the template for our conception of the mental faculty of the will (RV I.1, OCM I 41/LO 2).[50] In a later defense of this account of mental faculties, moreover, he noted that we can recognize that the understanding and the will are not entities distinct from the soul once we see in the idea of matter that the capacities for receiving shapes and motions are not distinct from body. He added that "if we had as clear an idea of the soul as we have of body, I am convinced that we would also see that its understanding and will are not different from itself" (*Écl. II*, OCM III 40/LO 560). According to Malebranche, then, we can know these features of the soul, not directly by means of a clear idea of the soul, but only indirectly by means of the clear idea of matter.

In the *Recherche* Malebranche used this sort of indirect argument to show that "the mind has a capacity to receive successively an infinity of different modifications the same mind does not know" (RV III–1.1, OCM I 384/LO 199). There is no direct route to this conclusion, since we have no access to an idea of the soul that reveals the modifications of which it is capable. Rather, we must consider that because each of the infinitely many different kinds of shapes is itself infinitely diverse, a particular body such as a piece of wax is "capable of an infinite number, or rather an infinitely infinite number of modifications that no mind can comprehend" (OCM I 384/LO 199). Malebranche extended the analogy, moreover, claiming that just as the matter of our body "is capable of but few modifications during our lifetime [since] it has to be flesh, brain, nerves, and the rest of the body of a man so that the soul may be united to it," so our soul, while it is joined to this body, has only a portion of the modifications of which it is capable (OCM I 385/LO 200). He later argued, along similar lines, that "when the soul is separated from its body, it will be free to receive all sorts of ideas and modifications quite different from those that it has presently, as our body for its part will be capable of all sorts of shapes and configurations quite different from those that it must have to be the body of a living man" (RV IV.2, OCM II 25/LO 274).

Malebranche therefore took the idea of matter to play a role in our knowledge of immortality beyond that of revealing the indivisibility of the soul and its consequent difference from body. While he apparently did not realize it, moreover, he has reason as well to say that we need this idea to see that the indivisible soul is indestructible. Since we have no access to a clear idea of spiritual substance, the only clear idea of substance from which we could begin to argue for indestructibility would be that of matter. The argument here, patterned on Malebranche's discussion of mental faculties and modifications, would be that the soul, qua substance, is no more subject to natural destruction than is material substance.

The position that our knowledge of the soul's indestructibility must be indirect in this manner actually serves to strengthen Malebranche's claim to Arnauld that "the idea that one has of bodies suffices to demonstrate that the soul is immortal" (*Réponse*, c. 23, OCM VI 160). Malebranche himself failed to take full advantage of this sort of position, suggesting instead that we can see directly that the indivisible soul is by nature indestructible; here he may simply have been blinded by Descartes' argument for immortality in the *Synopsis*. It is clear from the discussion of immortality in the *Recherche*, in any case, that Malebranche did not carry to the end his critique of Descartes' doctrine that the nature of mind is better known than the nature of body.

5.2.3 The Proof in the *Entretiens sur la mort*

In the 1674 *Recherche* Malebranche spoke of the question of the immortality of the soul as "one of the easiest questions to resolve" (RV IV.2, OCM II 25/LO 274). What he claimed to resolve, however, was only the question of whether the soul can be annihilated by the ordinary forces of nature. As he recognized in the 1696 *Entretiens sur la mort*, there are complications deriving from the fact that any complete argument for immortality must go beyond the claim that the soul is naturally indestructible. This work, which was first published with the third edition of the *Entretiens sur la Métaphysique*, is a continuation of the discussion between Ariste and Theodore in the original *Entretiens*. In the sequel Theodore attempts to calm Ariste's fears concerning death by invoking the familiar position that the annihilation of soul and body "is equally impossible for the ordinary forces of nature" (*E. mort I*, OCM XIII 367). Although Ariste conceded that it is impossible for substances to be annihilated by natural means, he objected that he still has reason for fear since it is the case that "God can annihilate me" (OCM XIII 370).

An important source for this objection is undoubtedly Descartes' claim in the *Second Replies* that God can annihilate any created substance by means of his absolute power (AT VII 154/CSM II 109). Furthermore, such a possibility can be derived from his official view, which profoundly influenced Malebranche, that conservation is simply continual divine creation. Descartes argued that since there is only a contingent connection between the different parts of the duration of an object, that object can be conserved in existence only by means of God's continued creative activity.[51] At one point he took such a view to imply that "there is no imaginable time before the creation of the world in which God could not have created it if he had so willed" (*To Chanut*, 6 June 1647, AT V 52–53/CSMK 320). By taking this argument in the other direction, one can conclude that there is no imaginable time after the present moment in which God could not annihilate the world if he so wills.

Malebranche himself emphasized in a 1685 response to Arnauld that since creatures continually depend on God for their existence, "if God merely ceases to will that they be, from that only they cease to be" (*Rép. Diss.*, c. 7, OCM VII 514). He drew on this view three years later in the *Entretiens sur la Métaphysique*, where he had Theodore correct Ariste's view that bodies can continue to exist once the instant of their creation is past.

> *The instant of creation past!* But if that instant does not pass, then you are up against the wall; it is necessary that you give in. Now observe. God wills that there be a world. His will is all-powerful: thus this world is made. Let God no longer will that there be a world: it is thus annihilated. For certainly the world depends on the volitions of the Creator. If the world subsists, it is thus the case that God continues to will that the world be. The conservation of creatures on the part of God is thus only their continued creation. (*EM VII*, OCM XII 156–57/D 153)

Theodore went on to conclude that it is within God's power to annihilate anything he has created because "he can cease willing what he has freely willed" (OCM XII 159/D 157). Thus does he concede to Ariste in the *Entretiens sur la mort* that "at death God can annihilate our souls" (*E. mort I*, OCM XIII 369).

As we have seen, Descartes conceded that he cannot refute the view that God has decreed that our soul be destroyed at death since no one can "use the power of human reason to settle any of those matters that depend on the free will of God." The certainty that God has not made any such decree derives not from reason but from the faith that "God himself has revealed to us that this [i.e., the destruction of the soul at death] will not occur" (*Second Rep.*, AT VII 153/CSM II 109). Malebranche himself granted in a 1693 letter that because all creatures depend on God's free will for their existence, there is no possibility of a *demonstration mathematique* that the soul will exist eternally (*To De Torssac*, 31 Mar. 1693, OCM XIX 605). This concession is, in fact, required by his position that one can have a rigorous mathematical demonstration only of those properties that follow necessarily from the nature of an object alone and thus do not depend on the free will of God.[52]

Even so, Malebranche went on to stress in this letter that there are *bonnes preuves* of immortality that appeal to the divine attributes (OCM XIX 605–6). In an earlier exchange with Arnauld, he had held that the conclusions of *preuves*, in contrast to those of *démonstrations*, are merely probable.[53] In the later letter, though, Malebranche made clear that the proof of immortality produces a conclusion that is demonstratively certain. His position there, in particular, is that, given the divine attributes of goodness and justice, it is necessary that God refrain from exercising the power he has to annihilate the soul.[54] Malebranche reaffirmed this position three years later in the *Entretiens sur la mort*, where he had Theodore ask rhetorically whether "the annihilation of the most noble of [God's] creatures accords with his wisdom and his immutability, as well as his justice and his goodness." Theodore concludes, on Malebranche's behalf, that since divine justice requires that God provide for the immortality of the soul, it is "not only faith that reveals this truth [of the soul's immortality]; metaphysics demonstrates it to us" (*E. mort I*, OCM XIII 378).

Malebranche therefore rejected the view, which Descartes had explicitly endorsed, that reason can yield no certain argument for the actual immortality of the soul.[55] Given this difference, there is some irony in Arnauld's objection to Malebranche that Descartes appealed to a clear idea of the soul in order to prove that "the soul can exist being separated from body, from which he brought about his proof of the spirituality and the immortality of the soul."[56] It was Malebranche, not Descartes, who claimed to provide a demonstrative proof of the actual immortality of the soul. Moreover, Malebranche attempted to secure such a proof by appealing not to a clear idea of the soul but rather to the nature of the divine will. It would have been difficult for Descartes to attempt to secure the proof in this manner, given his claim that God's purposes "are all equally hidden in the inscrutable abyss of his wisdom" (*Fifth Rep.*, AT VII 375/CSM II 258).[57] Thus it was left to Malebranche, who was less reluctant to appeal to the nature of divine wisdom, to try to complete the proof of immorality by ruling out the possibility that God will exercise his absolute power to annihilate the soul.

This is not to say that such an attempt was successful. One difficulty here is that Malebranche failed at times to distance himself from Descartes' position that we have only a very limited access to the divine will. Indeed, in the *Lois de la communication des mouvemens* (1712), he made the point (directed, interestingly enough, against Descartes)[58] that the principle of the conservation of the quantity motion can be discovered only by "a species of revelation, such as that which experience [*expérience*] gives, [since] one can neither encompass [*embrasser*] the designs of the Creator, nor comprehend all the relations that they have to his attributes" (OCM XVII–1 55).[59] The more Malebranche stresses our inability to comprehend the relation God's designs bear to his attributes, the more difficult it is for him to argue that any plan that includes the annihilation of the soul is incompatible with God's justice and goodness.

There is another question: whether Malebranche's appeal to the divine attributes allows him to conclude that our soul must have an eternal existence, as opposed to some sort of limited existence in an afterlife. In his 1693 letter on immortality, Malebranche urged that since "the best people are more unhappy in this world than the most evil," it must be the case "that we subsist after death, in order that each receive according to his deeds." Although he recognized the objection that this period of subsistence "may perhaps be for 20 or 30 years, after which God will annihilate us," he responded that "we can receive a reward infinitely worthy of the infinite greatness and liberty of God only through the infinite duration of our happiness" (OCM XIX 605–6). However, Malebranche also admitted in the *Traité de l'amour de Dieu* (1697) that the annihilation of the souls of the just is not inconsistent with God's nature (OCM XIV 25).[60] Even if God's nature requires that some being receive a reward infinitely worthy of him, moreover, it is not clear why human souls must be among the recipients.[61] In the *Entretiens sur la mort* Malebranche made the further point that God must esteem human souls more than he does the bodies to which they are united. Theodore there counters Ariste's objection that God may have limited the life of the human soul to that of its body by arguing that "all that God wills necessarily conforms to order. He loves, he always esteems the things in proportion to which they are more perfect; because loving invincibly his substance, and all that is, the love he has for his creatures is ruled by the relation that they have with him, through the perfections of their being" (E. mort I, OCM XIII 371). Here again, however, the argument entails only that the human soul must live on for some time after the death of the human body.[62]

Malebranche's argument from the divine attributes to the immortality of the soul is therefore not entirely secure. This result raises the question of whether there is open to him another route to immortality that relies on reason alone. I believe that one possible direction he could go is indicated in the writings of Desgabets, one of Malebranche's most unorthodox Cartesian critics. Like Malebranche but unlike Descartes, Desgabets attempted to reconcile the rational certainty of immortality with the fact that God can annihilate the soul by means of his absolute power. His understanding of God's absolute power admittedly differs from Malebranche's since he explained such a power in terms of Descartes' doctrine of the divine creation of the eternal truths, a doctrine that Malebranche himself adamantly opposed. In a move that should have been of interest to Malebranche, however, Desgabets attempted to secure the "indefectibility" (his term for the indestructibility)[63] of substance by appealing to the impossibility of the annihilation of body. Desgabets' novel argument is that such an annihilation is precluded by Descartes' view, deriving from his identification of matter with extension, that there can be no void in nature. Although Desgabets insisted against Malebranche that we have an idea of the soul that yields knowledge of its nature (see §2.2.2 [1]), his remarks on indefectibility are in line with the position, which Malebranche had suggested to Arnauld, that for Cartesians the idea of body best reveals the immortality of our soul.

5.3 Desgabets on the Indefectibility of Substance

5.3.1 Matter, the Void, and Indefectibility

In a 1674 letter Desgabets told his correspondent that "it was 20 years ago that I commenced with the Indefectibility of Creatures that Descartes has not seen, although he has revealed to us the immense extension of the world of which no single atom can be annihilated."[64] This remark corresponds to the argument in Desgabets' unpublished text, the *Traité de l'indéfectibilité des créatures*,[65] that

> it is not possible that the least atom is annihilated and reduced to nothing since there being a void in nature and each body rightly filling its place, there would be no means to reestablish the continuity of all the parts of the world. But I do not think that what one says of the least parcel of matter need not be said also of the world as a whole [*le monde tout entier*], which by this means finds itself perfectly indefectible.[66]

This account of "the world as a whole" serves to counterbalance the view of one scholar that Desgabets was "closer to Gassendi than to Descartes."[67] In his *Traité* Desgabets rejected Gassendi's appeal to imaginary spaces (*espaces imaginaires*) distinct from corporeal substance,[68] professing his loyalty to Descartes' view that "extension in length, breadth and width is the first attribute of matter, or of corporeal substance," and thus that "in the idea of . . . space this same extension is contained and nothing else."[69] Desgabets went on to conclude in this same text that God "has created an extension . . . containing all matter,"[70] a conclusion that undoubtedly is linked to Descartes' claim in the *Principles* that there can be no plurality of worlds given that "this matter, whose nature consists solely in its being an extended substance, already occupies absolutely all the imaginable space in which the other worlds themselves would have to be located" (PP II.22, AT VIII–1 52/CSM I 232).[71] Desgabets simply took over from Descartes the view that all existing bodies are located in the same world in virtue of the fact that there is a single matter or extension that fills every possible space in that world.

In the passage just quoted, Desgabets held that the indefectibility of this single matter follows from the fact that "the least parcel of matter" cannot be annihilated. The argument in his *Traité* against the possibility of such an annihilation again bears the imprint of Descartes' work. In the *Principles* Descartes had considered the suggestion that God can remove a body from a vessel with a concave shape while at the same time preventing any other body from taking its place, concluding that

> it is no less contradictory for us to conceive of a mountain without a valley than it is for us to think of the concavity apart from the extension contained in it, or the extension apart from the substance that is extended ... For when there is nothing between two bodies, it is necessary that they touch each other; and it is manifestly repugnant that they be apart, or have a distance between them, and that this same distance however be nothing: for every distance is a mode of extension, and thus cannot exist without extended substance. (PP II.18, AT VIII–1 50/CSM I 230–31)[72]

Desgabets echoed these remarks when he noted in his *Traité* that "bodies cannot enclose nothingness and be hollow or concave, without containing a real space that is the foundation of the distance there is between the opposite sides, which would no longer be separated from one another, but would touch immediately without any concavity."[73] What is familiar from Descartes is the view here that the sides of the vessel must touch if the vessel itself does not contain something real that is extended. Desgabets' suggestion that there must be a foundation of distance between the sides raises an additional point related to Descartes' claim that there must be a single matter that occupies all possible space. According to Desgabets, the existence of a real space between the sides is required if they are to bear relations of distance to each other. The annihilation of such a space thus brings it about that there are "no means to reestablish the continuity of all parts of the world."[74] While there may seem to be no impossibility in the notion of such an annihilation, Desgabets appears to have assumed that different parts cannot belong to the same world without the continuity that binds them together. Given this assumption, the conception of a single world with an annihilated portion of space must involve the conception of parts belonging to the same world that cannot be parts of the same world. For Desgabets it is impossible for a portion of space, that is, a parcel of matter, to be annihilated. He took it to follow from this result that space or matter as a whole cannot be annihilated and thus is "perfectly indefectible."

This final step in Desgabets' argument is admittedly questionable. Even if no particular portion of matter can be annihilated while the other portions remain, it does not seem to follow that all portions of matter cannot be annihilated at once. Desgabets' full argument for the indefectibility of matter as a whole, however, relies on his claim that "it is properly only modes that coexist in time and that matter considered according to what it is absolutely and essentially contains no time, present, past, or future."[75] On his official view, modifications have a temporal duration that is measured by the succession of motion (see §1.2.3 [1]). Desgabets insisted in his *Traité*, however, that temporal changes pertaining to the modifications of matter are extrinsic to matter itself, just as spatial changes in one who travels from Paris to Rome are extrinsic to that traveler, who remains "the same as before with respect to his person [*quant à sa personne*]."[76] The result here is that matter is not subject to temporal duration since it exists "simply and indivisibly, without duration, with neither beginning nor end."[77] However, for Desgabets the conception of the annihilation of matter as a whole can be only the impossible conception of something that eternally both has existence and lacks it. Thus he concluded that the entire material realm must be as indefectible as portions of it.

This metaphysical argument is rather dense but nonetheless had a profound influence on Regis. The influence is most evident in the *Usage de la raison*, where Regis distinguished between bodily modes, which have temporal duration and thus can come to be and perish, and matter considered simply as unlimited extension or "body in itself," which is eternal and thus absolutely indefectible.[78] In order to illustrate the view that temporal change is extrinsic to matter, moreover, he modified only slightly Desgabets' example in the *Traité*, noting that while a traveler who "comes to Paris from Rome [is] changed extrinsically, and is not the same with respect to place," he is nonetheless "the same as before with respect to his person [*quant à sa personne*]."[79] Again true to Desgabets, Regis concluded in his text that because it is impossible that God wills that something at once both exist and fail to exist, it must be the case that indivisible and eternal substance, of which his primary example is body in itself, must be indefectible.[80]

The claim that matter is eternal is not recognizably Cartesian and, indeed, is linked to the rejection in Desgabets and Regis of Descartes' official doctrine that conservation is merely continuous creation. In *Descartes à l'alambic*, Desgabets took issue particularly with the view in the *Third Meditation* that since the different parts of our life are not dependent on the others, "we cannot subsist, if that which produced us does not conserve us."[81] His response is that Descartes has confounded "the successive duration of our life with our substantial being" and thus has overlooked the fact that while "the parts of the duration of our life need to be conserved, . . . it is false that there are any parts in our substantial being."[82] Desgabets went on to apply this point to the specific case of matter, noting that instead of saying that "God has created matter with movement and repose," Descartes should have said that "God has created matter, and following that he has given it movement, and the repose of its parts, etc."[83] Regis picked up on this radical critique of Descartes, distinguishing in his *Usage de la raison* between God's immediate creation of immutable matter, on the one hand, and his conservation of changes in bodily modes that he brings about mediately by means of secondary causes, on the other.[84]

From a Cartesian standpoint, one weak element of this argument for the distinction between creation and conservation is its premise that matter is not subject to the duration of its modes. In his discussions with Desgabets at the Commercy conferences, the Cardinal de Retz argued on Descartes' behalf that temporal relations among the modifications of a substance serve to measure the duration of that substance.[85] Such an argument is strengthened by Malebranche's own claim that a mode or manner of being "is only the being or substance itself in a certain way" (MC IX, OCM X 105). This claim leaves little room for the position that changes in the modes of matter are merely extrinsic to matter itself.[86] There seem to be Cartesian grounds for rejecting the claim in Desgabets and Regis, central to their argument for the indefectibility of matter as a whole, that matter does not change when its modes do.

While Desgabets' argument for the indefectibility of matter as a whole may not have a solid Cartesian foundation, his argument for the indefectibility of portions of matter does since it is built directly on Descartes' rejection of the possibility of a void in nature. Indeed, to my mind this latter argument provides a more directly Cartesian derivation of the conclusion in the *Synopsis* that "body in general" (portions of extension, not the realm of extension as a whole) cannot perish than does Malebranche's own appeal to the nature of the divine will. Desgabets was in a position to offer such a Cartesian derivation because he considered with more care than did Malebranche the implications of the Cartesian identification of matter with an indefinite extension that must fill all possible space.

To be sure, Desgabets conceded in the passage from his 1674 letter cited above that Descartes himself "has not seen" the indefectibility of creatures. He had in mind here Descartes' concession in the *Second Replies* that reason cannot settle the issue of whether God will annihilate a created substance by means of his "absolute power."[87] I have urged that related considerations involving God's absolute power help to explain why Malebranche did not attempt to derive the property of indestructibility from the clear idea of matter. Desgabets wanted to allow that the existence of created substance is in some sense subject to God's power, while still retaining the claim that such a substance is necessarily and by nature indefectible. His strategy here, unacceptable to Malebranche but related in an interesting way to Descartes' writings, was to invoke the doctrine of the divine creation of the eternal truths.

5.3.2 Eternal Truths, Substance, and the Divine Will

At the Commercy conferences, the Cardinal de Retz objected that Desgabets' claim that *"the will of the Creator is the nature of each thing,* that is to say that each thing is what God has willed it to be" explicitly contradicts his doctrine of the indefectibility of substance and, in particular, its implication that it is not within God's power to make a substance to be corruptible.[88] Retz took this claim from a summary of Desgabets' *Traité*;[89] the claim itself derives from the view in this work that eternal truths such as "that two and two make four, that the whole is greater than its parts, that the three angles of a triangle are equal to two right [angles]"[90] are "necessary and immutable only because God has made them such."[91] The position that eternal truths depend on the divine will is, by Desgabets' own admission, simply borrowed from Descartes.[92] Following Descartes, Desgabets claimed to see in Augustine the view that everything is governed by the divine will.[93] Desgabets' merely repeated Descartes' own words, moreover, when he asserted that "God has produced these truths as their true efficient cause, in the manner in which kings are efficient causes of their laws."[94] What puzzled Retz was how someone faithful to Descartes' view that God's free will extends even to eternal truths, as Desgabets was, could nonetheless adopt of doctrine of the essential indefectibility of substance that "strikes directly against the principles of Augustine and those of Descartes."[95]

Desgabets himself took his doctrine of substantial indefectibility to complement, rather than contradict, Descartes' account of the eternal truths. He emphasized in the *Traité* that truths and substances "are equally immutable and indefectible with a participated and consequent [*participée et de conséquence*] immutability and indefectibility."[96] He went on to argue that just as Descartes can say that eternal truths are immutable "notwithstanding their dependence on God," so he can claim that "immense spaces . . . are no less indefectible, notwithstanding their dependence on the first cause."[97] While there is to my knowledge no record of Desgabets' reaction to the charge of contradiction at the Commercy conferences, his unpublished writings suggest the response that the fact that the indefectibility of substance derives from an immutable divine decree shows that it is perfectly compatible with the principles that underlie the account of the eternal truths that he borrowed from Descartes.[98]

It is noteworthy that Desgabets' reconciliation of substantial indefectibility with this doctrine focuses on the particular case of space or matter. Indeed, he suggested at one point that Descartes himself took this case to be connected in a special way to such a doctrine when he claimed that Descartes attempted "to establish the dependence [on God] of these equally indefectible truths and spaces."[99] Desgabets was on to something here; Descartes had in fact broached the issue of the divine creation of the eternal truths in the course of defending his argument for the impossibility of a void.[100] Arnauld provided the occasion for a discussion of this issue when he expressed to Descartes the worry that the argument against the void in the *Principles* places unacceptable limitations on God's power since it implies that God could not "reduce a body to nothing without being bound immediately to create another [body] of equal quantity, indeed, without the space, which the annihilated body occupied, being understood to be a true and real body in the absence of any new creation."[101] Descartes responded that the difficulty in recognizing the impossibility of a void arises "because we have recourse to the divine power, which you know to be infinite; we attribute to it an effect, without noticing that it involves a contradiction in concept, that is, what cannot be conceived by us." He added, however, that "since every reason for truth and goodness depends on [God's] omnipotence, I would not dare to say that God cannot make a mountain without a valley, or bring it about that one and two are not three. . . . I think the same should be said of a space that is wholly a vacuum, or of nothing that is extended" (29 July 1648, AT V 223–24/CSMK 358–59). This suggests that it is within God's power to create an empty space only in the sense that it is within his power to bring it about from eternity that one and two not be three. However, this suggestion need not conflict with his claim in the *Principles* that the existence of a vacuum is impossible (*PP* I.16, AT VIII–1 49/CSM I 229). In fact, just as Descartes held that it is now the case that one and two necessarily equal three, given that God has ordained it,[102] so he could hold that it is the case due to divine decree that there can be no vacuum in nature. Descartes did not address here the issue of indefectibility, but on Desgabets' view he is committed to the indestructibility of matter since it simply follows from the fact that God cannot create a space without matter that he cannot annihilate a portion of matter.[103]

Desgabets could grant Descartes that God can annihilate matter by means of his absolute power once it is agreed that this power does not differ in kind from God's power over the eternal truths. Yet his main point in the *Traité* is that the view that God has the power to annihilate matter in this sense no more compromises its necessary indestructibility than Descartes' view that God had the power to change the eternal truths from eternity compromises their necessary immutability. Desgabets' use of Descartes' account of the eternal truths is admittedly suspect at times. He argued, for instance, that such an account commits Descartes to the view that substance is as eternal and immutable as the divine act which creates it.[104] It seems open to the Cartesian to object that the eternal and immutable divine act can produce a substance that undergoes changes in time. Desgabets was not far from Descartes, however, when he appealed to the doctrine of the creation of the eternal truths in order to reconcile the indefectibility of matter with the fact that God can by his absolute power create a void by annihilating a portion of matter or extension.[105]

The very fact that this Cartesian reconciliation draws on Descartes' account of the eternal truths reveals that it is not open to Malebranche. In his *Critique de la Critique*, a response to Foucher's criticisms of the *Recherche*, Desgabets believed he was defending Malebranche, as well as Augustinian orthodoxy, when he argued that eternal truths have been "made and established" by God "with a sovereign indifference."[106] Yet Malebranche made clear that he could accept Desgabets' reading neither of Augustine nor of his own work.[107] Malebranche claimed to inherit from Augustine an account of the vision of ideas in the divine intellect that is directly incompatible with the position, found principally in Descartes, that eternal truths depend on God's free will.[108] The view that the annihilation of portions of matter is impossible yet still within the scope of God's absolute power, which Desgabets tied to Descartes' doctrine of the creation of the eternal truths, is simply a nonstarter for Malebranche.

As we have seen, Malebranche himself admitted that the annihilation of any created substance is possible, yet he attempted to save the demonstrability of substantial indestructibility by appealing to the fact that such an annihilation is incompatible with the divine attributes of justice and goodness. Another way of saving demonstrability, which is opened up by Desgabets' remarks, is to argue that the distinctively Cartesian doctrine that the nature of matter consists in extension precludes a certain sort of destruction of matter. It was clear to Descartes that the identification of matter with extension rules out the possibility of space without matter, but if it were granted Desgabets that the destruction of a portion of matter entails the creation of space without matter, Descartes' argument could be extended to rule out the possibility of such destruction. Since Malebranche accepted Descartes' identification of matter with extension, this concession to Desgabets would commit him to ruling out as well the possibility of the destruction of particular portions of matter. Such a commitment need not be inconsistent with Malebranche's belief that God is free to annihilate matter as a whole since it precludes only the claim that God can annihilate this matter in a piecemeal fashion by destroying certain portions of it.

Desgabets urged in *Descartes à l'alambic* that Descartes should have carried his "insight" (*lumière*) that the notion of a void implies a contradiction "right to the indefectibility of creatures, . . . because if God would annihilate a grain of sand, there would be space without body."[109] What is significant, in light of Malebranche's writings, is that the insight that carries the Cartesian to the doctrine of substantial indefectibility concerns the nature of body rather than the nature of the soul. Malebranche held that Cartesians need the idea of body in order to see by way of contrast that the soul is an indivisible substance and thus indestructible and immortal, but Desgabets' remark indicates that body yields what for Cartesians is the best case for the claim that substance is by nature indestructible.

Desgabets' own account of substantial indefectibility does not focus exclusively on the case of matter. After all, he urged that such indefectibility is required by the fact that substance, as opposed to its modes, is eternal by nature. I have urged, however, that this sort of distinction between substance and mode is questionable from a Cartesian perspective. Desgabets was most securely Cartesian when he attempted to derive the indefectibility of substance from the impossibility of a void in nature. It is true that this impossibility directly yields, at most, only the indefectibility of portions of matter. However, perhaps the most natural way to go beyond this limited conclusion is by arguing that because the soul is a substance, it must have the same property of indefectibility that substantial portions of matter possess. Regis in fact offered just this sort of argument when he noted in his *Système* that since "an extension, which is the essential attribute of body, never corrupts itself; and it is only the modes that make it such and such a body, that perish," it is obvious that "thought, which is the essential attribute of mind, cannot be corrupted. And it is only the modes that determine it to be such and such a mind, for example, to be the soul of Pierre, of Paul, of Jean, etc. that are destroyed."[110]

Regis' claim that death destroys the modes that determine thought to be "such and such a mind" broaches difficulties related to the issue of the survival of the person, difficulties that, as I have indicated, neither Descartes nor Malebranche forthrightly addressed. For our present purposes, however, the most salient feature of Regis' remarks is its appeal to the incorruptibility of extension in support of the conclusion that thought, or thinking substance, is incorruptible. While Malebranche himself did not see fit to support the doctrine of the indestructibility of the soul in precisely this manner, Regis' argument is similar in structure to the argument in the *Recherche* that the soul must be capable of an infinity of different modifications after death since body is so capable.

At one point in the *Supplément* Desgabets himself claimed that the soul must be capable of an infinity of different thoughts given that matter can over time receive an infinity of different forms. He went on to note that he rather preferred to discuss changes "that occur or can occur in matter than those of angels, of souls, because it is commonly believed that corporeal things are better known than spiritual ones."[111] This common belief was, of course, the very one to which Malebranche took the Cartesians to be committed, yet it was Desgabets rather than Malebranche who emphasized that the Cartesian can see the property of indestructibility most clearly in the nature of body. I mentioned previously that Arnauld's objection to Malebranche that Descartes had a clear idea of the soul that allowed him to establish its immortality is ironic since it was Malebranche, not Descartes, who attempted to establish by reason that the soul is actually immortal. I would simply note, in closing, the further irony that Malebranche's thesis that any knowledge of the nature of the soul must derive from the clear idea of body is better reflected in the discussion of substantial indefectibility in the work of his critic, Desgabets, than it is in his own account of immortality.

six

FREEDOM

Arnauld offered spirituality, immortality, and freedom as examples of properties that Cartesians cannot demonstrate of the soul without the help of a "clear and distinct vision" of its nature. Although Arnauld's example of immortality raises some difficulties, as I have pointed out in the previous chapter, it is the example of freedom (*liberté*) that is perhaps the most problematic for him. We will discover that Arnauld's theological sensibilities led him, in fact, to reject Descartes' account of our property of freedom in terms of an undetermined power of choice. Malebranche himself readily accepted such an account, however, holding throughout his philosophical career that we have in us this sort of undetermined power. Of the two Cartesians, then, it was Malebranche rather than Arnauld who worked with Descartes' own notion of freedom.

Admittedly, the relation between Descartes and Malebranche on the issue of the freedom of the will is not entirely straightforward. An initial complication is that the two had different conceptions of the relation between freedom and the will. Descartes' comment that we experience that all our volitional actions "come directly from our soul, and seem to depend on it alone" (PS I.17, AT XI 342/CSM I 335) virtually identifies the will with the power to act freely.[1] By contrast, Malebranche insisted from the start that since there are features of our will that derive from God rather than from us, our will itself must be distinguished from the power involved in our free actions. That there is nothing in Descartes that matches Malebranche's complex account of the different kinds of acts and dispositions of the will further complicates the issue.

Nevertheless, Malebranche's discussion of freedom and the will does overlap with Descartes' remarks on these matters. I want to argue that the overlap is such that Cartesians cannot simply dismiss Malebranche's conclusion that we know our own will only in a confused way and thus do not know it through a clear idea of the soul. The defense of this conclusion that derives from his discussion of the will in general (as opposed to free will in particular) draws on the claim, which Descartes explicitly endorsed in at least one text, that our will has certain habits or dispositions that are distinct from its volitional acts. On the other hand, the defense of the conclusion indicated by Malebranche's discussion of free will in particular draws on the position, broached in Descartes' later writings, that we cannot comprehend how God could know which actions will arise from our undetermined and free will.

The starting point for Malebranche's discussion of the will in general is a conception of the will in terms of bodily motion. He subsequently came to emphasize, however, that such a conception fails to reveal the nature of the habits or dispositions of the will that prepare for its actions. Arnauld took particular pains to respond on Descartes' behalf to this later and more negative view. Here as elsewhere, though, Arnauld revealed surface difficulties with Malebranche's position while overlooking its deeper point. In this case Arnauld failed to come to grips with Malebranche's claim that those who are faithful to Descartes' own views must take the will to have a hidden structure the nature of which they cannot clearly understand.

Malebranche's discussion of free will in particular begins with the claim, inherited from Descartes, that we are conscious of a power of action in us that is undetermined. What is most interesting here is not Malebranche's unconvincing defense of this claim, but rather his attempt to respond to the objection that our freedom encroaches on God's power. This objection was, of course, especially pressing for Malebranche, given his occasionalist position that God alone can be a real cause. Yet his response to this objection is related in important ways to the writings of Descartes and the Cartesians. Descartes himself had raised, without fully addressing, the basic difficulty that our undetermined freedom seems to be incompatible with God's preordination of our actions. There is reason to think, moreover, that Malebranche's own attempts to extricate himself from this difficulty draw on the treatment of the relation between God's creation of motion and our freedom to move body provided by Claude Clerselier (1614–84) and Johann Clauberg (1622–65), two Cartesians with special ties to Descartes. Whereas Malebranche was confident that he could give an account in Cartesian terms of how God's power leaves our free actions undetermined, however, he emphasized in his final work that we cannot understand how God could have infallible knowledge of such actions. The discussion of this negative point concerning God's knowledge returns us to a persistent, if somewhat overlooked, theme in Malebranche's work that Cartesians do not know the soul through a clear idea of its nature.

6.1 The Nature of the Will

6.1.1 Bodily Motion and the Will

In §5.2.2 (2) I mentioned Malebranche's claim that since we cannot know mental faculties through a clear idea of the soul, we must conceive them on analogy with the faculties revealed by the clear idea of matter or extension. At this point I want to focus in particular on his comparison of the mental faculty of will to the bodily faculty of motion. Toward the start of the *Recherche*, Malebranche held that just as matter has the capacity to receive various motions, so the soul is capable of receiving various "inclinations" (RV I.1, OCM I 45/LO 4). He also noted that inclinations, like motions, involve relations to something external; motions relate a body to other bodies while inclinations relate the soul to various goods (OCM I 42/LO 2–3). For Malebranche all of these inclinations are related to something external. The inclinations that we have in virtue of our union with the body (our passions) lead us to love of our body,[2] while the inclinations toward the general good that we have in virtue of our union with God, (our natural inclinations) lead us to love of God himself, "who alone is the general good because he alone contains in himself all goods" (OCM I 47/LO 5).[3]

Malebranche defined the will itself as "the impression or natural movement that carries us toward general and indeterminate good" that is God (OCM I 46/LO 5). Such a definition is, to be sure, more Augustinian than Cartesian. As Alquié has noted, Malebranche's account of the will is "faithful to Saint Augustine, for whom the tendency toward God and the desire for happiness are one and the same."[4] There is in Descartes no similar identification of the will with a tendency toward God, yet he did anticipate the Malebranchean account of the will in terms of motion when he spoke of "the movements of the will that constitute joy, sadness and desire" (*To Chanut*, 1 Feb. 1647, AT IV 602/CSMK 306).[5] While the claim that the will involves a movement of the soul is admittedly infrequent in Descartes,[6] Malebranche's talk of the will as a kind of motion is not entirely foreign to his system.

In Book Four of the *Recherche*, entitled "Of Inclinations, or of the Natural Movements of Mind" (OCM II 9/LO 265), Malebranche attempted to extend the analogy to bodily motion that he had introduced at the start of this work. In this later section he began by noting that "if God in creating this world had produced an infinitely extended matter without impressing any movement on it, no body would have been different from any other" (RV IV.1, OCM II 10/LO 265). Thinking no doubt of the claim in Descartes that "all variety in matter, all the diversity of its forms, depends on motion" (PP II.23, AT VIII-1 52/CSM I 232), Malebranche held that a world without motion would be one without "this succession of forms and this variety of bodies that bring about the entire beauty of the universe, and that lead all minds to admire the infinite wisdom of him who governs it." However, since "the inclinations of minds are to the spiritual world as movement is to the material world," it follows that "the difference inclinations make in minds is rather like [*assez semblable*] the difference that movements make in bodies" and that "the inclinations of minds and the movements of bodies together make all there is of beauty among created things." Because the divine attributes require that God create a world that is beautiful, "every mind must have some inclinations just as bodies have different kinds of movements" (OCM II 10/LO 265).

Whereas in this passage Malebranche claimed that minds must have inclinations, earlier in the *Recherche* he had made the contrasting point that the will is not essential to mind. In his discussion of "pure mind" in Book Three, he defended the thesis that thought constitutes the essence of mind by noting that while "no mind can be conceived of that does not think," still "it is quite easy to conceive of one that does not sense or imagine, and that does not even will, just as unextended matter cannot be conceived of, though it is possible to conceive of matter that is neither earth nor metal, neither round nor square, and that even has no movement" (RV III–1.1, OCM I 382/LO 198). That mind without will and matter without motion are equally conceivable may seem to conflict not only with the point, expressed in Book Four, that minds must have inclinations but even more directly with the claim, immediately following this passage, that "just as immovable matter is inconceivable, so a mind incapable of willing or of some natural inclination is inconceivable." Such a claim, however, is prefaced by the remark that it follows from God's nature that he would create nothing as useless as mind without will or matter without motion (OCM I 382/LO 198). The indication here is that the inconceivability of mind without inclination or matter without motion derives from something other than the nature of mind or of matter. I believe that Malebranche was attempting to indicate the external source of this inconceivability when he concluded that the power to will is "inseparable from" though not "essential to" mind, just as the capacity to be moved is inseparable from though not essential to matter (OCM I 383/LO 199).[7]

There is, however, an important disanalogy between inclination and motion. In Book Four Malebranche noted that without motion there would be absolutely no difference among various bodies; the material world would be "but a mass of matter or extension" (RV IV.1, OCM II /LO 265). Although he did not address the issue explicitly, Malebranche surely would have wanted to allow that minds can be distinguished even apart from inclination.[8] In fact, he did say that the difference inclinations make among minds is only "rather like" the difference motions make among bodies. Malebranche's considered view appears to be that minds without inclinations can differ from each other but cannot have the wondrous variety of desires and strivings that our minds have. Whereas motion is required for the diversity as well as the beauty of the material world, then, inclination is required only for the beauty of the spiritual world.[9]

After drawing the analogy in Book Four between the beauty deriving from the inclination of the will and the beauty deriving from bodily motion, Malebranche added that we can know the sort of inclinations the soul must have only through reason. Had our nature not been corrupted, "all we would have to do would be to consult ourselves, and we would recognize through the inner sentiment that we have of what occurs in us all the inclinations we naturally must have" (OCM II 10–11/LO 266). The distinction between inner sentiment and reason is elsewhere linked to the thesis that inner sentiment yields only a confused knowledge of the soul. However, such a thesis is not suggested by the implication, expressed in this passage, that were our nature not corrupted we could know through inner sentiment which inclinations our soul naturally must have. Malebranche went on to note that even this corruption does not prevent us from being "internally convinced" [*intérieurement convaincus*] that pleasure is good and that whatever is the cause of our pleasure is worthy of love. The corruption of our nature merely prevents us from seeing that God alone can be worthy of our love since he alone is capable of causing our pleasure (RV IV.10, OCM II 82–83/LO 310).

The *Recherche*, in fact, does not emphasize that our inner sentiment of the will is confused. There is no mention of inclinations, for instance, in the discussion in this text of the thesis that we know the soul only through consciousness and not through an idea (RV III–2.7, OCM I 451–53/LO 237–39).[10] The point that we do not know our will through a clear idea of our soul emerges only later, in the commentary on the *Recherche* in the *Éclaircissements*. For instance, in *Éclaircissement I*, which concerns the brief discussion of human freedom toward the start of the *Recherche*, Malebranche stressed that "we have no clear idea, nor even an inner sentiment, of this constancy or impression or natural impulse toward the good" (OCM III 22/LO 550). It is true that his subsequent explanation focuses more on the fact that we lack an inner sentiment of this impulse than on the fact that our knowledge of the impulse is confused. Thus he emphasized that we both "do not sense in us what is natural, commonplace, and always the same [and] are not even aware of our habits, and whether we are worthy of the love or wrath of God." Yet he also noted that our knowledge of volitional impulses must be confused since if we had never desired particular goods inner sentiment "would not enable us to discover whether we were capable of ... wishing for such goods" (OCM III 23/LO 550). We have applied to the case of inclination Malebranche's conclusion that since we can know the sensations of which the soul is capable only through *expérience*, it must be that we do not know the nature of these sensations through a clear idea of the soul (see §2.3.2 [1]).

I have urged that we understand the conclusion that we do not know our sensations through a clear idea to say that we do not have a clear objective view of the way in which these states modify the soul. In light of this understanding, it is signficant that toward the end of his defense in *Éclaircissement XI* of the thesis in the *Recherche* that we do not know our soul through its idea, Malebranche made the point that "we do not know what the soul's dispositions consist in which make it readier to act and to represent objects to itself [and] cannot even conceive what such dispositions could consist in" (OCM III 169/LO 636). In this passage he emphasizes in particular the limitations of our knowledge of the spiritual habits that ready us for action as well as our knowledge of the moral worth of our will. His brief remarks in this text concerning these matters, especially those regarding moral worth, are problematic in certain respects, yet these remarks, when read in light of Malebranche's more detailed discussions in other writings, serve to reinforce his basic position that Cartesians do not know the faculty of the will in the clear, objective manner in which they know bodily faculties.

6.1.2 Spiritual Habits, Moral Worth, and the Will

(1) Spiritual Habits and Inner Dispositions. In Éclaircissement XI Malebranche attempted to illustrate our ignorance of the dispositions of the soul by noting that "we cannot ascertain through reason whether the soul by itself separated from body, or considered apart from the relation to body, is capable of habits and memory." The fact that one cannot ascertain whether the soul considered by itself has such elements is contrasted with the fact that "one sees without pain in what consists the facility that the animal spirits have to be distributed in the nerves, in which they have already flowed several times" (OCM III 169/ LO 637). Malebranche was drawing here on his discussion of memory and the habits in Book Two of the *Recherche*. In this discussion he had identified memory with the traces imprinted in the brain by the flow of the "animal spirits" (i.e., the rarefied parts of the blood),[11] which traces explain the facility with which the brain receives the same impressions at different times (RV II–1.5, OCM I 224–25/LO 106).[12] He went on to note that since habits "consist in the facility the spirits have acquired for flowing to certain places in our body" (OCM I 228/LO 108), there is, in fact, no intrinsic difference between memory and other habits.[13] Malebranche admitted that his account of memory and the habits is not "perfectly demonstrated in every detail" but nonetheless held in effect that any other account must be similar to his own in order to have any hope of being intelligible as well as empirically adequate (OCM I 227/LO 108).

The identification in this section of the *Recherche* of memory and other habits with features of the body is somewhat odd, given that Book Two as a whole is devoted to a discussion of the imagination as a faculty of the soul.[14] Malebranche himself acknowledged the oddity in Éclaircissement VII, a brief commentary on this section. He excused himself, though, by pointing out that since neither he nor anyone else has a clear idea of the soul, there is little that can be said about the nature of its dispositions. "For what means is there to explain clearly what the dispositions are that the operations of the soul leave in it, which dispositions are its habits, since we do not distinctly know the nature of the soul?" (OCM III 67/LO 577). According to Malebranche, it is even possible that the facility for thought and action consists solely in the manner in which God causes certain occurrent thoughts in the soul. In this case there would be nothing in the soul itself corresponding to dispositional memory and habits (OCM III 67–68/LO 577). This conclusion, namely, that one cannot simply rule out the identification of spiritual memory and habits with features of the divine will, helps to explain the claim in Éclaircissement XI that reason alone cannot determine whether the soul considered in itself is capable of these elements.

Nonetheless, Malebranche held in Éclaircissement VII that certain "proofs from Theology" lead him to believe that "after the soul's action there remain in its substance certain changes that really dispose it to the same action" (OCM III 68/LO 578). While he did not elaborate on these proofs in this 1678 text, he did indicate the nature of one such proof in the 1684 *Traité de Morale*. In the later work he made the point that God "does not judge a soul according to actual and passing movements; he judges it according to what he finds in it that is stable and permanent" (*Mor.* I.3, OCM XI 48).[15] Thus there must be stable and permanent dispositions in the soul for God to judge. Malebranche admitted that the soul does not have the sort of immediate access to its dispositions that it has to its actual and passing thoughts since "one does not sense habits, as one knows only what passes actually in the soul" (OCM XI 48).[16] This admission is in line with his claim in *Éclaircissement* XI that if he did not have counterbalancing reasons to conclude that the soul has dispositions, he would be led by inner sentiment to judge that his soul has no habits (OCM III 169/LO 637). Nevertheless, his argument in the *Traité de Morale*, which is not clearly anticipated in the *Recherche*, is that theological considerations involving the nature of divine judgment provide sufficient reason to infer that the soul has habits distinct from its actual thoughts and volitions.

Some of Malebranche's remarks give the impression that the conclusion that we do not have a clear idea of the soul follows simply from the premise that we cannot know the existence of spiritual habits directly by means of inner sentiment.[17] However, he allowed that we can know corporeal habits through a clear idea of body even though we can only infer the existence of particular habits on the basis of the evidence. His more considered position is that since no sort of investigation of the self can clearly reveal the nature of spiritual habits, it must be the case that we have no clear idea of the soul. Malebranche had this sort of position in mind when he asked his Cartesian critics in *Éclaircissement* XI: "[W]hat could one conceive that is capable of augmenting the facility that the soul has to act or to think? For my part, I must admit that I comprehend none of this. In vain do I consult myself in order to discover these dispositions; I have no answer for myself" (OCM III 169/LO 637).[18] According to Malebranche, we can readily understand corporeal habits in terms of the well-worn paths in the body that allow for the motion of the animal spirits. While he allowed that we can have some (very imperfect) understanding of our actual inclinations when we conceive of them in terms of the motion of the animal spirits, he also held that we have absolutely no understanding of what in the ectoplasm of the soul could possibly correspond to the open bodily pathways.[19]

For various reasons, some of which I have already mentioned, Malebranche held that our ignorance of the nature of spiritual habits does not prevent us from positing habitual dispositions in the soul. Despite his disdain for scholastic qualities and powers, Descartes himself had accepted the existence of such dispositions. Thus in a letter that addresses the critique of the schoolmen offered on his behalf by Regius, Descartes cautioned against a blanket rejection of active qualities by pointing out that on his own view there are two different kinds of dispositions that serve as the principle of actions in objects: the first "are purely material and depend only on the configuration or other arrangement of the parts [of bodies]," whereas the second "are immaterial or spiritual, like the states of faith, grace and so on of which the theologians speak" (*To Regius*, Jan. 1642, AT III 503–4/CSMK 208). This suggestion that dispositions involve causal activity conflicts with Malebranche's occasionalism. Moreover, Descartes' offhand reference in this letter to spiritual dispositions "like the states of faith, grace and so on," which fairly reflects his lack of concern with these dispositions, can be contrasted with the detailed account in Malebranche of the habitual dispositions that derive from the necessary and the free action of the soul as well as from divine grace.[20] Nonetheless, Descartes' remarks to Regius indicate a basic, if unexplored, commitment to spiritual dispositions. Such a commitment is strengthened by remarks in the *Passions of the Soul*, Descartes' final work, that appeal to "habits in the soul that dispose it to certain thoughts; they are different from these thoughts, but they can produce them, and reciprocally be produced by them" (*PS* III.161, AT XI 453/CSM I 387). These texts thus reveal a precedent in Descartes for the fundamental tenet in Malebranche's *Traité de Morale* that the soul has habitual dispositions that are distinct from but nonetheless linked to its acts.[21]

The fact that Descartes allowed for habitual dispositions distinct from occurrent thoughts is not too surprising; he held, after all, that innate ideas exist only in a mental faculty or power when they are not actually perceived (see §3.1.1 [2]). He had prepared for the admission of unperceived features of mind, moreover, when he told Arnauld that while "we are always actually conscious of those acts or operations of our mind," we are not always conscious of "faculties, or potentialities [*potentiarum*], ... unless potentially [*potentiâ*]" (*Fourth Rep.*, AT VII 246/CSM II 172). Thus Malebranche was simply following Descartes' lead when he asserted in the *Traité de Morale* that "one knows only what passes actually in the soul." To be sure, Descartes went on to say to Arnauld that "we may deny that [a faculty] to be in the mind, if we are not capable of becoming conscious of it" (AT VII 247/CSM II 172). Descartes himself did not fully anticipate the conclusion in Malebranche that "we do not have an inner sentiment of all that we are" (*Écl. I*, OCM III 23/LO 550). The remarks in the *Passions*, however, can be seen as supporting such a conclusion. Descartes' position in this work, namely, that the habits or dispositions of the soul are distinct from its thoughts, together with his view elsewhere that all of its acts or operations are thoughts,[22] entail that the soul's habitual dispositions are distinct from its acts or operations. It simply follows from the claim to Arnauld that the soul can be conscious only of its acts and operations, then, that it cannot be conscious of such dispositions. The admission of habits in the *Passions* thus creates difficulties for Descartes' official position that "there can be nothing in me of which I am in no manner conscious" (*First Rep.*, AT VII 107/CSM II 77).

This admission creates difficulties as well for Descartes' response to Gassendi's point that one can know the nature of the soul only by means of "a certain chemical-like labor." We have seen in §1.3.2 that Descartes rejected out of hand the need for such labor and that Arnauld defended such a rejection in his *Vraies et fausses idées* (1683) by claiming that we can distinctly know our thoughts merely by means of consciousness. Arnauld applied this defense to the case of the will in the third volume of his *Réflexions Philosophiques et Théologiques* (1686), which concerns the theory of divine grace in Malebranche's *Traité de la Nature et de la Grâce*. In prefatory remarks in this volume, Arnauld cited Augustine in support of the view that "each of us knows what he wills, what he desires, or the design that he has had in making such a choice, with the same evidence that he sees with the eyes of the body." He went on to counter the suggestion in Malebranche that he is confused about the nature of his inner dispositions by asserting that "this M. Arnauld is not as stupid as you represent. He knows as other men what passes in himself."[23] These remarks seem to me to leave Arnauld rather vulnerable to Malebranche's 1687 response, in the first of his *Deux Lettres* on the *Réflexions Philosophiques et Théologiques*, that "there is a great difference between *what actually passes* in the soul, and its *inner dispositions*." Malebranche insisted that Arnauld's claim that "*one knows certainly what one wills, and what one desires*" is perfectly compatible with the view that "man does not know his *inner dispositions* if they are not actually excited" (OCM VIII 796).[24] While Malebranche allowed that Augustine's remarks support the thesis that "we have an inner sentiment of what passes actually in us," he also noted that there is nothing in Augustine's writings that implies that "we know well our inner dispositions, when they are not actually aroused" (OCM VIII 797).

Neither Malebranche nor Arnauld explicitly cite Descartes in this exchange. Although Descartes' denial of mental faculties inaccessible to consciousness is in line with Arnauld's contention that the mind has access to all of its states, his admission in the *Passions* that the soul has habits or dispositions distinct from its thoughts supports rather Malebranche's claim that the mind has a structure hidden from inner sentiment. There is no doubt that Descartes and Arnauld alike affirmed what Margaret Wilson has called the doctrine of the "epistemological transparency" of the mind, according to which the mind in some sense knows all of its own states "through and through, unproblematically."[25] Malebranche's remarks on the dispositions of the will help us to see, however, that this doctrine itself is far from unproblematic on Descartes' own terms.[26]

It should now be clear why I said earlier that Malebranche could not have accepted Process Cartesianism, the thesis that we have incorrigible knowledge of inner mental processes or structures connected to our thoughts. In his response to Arnauld's claim that we are conscious of all that passes within us, Malebranche stressed that inner sentiment can yield no knowledge of the existence of dispositions that are linked to the acts of the soul. As we have seen, though, he also made the point that we do not clearly know the nature of such dispositions. With respect to this point, Malebranche could again draw on Descartes' remarks for support. In his letter to Regius, Descartes held that corporeal dispositions depend on the configuration and arrangement of bodily parts. He also alluded to spiritual dispositions but failed to indicate the specific features of the soul on which these dispositions depend. It is difficult to see what more he could say here; as Malebranche urged, consciousness does not clearly reveal the nondispositional states of the soul that serve to ground its dispositions in the same manner in which the configurations of a body ground its dispositions. Given his discussion of the cogito argument, to be sure, Malebranche could hardly deny Descartes' claim that "we cannot will without knowing that we will"

(*To Mersenne*, 28 Jan. 1641, AT III 295/CSMK 172). Yet though he was bound to the position that the soul has immediate and incorrigible knowledge of the existence of acts of the will, Malebranche was able to argue that neither Descartes nor other Cartesians have the resources to explain the nature of the dispositions of this mental faculty. He thus provided powerful Cartesian reasons for rejecting Process Cartesianism.

(2) *Moral Worth and Knowledge of the Will.* After claiming in *Éclaircissement XI* that he cannot understand what in the soul could correspond to its habits, Malebranche made the point that "the enlightened man does not know with evidence whether he is worthy of love or hatred" (OCM III 170/LO 637). As in the case of the claim concerning spiritual habits, it is helpful to interpret this point about our moral worth in light of his detailed account of the will in the *Traité de Morale*. I have noted the view in this work that God judges the soul according to its stable dispositions rather than according to its temporary acts. Malebranche held there that the soul can be justified before God only if it has a love of God "from immutable order [that is] habitual, free and dominant" (*Mor.* I.3, OCM XI 50). This love must be habitual and free in the sense that it is a habitual disposition tied exclusively to inclinations that we freely choose and thus are in our power to reject. Such a disposition differs in kind from habitual dispositions tied exclusively to the natural inclinations, which are voluntary and unconstrained but not in our power to reject.[27] The habitual love that justifies, moreover, must be in accord with an immutable order that explicates "relations of perfection" (*rapports de perfection*).[28] Since God is infinitely more perfect than we are, such an order dictates that we take God to have more importance than we ourselves have.[29] The love that derives from the immutable order of perfections is therefore one that is directed primarily toward God and only secondarily toward the self.[30]

According to Malebranche, however, the mere fact that an individual possesses a free habitual disposition in accord with immutable order cannot make that person morally worthy before God. The *Traité* indicates that even the sinner who is morally unworthy must possess such a disposition. Malebranche insisted in this text that such a person has the power to freely choose to act from a love of immutable order, and that he could not have this power if he lacked any free habitual disposition to act in this manner (*Mor.* I.4, OCM XI 53–55). What renders this sinner reprobate rather than just is simply the fact that this disposition in him is subordinate to the disposition to act out of a disordered love of self. Thus did Malebranche conclude that one who is morally worthy must have a habitual disposition that is not only free, but also dominant.

The discussion in the *Traité de Morale* reveals, then, that the difficulty of determining whether we are morally worthy reduces to the difficulty of determining whether we have a free habitual disposition that both reflects immutable order and is dominant. In *Éclaircissement XI* Malebranche took the very fact that we have this sort of difficulty to reveal that our inner sentiment does not yield a clear idea of our soul. Citing Saint Paul's remark that God alone can judge,[31]

Malebranche concluded that "as one has a clear idea of order, if one also had a clear idea of the soul through the inner sentiment that one has of oneself, one would know clearly whether the soul conformed to order; one would know whether one is righteous or not" (OCM III 170/LO 637). Since we have a clear idea of order, we can determine whether or not an action is morally correct. From the fact that our inner sentiment does not reveal whether we have a dominant and free disposition that conforms to order, however, it follows that such a sentiment does not provide access to a clear idea of the soul.

In his *Vraies et fausses idées*, Arnauld was concerned to respond to this argument in order to defend the more orthodox position that inner sentiment yields clear and perfect knowledge of the soul. He argued initially that to be acceptable the claim that we have a clear idea of order must allow for the evident fact that we can be mistaken about whether an action conforms to order. He then went on to note that "if I can be deceived in thinking that something conforms to order which is not so conformed, I could know perfectly the state of my soul without knowing with evidence whether it was conformed to order." Arnauld used the example of Saint Paul, who, prior to his conversion, thought he was conforming to order in subjecting the Christians to persecution. His error did not derive from any deficiency in his knowledge of his soul; Paul knew clearly his intention to persecute the Christians. According to Arnauld, he was mistaken rather because he did not see clearly that the action he intended did not conform to order.[32]

Malebranche was in no position to reject Arnauld's claim that Paul knew through inner sentiment the existence of his actual intention to persecute the Christians. Though the view that the clear idea of order does not allow for error is perhaps suggested by Malebranche's unfortunate claim that clear ideas yield knowledge through a simple view, moreover, his considered position is that we can be mistaken about what conforms to order even though we have access to a clear idea of its nature.[33] He therefore need not deny that ignorance of order was the primary source of Saint Paul's mistaken beliefs concerning his persecution of the Christians. Nonetheless, Malebranche could protest that Arnauld's example does not fairly address his view in *Éclaircissement* XI that even those who know what conforms to order cannot know whether they are righteous. In this text, after all, he had emphasized Saint Peter's ignorance of the weakness in his character that led to his denial of Christ (OCM III 170/LO 637). It is clear that Saint Peter was ignorant not of what conforms to order but rather of how he was disposed to act.

In his *Vraies et fausses idées*, however, Arnauld did address the point of this particular example in a manner that draws attention to his claim elsewhere in this text that even Malebranche must admit the knowledge that we have through a clear idea of particular bodily properties relies essentially on *expérience* and thus is irreducibly empirical (see §2.2.1 [2]). If Malebranche is sharp enough to realize that he must admit this, Arnauld asked, "why then does he claim that it is a proof that we do not have a clear idea of our soul that we often need experience [*expérience*] in order to know what the inner dispositions are concerning virtue, or what [the soul's] forces are for remaining firm in its duty?"[34] In one sense Malebranche must deny that experience can afford the soul access to its inner dispositions. His talk of our sensing these dispositions notwithstanding,[35] Malebranche's official position is that inner sentiment can directly reveal only the acts of the soul and not its dispositions. When he spoke of our ignorance concerning our moral worth, he sometimes had in mind our inability to contemplate directly our inner dispositions.[36]

Arnauld tended to discount the possibility that our soul has certain features that are inaccessible to consciousness; on this issue, I think, he exhibited less insight than Malebranche. However, in the previous passage Arnauld made the interesting point that the existence of such features poses no threat to the doctrine that we have a clear idea of our soul. He suggested that we could infer to the existence of hidden inner dispositions on the basis of acts accessible to consciousness, in much the same way that we infer to the existence of unobservable inner structures of bodies on the basis of their observable features. Given that the necessity of an inference to inner bodily structures is consistent with our possession of a clear idea of body, so the objection goes, the necessity of an inference to inner mental dispositions need not be inconsistent with our possession of a clear idea of our soul.

Malebranche left himself open to this line of objection; his comments regarding Saint Peter suggest that the mere fact that our knowledge of our dispositions is subject to disconfirmation reveals that we do not have a clear idea of our soul. Nonetheless, Arnauld's claim that we can know through experience "what the inner dispositions are" is itself open to objection. Such a claim seems to concern knowledge not only of the existence of the dispositions, but also of their nature. While Malebranche would have some difficulty in denying that experience can yield the knowledge that certain dispositions exist, he had well-founded reasons to deny that it can yield knowledge of their nature. Even though experience allows us to posit spiritual dispositions as well as unobservable bodily structures, it does not reveal what in the soul grounds these dispositions in the way in which the structures ground bodily dispositions. A spiritual disposition is for us merely a "something-I-know-not-what" that underlies and is somehow linked to the various acts of the soul.

There is a hint of this point about the obscurity of the nature of dispositions in Malebranche's comment in *Éclaircissement* XI that if we had access to a clear idea of the soul we would "know exactly all its inner dispositions toward good and evil" (OCM III 170/LO 637). It is true that his main argument in this text from our ignorance concerning our moral worth to our lack of access to such an idea focuses on the fact that we do not know with certainty the existence of certain spiritual dispositions. Such an argument is problematic for reasons indicated by Arnauld. Given Malebranche's view in the *Traité de Morale* that our moral worth depends on which free habitual disposition dominates in us, however, it simply follows from the fact that we do not in general understand the nature of our spiritual dispositions that we lack in particular a clear knowledge of that which renders us morally worthy. Arnauld could perhaps be excused for overlooking the point that we lack this sort of knowledge of our moral worth; after all, Malebranche had failed to draw attention to its importance in *Éclaircissement XI*. Yet Malebranche did emphasize to Arnauld our lack of an understanding of the nature of our spiritual dispositions. Because Arnauld overlooked this position, he failed to address an element of Malebranche's account of our moral worth that provides particularly direct support for the thesis that we do not have a clear idea of the nature of the soul.

Malebranche's claim that our moral worth depends on habitual dispositions is not the only element of his account that bears on this thesis; his claim that these dispositions are free is also important. I have indicated that the dispositions are free for Malebranche in the sense that they are linked to the free acts of the will, as opposed to its natural and necessary actions. In the 1678 *Éclaircissement I*, Malebranche first broached the point that we have only a confused inner sentiment, not a clear idea, of the source of our free actions (OCM III 30/LO 554). He returned to this point in 1715, noting in his final work that while inner sentiment reveals our freedom, it does not display those features of our soul that explain God's certain knowledge of our free actions (*Pré. phy.*, sec. IX, OCM XVI 32–33). It has been said quite properly that Malebranche's defense of the claim that inner sentiment directly reveals our freedom is "perfunctory" and "borrowed without noteworthy modification from Descartes";[37] I offer only a brief consideration of this defense. On the other hand, Malebranche's discussion of the conclusion that we do not know our free actions in the clear and evident manner in which God knows them draws in a quite original manner on the accounts of human freedom in the writings of Descartes and the Cartesians. I believe that an extended consideration of the Cartesian context of Malebranche's discussion will help us to see why he took the Cartesian proof of freedom to complement his own thesis that we know the soul through a confused inner sentiment rather than through a clear idea of its nature.

6.2 The Nature of Freedom

6.2.1 The Cartesian Proof of Freedom

In response to Arnauld's objection that one must have a "clear and distinct vision" of the soul in order to demonstrate its freedom, Malebranche asserted that "the inner sentiment" that one has of the soul "suffices to demonstrate" its freedom. Anticipating Arnauld's response that inner sentiment yields a clear knowledge of the soul, Malebranche drew attention to the difference between a vivid awareness of the existence of a thing and a clear knowledge of its nature. He indicated to Arnauld that "I have an inner sentiment that I suffer pain," but that "I do not know what my pain is. God knows it without sensing it, and on my part I sense it without knowing it." We are already familiar with the view here that our inner sentiment of our own sensations is confused in this way (see §2.2.2). What is new, though, is Malebranche's claim that our inner sentiment of our own freedom is confused in just the same manner. Thus he insisted to

Arnauld that while he senses his freedom (*liberté*) "vividly and sensibly," he "does not know it intelligibly" (*Réponse*, c. 23, OCM VI 163).

I will return to Malebranche's negative point that he does not know in an intelligible manner the nature of his freedom. For the moment, though, I want to pause a bit over his positive point that the fact that he has a vivid sensation of his freedom suffices to demonstrate its existence. In particular, Malebranche took such a sensation to reveal that certain actions are within our power and thus are not determined by anything external to us. His position bears more than a little resemblance to Descartes' assertion in the *Principles* that "we are so conscious [*conscios esse*] of the freedom and indifference which is in us, that there is nothing we comprehend more evidently and more perfectly" (PP I.41, AT VIII–1 20/CSM I 206). Malebranche would, of course, dispute the claim that we perfectly comprehend the nature of our freedom, but it will become clear shortly that the reference in the *Principles* to our "freedom and indifference" reflects a commitment to the view, which Malebranche adopted, that we have an undetermined power of action in us. Moreover, Descartes' claim in this text that we are conscious of such freedom and indifference is in line with Malebranche's own position that our inner sentiment provides direct access to our freedom.

There is a passage from Leibniz's 1710 *Essais de Theodicée* that reveals the extent to which the proofs of freedom in Malebranche and Descartes can be run together. In the course of his defense, in this work, of the view that our actions are completely determined, Leibniz urged that

> the reason M. Descartes alleged to prove the independence of our free actions by a pretended vivid internal sentiment has no force. We cannot strictly sense our independence, and we are not always aware of the causes, often imperceptible, on which our resolution depends. It is as if the magnetic needle found pleasure in turning toward the north; for it would believe that it turned independently of any other cause, not being aware of the insensible movements of the magnetic matter.[38]

It is interesting that Leibniz's talk of a "vivid internal sentiment" of freedom is closer to Malebranche's remarks than to anything in Descartes.[39] We will discover, moreover, that Malebranche insisted more consistently than Descartes that our freedom renders us independent even of God's power. For these reasons Malebranche is a clearer target for Leibniz's critique than is Descartes. Nonetheless, the passage from the *Principles* just cited shows that Descartes anticipated the basic position in Malebranche that we know simply by introspection that we are free in the sense that we are not causally determined.

It must be said, however, that it is difficult in light of Leibniz's critical remarks to accept the introspectionist proof of freedom common to Descartes and Malebranche. Leibniz's example of the magnetic needle effectively brings home the point that our actions could appear to us to be free and independent and yet still be determined by causes of which we are ignorant. Even if it is not intelligible to suppose that we do not have a certain sensation when there is the appearance of this sensation in us, certainly it is intelligible to suppose that we are not free when there is the appearance of freedom in us. Malebranche's claim to Arnauld that our inner sentiment of freedom yields certain knowledge of the existence of our freedom in just the same way that our inner sentiment of pain yields certain knowledge of the existence of pain simply lacks persuasive force.

Although Malebranche himself took the argument from inner sentiment for our freedom to be decisive, in his *Réponse* directed against Arnauld, he introduced an additional (if merely subsidiary) argument that derives from reason.[40] Malebranche noted there that it is not in our power to refrain from loving the good in general since our desire to be happy does not depend on us. Rather, God produces this desire when he carries us invincibly to the good in general. It is in our power to refrain from the sin of loving particular goods more than God, however, since God does not invincibly carry us to these goods. If it were not in our power to refrain from this sinful love, this could be only because God leads us invincibly to the particular goods; but then God would be as much the author of our sinful love as he is the author of our love of the good in general (*Réponse*, c. 23, OCM VI 164). The assumption here is that God's perfection prevents him from being the author of our sin. According to this argument from reason, therefore, reflection on the nature of God yields the conclusion that our sinful acts are free in the sense that it is in our power to refrain from them.[41]

While there is no clear analogue of this argument from reason in Descartes' writings, I believe that the following discussion of his mature account of freedom will reveal that he was sympathetic to the conclusion that God is not responsible for our free actions since it is in our power to refrain from them. It is interesting, however, that there seems to be in Descartes and Malebranche alike the concession that a rational consideration of the nature of God can yield results that are at odds with the conclusion that we are free. Just prior to his claim in the *Principles* that we are conscious of our freedom and indifference, for instance, Descartes held that our knowledge of God renders it impossible to think that there is anything that is not preordained by him. His conclusion is that we cannot reconcile the freedom of our actions with the undeniable fact that God has with infinite power preordained such actions (*PP* I.40, AT VIII-1 20/CSM I 206). Likewise, Malebranche noted in *Éclaircissement I* that even though inner sentiment convinces us that we are free, when

> we attend to abstract reasons, which turn us away from thought about ourselves, then perhaps in losing the view of ourselves, we shall forget what we are; and in wishing to harmonize [*accorder*] God's knowledge [*la science de Dieu*] and the absolute power he has over our wills, we shall doubt that we are free, and we shall fall into an error that upsets all the principles of religion and morality. (OCM III 30/LO 554)

Nonetheless, there is some difference in the reaction to this difficulty in Descartes and Malebranche. Whereas Descartes indicated in the *Principles* that there is no need to reconcile our freedom with God's power (a view that drops out of his later writings), Malebranche suggested that such a reconciliation is necessary to avoid falling into an error that upsets religion and morality. This difference helps to explain why Malebranche was more consistently concerned than was Descartes to offer an account of our freedom that allows for such a reconciliation. While none of the various accounts that he offered over time correspond exactly to anything in Descartes, we will see that these accounts draw on various metaphysical notions that Clerselier and Clauberg employed in the course of their attempt to show that our freedom to move body is compatible with the fact that God alone can create motion. The writings of these Cartesians, as well as those of Descartes, thus prepare the way for Malebranche's complex and evolving account of our freedom.

6.2.2 Descartes on Freedom, Indifference, and Divine Power

(1) Human Freedom and Indifference. In the *Principles* Descartes considered our consciousness of freedom in the context of providing a solution to the theological problem of how error could be consistent with the existence of an omnibenevolent and omnipotent God. He was concerned to argue that our error derives not from God but from our own misuse of the freedom of our will. The solution in this text starts from the position that all operations of mind consist either in the perceptions of the faculty of intellect (understood in a broad way to include sensory faculties) or in the volitions of the faculty of will. Descartes emphasized that judgment involves both sorts of operation when he wrote, "In order to make a judgment the intellect is of course required, since we can judge nothing about the thing that we perceive in no way; but the will is also required, so that assent may be given to the thing perceived in some manner" (PP I.34, AT VIII–1 18/ CSM I 204). The view that an act of will is a constituent element of judgment, which is arguably without precedent in medieval or scholastic philosophy,[42] is important to Descartes' explanation of error. He emphasized that although the intellect is limited in the objects it can perceive clearly and distinctly, the will is infinite in the sense that it can assent to or deny anything that can be perceived in any way. Error is possible because the assent or denial of the will can be directed toward something not clearly and distinctly perceived by the intellect.

In this text Descartes held that God cannot be blamed for those features of the mental faculties that allow for our error. He cannot be blamed for giving us a limited intellect since no created intellect can be omniscient,[43] and he cannot be blamed for giving us an infinite will since this infinity is a sign of perfection.[44] However, Descartes also emphasized that we have experienced within ourselves a freedom of will "so great as to enable us to abstain from believing what was not completely certain and examined" (PP I.39, AT VIII–1 20/CSM I 206). This suggests that we, rather than God, are responsible for our errors in judgment that are blameworthy[45] because we judge freely in the sense that we have the power to reign in the will by abstaining from judgment.[46]

At one point in the *Principles* Descartes spoke of our free actions as "undetermined" (*indeterminatas*) (PP I.41, AT VIII–1 20/CSM I 206), thus implying that the power involved in such actions is contra-causal. This is the very same passage in which he referred to our consciousness of "freedom and indifference." Descartes seems to have been drawing here on the standard Jesuit position that human freedom requires not only spontaneity (i.e., the absence of coercion) but also indifference (i.e., the presence of an undetermined power to act or not to act). In light of such a position, Descartes' claim in the *Principles* that our assent or dissent is free and indifferent indicates that we have the power to abstain and thus are not determined to make a judgment.

The suggestion in the 1644 *Principles* that freedom requires indifference and a lack of determination, however, appears to be at odds with the view in the 1641 *Meditations* that spontaneity, rather than indifference, is essential to freedom. In the *Fourth Meditation* Descartes proposed initially that will consists in the ability "to do or not to do (that is to affirm or to deny, to pursue or to avoid)," an ability that seems to require indifference. However, he added that will consists "rather" (*potius*) in the fact that when the intellect puts something forward for affirmation or denial, pursuit or avoidance, "we sense that we are determined by no external force to it" (AT VII 57/CSM II 40). The ability to act apparently requires not indifference but rather the lack of coercive determination by an external force. Descartes emphasized that indifference provides evidence of "a defect in knowledge [and] a kind of negation", and that such indifference is in no way a prerequisite of freedom. Thus he concluded that

> the more I incline one direction, either because I evidently understand the reasons of truth and goodness [that point] in that direction, or because God thus disposes the innermost of my thoughts, the freer is my choice; neither divine grace nor natural knowledge diminishes freedom in any way, but rather they augment and strengthen it. (AT VII 58/CSM II 40)

This position leads Descartes to say that whenever he had clear and distinct perceptions in the past, "a great light of intellect was followed by a great propensity in the will, and thus the spontaneity and freedom of that belief were all the greater in proportion to my lack of indifference" (AT VII 59/CSM II 41).[47] Whereas Descartes aligned himself with the Jesuits when he spoke in the *Principles* of "freedom and indifference," in a 1641 letter to Mersenne he noted that the account of freedom in the *Meditations* is perfectly in accord with the view in the *De libertate dei et creaturae* (1630) of the Oratorian Guillaume Gibieuf, which was itself directed against the Jesuits, that indifference is not essential to human freedom (21 Apr. 1641, AT III 360/CSMK 179).[48]

One could downplay the differences between the *Meditations* and the *Principles* by emphasizing the view in the latter text that the indifference of the will pertains primarily to matters not clearly and distinctly perceived by intellect. In the *Principles*, after all, freedom is defined in terms of the ability "to assent or not to assent at will," not in *all* but merely in *many* cases. In the portion of this text just cited, Descartes indicated that this power is limited to matters that are "not completely certain and examined" (PP I.39, AT VIII–1 19–20/CSM I 205–

6). He stressed in a later passage, moreover, that our nature is such that "whenever we perceive anything clearly, we assent to it spontaneously, and can in no way doubt that it is true" (PP I.43, AT VIII–1 21/CSM I 207). The *Principles* therefore allows that our assent follows spontaneously and inevitably at the moment we have a clear and distinct perception.[49]

While these considerations seem to support the view of certain commentators that Descartes held consistently to a single account of human freedom,[50] I would argue with Ferdinand Alquié that this view ignores the significant difference in emphasis between *Fourth Meditation* and the *Principles*. The *Fourth Meditation* focuses on what Alquié has called *la liberté eclairée*—"the enlightened freedom" that occurs when the spontaneous assent of the will is determined by the clear and distinct perceptions of the intellect. In line with the critique of the Jesuits in Gibieuf, this text takes indifference to be incidental to freedom. However, the *Principles* focuses on what Alquié has called *la liberté positive*—"the positive freedom" that occurs when the act of will is undetermined and indifferent.[51] This latter sort of freedom is prominent also in later correspondence where Descartes emphasized his sympathy with the Jesuit account of freedom. Thus, in a 1644 letter Descartes told Denis Mesland, a rare Jesuit supporter, "[S]ince you regard freedom not simply as indifference but rather as a real and positive power to determine oneself, the difference between us is merely a verbal one, for I agree that the soul has such a power" (2 May 1644, AT IV 116/CSMK 233–34). In another letter that is traditionally held to have been sent to Mesland in 1645 (though the recipient and date of the letter are uncertain),[52] Descartes agreed with his correspondent that the will is indifferent in the sense that one has "a positive faculty of determining oneself to one or the other of two contraries, that is to pursuing or avoiding, affirming or denying" (AT IV 173/CSMK 245). The *Principles* and these two letters thus work toward the Jesuit view that identifies indifference with an undetermined power essential to human freedom. John Cottingham's recent contention that "Descartes did not make the notion of a two-way contra-causal power central to his account of freedom,"[53] while true of the *Fourth Meditation*, does not hold for the *Principles* and the two letters on human freedom.

(2) Human Freedom and Divine Power. In a 1647 letter to Queen Christina of Sweden, Descartes noted that "free will is in itself the noblest thing we can have, since it makes us in a way equal to God and seems to exempt us from being his subjects" (20 Nov. 1647, AT V 85/CSMK 326). This startling remark reveals that the new account of freedom broached in the *Principles* was not without theological difficulties. The theologian Arnauld, who as we have seen was accustomed to defending Descartes, emphasized such difficulties in a 1669 letter when he wrote, with reference to Robert Desgabets,

> I find it quite strange that this good religious man takes Descartes to be exceedingly enlightened in matters of religion, whereas his letters are full of Pelagianism and, outside of the points of which he was convinced by his

philosophy—like the existence of God and the immortality of the soul—all that can be said of him to his greatest advantage is that he always seemed to submit to the Church.[54]

Given his Jansenist position that we cannot freely will to do what is right without divine grace, Arnauld certainly would have endorsed the claim in the *Fourth Meditation* that such grace strengthens our freedom. What he could not have accepted is the later position in Descartes' two letters that an undetermined power of choice is essential to human freedom. Arnauld would have seen in such a position, as he saw in the standard Jesuit account of freedom, the heretical Pelagian view that certain human actions are independent of God's control.[55]

Arnauld was not the first to charge Descartes with Pelagianism. Over two decades before Arnauld's letter, a thesis containing this charge was offered at the University of Leiden by the Calvinist theologian Jacob Trigland with the support of Jacobus Revius, the Regent of the College of Theologians. In a 1647 letter to the curators of the university, Descartes himself disputed the thesis and particularly emphasized that it wrongly interpreted him as claiming that we apprehend our freedom more clearly even than the idea of God (4 May 1647, AT V 4). Indeed, in a previously mentioned passage from the *Principles* he already had made a concession to those who assert the primacy of divine providence when he interrupted his discussion of human freedom to note that we perceive in God "a power so immense that we regard it to be impious to hold that there is anything that can be done by us that was not already preordained by him" (*PP* I.40, AT VIII-1 20/CSM I 206).

In a letter that initiated an important exchange on the compatibility of divine providence and human freedom, Princess Elisabeth was prompted by remarks in the *Principles* to write that while reason can show that God controls "the ordinary course of nature," faith alone reveals that he regulates as well the actions of a human will that "seems entirely free" (22 June 1645, AT IV 302). Descartes responded that

> all the reasons that prove the existence of God, and that he is the first and immutable cause of all the effects that do not depend on the free will of humans, proves it seems to me, in the same way, that he is also the cause of all those that do depend. Because the only way to demonstrate that he exists is to consider him as a supremely perfect being; and he would not be supremely perfect if something could happen in the world that did not come entirely from him.

He went on to note that the scholastic distinction between universal and particular causes does not provide a way around his position since "God is the universal cause of all in such a way that he is in the same way the total cause; and thus nothing could happen without his will" (6 Oct. 1645, AT IV 313–14/ CSMK 272).

Descartes' claim that everything comes entirely from God may seem to suggest that God is the only cause of human actions, but he held in general that the fact that something derives from a total cause need not preclude the fact that it derives from other partial causes.[56] Thus he would not have seen a tension between the claim that God is the total cause of human actions and the claim that the human will is a partial cause of these actions. Even if there is no difficulty here, however, there does seem to be a tension between his claim that God is the total cause of free human actions and the doctrine of the *Principles* that such actions are undetermined. Descartes admitted in this text that "we can easily entangle ourselves in great difficulties if we try to reconcile this divine preordination with the freedom of our will, and to comprehend both together" (PP I.40, AT VIII–1 20; CSM I 206). However, he went on to say that we can avoid such entanglement once we

> remember that our mind is finite; however God's power by which he not only knew from eternity whatever is or can be, but also willed it and preordained it, is infinite; and thus this power is comprehended by us enough so that we clearly and distinctly perceive that it is in God; however it is not comprehended enough so that we see how it leaves the free actions of men undetermined.

Descartes concluded that "it would be absurd, simply because we do not grasp one thing, which we know must be by its nature incomprehensible to us, to doubt another, which we comprehend intimately [*intime comprehendimus*], and experience [*experimur*] within ourselves" (PP I.41, AT VIII–1 20/CSM I 206). Since we intimately comprehend our freedom but do not comprehend divine preordination, we need not attempt to reconcile the two but can simply accept that our free actions are undetermined.

Descartes noted in his 1644 letter to Mesland that he did not address the issue of our freedom to do good or evil since "I wanted to avoid as far as possible all theological controversies and stay within the limits of natural philosophy" (AT IV 177/CSMK 234). It is tempting to think that in the *Principles* he treated difficulties concerning divine power in a perfunctory manner so as to avoid entanglement in the rancorous theological disputes then prevalent regarding the nature of divine providence. Nevertheless, his quick dismissal of such difficulties is unsatisfactory for philosophical reasons. In the *Principles* he derived the incomprehensibility of divine preordination from the purported fact that our free actions are undetermined. He simply assumed that his experience reveals directly the existence of undetermined action. However, it seems that he must show that his metaphysical results and, in particular, his result that God exists as the total cause of all effects, allow for the veridicality of this experience.[57] As Elisabeth emphasized in her response to Descartes' letter, there is some question whether this result so allows since the freedom we experience seems to require a lack of any sort of dependence on God (28 Oct. 1645, AT IV 323).

It is significant that in his next letter to Elisabeth, Descartes did not take refuge in the fact that divine preordination is incomprehensible. Rather, he asserted that "the independence that we experience and sense in ourselves, and that suffices to render our actions praiseworthy or blameworthy, is not incompatible with a dependence that is of another nature, whereby all things are subject to God" (3 Nov. 1645, AT IV 333/CSMK 277). When Elisabeth pressed again, raising doubts that "this dependence of the will can be of another nature than its freedom" (30 Nov. 1645, AT IV 336), Descartes was forced to play his hand. In the final letter of the exchange, he attempted to illustrate the sense in which the human will is both dependent on God and free. He asked Elisabeth to suppose that a king who has forbidden duels orders one of his subjects to travel to the town of another even though he knows with certainty that the two will fight when they meet. He then argued that the king may justly punish the two for disobeying his prohibition on the grounds that this king "does not constrain them; and his knowledge, and even his will to determine them in the manner that he has, does not prevent their fighting when they come to meet from being as voluntary and as free, as it would have been if he had known nothing and they had met on some other occasion" (Jan. 1646, AT IV 353/CSMK 282). Descartes concluded that just as a king can know and will the actions of his subjects without depriving them of their freedom, so God can with infinite foresight and power know and will our own actions even while leaving those actions free.

> Before he sent us into the world he knew exactly what all the inclinations of our will would be; it is he himself who gave them to us, it is he who has disposed all other things that are outside us, so that such and such objects would present themselves to our senses at such and such times, on the occasion of which he knew that our free will would determine us to such and such a choice; and he has so willed, but has not willed that we be constrained to [that choice]. (AT IV 353–54/CSMK 282)

This passage indicates that God is the cause of the elements that provide the background conditions for such action, including the inclinations of the human will and the sensory dispositions of external objects, yet it also suggests that this will itself, rather than God, ultimately determines which choice is made in this context. Descartes' view in this letter thus appears to be that God does not causally determine the actual choice but merely knows infallibly which choice would be made in such and such conditions, and with infinite power wills that those conditions obtain.

One could wish for a more precise account here of what in our free action is caused by God and what by us. There is also the need for a more detailed defense of the consistency of the position in this letter that we cause some element of free action with the claim in the earlier letter that God is the total cause of such action. Nonetheless, it is clear that the remarks in the letters to Elisabeth deviate from the position in the *Principles*. In the final letter Descartes did not emphasize the incomprehensibility of God's preordination of our free action, indicating instead that God does not determine our free choice. The difficulty broached in this letter concerns God's infallible knowledge rather than his infinite power. One particular difficulty is how God could infallibly know that "our free will would determine us to such and such a choice," given that our act of will is itself undetermined. It may well be that by the time of his exchange with Elisabeth, Descartes thought that we cannot comprehend how

God's knowledge could extend to our free and undetermined actions; but he tried to show his correspondent what he took to be impossible in the *Principles*, namely, that we can comprehend that God's power leaves our free actions undetermined.

6.2.3 The Cartesians on Mental Causation and Motion

(1) Descartes on Voluntary Motion. Descartes held that we experience in ourselves the power not only to give or to withhold assent, but also to move our body at will. Thus he wrote to Arnauld:

> That the mind however, which is incorporeal, can impel [*impellere*] the body is something that is shown to us without the need for any reasoning or comparison with other things, but every day by the most certain and most evident experience [*certissima et evidentissima experientia*]; for this is one of those things known per se, which we obscure when we try to explain through other things. (29 July 1648, AT V 222/CSMK 358)

We have considered the apparent tension between Descartes' remark to Elisabeth that God is the total cause of all effects and his conclusion that we have an undetermined power to give or to withhold assent. Now there is some question whether this remark allows for his conclusion that we have the power to impel body. The problem here derives from Descartes' view in the *Principles* that God is "the universal and primary, that is the general cause of all motions that are in the world" since he "in the beginning created matter at once with motion and rest, and now, through his ordinary concourse alone, conserves just as much motion and rest in it as he put there at that time." Drawing on his earlier claim in the *Third Meditation* that "conservation differs only by reason from creation [since] the same power and action are needed to conserve a work at each moment that it endures as would be needed to create the work anew at each [moment] if it did not yet exist" (AT VII 49/CSM II 33), Descartes concluded that God conserves motion and rest "in the same manner and by the same process that he first created it" (PP II.36, AT VIII-1 61–62/CSM I 240). According to the account in the *Principles*, the law of the conservation of the total quantity of motion (where the quantity of the motion of each body is measured by the speed of the motion multiplied by the size of the body) derives from God's continued creation of "all motions that are in the world." However, the view that God is the total cause of motion in this sense seems to leave no room for the position, implicit in Descartes' remarks to Arnauld, that the human mind can add to the quantity of motion in the world by impelling a body.

In his *Theodicée* Leibniz recalled that Descartes not only grappled with this difficulty but also offered a solution to it:

> M. Descartes wished . . . to make a part of the action of the body depend on the mind. He thought he knew a rule of nature that, according to him, holds that the same quantity of motion is conserved in bodies. He did not judge it possible that the influence of the mind could violate this law of bodies, but he

believed, however, that the mind could have the power to change the direction of the motions that are in bodies; much as a rider, though he gives no force to the horse he mounts, nevertheless governs it by guiding this force in any direction that seems good to him.[58]

In taking Descartes to hold that the human mind can alter the direction of body without changing the quantity of motion, Leibniz assumed that he distinguished between direction and the motion quantified. Indeed, Descartes suggested something akin to this distinction when, drawing on a view found in his earlier scientific works, he remarked in the *Principles* that "there is a difference between motion considered in itself and its determination in a certain direction [*determinationem versus certam partem*], since the determination can be altered while the motion remains in its entirety" (PP II.41, AT VIII–1 65/CSM I 243). Descartes' account of the nature of the determination of motion is complex and perhaps not entirely clear,[59] but it is clear enough from the remark in the *Principles* that he took determination to be an aspect of motion that is characterized in terms of the direction of that motion. In response to an earlier version of the position outlined in this remark, Hobbes had objected that Descartes' suggestion that determination in a certain direction inheres in motion commits him to the implausible position that motion is itself a substance, rather than merely a mode of bodily substance.[60] Descartes replied in a letter to Mersenne that

> there is no awkwardness or absurdity in saying that an accident is the subject of another accident . . . When I said that motion is to its determination as a flat body is to its top or surface, I certainly did not mean to compare the motion and the body as if they were two substances; I was comparing them merely as one would compare two concrete things, to show that they were different from things that could be treated merely as abstractions. (21 Apr. 1641, AT III 355–56/CSMK 178)

Descartes' position here is that motion is a mode of body that is, in turn, the subject of two different modes: determination and "motion considered in itself," or the speed of the motion. Moreover, the *Principles* allows for the case in which the speed of the motion remains constant even while the determination of that motion changes. Since the conservation law concerns speed but not determination, in such a case there would be no violation of this law.

On Descartes' view, then, the human mind would not violate the conservation law if it merely altered the determination of motion by changing the direction of that motion. But there is some reason to distrust Leibniz's recollection that Descartes held that such a mind cannot violate this law and, therefore, that it can move body only by changing the direction of its motion. It is significant, for instance, that Descartes wrote in the *Principles* that the quantity of motion remains constant "excepting those changes that evident experience [*evidens experientia*] or divine revelation renders certain, and that we perceive or believe to occur without any change in the Creator" (PP I.36, AT VIII–1 61/CSM I 240). The fact that those changes rendered certain by "evident experience" include the movement of body by our mind is indicated by the claim to

Arnauld that the fact that we can set body in motion is shown to us "every day by the most certain and most evident experience."[61] Read in light of this claim, the "escape clause" in the *Principles* allows for a causation of motion by the human mind that violates the conservation law deriving from God's creative activity. Such a clause therefore directly conflicts with Leibniz's view that Descartes did not think it possible for the action of mind on body to violate the law governing the conservation of motion.[62]

(2) Clerselier and Clauberg on Mental Causation. Leibniz's recollections of Descartes may well have been shaped by his reading of other Cartesians. One possible influence is Claude Clerselier, Descartes' friend, translator, and editor, who was well known to Leibniz.[63] The central text here is a 1660 letter to La Forge, "Observations de Monsieur Clerselier, touchant l'action de l'Ame sur le Corps," which Clerselier placed at the end of the third and last volume of his *Lettres de Descartes*.[64] Clerselier wrote in the preface to this volume that he intended to carry on the work started by Descartes and La Forge, and in the letter itself he repeated the standard Cartesian position that all properties belong either to corporeal or to spiritual substance. He then went on to note that only spiritual substance has the ability to "give the first movement to body, or to imprint in it a completely new motion that increases the quantity of that which is already in the world."[65] Moreover, only infinite spiritual substance (i.e., God) can have such an ability since this substance alone "is capable of imprinting the first motion in body; . . . of creating, or of making a thing that is not, to be or to exist." There is the objection, which finds some support in Descartes' texts, that though an infinite power is required to create a body from nothing, it is not needed to create motion, which is, after all, merely a mode of body.[66] Clerselier responded to this objection by stating that the power to move and animate a body is of the same order as the power to create a body from nothing; thus no finite spirit could move a body "unless the will of the Creator were to join with that of it." Even if a body were moved and divided by the word of an angel, "his word would have been only an instrument of that of God, whose power [*vertu*] alone would have worked this marvel, it not being possible that the nothingness of movement [*neant du mouvement*] obey other than an infinite power."[67] These remarks therefore endorse the negative position, which the *Theodicée* attributes to Descartes, that it is impossible for "the influence of the mind" to add to the quantity of motion in the world.

In accord with the positive position that Leibniz' text claims to find in Descartes, Clerselier also claimed that the human mind "could have the power to change the direction of motion that is in bodies." He noted that finite spiritual substance, and the human mind in particular, can determine the motion (*determiner le mouvement*) that is already in the world, since

> the determination of motion . . . adds nothing real to nature, and . . . says nothing more than the motion itself, which cannot be without determination. So it is not to be marveled that the soul has a faculty to determine it, as our own

experience convinces us that it has; for that does not prevent God from being the author of all the forms [*formes*] that arrive successively in matter, which are all effects, consequences, and dependencies of the motion that he has introduced into it, and that he conserves in it, and thus does not prevent him from being really the Creator of all things.[68]

Following "the sentiment of Monsieur Descartes," Clerselier admitted that we do not know how spirit acts on body any more than we know how God created something from nothing.[69] However, he echoed the remarks in Descartes' letter to Arnauld when he wrote that the fact "that our soul, which is incorporeal, can move the body" is something "we can in no way doubt, since most certain and most evident experiences [*des experiences tres-certaines et tres-evidentes*] only convince us of it more every day."[70] What is not anticipated in Descartes' writings, though, is Clerselier's attempt to argue that the action of the human mind on body is compatible with the fact that God is the author of all forms that depend on the motion he creates and conserves, on the grounds that this mind merely alters the determination of that motion which God has already created, and thus "adds nothing real to nature."

The parallels I have noted between the remarks in Clerselier's letter to La Forge and those in the *Theodicée* provide some reason to suspect that the former helped to shape the latter. There is even stronger evidence, however, that Leibniz's remarks were influenced by the work of Johann Clauberg. Clauberg himself had strong Cartesian credentials, having worked as a young man on the edition of the conversation between Frans Burman and Descartes, and later having published the *Paraphrasis in Renati Des Cartes Meditationes*, his detailed commentary on the *Meditations*.[71] Leibniz may well have had the *Paraphrasis* in mind when he wrote in one letter that though Clauberg is "clearer than the master," neither Clauberg nor other Cartesians "added anything to the discoveries of their master," publishing as they did "only paraphrases of their leader."[72] What is more directly relevant to Leibniz's recollections in the *Theodicée*, however, is Clauberg's *Corporis et Animæ in Homine Conjunctio*.[73] In his text Clauberg noted that the commonsense view that "the mind produces certain changes in the body" seems contrary to the fact that "God is truly the efficient, creative, and conserving cause of all motions," which, given God's immutability, accounts for the fact that the quantity of motion in the world can be neither increased nor diminished.[74] He suggested that this tension can be overcome once it is recognized that "the human mind is not a physical cause [*causa . . . Physica*] of bodily motions in the man, but only a moral [*Moralis*] one, since it no more than guides and directs those other [motions], and forms those motions, which already are in the body, by which means that part [of the human body] is agitated." Clauberg elaborated on this claim by noting that the action of the human mind on the body resembles the case where "the driver joins the horse to the wagon, and turns to that place, and thus directs the motion of the wagon that the horse truly produces as the physical cause [*causa Physica*]."[75] The resemblance between this example and the one that Leibniz employed in the *Theodicée* is striking indeed. There is reason to think that when he attributed to Descartes the view that mind can influence body only by changing the direction of its motion, Leibniz was thinking of Clauberg's position in *Corporis et Animæ* that the human mind is not a physical cause that creates motion, but merely a moral cause that guides and directs the motion already created by God.

Whether it was Clerselier or Clauberg who influenced Leibniz's remarks in the *Théodicee*, it is important to recognize that these Cartesians offered fundamentally the same account of the causation of bodily motion by the human mind. It is true that they employed different terminology; Clerselier spoke of the mind as determining motion, for instance, whereas Clauberg spoke of the mind as being a moral cause of motion. Nevertheless, both held that the mind acts on body merely by changing the direction of its motion. Likewise, both claimed that such action is consistent with the principle that only God can introduce motion into the world, as Clerselier put it, and, in Clauberg's terms, that God alone can be a physical cause of motion. I have indicated that Descartes himself would not have accepted such a principle. I want to argue, however, that both Clerselier's claim that the mind's determination "adds nothing real to nature" and Clauberg's claim that mind is a moral but not a physical cause have interest beyond their application to the question, which so preoccupied Leibniz, of how Descartes could allow for the influence of the human mind on the body. Here I focus in particular on Malebranche's appeal to notions employed by Clerselier and Clauberg in order to provide elbow room for the sort of indeterministic freedom of action that Descartes claimed, in the *Principles* and elsewhere, to experience in himself.

6.2.4 Malebranche on Freedom and the Motion of the Will

(1) Divine Creation and the Motion of the Will. We have seen that for both Clerselier and Clauberg God alone can create bodily motion. None of these Cartesians provided a sufficiently deep argument, however, against Descartes' suggestion that the human mind, as well as God, can impel a body. Clerselier simply asserted that since the power needed to move a body is as great as the power needed to create it from nothing, only God can cause motion. However, at one point Descartes himself rejected the equality of these powers when he endorsed the traditional scholastic distinction between two kinds of causes: causes *secundum esse* (i.e., causes of the existence of an object) and causes *secundum fieri* (i.e., causes of a change in the state of an object).[76] The two causes must be distinct, according to Descartes, because while the effect of a cause *secundum fieri* (e.g., a house) does not depend on its cause (e.g., the architect) for its continued existence, all created things, which are effects of a cause *secundum esse* (viz. God), depend at each moment on the activity of this cause for their existence (*Fifth Rep.*, AT VII 369/CSM II 254–55). It was less than obvious to Descartes, then, that the power to impel a body, which is merely a power to cause a state of that body, is of the same order as the power to create that body from nothing. Moreover, I have urged that Descartes was not inclined

to the position, which Clauberg simply assumed, that the conservation law entails that there can be no addition to the quantity of motion that God originally created in the world.

However, Malebranche attempted to construct an occasionalist argument against Descartes' suggestion that human minds can cause motion that starts from the premise that the conservation of bodies at each moment of their existence depends on an act of God that does not differ from his act of creating the bodies. In his *Entretiens* Malebranche had Theodore assert that

> God himself, although all-powerful, cannot create a body that is nowhere, or does not have certain relations of distance to others. Every body is at rest when it has the same relation of distance to others; and it is in motion [*mouvement*] when this relation always changes. Now it is evident that every body either changes or does not change its relation of distance. There is no middle ground. ... Thus it is a contradiction that a body can be neither in motion nor at rest. (EM VII, OCM XII 155/D 153)

Given the Cartesian premise just mentioned, it follows that in the case of the conservation of a particular body, such as a chair "it is a contradiction that God should will that existence of the chair yet not will that it exist somewhere and, by the efficacy of His volition, not put it there, not conserve it there, not create it there" (OCM XII 160/D 157). In conserving the chair and all other surrounding bodies from moment to moment, God must cause them to exist in the precise positions they occupy at each moment. Since human minds cannot place a body where God has not placed it, Malebranche had Theodore conclude, such minds cannot cause motion in the material world.[77]

It may be that Descartes could resist this sort of argument,[78] but at least the argument addresses the sort of deep issues concerning the nature of divine creation and conservation which Clerselier and Clauberg overlooked. It is also noteworthy that Malebranche's argument against Descartes precludes the accounts of voluntary motion offered by Clauberg and Clerselier. Given Clerselier's own admission that motion "cannot be without determination," it follows from this argument that when God conserves a body in motion, he must also determine the direction of the motion by creating that body in the different positions it occupies from moment to moment. There is nothing left in the motion for the human mind to determine. Likewise, Clauberg's view that the human mind can be a moral cause of motion is undercut by the fact that God must conserve bodies by creating them at particular positions. Thus, when God creates the motion of body, that is, when he is a physical cause of the motion, he must at the same time guide and direct the motion, that is, he must be a moral cause of the motion. After God has created a body, there remains no aspect of the motion of that body for the human mind to guide or direct.

Indeed, Malebranche's argument seems to entail that the human mind cannot even causally determine its own acts of will. In the section of the *Recherche* that introduces the analogy of the mental faculty of the will to the bodily faculty for receiving motion, Malebranche wrote that just as God "is the universal cause of all motions [*mouvemens*] that are found in matter," so also is he "the general cause of all natural inclinations that are found in minds" (RV I.1, OCM I 45–46/LO 4–5). Yet it seems that just as God must create motion in a determinate manner, so must he create the natural motion of our will with all of its features. Our will would no more be able to causally determine its motion than it would be able to so determine the motion of body.

In this same section, however, Malebranche warned that the analogy between bodily and mental motion is limited since though body "is altogether without action," the will "in a sense can be said to be active." This activity consists in "the power [*puissance*] to will, or not to will, or even to will the contrary of that toward which our natural inclinations carry us" (OCM I 46–47/LO 4–5). Malebranche allowed that God is the cause not only of our inclination or motion toward the good in general, but also of our perceptions of particular objects. He also admitted that "although it is voluntarily and freely, or without constraint, that we love the good in general," we are not free to love this good with a freedom of indifference "since it is not in the power of our will not to wish to be happy" (OCM I 47/LO 5). However, he emphasized that when we perceive a good that we do not recognize to be our greatest good, it is always in our power to "suspend" our consent to love of that good (OCM I 48/LO 5). As the context of his remarks makes clear, Malebranche was most concerned to appeal to the fact that we have this power in order to absolve God of responsibility for our sins. Even though God causes all of our inclinations and perceptions, we are responsible for the sin of loving particular goods rather than God because our will is not determined even by God to consent to such love.

Though these remarks focus on sinful action, the *Recherche* considers as well the case of erroneous judgment. Malebranche sided with Descartes, and against the standard scholastic view, when he wrote in this text that assent to a proposition, no less than consent to a good, involves an act of will.[79] Just as Malebranche held that sin arises from the consent of the will to something not evidently perceived to be the ultimate good, moreover, so he claimed, in line with Descartes' position, that error arises from the assent of the will to something not clearly and distinctly perceived to be true (RV I.2, OCM I 51–52/LO 8). However, most significant for our purposes is Malebranche's claim that our assent to a proposition not clearly perceived to be true, in addition to our consent to love of a particular object not clearly perceived to be our greatest good, is indifferent in the sense that we have the power to refrain from judgment. Thus he concluded, in the spirit of the view of the *Principles*, that we should make use of our freedom in order "never to consent to anything until we are forced as it were to do so by the internal reproaches of our reason" (OCM I 55/LO 10). The emphasis on a freedom that involves a two-way contra-causal power of choice is a feature of the *Recherche* as well as of the *Principles* and Descartes' two letters on human freedom.

Perhaps unwittingly, Arnauld drew attention to this point of contact between the accounts of freedom in Malebranche and Descartes. In terms that recall his earlier criticism of Descartes, he objected in a 1684 text to Malebranche's claim that our consent derives from our will rather than from God: "I do not know whether Pelagius ever said anything more pelagian. For that means that God does not act in us when we act freely; and that he never has a part in the consent that we give to the truth, when we consent freely to it, and are able not to consent to it."[80] Malebranche was as concerned as Descartes to deny the charge of Pelagianism, though he was more willing than Descartes to address in detail the theological issues pertaining to this charge.[81] Malebranche insisted, in particular, that apart from divine grace we cannot have the sort of dominant free disposition that renders us morally worthy before God.[82] Nonetheless, he remained committed to the view that the soul has a power over its free acts that cannot be determined even by God's action through grace. Such a commitment, however, carries with it a difficulty for Malebranche. Just as Descartes must explain how our indeterministic freedom is compatible with the fact that God is the total cause of our actions, so must Malebranche explain how this sort of freedom is compatible with the fact that God creates all the inclinations of our soul. Admittedly, the two difficulties here are not precisely the same. Arnauld urged that Malebranche's occasionalist claim that God is the only true cause leaves no room for his position that we cause our actions.[83] As I have indicated, however, Descartes understood the claim that God is the total cause of our actions to mean that he is the ultimate, though not the only, cause of these actions. So the problem for Malebranche seems to derive more from his view that our soul is an undetermined *cause*, whereas the problem for Descartes seems to derive more from his view that our soul is an *undetermined* cause. However, the challenge for both consists in showing that our causal control of our free actions is consistent with God's power over these actions.

(2) Three Accounts of Human Freedom. We know by now that in the *Principles* Descartes attempted to sidestep problems concerning the compatibility of our freedom and divine power, though in remarks to Elisabeth he briefly suggested an approach to them. By contrast, Malebranche consistently saw the need to respond to such problems.[84] Here I will focus on the way in which this response is articulated in three different accounts of human freedom that he offered over the course of his philosophical career, the first in his first published work, the *Recherche* (1674), the second in his *Éclaircissement I* (1678) as well as in his *Réponse à la Dissertation de Arnauld* (1685), and the third in his final work, the *Réflexions sur la prémotion physique* (1715).

(i) The Determination of Inclination. I have noted Malebranche's claim toward the start of Book One of the *Recherche* that our will is "in a sense" active. He explained there that this activity consists in the fact that "our soul determines [*déterminer*] in various ways the inclination or impression that God gives it." Although the soul cannot stop the motion that God creates in it, "it can in a sense turn [*détourner*] it toward that which pleases it, and thus cause all the disorder in its inclinations, and all the miseries that are the certain and necessary results of sin" (RV I.1, OCM I 46/LO 4–5).[85] On Malebranche's view, then, there is a fundamental difference between God's control over bodily motion and his control over our inclinations. God is the sole cause of any motion of body; he creates in such a way as to completely determine the direction not only of motion that proceeds in a straight line, but also of motion that deviates from this path. While God also is the sole cause of our inclinations insofar as they proceed toward goodness or truth, our soul determines the direction of those inclinations created by God that deviate from this path when it consents to the love of some object not clearly perceived to be wholly good or assents to some proposition not clearly perceived to be wholly true (OCM I 45/LO 4).

The terminology here recalls Clerselier's remarks in his letter to La Forge. The *Recherche* speaks of our soul as being able to "determine" our inclinations, just as Clerselier's had spoken earlier of our soul as having "a faculty to determine" the motion of our body. Likewise, Malebranche's text refers to the ability of our soul to "turn" our inclinations, while Clerselier had referred to the power of our soul to "change the direction" of bodily motion. This similarity may be more than coincidental; we know that Malebranche owned the third volume of Clerselier's 1677 edition of Descartes, which contains his letter.[86] In composing his account of free human action in the *Recherche*, Malebranche may well have consulted his copy of this letter. In any case, it is clear that his first attempt to reconcile our causation of free action and God's creation of our inclinations is analogous to Clerselier's attempt to reconcile our causation of voluntary motion and God's creation of motion in general. For both, what allows for the reconciliation is the fact that our causal activity does not create anything new in the sense that it does not add to the quantity of motion since such activity merely redirects the motion that God has already created.

One difficulty with Malebranche's suggestion in Book One of the *Recherche* that our free act of consent brings about the turning of an inclination, however, is that it conflicts with a central feature of the account of inclination indicated in the section itself. Malebranche noted there that in the case where a person loves some particular honor, his impression is directed to that honor prior to any act of consent on his part (OCM I 48/LO 5). Elsewhere in the *Recherche* he held that the initial motion of the will toward a particular good comes from God since the soul is drawn to any object it perceives to be good even before it has consented to the motion toward that object (RV V.3, OCM II 142/LO 347). This view can be explained in terms of Malebranche's distinction in the *Traité de Morale* between natural love, which is produced independent of any activity of the soul, and free love, which arises only from the consent of the will.[87] On his considered position, our free love of a particular object cannot involve a turning of our inclination, since we already have a natural love of this object which God produced when, immediately after our perception of the object as good, he directed our inclination toward it.

Malebranche emphasized that God is the source of our natural love when he noted in *Éclaircissement I* that God leads us toward all particular goods, for since "God leads us to all that is good, it is a necessary consequence that he lead us toward particular goods when he produces the perception or sensation of them in our soul" (OCM III 18/LO 547–48). Thus in this text he affirmed that when we sense our freedom, we do not sense a "pure indifference [or] a power determining us to will something without any physical motive [*motif physic*]" (OCM III 29/LO 553).[88] Because it is always the case that a natural love for objects we perceive to be good precedes our free love of those objects, it is impossible that our freedom of consent render us independent "of God's control over us or of the physical motives that he produces in us, by which he knows and can make us will and freely execute all that he wills" (OCM III 29/LO 553). Malebranche intended *Éclaircissement I* to provide a commentary on the account of human freedom in Book One of the *Recherche*. However, in this commentary he disowned the view, suggested by talk in that section of the *Recherche* of our turning our own inclinations, that our act of consent rather than God initially moves us toward a particular object.

(ii) The Repose of Consent. It is to be expected, then, that Malebranche's attempt in *Éclaircissement I* to reconcile our freedom of consent and the divine creation of our inclinations will differ significantly from his attempt in the *Recherche*. At the outset of the former work, he noted that his primary aim is to address the objection that he must either allow "that man is capable of giving himself some new modification," and thus compromise God's omnipotence, or admit "that God is truly the author of sin," and thus compromise God's omnibenevolence (OCM III 18/LO 547). He responded that while God causes in us the perceptions or sensations that lead us to particular goods, and thereby "produces and also conserves in us all that is real and positive in the particular determinations of the movement of our soul" (OCM III 23/LO 550), still he does not invincibly impel us to love these particular goods. We are free, therefore, either to consent to the movement of our soul toward such goods, and thus to commit the sin of loving creatures more than God, or to suspend our consent, and therefore to continue the search for the greatest good. But if we consent, according to Malebranche, we do not cause any new modification. Rather, we do nothing, since we simply rest with a particular good, and thereby stop our search for greater goods. Thus it is that "our consent or our repose upon viewing a particular good is nothing real or positive on our part" (OCM III 20/LO 548).[89] Although God is the only cause of effects in us that derive from action, we are the author of the sinful effects in us because such effects are made possible by our inaction, particularly by our consent to love of particular goods.[90]

The emphasis in *Éclaircissement I* on the inactivity of our consent is found also in the later *Réponse à la Dissertation*. Reacting to Arnauld's contention that "intelligences are the real causes of the determinations of their will," Malebranche noted in the *Réponse* that our own consent is "only a simple repose, and thus that all there is physical and real [*de physique & de réel*] in our determinations, comes from the efficacy of the general laws, according to which God acts in us constantly" (*Rép. Diss.*, c. 12, OCM VII 564–65). He went on to explain that the free movements of our will "are determined by our judgments, and all our judgments are on our part only a simple repose or the cessation of searches; searches, I say, that we have made by the continual action of God in us by this invincible desire to be happy, and not by our own efficacy" (OCM VII 568). Because consent is merely a "simple repose or the cessation of searches," it does not produce anything physical and real in us. Malebranche therefore concluded that the fact that we cause our consent is perfectly consistent with the fact that God is the only cause of what is physical and real (or, to use the terminology of *Éclaircissement I*, what is real or positive) in our determinations.

There are at least two difficulties with Malebranche's claim that consent is merely an inaction that does not produce anything real or physical in us. The first is that his talk of our being the author of consent seems to suggest that there is some sort of activity involved in consent. The second and related difficulty is that even though consent may lack efficacy and thus fail to produce effects in us, it seems that we exercise causal power in bringing about the state of consent itself. I believe that Malebranche attempted to address the first difficulty in later additions to the *Réponse*. For instance, he replaced the comment in the first edition that "I do not change the modifications of my substance," with the remark in the second edition (1709) that "my consent is an immanent act of my will that produces no work [*rien au dehors*], and that does not change even the modifications of my substance, or which produces neither ideas nor sensations nor movements" (OCM VII 567b).[91] He replaced the original comment that "all there is of reality" in the movement of the soul comes from God with the later remark that "all that there is of physical reality [*realité physique*]" in this movement comes from God (OCM VII 568b). These additions highlight Malebranche's considered view that consent involves an immanent act, but an act that also is itself inactive in the sense that it produces none of the physical modifications of the soul—sensations, ideas (i.e., pure perceptions),[92] or motions.[93]

This considered view is reflected in the remark, which Malebranche added to the 1712 edition of *Éclaircissement I*, that consent is accomplished

> by an act, without doubt, but by an immanent act that produces nothing physical [*rien de physic*] in our substance; by an act that in this case does not even require a true cause of some physical effect [*effet physic*] in us, neither ideas nor new sensations; that is to say, in short, by an act that does nothing and makes the general cause do nothing as general, or in abstraction from his justice, for the repose of the soul as that of body has no force or physical efficacy [*force ou efficace physique*]. (OCM III 25/LO 551)

This passage repeats the claim in the second edition of the *Réponse* that consent is an immanent act that produces nothing physical, but it also adds the point that just as the repose of the body lacks force, so does the repose of the soul.[94] This point broaches an objection, however, that is related to my second difficulty with Malebranche's emphasis on the inactivity of consent. Even if it is granted that no force is required for the *continuation* of the repose of body and soul, it seems that some force is required for the *onset* of the repose of both kinds of substance. Malebranche did indicate an important difference between the two states of repose when he wrote in *Éclaircissement I* that while the repose of the body brings about the destruction of its motion, the repose of our soul does not bring about the destruction of our motion since God creates in us the same amount of motion whether or not we consent to love of a particular good (OCM III 22/LO 549). So one might respond, on Malebranche's behalf, that although force is needed to bring about the repose of body, since this repose requires the destruction of motion, it is not needed to bring about the repose of soul, since that repose does not require this sort of destruction. Nonetheless, Malebranche's admission that consent is an immanent act seems to entail that it involves some sort of change in us.

There remains the objection that some sort of force in us must bring about such a change. The remark in the passage added to *Éclaircissement I* that consent "does not even require a true cause of some physical effect in us," however, provides a response to this line of objection. One point here is that since consent is not among the physical modifications of soul, it does not require a true physical cause for its production. Given Malebranche's suggestion at the end of this passage that force is simply a physically efficacious cause, he clearly has reason to reject the claim that force is needed to bring about the state of consent. What is not so clear, though, is that he must reject the claim that since consent involves the production of some sort of change in us, albeit not a physical one, it must be produced by some sort of power in us, albeit not a force in his own sense. Some passages from the first editions of *Éclaircissement I* and the *Réponse* encourage the view that consent involves the production of no change in the soul since it is merely a repose that allows for the continuation of what was a natural love of a particular object. However, I think that the suggestion, particularly in passages from later editions of these texts, that consent is an immanent act and that it does not involve the production merely of physical modifications at least leaves room for the position that consent involves some change brought about by a power in us. Leaving room for this position is not the same as endorsing it, but I want to argue that Malebranche did endorse it in the course of the defense of his final account of human freedom in the *Réflexions sur la prémotion physique*.

(iii) The Moral Causation of Consent. Malebranche's *Prémotion physique* is a response to *De l'action de Dieu sur les créatures*, a work written by the somewhat unorthodox Thomistic theologian, Laurent Boursier.[95] In this 1713 tract, Boursier accepted Malebranche's occasionalist conclusion that the divine conservation of body must determine every feature of bodily motion, yet he rejected Malebranche's position that we produce our own consent when he claimed there that the divine conservation of the soul must also determine all features of its states. Boursier urged that it is more consistent with Malebranche's occasionalism to hold that God has preordained the actions of our will by means of a *prémotion physique*. In order for us to consent, on Boursier's view, it is necessary that God produce in us a physical premotion that irresistibly leads us to consent.[96]

Malebranche responded that since Boursier suggests that consent is a *motif physic* when he claims that God produces it by means of a *prémotion physique*, he "confounds the physical with the moral, or he does not distinguish enough the one from the other" (*Pré. phy.*, sec. X, OCM XVI 37). Malebranche himself held that "the soul is the true cause of its free acts," but that the acts themselves are merely moral aspects of the soul "since they produce nothing physical [*rien de physic*] by their own efficacy." The fact that the soul causes its own acts therefore is perfectly consistent with the consequence of his occasionalism that the soul "is not the true cause of its own modalities or of physical changes that it undergoes, following its acts morally good or bad" (OCM XVI 42–43).

It does seem that free acts are as much states of the soul as the modalities that follow on these acts, and thus that the distinction between moral and physical aspects of the soul is one without a difference. However, Malebranche attempted to indicate a difference to Boursier by means of an imaginary case of bodily motion:

> Suppose, for example, that God has created a body with a round shape, and with four degrees of speed [*vitesse*], such that it depends on it to determine its motion toward the Orient or toward the Occident, and that the Eternal Law demands that all bodies move themselves toward the Orient. In this absurd supposition, which I offer only to explain exactly my thought, it seems evident to me that if this body moves sometimes toward the Orient, and sometimes toward the Occident, motion of which it is not the cause, but which is not invincible: it seems to me, I say, that its determination contrary to the law, and morally evil, would remain such as it is, and would produce by itself a change neither in its roundness, nor in the degrees of speed of this ball; and that if this body becomes cubical or immobile, following its determination contrary to order, its change would never be produced by the efficacy of its disordered determination, but by the author of all beings, and of all their modalities. (OCM XVI 43)

The claim here is that both the shape of a ball and the quantity of its motion differ in kind from the direction of its motion toward the Orient or Occident. Such a claim can be understood in terms of the distinction in the *Recherche* (see §2.2.1 [1]) between the modifications of a body that consist in internal relations between its parts (modifications in a strict sense) and the modifications of the body that involve its relation to bodies external to it (modifications in a loose sense) (RV I.1, OCM I 42/LO 2–3). The imaginary case of bodily motion is naturally read as implying that the ball's shape and quantity of motion are modifications of it in a strict sense, while the direction of its motion is a modification of it only in a loose sense since this direction consists merely in an external relation to the Orient or Occident.[97] The supposition that the ball determines the direction of its motion toward the Occident thus does not require the attribution to the ball of the power to cause what is strictly speaking a modification of it. Likewise, the view that the soul determines the direction of its motion toward a particular good does not require the attribution to it of such a power. While the perceptions or sensations of the soul and the "quantity" of its motion toward the good in general involve internal or physical features that require God as a cause, the consent that consists in the determination of that motion involves only an external relation and thus is a moral rather than a physical feature of the soul.[98] God alone can create the physical aspects of the motion of our soul, according to Malebranche, but we can be the cause of the moral aspects of that motion, and in particular of the determination that constitutes consent.

Malebranche's attempt to reconcile our causation of consent and God's causation of the motion of our soul is reminiscent of Clauberg's attempt in *Corporis et Animæ* to reconcile our causation of the motion of our body and God's causation of all bodily motion. Just as Clauberg had distinguished between the quantity of bodily motion, which requires a physical cause, and the direction of that motion, which requires only a moral cause, so Malebranche distinguished between the physical aspects of the motion of the soul and the determination of that motion, the latter of which is merely a moral aspect. And just as Clauberg had argued that the fact that God alone can be a physical cause of bodily motion does not show that we cannot be a moral cause that guides and directs such motion, so Malebranche argued that the fact that God alone can cause the physical aspects of our volitional motion does not show that we cannot cause a certain moral aspect of it, namely, its determination toward a particular good. It is interesting that talk of the physical and moral aspects of the motion of the will entered into Malebranche's writings only after the publication in 1690 of the collection of Clauberg's writings that contains the *Corporis et Animæ*.[99] Although there is no indication that Malebranche owned this collection, it is tempting to suppose that in his later years he somehow learned of the distinction in Clauberg's text between moral and physical causes and made use of such a distinction in order to respond to Boursier's position that all aspects of our soul are determined by God's *prémotion physique*.

At this point, however, one might wonder whether anything prevents Malebranche from following Clauberg further by allowing that our soul can determine the motion of body. After all, the determination of this motion involves only an external relation. It seems that we could produce this determination without causing any physical effect. However, Malebranche in essence argued against this possibility in the *Réponse* when he told Arnauld that it is contradictory to hold that

> God can move a body in an indeterminate manner, or towards a body in general. But the natural movement of the soul is an indeterminate movement; it is the love of the good in general. In order to determine this indeterminate movement toward such and such goods, it suffices to represent them to the soul. And by consequence, since man can have different ideas of good by its union with universal Reason, he can change at every instant the determinations of his love: it is never necessary that for this he exceed the power of God, the particular

movements of the soul not being invincible, as the particular movements of body, because they are not, as are those of body, in any way necessary for their conservation, or their continued creation. (OCM VII 569)

Malebranche is, in fact, committed to the position—which perhaps conflicts with the coupling of quantity of motion with shape in the *Prémotion physique*—that the motion of a body cannot be a physical feature of the body since such motion consists merely in the change in relations of distance between that body and other bodies external to it.[100] As we have seen, however, he had argued in the 1688 *Entretiens* that only God can fix the relations of distance between that body and the other bodies since he alone has the power to create these bodies in their determinate positions. This argument supports the claim in the earlier *Réponse* that God cannot move body in an indeterminate manner and that the particular movements of body are invincible. Malebranche indicated an important difference between bodily motion and the motion of soul, however, when he told Arnauld that the determinate movements of the soul are not invincible because these movements are not necessary for the continued creation of the soul. Whereas God must create the moving body by determining its relations to other bodies, he can create the motion of the soul without creating it in a certain relation to particular goods.

The passage from the *Réponse*, read in light of the discussion of the motion of the imaginary ball in the *Prémotion physique*, provides the material for an account of consent that can be distinguished from Malebranche's previous two accounts. Malebranche supposed in his final work that the ball had the power to determine its motion to the Occident. The analogy indicates that by means of its consent, the soul determines its motion toward a particular good. This text therefore returns to the claim early in the *Recherche* that the soul determines its own motion when it consents. I have noted that such a claim seems inconsistent with Malebranche's position, emphasized in *Éclaircissement I*, that God determines the natural movement of the soul toward a particular good. However, one could draw on the distinction in the 1683 *Traité de Morale*, mentioned earlier, between our natural and free love. Prior to our free action, God does indeed determine our natural movements, yet while this sort of movement provides a motive for our free movement toward that good, it does not itself determine the free movement. Malebranche referred in the *Réponse* to God's causation of an indeterminate natural movement in the soul, but a better position for him seems to be that God causes there an indeterminate free movement that the soul itself determines by causing its free consent.[101]

Of course, Malebranche emphasized that when we consent, it is in our power to suspend this consent. He noted in *Éclaircissement I* that when we, in fact, suspend our consent we produce nothing real and positive because we merely "do everything that God does in us, for we do not limit to a particular good or, rather, to a false good the love that God impresses in us for the true good" (OCM III 24/LO 551).[102] However, the emphasis in this text on the fact that consent is an inaction because it is a mere repose makes it difficult to determine the sense in which suspension, which is not a mere repose, is nonetheless an inaction. On the view I have attributed to him, however, the suspension of consent consists in resisting the urge to determine the indeterminate free motion that God creates in us, which resistance leaves this motion in its indeterminate state. These remarks, therefore, indicate how it is that we simply "do everything that God does in us" when we suspend our consent. Moreover, they allow Malebranche to say that whether we consent or suspend we produce nothing real and positive in the sense that we neither produce perceptions nor add to the quantity of the motion of our will.

Nevertheless, Malebranche insisted in the *Prémotion physique* that when the soul suspends its consent, it directs its attention away from a particular good (*Pré. phy.*, sec. XII, OCM XVI 48–49). This act of redirection merely changes the relation between the soul and the object of attention and therefore does not itself cause a real being. However, Malebranche held that such an act serves to extinguish the natural love of a particular good that existed prior to the act of suspension; thus his claim to Arnauld that by this sort of act the soul "can change the determinations of its love." Just as by its act of consent the soul causes its free love to be determined toward a particular good, then, so by its act of suspension it causes a redirection of attention, which redirection is in turn the (occasional) cause of a change in the determinations of its natural love. While Malebranche continued to believe that consent and suspension involve the production of *rien de physic*, he also can be interpreted as holding that they are "acts without doubt" that either directly produce certain free motions or indirectly bring about the elimination of certain natural motions.

(3) Freedom, God, and the Clear Idea of the Soul. We have seen that on Malebranche's view, as well as on the mature view of Descartes, the free causal activity of the soul is itself undetermined. Boursier had objected that such a view compromises divine omniscience since God can know infallibly only what his decrees have predetermined.[103] In response Malebranche admitted that we cannot determine how God could know with certainty, for instance, that Eve would freely consent to the suggestions of the serpent and Adam to the entreaties of Eve. He continued, however, that this is only because we do not have "a clear idea of the soul or of its faculties," and, thus, we know the soul and its faculties "only by consciousness or inner sentiment." According to Malebranche, consciousness or inner sentiment reveals that we are free to consent but does not render intelligible the nature of that in us which produces the free action. There is undoubtedly an idea of the soul in God that explains how he could know with certainty which free actions this power would produce in certain circumstances, but since we do not have access to this idea, we cannot provide such an explanation (*Pré. phy.*, sec. VIII, OCM XVI 24).

The central difficulty that Malebranche's remarks address is a version of the old problem of God's knowledge of future contingents.[104] The debate between Boursier and Malebranche, moreover, to a considerable extent replicates the earlier dispute between the partisans of two sixteenth-century Spanish theologians, the Jesuit Luis de Molina and the Dominican Domingo Bañez. Boursier defended the Bañezian line that God can know our free actions because he himself has determined them. His talk of the divine determination of these actions through a "physical premotion," moreover, is anticipated in the work of the sixteenth-century Thomists.[105] On the other hand, Malebranche held with the Molinists that since we can act freely only if it is possible for us to act otherwise, it cannot be the case that God comes to know our free actions by determining them. He therefore followed the Molinist line prominent among the Jesuits; God does not determine these actions by means of a physical premotion.

Molina and his followers proposed the alternative position that God knows that we will act freely in certain ways through his *scientia media*, a middle knowledge standing between his natural knowledge of the properties that objects can or must possess if they exist, on the one hand, and his free knowledge of the properties that objects in fact possess due to a free act of his will, on the other.[106] I suggest reading Malebranche as offering a similar sort of position. Such a reading is complicated by the fact that Malebranche did not present himself as a Molinist. Thus, when Arnauld charged that he was a "nouveau protecteur de la Grace Molinienne,"[107] Malebranche responded in a 1687 letter that he had in fact never read any of Molina's writings and had no knowledge of his views on grace (*Quarte lettres III*, OCM VII 416). Drawing on his own position that we cannot be morally justified apart from divine grace, Malebranche went on in this letter to reject "the use that the Demipelagians make of middle knowledge [*la science moyenne*] to defend purely human merits, and to find in us the reason for our choice" (OCM VII 415).[108] Nonetheless, he concluded by telling Arnauld that if it is in fact the sentiment of Molina that God knows our free actions without leading us invincibly to them, then he readily accepts it since "it is also the sentiment most approved in the Church, and even that which Augustine supposes as incontestable" (OCM VII 416). It was this same Molinist sentiment that Malebranche reaffirmed toward the end of his life when he claimed to Boursier that God had certain knowledge of the sin of Adam before it occurred even though he in no way determined Adam's consent to it (*Pré. phy.*, sec. VIII, OCM XVI 24).

Faced with the question of how God could possibly know our free actions that are not determined beforehand, Molina himself had referred in a terse manner to the "*absolutely profound and absolutely preeminent comprehension, such as is found only in God with respect to creatures.*"[109] When Boursier confronted him with a related question, Malebranche referred in a similarly terse way to the "clear idea of the soul, such as is in God" (OCM XVI 24). Here I think one could fill out Malebranche's account of the role of this clear idea in God's knowledge of our free actions by drawing on Calvin Normore's helpful development of the Molinist account of middle knowledge. Normore has us imagine that God contains a perfect model of our mind, and that he "sees" how we would freely behave in certain circumstances by simulating those circumstances and running the model.[110] God's perfect model of the mind corresponds roughly to Malebranche's clear idea of the soul in God. Just as on Normore's picture our perfect model provides the resources for divine knowledge of how we would freely behave in certain circumstances, so on Malebranche's view God's clear idea of our soul yields determinate knowledge of our free actions. Malebranche's suggestion to Boursier is that we cannot comprehend divine knowledge of our free actions because we do not have access to the clear idea—in Normore's terms, the perfect model—of our soul on which this knowledge depends.

Malebranche emphasized to Boursier an argument for our lack of access to such an idea that focuses on the fact that we cannot discover apart from our internal experience "that we are capable of such and such modifications, and even less in what they consist" (Pré. phy., sec. XIV, OCM XVI 61). The case of our free action raises different considerations, though, since it does not follow from the nature of the soul that we will freely act in particular ways in just the manner that it follows from this nature that we are capable of certain modifications. Malebranche can be faulted for failing to stress these differences; it is a weakness of his discussion in the *Prémotion physique* of God's knowledge of our soul that it does not draw attention to the Molinist distinction between God's natural knowledge of our modifications, on the one hand, and his middle knowledge of our free actions, on the other.

We can see the importance of this distinction by returning to my suggestion in §2.2.2 that Malebranche must take God's knowledge of our free action to depend on ideas of particular souls. It is clear that for him God's knowledge of the modifications of which the soul is capable depends only on his idea of the soul in general, just as God's knowledge of the modifications of which body is capable depends only on his idea of extension. Malebranche also admitted that in order to know which modifications particular bodies actually possess, God must consider not only his idea of extension, but also his volitions to create a certain world and to establish the laws of motion in that world.[111] Given his view that the divine volitions completely determine the modifications of particular bodies in that world, Malebranche can claim that God does not require ideas of particular bodies, in addition to his idea of extension, in order to know which modifications bodies actually possess. Since he stressed that divine volitions cannot completely determine the free acts of our will, on the other hand, it is difficult to see how he could avoid saying that God's knowledge of these acts depends on some idea of our soul in particular that differs from his idea of the soul in general.

Malebranche noted to Boursier that "the soul, although finite, contains several mysteries that it senses in itself, and that it cannot explain" (Pré. phy., sec. XXIII, OCM XVI 131). The sensations that the soul senses in itself are mysterious since we lack access to a clear idea of the soul that is akin to the clear idea of extension. If I am correct, the freedom that the soul senses in itself must for Malebranche be doubly mysterious since we lack access not only to this sort of idea of the soul, but also to a further idea that has no counterpart in the case of body. Indeed, the remarks at the start of the *Recherche* make clear that the analogy between the will and the bodily faculty for motion simply breaks down in the case of our free action. Malebranche emphasized the "very considerable difference" between the motions that God impresses in matter and the motions he impresses in the soul. The difference is revealed, in particular, by the fact that whereas matter is "altogether without action," and thus must have its motion directed by God, our own will "in a sense can be said to be active" since it can direct our free impressions (RV I.1, OCM I 46/LO 4). The point here, which is related to Malebranche's remarks in the *Prémotion physique*, is that nothing in matter allows us to conceive the power that the will has to determine its free movements.

The passage from the *Recherche* also indicates that the motion of the will, in addition to its active power, cannot be clearly understood in terms of something in body. The view suggested in Malebranche's later writings is that the motion that God impresses in the will can, as the motion that he impresses in matter cannot, be completely indeterminate. Thus, as in the case of our active power, so in the case of the free motion of our will, the analogy to matter fails to provide a complete understanding. However, we cannot fill in this gap in our understanding, according to Malebranche, since we lack access to a clear idea of the soul in general. In the end, therefore, we can no more know in what the indeterminate motions of the will consist than we can know in what its dispositions consist. This conclusion that we have only a confused knowledge of our indeterminate motions serves to address Arnauld's objection that the proof of freedom requires a clear vision of the soul. On the position I attribute to Malebranche, it is because the free motion that God impresses in the soul is indeterminate that we can have the power to determine that motion. The very same indeterminateness that reveals the inconceivability of our free motion thus also provides room for our freedom. The response to Arnauld, then, is that the claim that our knowledge of our own soul is radically imperfect, far from precluding the proof of our freedom, actually allows for its possibility.

Though Descartes himself spoke of the movement of the will in passages cited previously, he did not explicitly allow that this movement could be undirected. The Malebranchean argument from the premise that the motion of our will can be indeterminate to the conclusion that we do not know the will through a clear idea of the soul thus bears no direct relation to Descartes' writings. However, the main argument in the *Prémotion physique* to such a conclusion from the premise that we have a contra-causal power to determine our will is more directly Cartesian since Descartes clearly embraced this premise in his mature works. It is true that Malebranche's inference from such a premise is not compatible with Descartes' view in the *Principles* that "we are so conscious of the freedom and indifference that is in us" that "there is nothing we comprehend more evidently and more perfectly" (PP I.41, AT VIII–1 20/CSM I 206). Yet it must be said that Descartes focused more on our consciousness of freedom than on our perfect comprehension of it. He therefore was not in a good position to respond to the position that our freedom is, like our union with the body, something we sense rather than clearly understand.

In any event, the response that Descartes did provide in the passage from the *Principles* is inadequate. He argued that it follows merely from the fact that we are conscious of our freedom that we perfectly comprehend it. But surely we could be conscious *that* our soul acts in a certain way without comprehending *how* it so acts. Clerselier indicated as much when he proposed in his letter to La Forge (ironically enough, "following the sentiment of Descartes") that even though we experience with certainty that our soul moves our body, we do not know how our soul brings about that motion. Likewise, Malebranche took the claim that we have a consciousness or inner sentiment of our freedom to be wholly compatible with the conclusion that we cannot comprehend the power that brings about our free actions. Reasonably enough, he also argued that such a conclusion is plausible given that we cannot comprehend God's infallible knowledge of the actions deriving from this power. It is the fact that the power is undetermined, after all, that renders God's knowledge of the actions so incomprehensible to us. Malebranche therefore saw in a way Descartes never could that the claim that our free actions are indifferent or undetermined is at odds with the doctrine that our knowledge of our own soul is clear and distinct.

I believe it is helpful to consider Malebranche's negative point regarding our knowledge of our freedom in light of Thomas Nagel's recent claim that our internal, subjective view of ourselves as autonomous agents does not provide an explanation of our action that is satisfactory from an external, objective view.[112] From a subjective view it appears that while reasons may motivate us to act in a certain manner, we are free to refrain from such action. From an objective view, according to Nagel, it seems that these reasons can explain our action only if they causally determine that we act in a particular manner. What is so difficult to capture from this view is that in us which is distinct from our reasons and from other constraining features of our character and personality but which nonetheless is the source of our action. Nagel's conclusion is that it seems impossible to say "what would, if it were true, support our sense that our free actions originate with us."[113] I take Malebranche's appeal to the incomprehensibility of God's knowledge to indicate a similar difficulty in conceiving the source of our free action. To be sure, Malebranche assumed that a God's-eye view yields a transparent explanation of this source in objective terms, just as he assumed that such a view yields a transparent explanation of subjective sensory appearances in these same terms. In this respect his view of our freedom is more optimistic than Nagel's. However, he shared Nagel's pessimism concerning our own ability to provide a transparent objective explanation of our autonomy or freedom of action. I take such pessimism to be reflected in Malebranche's claim in the *Prémotion physique* that a consideration of our freedom reveals that we lack access to a clear idea of our soul.

In the first chapter of this study I emphasized the result of Malebranche's discussion of the cogito argument that the same subjective view that provides immediate access to our modifications, particularly to our sensations, also produces only a confused knowledge of their nature. As I noted there, he took these positive and negative claims concerning our view of our own modifications to be two sides of the same Cartesian coin. Now we are in a position to see that his account of freedom similarly has two related sides. From the beginning Malebranche held with Descartes that we are conscious of our freedom. Nonetheless, he came to believe that we can allow for such a consciousness only by admitting that we do not have a clear knowledge of our soul. Malebranche could not, in the end, accept the view of Clerselier and Clauberg, found also in Descartes, that we are conscious of a power in ourselves to move our own body. He understood our clear knowledge of matter to reveal that God cannot create or conserve bodily motion without fully determining it. Yet he also held that since we do not have a clear idea of the soul, we cannot rule out the claim that God creates and conserves our will without fully directing it. Thus, it is the fact that our mind differs from matter in an inexplicable manner that allows us to posit an equally inexplicable power in ourselves to direct our own will. I have suggested that Descartes may be able to resist Malebranche's argument against our power to move our body.[114] However, it is difficult to see how he could resist Malebranche's conclusion that we know neither the nature of our undetermined power of action nor the nature of the habits or dispositions of our will in the same clear manner in which we know the nature of the geometrical and kinematic features of body.

Contemporary compatibilists will of course reject Malebranche's conclusion that inner sentiment reveals that we have an undetermined power to act freely, just as contemporary eliminativists will reject his conclusion that consciousness establishes the existence of our sensations. It has proven rather difficult, however, to eliminate the belief in sensation. While it may not be as difficult to eliminate the belief in undetermined freedom, there seems to be something vaguely unsettling about the compatibilist alternatives. At least some of Malebranche's specific claims regarding the soul continue to have a certain appeal.

Admittedly, Malebranche's project of providing Cartesian demonstrations of properties of the soul such as spirituality, immortality, and freedom is no longer appealing as it once was. Certainly nothing I have said here shows that this positive Cartesian project is still viable. Yet Malebranche's work continues to be useful insofar as it reveals a negative side to the Cartesian theory of mind that is often overlooked. His remarks concerning freedom, in particular, serve to indicate that Cartesians who follow Descartes in positing an undetermined power of action must admit that they do not have a clear understanding of the nature of this power. These remarks thus strengthen Malebranche's general point that the knowledge that Cartesians have of the nature of the properties of the immaterial soul is inferior in kind to the knowledge that they have of the nature of the properties of body. Critics such as Arnauld struggled valiantly to defend Descartes' own official line, which La Forge also had attempted to strengthen, that we have a clear and distinct perception of our own soul. To my mind, however, what wins out in the end is Malebranche's revisionist claim, which sets him apart even from Desgabets and Regis, that on the Cartesian view we can know only in a confused manner what consciousness reveals to us.

Such a claim may seem to be of limited interest, given that the Cartesian tradition in philosophical psychology is widely regarded to be dead. But just as

Malebranche drew attention to the pretense of Cartesians who claimed that the nature of the soul as an immaterial thing is wholly intelligible, so his works may even today speak against the pretensions of those who would hold that there is a wholly intelligible materialistic explanation of the nature of mind. In any case, recent work in the philosophy of mind has made clear that the phenomenon of consciousness yields important difficulties or challenges for such an explanation. For this reason it can be said that it is Malebranche, more than any other Cartesian, including Descartes, who shows us what remains alive in the Cartesian theory of the soul.

NOTES

N.B.: References in the notes and text are cited by abbreviations or by short names and titles; complete information is provided in the bibliography.

Introduction

1. Descartes noted at one point that he preferred to speak of the "mind" (*mens* or *l'esprit*) in order to distance himself from the Aristotelians (see *Fifth Rep.*, AT VII 355–56/CSM II 246), though he also referred frequently to the "soul" (*anima* or *l'âme*). On the other hand, Malebranche preferred the more traditional term 'soul' (*l'âme*), but at times employed the term 'mind' (*l'esprit*). I follow Malebranche and Descartes in taking both terms to denote thinking substance.

2. Entries separated by a slash refer to the original and an English translation of the same passage. For information concerning the translation of passages from foreign-language sources, see bibliography.

3 See Yolton, *Perceptual Acquaintance*, c. 2–3; Nadler, *Malebranche and Ideas*; and Jolley, *Light of the Soul*, c. 2–7. I do not mean to suggest that such work entirely ignores those features of Malebranche's theory of the soul that I want to emphasize—Jolley in particular devotes a chapter to Malebranche's views on self-knowledge that is relevant to the discussion in my study—but I think it is fair to say that the discussions in the recent English literature of Malebranche's account of ideas have been more prominent and more detailed than the discussions there of these other features. In the French literature, by contrast, there is a tradition of concentrated work on Malebranche's psychology that derives from Bièma's "Comment Malebranche conçoit la psychologie" (1916) and Gueroult's *Étendue et psychologie chez Malebranche* (1939).

4. Malebranche first cited Augustine in his initial discussion of the doctrine of the vision in God in Book Three of the *Recherche de la Vérité* (RV III–2.6, OCM I 443–44/ LO 233) and often appealed to Augustine in the course of his decade-long dispute with Arnauld over the nature of ideas. In a preface first added to the third edition (1696) of the *Entretiens sur la Métaphysique*, Malebranche cited at length several passages from Augustine that he took to anticipate his own account of ideas. For a discussion of the

distinctively Augustinian features of Malebranche's system, see Rodis-Lewis, "Les limites initiales du cartésianisme de Malebranche."

5. See chapter 5, note 108.

6. When Arnauld charged that Descartes had held that ideas are modifications of our soul rather than features of God, Malebranche admitted that this is so but went on to say that this is only because "unlike me he does not take the work *idea* for signifying uniquely *the objective reality*, but for [signifying] those sorts of *thoughts* by which one perceives a man, an angel, etc." (*TL* I, OCM VI 217). This suggests that Descartes' position is consistent with the claim that the objective reality of our thoughts exists in God, even though Descartes himself did not endorse such a claim. Moreover, at one point Malebranche cited Augustine's dictum that only God can enlighten us in order to support his position that the nature of our soul is obscure (*Écl.* X, OCM III 150–51/LO 625–26). These remarks reflect Malebranche's tendency to smooth over differences between the views of Augustine and Descartes. Nonetheless, he did say that his recollection of what he read in Augustine allowed him to conclude that ideas are located in God (*TL* I, OCM VI 199) and that it was Descartes who taught him that "color, heat, pain are only modalities of the soul" (*TL* I, OCM VI 201). Malebranche therefore emphasized more what Augustine said about the nature of ideas and what Descartes said about the nature of the soul.

7. In "Gassendi and the Genesis of Malebranche's Philosophy," Connell has claimed that the remark in the *Recherche* concerning the opposition between those who say that we know nothing more than the soul and those who say that we know nothing less is in fact an allusion to this exchange. While there is some evidence that Malebranche was influenced by Gassendi's objections to Descartes, in the *Recherche* he took Michel de Montaigne rather than Gassendi to be the representative of those who assert that they know nothing less than the soul (see §4.1.1 [1]).

8. See the discussion of this exchange in §1.3.2 (1).

9. *Disquisitio*, Med. II, Dub. VIII, in *Opera Omnia* III 313.

10. Connell, "Gassendi and the Genesis of Malebranche's Philosophy," 111–12. I must take issue, however, with Connell's claim that the Gassendist argument is the only one that Malebranche offered in the first edition of the *Recherche* against the claim that we know the soul through an idea of its nature. Malebranche in fact offered the additional point—which to my knowledge Gassendi did not anticipate—that we cannot know our sensory modifications through definitions (RV III-2.7, OCM I 452–53/LO 238). I discuss this additional Malebranchean point in §1.3.3.

11. Connell, "La passivité de l'entendement selon Malebranche," 550.

12. *Cartésianisme de Malebranche*, 94.

13. For this view see Blondel, "L'anticartésianisme de Malebranche," 75–78; and Gueroult, *Étendue et psychologie chez Malebranche*, 41–45.

14. This perspective also informs Alquié's remarks on Malebranche's theory of the soul in *Cartésianisme de Malebranche* as well as in his "Sources cartésiennes de Malebranche." Although I differ with Alquié over some features of the relation between Malebranche and Descartes and emphasize other features not discussed by him in any detail, my general approach here owes much to his work.

15. Malebranche was referring explicitly in this passage to his rejection of Descartes' laws of motion on the grounds that bodily rest has no force to resist motion. He asserted that "there is reason to believe that if M. Descartes himself had examined his principles anew without bias, and by thinking of explanations [*raisons*] similar to those I have stated, he would not have believed that the effects of nature had confirmed his rules . . ." (OCM

II 449/LO 526). I suggest that Malebranche also believed that Descartes would not have endorsed the thesis that the nature of mind is better known than the nature of body had he examined without bias other fundamental tenets of his system.

16. To Quesnel, 18 Jan. 1680, OA II 73–74.

17. VFI, c. 21–24, OA XXXVIII 293–331/TFI 116–52. Arnauld elaborated on this critique in his *Défense* (1684), OA XXXVIII 603–35.

18. Malebranche defended this doctrine in the *Réponse à la Dissertation* (1685) in responding to Arnauld's objections to his account of freedom (*Rép. Diss.*, c. 12, OCM VII 568) and in the *Réponse à la troisième lettre de Arnauld* (1699) in replying to Arnauld's objections to his distinction between perceptions and ideas (*Lettre III*, OCM IX 923–24, 956–58). I discuss the remarks in the 1699 text in §3.2.2 (3) and the remarks in the 1685 text in §6.2.4 (2).

19. Cf. La Forge's comment in his *Remarques* that "I have sought to introduce all that M. Descartes has already said within, and to add what I believed he would have said if he had continued his plan" (*L'Homme de Descartes*, 334).

20. *Traité*, c. 2, LF 110. In chapter 1, note 83, however, I indicate that Descartes did not anticipate some features of La Forge's position in this remark.

21. The inventory of Malebranche's library composed by his friend Jacques Lelong lists the first edition (1666) of *L'esprit de l'homme par de la Forge* as item number 139 (OCM XX 237, 267). In §1.1.1 I argue that this work influenced Malebranche's discussion of our knowledge of the existence of the soul in Book Six of the *Recherche*. We know that Malebranche went to Saumur in 1661, and it is possible that he attended the lectures of La Forge. However, Gouhier has urged that Malebranche had little reason to attend these lectures since he "did not enter the Oratory to occupy himself with philosophy" and since he was not then "of the intelligence capable of interesting him in the discourses of de La Forge" (*Vocation de Malebranche*, 23).

22. One of Foucher's objections was that we know the essence neither of mind nor of body (*Critique*, 20–23). In a 1678 letter to Leibniz, Foucher suggested that this objection led Malebranche to claim in his *Éclaircissments* that "we have no clear idea of the nature of our soul" (*To Leibniz*, 12 Aug. 1678, in Leibniz, *Philosophische Schriften* I 375). In fact, Malebranche made the similar claim that we do not know the soul through its idea in the first edition of the *Recherche* prior to seeing Foucher's *Critique*. Nonetheless, Foucher's criticisms may have prompted him to revise certain passage in the first edition that imply that we have a clear idea of the soul (see RV I.12, OCM I 141d; III–2.9, OCM I 471h; and IV.2, OCM II 25h).

23. The first volume of the *Recherche* appeared in 1674, Foucher's *Critique* in January 1675, and Desgabets' *Critique de la Critique* and the second volume of the *Recherche* (containing the last three books) in September 1675. Desgabets announced in 1676 that he had started work on a commentary on the *Recherche* (OCM XVIII 122) and referred in 1677 to his "long examination" of this text that focuses on Malebranche's critique of the Cartesian laws of motion (OCM XVIII 126). This work, which is cited in the list of Desgabets' manuscripts with the title *Examen des fondements de la doctrine contenue dans les deux tomes de la Recherche de la vérité*, is now lost.

24. In the "Préface pour servir de Réponse à la critique du premier Volume," also added to the second volume of the *Recherche*, Malebranche made the similar objection to Foucher that "when one Critiques a Book, it seems to me that one must at least have read it" (OCM II 496). Following the death of Desgabets, he dropped both the "Préface" and the "Avertissement" from the fourth (1678) and subsequent editions of this volume. For more on Malebranche's confrontation with Foucher and Desgabets, see Gouhier, "La

première polémique"; Robinet, "Dom Robert Desgabets"; and Watson, *Breakdown of Cartesian Metaphysics*, c. 5–6.

25. In his "Préface" Malebranche responded to Foucher's criticism of the view that "our ideas are only manners of being of our soul" and that "the ideas that we receive from the senses represent to us only the effects that external objects produce in us" by noting that in the *Recherche* he had explicitly denied these views (OCM II 496). Desgabets attempted to defend both views in *Critique de Crit.*, 104–22. To be fair to Desgabets, however, it must be said that he did not simply overlook Malebranche's doctrine of the vision in God. An entire section of the Desgabets' text is in fact devoted to this doctrine (198–216), and his final judgment there is that the vision in God "appears wholly mystical and . . . it is very difficult to find anything solid there" (214).

26. For the claim that Arnauld's identification of ideas with perceptual acts reflects Descartes' own considered position, see Nadler, *Arnauld and the Cartesian Philosophy of Ideas*, 126–30.

27. See *Supplément* I.2.vi, RD V 177–78. In the preface to this unpublished work, Desgabets contrasted his "première supplément," which serves to correct Descartes, with the "second supplément" of writers such as Geraud de Cordemoy, Johann Clauberg, Jacques Rohault, and La Forge, which merely applies Descartes' principles to new phenomena (RD V 156).

28. *Supplément* I.2.iv–v, RD V 171–74.

29. Desgabets not only defended Descartes' identification of matter with extension against the views of the atomists (see chapter 5, note 69), but he also was one of the few Cartesians to adopt Descartes' doctrine of the divine creation of the eternal truths (see §5.3.2).

30. *Usage* III.7, 328.

31. In §§1.2.3 (2), 2.2.1 (1), and 2.3.2 (3) I indicate the specific ways in which Desgabets' work helped to shape Regis' critique of Malebranche's view that the nature of body is better known than the nature of the soul.

32. Retz may well have initiated discussions on Cartesian topics after he secluded himself in the Benedictine abbey of Saint-Mihiel in June 1675, but it is more likely that he organized the formal conferences after taking his full retirement in Commercy in 1677. The manuscripts pertaining to these conferences were discovered in the Bibliothèque municipale in Epinal by Cousin and Hennequin. Cousin published these manuscripts initially in the *Journal des savants* in 1842, with some corrections in the 1845 *Fragments de philosophie cartésienne*, and with further corrections—some due to the suggestions of Cerquand—in the 1866 *Fragments philosophiques*. Hennequin published the manuscripts in *La France littéraire* in 1842. The most complete record was edited by Chantelauze, and appeared in 1887 as the ninth volume of the *Œuvres du Cardinal de Retz*; this is the record I cite. For an indication of the variations among the different editions of the record of the conferences, see Rodis-Lewis, "Les diverses éditions." For further discussion of the conferences themselves, see Delon, "Les conférences de Retz sur le cartésianisme"; and Plaisance, "Corbinelli auteur de comptes rendues de séances cartésiennes?"

33. This work is found in PL 320–25. For the rejection of Descartes' view that mind is better known than body, see *Alambic* I.8 and 11, PL 320–21; for the rejection of Descartes' method of doubt, see *Alambic* I.1, 2 and 9, PL 320. Other works contributed by Desgabets include *Des défauts de la méthode de M. Descartes* and the *Traité de l'indéfectibilité des créatures*.

34. We know the approximate time of Corbinelli's arrivals and departures from the

correspondence of his friend, Mme de Sévigné, who also was a friend of Cardinal de Retz. See her letters to her daughter, Mme de Grignan, 14–15 June and 21 and 22 September 1677, in *Correspondance* II 268, 355, and 356.

35. I present such evidence in §§2.3.1 (2) and 4.2.2.

36. For the difference between Malebranche and Desgabets on this point, see §3.1.1 (1).

37. *VFI*, c. 24, OA XXXVIII 326/TFI 148.

38. *Étendue et psychologie chez Malebranche*, 91.

Chapter One

1. Gueroult, *Malebranche* 1:3–61. Cf. Alquié, *Cartésianisme de Malebranche*, 91–93; Robinet, *Système et existence*, 344–46; and Rodis-Lewis, *Malebranche*, 23–25.

2. *Traité*, c. 27, LF 334. Cf. Descartes' remark in Part Four of the *Discourse* that the truth, *Je pense donc je suis*, was "the first principle of the philosophy I was seeking" (AT VI 32/CSM I 127).

3. *Fifth Rep.*, AT VII 352/CSM II 244; *PP* I.9, AT VIII-1 7–8/CSM I 195.

4. *Traité*, c. 27, LF 334.

5. The fact that Malebranche did not explicitly cite La Forge in this section of the *Recherche* is explained by Prost's comment that Malebranche cited "only those authorities absolutely necessary for certain discussions. But La Forge did not present himself to [Malebranche] as an authority." Thus La Forge was for Malebranche "only a commentator, a clear and faithful disciple. It was Descartes, in essence, that the young oratorian believed he read in reading La Forge; he therefore did not have to name him, it being always from the same source that he borrowed" (*Essai sur l'atomisme*, 189–90. Cited with approval in Gouhier, *Vocation de Malebranche*, 88 n.4).

6. Thus Book One is devoted to an investigation of the errors of the senses, Book Two to the errors of the imagination, Book Three to the errors of the pure intellect, Book Four to the errors of the inclinations, and Book Five to the errors of the passions. The final Book Six concerns the method for the search after truth. See RV I.4, OCM I 68/LO 17–18.

7. *Traité*, c. 27, LF 332.

8. *Traité*, c. 27, LF 336. Cf. Descartes' second and third rules in Part Two of the *Discourse* at AT VI 18–19/CSM I 120.

9. *Traité*, c. 27, LF 335.

10. It is conceivable, of course, that Malebranche took these views directly from Descartes rather than from La Forge, but whereas in the *Recherche* Malebranche did not hesitate to mention when he borrowed from Descartes (see, e.g., RV I.10, OCM I 123/LO 49; IV.11, OCM II 93/LO 317), he never cited La Forge by name. This provides some reason to suspect that Malebranche was thinking more of La Forge's *Traité* than of Descartes' *Discourse* when he referred in Book Six to "the works of others."

11. RV III–2.7, OCM I 451/LO 237. Cf. *Écl.* XI, OCM III 167/LO 635.

12. Thus he was willing to speak of a knowledge of the soul "*par conscience ou par sentiment interieur*" (e.g., at RV III–1.1, OCM I 382/LO198; III–2.7, OCM I 4/LO 239). Cf. *Réponse*, c. 6, OCM VI 56. Malebranche had a preference for the term *sentiment*, however, as shown by the fact that in several passages from the fourth and subsequent editions of the *Recherche* he excised previous references to knowledge of the soul *par conscience* and referred only to knowledge *par sentiment intérieur* (e.g., RV I.12, OCM I

139g; I.13, OCM 147d). This preference can be explained by the fact, noted below, that it the use of the term *conscience* in a nonmoral sense was relatively new and unfamiliar to some of Malebranche's Cartesian contemporaries.

13. *Traité*, c. 6, LF 134.

14. *Le problème de l'inconscient*, 39. Cf. the discussion of the transformation of the use in early modern France of the use of the term *conscience*, in Davies, *Conscience as consciousness*, c. 1.

15. See Rodis-Lewis, *Malebranche*, 175.

16. *Traité*, c. 6, LF 134.

17. In this passage he explained that we have felt an inward pain and secret reproach of reason whenever "we clearly knew that ill use would be made of our freedom if consent were not willed, or if we willed to extend its power over things no longer in its power" (OCM I 55/LO 10). In §6.2.4 I consider the notions of freedom and consent that are broached by Malebranche's explanatory remarks.

18. *Traité*, c. 27, LF 334. I take La Forge to have understood knowing a thought through itself to consist in knowing that thought immediately and not by an act of reflection.

19. *Traité*, c. 6, LF 133. Cf. Descartes' remark in the *Sixth Replies* that one knows that one is thinking and what thought is "by that inner cognition [*cognitione illa interna*] which always precedes reflection [*reflexam*]" (AT VII 422/CSM II 285).

20. In his 1690 *Système de philosophie*, Regis endorsed the view, which he claimed to find in Augustine, that "the soul knows its sensations through themselves [*par elles-mêmes*]; and in effect if the soul knows a sensation through another, it would know also another sensation through another, and thus it would progress to infinity" (*Système*, Meta., I-2.13, I 150). Regis no doubt was thinking here of the charge in the 1689 *Censura philosophiae cartesianae*, written by the Jesuit Pierre-Daniel Huet, that Cartesians are committed to an infinite regress of thoughts. In response to Regis, Huet argued in the 1694 edition of his work that the act of thinking about a thought must be temporally posterior to that very thought and thus cannot be identical to it (*Censura philosophiae cartesianae*, c. 1, 35–36). In his response to Huet, Regis simply repeated that reflection on thought does not require a distinct act (*Réponse au livre*, c. 1, 43). This line is emphasized as well in replies to Huet by Dutch Cartesians that date from the same period. For a discussion of these replies, as well as of Regis' exchange with Huet, see (Rodis-) Lewis, *Le problème de l'inconscient*, 116–23.

21. See Rorty's view that Descartes held in effect that indubitability distinguishes the mental from the physical (*Philosophy and the Mirror of Nature*, 58) and Jolley's claim that Cartesians such as Descartes and Arnauld took incorrigibility to be a criterion of the mental (*Light of the Soul*, 128).

22. In the *Passions* Descartes distinguished passions in this restricted sense from passions in the more general sense of perceptions or nonvolitional states of the soul (PS I.25, AT XI 347–48/CSM I 337–38).

23. See Voss' reading of this passage in his edition of *The Passions of the Soul*, 34 n.29. One problem for this reading is that the passage itself affirms that we are typically ignorant of the proximate bodily cause, and not only when we are strongly agitated (PS I.25, AT XI 347–48/CSM I 337–38). It is thus difficult to see how Descartes could take ignorance of bodily causes alone to distinguish those who are strongly agitated from those who are not.

24. Descartes used this example to illustrate that attention to internal emotions that arise from our soul allows us to be unaffected by "the most violent assaults of the pas-

sions," which passions derive from motions in our bodies (*PS* II.148, AT XI 442/CSM I 382). Though he did not say this explicitly, it seems that the illustration is needed because the assaults cause us to overlook these emotions, or at least to confuse them with the passions. Compare the point in an earlier article of this text that we often fail "to distinguish adequately between the things that depend wholly on us from those that do not depend on us at all" (*PS* II.144, AT XI 436/CSM I 379). Curley has argued that the example of the grieving husband in *Passions* II.147 helps to explain the claim in I.28 that those who are strongly agitated by the passions do not know them best (*Descartes against the Skeptics*, 178).

25. Malebranche went on to say that "the same objects do not make everyone sense [the same sensation] because of the different dispositions of the sensory organs," and that "this is of the utmost consequence to note for physics and for morals" (OCM I 151/ LO 65). In Book Six he indicated that one reason this result is important for physics is that it shows not only that there is a distinction between sensible qualities and the bodily dispositions that give rise to them, but also that there is no neat correspondence between the qualities and dispositions (RV VI–2.2, OCM II 303/LO 441–42). For more on Malebranche's rejection of such a correspondence, see §2.1.2 (2).

26. As I indicate in chapter 3, note 25, Malebranche in fact said very little about the nature of reflective consciousness or thought. It can hardly be claimed, then, that the doctrine of the incorrigibility of reflective thought is a central feature of his theory of the soul.

27. Flanagan, *Science of the Mind*, 194–95. Flanagan's descriptions of Simple and Process Cartesianism differ slightly from my own, and my Content Cartesianism combines elements of Flanagan's State and Content Cartesianism. Moreover, Flanagan discusses an additional thesis, Causal Cartesianism, that I do not consider.

28. In his response to Huet, Regis attributed this distinction to "the Cartesians" (*Réponse au livre*, c. 1, 48–49). He also attributed the more elaborate distinction among *simple perception, jugement,* and *raisonnement* to Descartes (c. 2, 97). While to my knowledge Descartes did not invoke this further distinction, it is found in Rohault's *Traité de physique* (1671) (Bk. I, c. 2, pp. 5–6) and in Malebranche's *Recherche.*

29. In this passage Malebranche endorsed the traditional Cartesian postion that strictly speaking the understanding does not judge since judgment is an act of will (RV I.2, OCM I 49/LO 7). However, he went on to speak of *jugement* in a looser sense that pertains to perceptions of the understanding.

30. The translation in LO of *raisonnement* as "inference" can be misleading since, as I will shortly argue, the inferential derivation of existence from thought is for Malebranche more akin to a perceptual judgment than to reasoning.

31. One possible difficulty is raised by the claim in Book One that a simple perception is a pure perception (RV I.2, OCM I 50/LO 7). I have indicated that Malebranche allowed that the perception of a sensation can be an aspect of that very sensation. But he seems to be committed to holding that this aspect cannot be a simple perception, given his view that sensations differ in kind from pure perceptions (RV I.4, OCM I 66–67/LO 16). In a footnote to his discussion of simple perception added to the sixth edition of the *Recherche* (1712), however, Malebranche wrote that the operations of the understanding that he calls pure perceptions "are only modifications produced in the soul by the efficacy of divine ideas, in consequence of the laws of the union of the soul with the Sovereign reason and with its own body" (OCM I 50/LO 16). Since sensations are modifications that the soul has in virtue of its union with body (RV I.13, OCM I 143/LO 61), this footnote suggests that sensations are pure perceptions in some broad sense,

perhaps in the sense that they pertain to the understanding rather than to the will. In chapter 3 I discuss Malebranche's view of pure perceptions in a narrow sense, namely, those modifications of the soul that are distinct from sensations in virtue of the fact that they result from the laws of the union of the soul with "the Sovereign reason."

32. Huet had, in fact, objected to Regis that Cartesians cannot maintain that the existence of the soul is known by a simple view since reasoning it required to derive the conclusion, *sum*, from the premise, *cogito*; see *Censura*, c. 1, 54–61.

33. There is one noteworthy difference, however. Whereas Malebranche held that the perception of relations among relations requires an act of memory, Descartes stated in the *Rules* that he can run through a series of relations "until I have learned to pass from the first to the last so swiftly that memory retains hardly any part," so that "I seem to intuit the thing all at once" (*RM* VII, AT X 388/CSM I 25). It is perhaps significant, however, that Descartes said that memory "hardly" (*fere*) retains a part in the reasoning, and that he only "seems" (*videor*) to intuit the relations.

34. The *Rules* was among the works inherited by Clerselier after the death of Descartes in 1650. The Latin edition of this work was not published until 1701, but Clerselier allowed scholars to see the original manuscript (now lost). This explains the references to the *Rules* in the second edition (1664) of *Art de penser*, written by Arnauld and Nicole (see IV.2, OA XLI 362n.), as well as in the *Commentaire ou remarques sur la méthode de Descartes* (1671), written by a Cartesian member of the Oratory, Nicolas Poisson (see p. 76 of this text). Adam and Tannery have suggested that Clerselier showed the manuscript to Malebranche as well (AT X 352). This suggestion is supported by the fact that several remarks in Malebranche's *Recherche* are linked to passages from Descartes' text and that some of these passages were mentioned neither in *Art de penser* nor in Poisson's *Commentaire* (see OCM I 513 nn.242–43; II 535 n.8, 548–49 n.144, 551 n.168, 557 n.270, 559 nn.289–90).

35. *Système et existence*, 345–46. Cf. Gueroult, *Malebranche* 1:44. In *Système et existence* (346 n.6) Robinet grants that Descartes' cogito argument might involve a general principle but cites Gueroult's position that this principle differs from the principle that Malebranche invoked. I consider this position presently.

36. Malebranche raised this objection in order to respond to Arnauld's remarks in a 1694 letter concerning the claim in the *Recherche* that "the loftiest and most beautiful" argument for the existence of God is that we have an idea of God in virtue of our union with him (RV III–2.6, OCM I 441/LO 232). Arnauld charged that since this argument assumes that we must be united to God in order to perceive him, it supposes that God exists prior to concluding that he exists, and thus is "une des plus vicieuses manières de raisonner" (OCM IX 1032). Malebranche's suggested in response that since his argument is similar in nature to Descartes' cogito argument and since the cogito argument can be defended against the charge of circularity, so too can his argument for the existence of God.

37. Leibniz, *New Essays*, Bk. IV, c. vii, sec. 7, p. 411; Kant, *Critique of Pure Reason*, B422–23n., p. 378.

38. *Malebranche* 1:57–61.

39. *Malebranche* 1:57 n.40.

40. *Pensée métaphysique de Descartes*, 281. Cf. Alquié, *Cartésianisme de Malebranche*, 65.

41. *New Essays*, Bk. IV, c. ix, p. 434.

42. This appearance is strengthened by the translation in CSM of *concludimus* as "infer."

43. Such a position is related to the remark later in this text that "it is much easier

to have an understanding of extended substance or thinking substance than it is for us to understand substance on its own, leaving out the fact that it thinks or is extended" (*PP* I.63, AT VIII-1 31/CSM I 215).

44. Such an assumption is behind Descartes' claim in the *Second Meditation* that the same *I* can have very different thoughts (AT VII 28–29/CSM II 19). In his *Essay concerning Human Understanding*, Locke raised the possibility of the transference of consciousness from one immaterial thinking substance to another (II.xxviii.8), a possibility Kant later used to illustrate the difference between the logical identity of the self and the numerical identity of substance (*Critique of Pure Reason*, A364n., p. 342). Malebranche himself failed to discuss the relation between the awareness of the self and the identity of thinking substance. Indeed, as I argue in chapter 5, his account of personal immortality is similar to the account in the writings of Descartes and the other Cartesians in focusing exclusively on the permanence of immaterial substance and thus in overlooking entirely the importance of a personal identity rooted in a continuing sense of self.

45. In a note to this record, Robinet asks, "Who speaks for Desgabets, if it is not Desgabets himself?" (OCM XVIII 122 n.4). The answer to this question, offered some time ago by Gouhier ("La première polemique," 100–102) and more recently by Rodis-Lewis ("Les diverses éditions," 163) and Plaisance ("Corbinelli auteur?", 47), is that it is Corbinelli who spoke. All three indicate that the author's comment at the end of the record that he had to withdraw from discussion "comme la fièvre me prit" (OCM XVIII 124) is telling given the remark by Mme de Sévigné in correspondence that Corbinelli had been struck by "une fièvre tierce" during his time in Paris (21 and 22 Sept. 1677, *Correspondance* II, 355 and 356). It seems that Desgabets himself did not attend the Paris conference since, as Robinet's question indicates, he most likely would have spoken for himself had he been present.

46. The author of the record wrote that when he first pressed Malebranche to pronounce on Desgabets' position, "Malebranche responded to me that D. Robert has known well that he was not of his [i.e., Malebranche's] opinion, in what he has written in his work *De la Recherche de la Vérité*." Malebranche agreed to respond only after concceeding that he had not answered Desgabets' specific objections to the cogito argument (OCM XVIII 123).

47. *Critique de Crit.*, 186–87. Desgabets was arguing here against the thesis of the *Recherche* that the nature of body is better known than the nature of the soul.

48. *Alambic* I.8, PL 320. In his *Supplément* Desgabets held that the doctrine of the resurrection of the body reveals that even in the afterlife our thoughts depend on body (I.4.ix, RD V 187–88).

49. *Alambic* I.7, PL 320.

50. Retz often spoke on Descartes' behalf, though sometimes the participants looked to him as an impartial moderator (OR IX 270), and at other times Retz was content merely to clarify the differences between Desgabets and Descartes (OR IX 224–25, 228, 232–33). There is a discussion of Retz' role at the conferences in Delon, "Les conférences de Retz," 270–76.

51. OR IX 226. The "disciples of Descartes" chimed in that for Descartes "it is possible that this idea [of thought] represents what it is to think, without representing as well and as clearly the efficient cause of this idea" (OR IX 229). The Cartesians went on to argue that since it is possible that thoughts derive from something other than body, we cannot be immediately certain that they actually do derive from body (OR IX 231–32).

52. *Alambic* I.53, PL 322.

53. *PP* I.57, AT VIII-1 26–27/CSM I 212.

54. *Alambic* I.21, PL 322. At the Commercy conferences, Retz took Desgabets to hold that Descartes "has believed as [Desgabets] has that duration is corporeal" (OR IX 297).

55. *Alambic* I.48, PL 322. For Descartes' position, see *PP* I.48, AT VIII-1 22–23/CSM I 208. As Retz indicated (OR IX 297), Desgabets charged that Descartes did not offer a consistent view of duration.

56. *Supplément* I.2.vi, RD V 179. This passage provides the background to the remark in *Descates à l'alambic* that Descartes went wrong in mistaking his thought for that of an angel (*Alambic* I.11, PL 321).

57. At the Commercy conferences, "the disciples of Descartes" objected that the "primary inconvenience" of Desgabets' position is its implication that "the soul knows very clearly by an intuitive notion that it is a body" (OR IX 243). Desgabets had attempted to distance himself from materialism when he claimed in *Descartes à l'alambic* that there is a connection that "all thought has to motion, although it is not motion" (*Alambic* I.12, PL 321).

58. *Supplément* I.5.ii, RD V 189.

59. *Indéfectibilité*, c. 6, RD II 40.

60. *Supplément* I.5.vi, RD V 178–79. Cf. *Alambic* I.11, PL 321.

61. Desgabets' defender noted, as Desgabets himself had, that "duration and succession are the same thing" (OCM XVIII 123). It may be that, as in the case of Desgabets, we are to take the claim that the duration of thought just is the succession of motion to mean that the former is inseparable from the latter.

62. This position was also suggested by Retz at the Commercy conferences; see OR IX 299–300.

63. *To Arnauld*, 29 July 1648, AT V 223/CSMK 358. Cf. *To Arnauld*, 4 June 1648, AT V 193/CSMK 355. In these passages Descartes was responding to Arnauld's proposal that while the duration of motion involves succession, the duration of spiritual beings is "permanent and *totum simul*" (AT V 188). Perhaps in order to balance the suggestion in the *Principles* that time is the measure of motion (see the passage cited in note 53), Descartes emphasized to Arnauld that our knowledge of duration derives from our knowledge of the succession of our own thoughts. The account in this correspondence is linked to the view in the *Third Meditation* of the acquisition of the idea of duration (AT VII 44–45/CSM II 30–31).

64. RV I.9, OCM I 116/LO 45. At the Paris conference Malebranche claimed that duration belongs to God "properly" and to creatures "only by participation." He went on to say that the eternal truths lack duration since they do not exist outside of God's understanding (OCM XVIII 124). While this position is not fully worked out, Malebranche perhaps could say, in line with his remarks in the *Recherche*, that while God's duration is nonsuccessive, the duration that creatures have by participation is successive. When Malebranche said that eternal truths lack duration, then, he could have meant only that they lack the successive duration of creatures.

65. OR IX 302. At OR IX 299–300, Retz referred, as Desgabets had (OR IX 287–88), to Descartes' remarks on duration in his 1648 correspondence with Arnauld (see note 63). For an interesting discussion of Descartes' account of duration in relation to the discussions at Commercy, see Rodis-Lewis, "L'âme et la durée."

66. OR IX 316. As I indicate in §2.3.2, Desgabets' position that human sensory thought is a mode of the soul united to a body, rather than a mode of the soul itself, was anticipated somewhat by Descartes in his 1643 correspondence with Princess Elisabeth.

67. Such an argument would, however, fail to defeat Kant's "Refutation of Idealism" in the second edition of the *Critique of Pure Reason* since his refutation takes the mere fact that determinate knowledge of our existence depends on outer sense to reveal that such knowledge depends on sensory knowledge of external phenomena (*Critique* B274–79, pp. 244–47). It would be interesting to compare Desgabets' argument against Descartes with Kant's own position.

68. In *Descartes à l'alambic*, Desgabets presented a garbled version of this response to Descartes when he stated that "the soul and the body know themselves together, and with the same clarity" (*Alambic* I.11, PL 321). I take it that he wanted to say that we clearly know the existence of soul and body at the same time.

69. *Critique de Crit.*, 124.

70. *Critique de Crit.*, 189.

71. For the claim that soul is distinct from mind, see *Système*, Meta., I–2.1, I 113; for the claim that all thoughts of the soul derive from the body, see *Système*, Meta., I–2.4, I 122.

72. *Système*, Meta., I–1.1, I 68.

73. *Système*, Meta., II–1.6, I 164–67. I discuss Regis' defense of this thesis in §§2.2.1 (1) and 2.3.2 (3).

74. *Usage* I–2.6, 118.

75. *Usage* I–2.8–9, 123–30. There is an anticipation of this position in *Système*, Meta., I–1.3, I 76.

76. Though Regis did not follow Desgabets in appealing to the nature of duration in order to show that it is not the case that mind is better known than body, his thought on the nature of duration likewise evolved toward Desgabets' own view. In the *Système* Regis had indicated, in line with the position in Descartes' correspondence with Arnauld (see note 63), that knowledge of duration derives primarily from awareness of the succession of thoughts (Meta., I–1.14, I 106). In the *Usage*, however, he followed Desgabets in holding that the conception of succession presupposes that of bodily motion (I–2.3, 107; I–2.18, 153).

77. In the fourth (1678) and subsequent editions Malebranche wrote, "to prove demonstratively" (OCM I 122/LO 48).

78. *Critique*, 61–64.

79. It is interesting that in a section added to the fifth edition (1700) of the *Recherche*, Malebranche appealed to the strikingly similar principle that "nothingness is not perceptible, and that everything we see [*voit*] clearly, directly, immediately, necessarily exists." However, he went on to say that "the objects we immediately see are very different from those we see externally, or rather from those we think we see or look at [*regarde*]" (RV IV.11, OCM II 99/LO 320). So whereas Desgabets took the principle that what we see must exist to establish the existence of extended substance, Malebranche took it to establish the existence of ideas that are distinct from bodies and from our own thoughts.

80. There is a similar coupling of positive and negative claims concerning the soul in Malebranche's later works. See, for instance, the *Méditations Chrétiennes* (1683) (MC IX, OCM X 103), the *Réponse au Livre de Arnauld* (1684) (*Réponse*, c. 23, OCM VI 161), and the *Entretiens sur la Métaphysique* (1688) (EM I, OCM XII 32/D 25).

81. *Malebranche* 1:48–49. Gueroult argues that another source of this *déchéance* is Malebranche's refusal to doubt our clear ideas (1:42–48). He takes Malebranche to deviate in particular from Descartes' procedure of subjecting everything to doubt prior to a consideration of the cogito argument. Gueroult concludes that Malebranche grounds knowledge not on the cogito but on the vision of ideas in God. I am not in a position to

discuss Gueroult's position in any detail since I am concerned more with the details of the cogito argument than with the relation between this argument and Descartes' method of doubt. I can only note that Descartes' own responses to the so-called problem of the Cartesian Circle tend to indicate that clear and distinct ideas are in some sense immune from radical doubt. At the very least it is not clear that Malebranche's deviation from Descartes is as radical as Gueroult suggests.

82. This is Malebranche's paraphrase of Descartes' remarks in *Fifth Rep.*, AT VII 360/CSM II 249.

83. *Traité*, c. 2, LF 110. To my knowledge Descartes did not claim that he knows an infinite number of properties of his mind. Moreover, he did not anticipate La Forge's point that we know properties of mind before we know any properties of body. In fact, we will see that he discussed his knowledge of properties of his own mind in the context of a consideration of his knowledge of the observable properties of the piece of wax.

84. The second edition (1701) of Furetière's *Dictionnaire universel* states that "the philosophers understand by consciousness the inner sentiment that one has of a thing of which one cannot form a clear and distinct idea. In this sense they say that we know our soul, and that we are assured of the existence of our thoughts, only by consciousness, that is to say, by the inner sentiment of what passes in ourselves. MALEB."

85. Descartes claim that the mind "is best known of all" must be interpreted as concerning only created things given the position in the *Meditations* that the nature of God is the one that is known most clearly and distinctly (*Third Med.*, AT VII 46/CSM II 32; *Fifth Med.*, AT VII 69/CSM II 47). Since on Descartes' official dualistic position there are only two kinds of created substances, minds and bodies, it follows from the fact that the nature of mind is better known than the nature of body that the nature of mind is the best known of all created substances.

86. According to Descartes, attributes in a narrow sense are only invariable properties of substances, but in a broad sense they can be any sort of property, whether attribute (in a narrow sense) or variable mode (*PP* I.56, AT VIII-1 26/CSM I 211; *Notes*, AT VIII-2 348–49/CSM I 297). It is clear that in the *Fifth Replies* he was referring to attributes in the broad sense.

87. In a later writing Gassendi raised further objections to Descartes' position that, as I have indicated in the Introduction, are related to Malebranche's own remarks; see *Disquisitio Metaphysica*, Med. II, Dub. VIII, in *Opera Omnia* III 310–14.

88. Descartes, 96–97. Cf. Jolley, *Light of the Soul*, 116–17.

89. VFI, c. 24, OA XXXVIII 330/TFI 151.

90. OA XXXVIII 317/TFI 139. Arnauld cited here Descartes' remarks in *PP* I.68, AT VIII-1 33/CSM II 217.

91. VFI, c. 24, OA XXXVIII 324/TFI 146. Cf. Arnauld's development of this objection in *Défense*, OA XXXVIII 603–10.

92. Indeed, Malebranche suggested to Arnauld that strictly speaking our confused awareness of our own modifications is a sentiment (*sentiment interieur*) rather than a form of clear knowledge (*connaisance*) (*Réponse*, c. 6, OCM VI 55). Here I follow the view of the *Recherche*, which differs only verbally from that of the *Réponse*, that inner sentiment does yield a form of knowledge, though one that is radically inferior to knowledge through a clear idea (RV III-2.7, OCM I 448/LO 236).

93. Malebranche's view that geometrical shapes are definable while sensations are not is connected to this account of the difference between the laws governing the soul's union with the body and those governing its union with God. I discuss his account of this difference in §3.2.2 (2).

94. *Art de penser* I.1, OA XLI 130.

95. *Traité de physique*, Bk. I, c. 27, pp. 264–65.

96. Cf. his claim elsewhere in the *Recherche* that though we have ideas of geometrical shapes that allow us to "give to them good definitions" and "deduce ... all their properties," "one can define neither heat nor cold insofar as they are sensible qualities; because one does not know them distinctly and through an idea, one knows them only through consciousness or inner sentiment" (RV VI–2.5, OCM II 366/LO 478).

97. Prior to the work of Nagel, French commentators had understood Malebranche's position in terms of the distinction between objective and subjective knowledge. See for instance Blondel, "L'anticartésianisme de Malebranche," 77–78; Callot, *Problèmes du cartésianisme*, 191; and Gueroult, *Malebranche* 1:41.

98. Nagel, *View from Nowhere*, 4–5.

99. Cf. Blondel's remark that "it is precisely because Malebranche has an overly concrete experience of the inner life, an overly high regard for the soul, that he has resolutely turned his back on an abstract science of mind or an objective psychology" ("L'anticartésianisme," 77).

100. Jolley, *Light of the Soul*, 113.

Chapter Two

1. For the most part Malebranche cited the passages from Augustine in the 1667 *Philosophia christiana*, edited by the Cartesian Oratorian André Martin (pseud. Ambrosius Victor), which is listed as item number 592 in Lelong's inventory of Malebranche's library (OCM XX 248, 272). Gouhier has concluded, "L'augustinisme que Malebranche a connu, c'est celui de la Philosophia christiana" (*Philosophie de Malebranche*, 284). Gouhier's text provides the authoritative discussion of the influence of Martin's text on Malebranche (279–311) as well as a complete collation of passages from Augustine cited or quoted by Malebranche (411–20).

2. Malebranche held that his reading of Augustine not only encouraged him to offer his account of ideas, but also helped to shape this account. Thus he claimed in the 1696 preface to the *Entretiens sur la Métaphysique* that "I know and I protest that it is to St. Augustine that I owe the sentiment that I advance on the nature of ideas" (OCM XII 20). Connell claims, however, that "the teaching of St. Augustine had little if any influence upon Malebranche's original conception of the vision in God" (*The Vision in God*, 236). He argues in particular that scholastic sources played a more important role in the formation of this conception. Even if this is granted, though, it still can be said that Malebranche took his doctrine of the vision in God to have siginificant Augustinian features.

3. The question of the accuracy of Malebranche's interpretation of Augustine's theory of divine illumination is a contentious one. Gilson has rejected this interpretation as unsound in *The Christian Philosophy of Saint Augustine*, 94–96, for instance, whereas Hessen has defended it in "Malebranches Verhhältnis zu Augustin."

4. In the *Recherche* Malabranche claimed that a relation is "nothing real" (RV III–2.6, OCM I 444), but he meant by this not that the relation isn't real but merely that it is not a real *being*. For the view that eternal truths, as opposed to falsehoods, are real, see C III, OCM IV 66.

5. The discussion of the nature of ideas in the *Recherche* focuses on the question of how we perceive bodies external to our own (RV III–2.1, OCM I 413/LO 217). Malebranche often overlooked the fact that Augustine himself was not interested in employing

the theory of divine illumination to explain our knowledge of bodies. His use of Augustine thus involves some distortion of Augustine's own position.

6. Whereas in the 1674 *Recherche* Malebranche spoke of particular ideas of creatures (e.g., RV III–2.6, OCM I 443/LO 233), he claimed in the 1678 *Éclaircissement* X that God does not contain ideas that represent each particular thing, but rather "infinite intelligible extension" or the idea of infinite extension (OCM III 153–54/LO 627). When Arnauld claimed that the remarks in *Éclaircissement* X constitute a retraction of the view in the *Recherche* (VFI, c. 13, OA XXXVIII 241–42/TFI 63), Malebranche protested that they merely explicate the position in his earlier work (*Réponse*, c. 15, OCM VI 111–12). There is much scholarly dispute on the matter, but I will simply record here my own impression that Malebranche's early talk of ideas of particular extended things can easily be translated into his later talk of parts of intelligible questions.

7. *Light of the Soul*, 94. Cf. Nadler, *Malebranche and Ideas*, 106.

8. Malebranche attributed the claim that we see objects "in themselves" to Augustine in *EM*, Preface, OCM XII 20.

9. See *EM*, Preface, OCM XII 20; *Lettre III*, OCM IX 951; and *Contre le prévention*, OCM IX 1066.

10. He made this attribution initially in the third edition (1677).

11. At the end of his discussion in Book Three of the *Recherche* of the Peripatetic account of sensation, Malebranche claimed that the objections that he had raised concerning species "are not necessary after what has been said regarding this subject in Book One, where the errors of the senses were explained" (RV III–2.2, OCM I 421/LO 221). In Book One he had emphasized that the errors of the senses derive from "the prejudice common to all men, *that sensations are in the objects they sense*" (RV I.16, OCM I 169/LO 75).

12. As I note in §2.3.1 (1), Malebranche indicated in certain texts that those who project colors take them to be qualities of external objects that are joined to the soul in sensation. Thus, although the projected colors are themselves only sensations, on his view they are confusedly conceived to be qualities distinct from those sensations.

13. Malebranche sometimes took Augustine to hold that the nature of matter consists in extension; see *TL I*, OCM VI 242; RV III–2.8, OCM I 466/LO 247 (add. to sixth ed. [1712]). Here is another instance of Malebranche's tendency to smooth over differences between Augustine and Descartes (see introduction, note 6). Malebranche's more considered view, however, is that Descartes was the first to consistently identify matter with extension.

14. *Cartésianisme de Malebranche*, 187 n.11. Further support is provided by Malebranche's rejection of animal souls; see §5.2.1.

15. In this letter, Malebranche referred to the chapter from his initial response to Arnauld that contains the claim that color is, on Augustine's view, "a quality spread on the surface of bodies" (*Réponse*, c. 7 OCM VI 68).

16. This remark is from the 1695 "New System of the Nature and the Communication of Substances, as well as the Union between the Soul and the Body," in *Phil. Schriften* IV 483/*Philosophical Essays*, 143.

17. For the textbook account, see Coppleston, *Descartes to Leibniz*, 176–77; and Boas, *Dominant Themes*, 213. There is a more recent defense of this view in Radner, "Is There a Problem of Cartesian Interaction?" and "Rejoinder to Professors Loeb and Richardson."

18. See, for instance, Lennon, "Philosophical Commentary," 810–18; Loeb, *From Descartes to Hume*, c. 5; McCracken, *Malebranche and British Philosophy*, c. 3; and Rich-

ardson's and Loeb's "Replies to Daisie Radner's 'Is There a Problem of Cartesian Interaction?'"

19. La Forge, ed., *L'Homme de Descartes*, 411.

20. In later works Descartes continued to use occasionalist terminology to describe the relation between bodily motions and sensations in the soul. See the 1637 *Dioptrics* (AT VI 144/CSM I 166); the 1647 French edition of *Principles* (PP II.1, AT IX-2 64); and the 1647 *Notes* (AT VIII-2 358-60/CSM II 304-5).

21. *Traité*, c. 10, LF 178.

22. For this reading of Descartes, see Prost, *Essai sur l'atomisme*, 30-34; Yolton, *Perceptual Acquaintance*, 19-22; and Broughton, "Adequate Causes and Natural Change," 109-11. For a similar reading of La Forge, see Bouillier, *Histoire de la philosophie cartésienne* 1:513; Prost, *Essai sur l'atomisme*, c. 6; McCracken, *Malebranche and British Philosophy*, 95; and Lennon, "Philosophical Commentary," 811.

23. The view that Descartes did not take motions to be occasions in a noncausal sense has been prominent in the French literature for some time; see Gouhier, *Vocation de Malebranche*, 83-88; Laporte, *Rationalisme de Descartes*, 225-26; and Battail, *L'avocat philosophe*, 141-43.

24. I suggest below that he did not adhere to a single view either of the power of body to cause sensations or of the nature of the soul–body union. Nonetheless, I take him to have held consistently to the central position in the correspondence with Elisabeth that the union involves a bodily power to cause sensory states of the soul.

25. *Traité*, c. 16, LF 245.

26. *Traité*, c. 10, LF 176.

27. For discussion of the complications introduced by this account of sensation, see my "Descartes on Innate Ideas."

28. For this point, see Specht, *Commercium mentis et corporis*, c. 2.

29. *Traité*, c. 13, LF 213.

30. I defend this claim with respect to Descartes' remarks in the *Notes* in my "Sensation, Occasionalism, and Descartes' Causal Principles." For the view that La Forge took bodily motions to have causal efficacy, see Gouhier, *Vocation de Malebranche*, 88-95, 101; and Nadler, "The Occasionalism of Louis de la Forge," 63-68.

31. In the *Recherche* Malebranche indicated his high opinion of Cordemoy's text when he recommended it to the reader along with Augustine's *De quantitate animæ* and Descartes' *Meditations* (RV I.10, OCM I 123/LO 49).

32. *Discernement*, Disc. V, in Cordemoy's *Œuvres philosophiques*, 148-51. For a discussion of the use of the term "occasional cause" in the seventeenth century, see Clair, "Louis de la Forge."

33. OCM XVIII 88-90; cf. *Art de penser* I.1, OA XLI 133.

34. Desgabets' version of this view was not popular at the Commercy conferences, where the Cartesians took exception to the fact that he "gives [bodies] as the efficient cause, and not only as the occasional cause" (OR IX 228). Desgabets himself responded that "the action of the body on the soul is an efficient cause, not in a peripatetic sense, but in the sense of Descartes, who considered it as primitive in its kind" (OR IX 230). I take this to be an allusion to Descartes' claim in the correspondence with Elisabeth that we have a primitive notion of the soul–body union.

35. The terms *experience*, *apprendre*, and *cause* are prominent in the remarks cited from Desgabets' letter. In *Éclaircissement* X Malebranche linked the position that the senses cause ideas to the view of the Cartesians that the soul has a faculty, nature or power "by which it can produce ideas in itself" (OCM III 145/LO 622), a view that he

rejected on the grounds that "these terms are no more significant in their mouth than in that of the Peripatetics" (OCM III 144/LO 622). It is somewhat strange that Malebranche linked these two Cartesian accounts, given that in Desgabets' letter to him the view that body is the true cause of thought is offered as an alternative to the view in *Art de penser* that a mental faculty is such a cause. However, in light of Malebranche's argument in *Éclaircissement* X that both accounts fail to recognize that God alone can enlighten the soul, it is perhaps understandable that he was not concerned there to distinguish them.

36. Lelong's inventory of Malebranche's library lists Clerselier's three-volume edition of Descartes' letters as items 142–44 (OCM XX 237, 261). The first volume of this edition contains Descartes' 21 May and 28 June 1643 letters to Elisabeth (*Lettres de Descartes* I 89–96).

37. *Traité*, c. 16, LF 238.

38. *Traité*, c. 13, LF 213. La Forge here distinguished between a univocal cause, which causes something similar to itself, and an equivocal cause, which causes something that differs from itself. He argued that while body cannot impart motion that it has, and thus cannot be a univocal cause of motion, it can bring about the production of sensory thoughts, and thus can be an equivocal cause. For a discussion of this argument, see Nadler, "The Occasionalism of Louis de la Forge," 67.

39. *Traité*, c. 16, LF 240. La Forge seems to have allowed, however, as Malebranche did not, that the human mind can also be a cause of the motion of the body to which it is united. I return to the issue of the causation of voluntary motion in §6.2.

40. The claim that bodies are passive does not address the position, endorsed by Descartes as well as by Cartesians such as La Forge and Arnauld, that the mind has a faculty that produces sensory ideas. However, Malebranche elsewhere rejected this position by invoking the occasionalist doctrine that only God can create real changes in finite substances; see RV III–2.3, OCM I 422–28/LO 222–25; and *Écl.* X, OCM III 144–47/LO 622–24.

41. *Écl.* XV, OCM III 238/LO 677; *Traité*, c. 16, LF 243. For the view that Descartes in fact adopted an occasionalist account of motion, see Hatfield, "Force (God) in Descartes' Physics," as well as Garber, *Descartes' Metaphysical Physics*, c. 9.

42. For a detailed nonoccasionalist reading of Descartes' account of motion, see Gabbey, "Force and Inertia." Gabbey presents his reading as an extension of Gueoult's remarks in "The Metaphysics and Physics of Force."

43. *Système*, Phys., I–2.4, I 305.

44. *Système*, Phys., I–2.5, I 309.

45. *Usage* I–2.15, 143.

46. *Système*, Meta., I–2.5, I 124. Cf. Regis' more elaborate discussion of the causes of our ideas in *Usage*, I–2.35, 201–3. It is worth noting that Desgabets claimed without elaboration that "bodies do not move one another, and . . . it is God who produces all the motions in the world without exception" (PL 346). With respect to this particular point his view seems to be closer to La Forge's than to Regis'.

47. The original version of this passage in the 1644 Latin edition ends with the claim that dispositions in external objects enable those objects to set up motions in our nerves, while the version in the 1647 French edition adds that these motions are "required to excite in our soul all the different sensations [*sentimens*] that they [viz. the external objects] excite there" (AT IX–2 317).

48. In §1.3.2 (1) I mentioned Descartes' view in the *Principles* that the observable properties of bodies are to be explained in terms of their insensible parts (PP IV.203, AT

VIII–1 326/CSM I 288–89), and in §1.3.2 (2) I noted his reference in a letter to Chanut to "certain motions and shapes that cause the sensations we call light, heat, etc." (26 Feb. 1649, AT V 292/CSMK 369).

49. *Traité de physique*, Bk. I, c. 23, p. 195. Later in this work Rohault made the same point with respect to words for tastes (Bk. I, c. 24, p. 225), odors (Bk. I, c. 25, pp. 239–40), sounds (Bk. I, c. 26, pp. 244–45), and colors and light (Bk. I, c. 27, pp. 264–65). The influence of this discussion in the *Traité* is evident in the work of Regis, who was instructed in Cartesianism at Rohault's Wednesday conferences in Paris in the 1660s. In his own *Système*, Regis held that the terms for light, taste, odor, and sound are equivocal since they can denote either the *sentiment particulaire* of the soul or that in bodies by which they "cause" (*causent*) the particular sentiment (*Système*, Phy., VIII–2.9, III 137). On this point Regis differed from Desgabets, who tended to treat sensible qualities as modifications of the soul alone (see §2.3.1 [2]).

50. *Essay* II.viii.10.

51. Cf. Malebranche's remark later in the *Entretiens* that "often two different bodies may reflect light in the same way" (*EM XII*, OCM XII 281/D 283).

52. See Locke's claim that simple sensory ideas "must be suitable to those Powers, he [God] has placed in external Objects, or else they could not be produced in us" (*Essay* II.xxxii.13). To say that the ideas are suitable to the powers is thus to say simply that there is some quality in the external objects that (consistently) produces the ideas in us.

53. Malebranche made the related claim that "the qualities of bodies that cause totally different sensations in us are nearly the same. . . . Bitterness and sweetness in fruits differ . . . only more or less, and that is why there are people who find them sweet, when others find them bitter" (OCM II 303/LO 442; cf. RV I.13, OCM I 149–50/LO 64–65). Though the reference here to the bitterness and sweetness of fruits may seem to suggest a Lockean understanding of these sensible qualities, Malebranche's main point is that the motions that are the (occasional) causes of these different sensations vary only in degree and consequently that only relatively slight differences in the fibers of the tongue in different people are required for the same fruit to bring about different sensations.

54. Malebranche took this distinction to be related to the fact that sensations of color are only weak and languid and thus are perceived as belonging only to external objects whereas sensations of tastes and temperatures are strong and lively and thus are perceived as belonging to the self as well as to external objects; see §2.1.3.

55. In this section of the *Recherche* Malebranche claimed that we cannot "demonstrate" that this is so, but he went on to say that it is "more reasonable" to hold that God creates sensations in accord with general and constant laws of the soul–body union (OCM I 148/LO 64). The position here that we cannot demonstrate these laws is no doubt related to his view that there can be no a priori derivation of the laws of motion since these laws depend on God's will (see notes 83 and 85). Malebranche argued in a similar manner that no demonstration of the existence of the material world is possible since this existence depends on God's volitions (*Écl.* VI, OCM III 61/LO 574–75).

56. In "Malebranche's Cartesianism and Lockean Colors," I defend this judgment on Malebranche's account by comparing it to the recent critique in C. L. Hardin of broadly Lockean accounts of color.

57. Malebranche claimed that God has given us sensations "so that we may believe [objects] to be present, and so that we may have all the sentiments and passions that we should have in relation to them" (RV III–2.6, OCM I 445/LO 234; cf. *Écl.* X, OCM III 141–42/LO 621). This remark seems to indicate that the purpose of sensation is not only to aid the conservation of the body, but also to bring about the belief in the existence

of external objects. However, Malebranche held that these two purposes are inseparable since sensations can aid the conservation of the body only because they are linked to the natural judgment that they belong to existing bodies. (I will shortly return to this point.)

58. In the *Fourth Meditation* Descartes distinguished the intellect, or the passive faculty of perception, from the active faculty of the will, but he also emphasized there that judgment depends on both faculties (AT VII 56–57/CSM II 39–40). His claim in the *Sixth Replies* that sensory judgment pertains to the intellect rather than the senses thus does not imply that it belongs to intellect as opposed to the will, but says rather that it involves an act of will that is coupled with intellectual as well as sensory perceptions.

59. Descartes cited here his position in the *Dioptrics* (see AT VI 138–41/CSM I 170–72), though the account of sensory judgment in this earlier text differs in significant ways from the account in the *Sixth Replies*. For a discussion of the differences, see my "Descartes on Innate Ideas."

60. Cf. Descartes' claim in the *Sixth Replies* that in calculating the size, shape, and distance of a body, reason "works out any one feature from other features" (AT VII 438/CSM II 295); and Malebranche's position in the *Recherche* that the sensation of size is compound because it depends on "two or more impressions occurring in the eye at the same time" (RV I.7, OCM I 97/LO 34).

61. Cf. the parenthetical remark that "the soul does not make all the judgments that I attribute to it—these natural judgments are only sensations" (RV I.9, OCM I 109/LO 41). Both this remark from chapter 9 and the passage from chapter 7 were added to the second edition (1675) of the *Recherche*. In the first edition (1674), Malebranche did not claim that these judgments depend on God, and indeed even suggested that they are states distinct from sensations that depend on us. For discussion of the shift in Malebranche's account of natural judgment, see Bréhier, "Les 'jugements naturels' chez Malebranche;" Gueroult, *Malebranche* 3:69–79, 385–89; Robinet, *Système et existence*, 305–15; and Alquié, *Cartésianisme de Malebranche*, 167–73.

62. Malebranche held that even natural judgments concerning extension, "although very useful, often lead us to some error" since they "deceive us not only with regard to the distance and the size of bodies, but also by making us see their shape as something other than it is" (RV I.7, OCM I 99–100/LO 35–36). While Malebranche claimed that these judgments lead us to the true conclusion that there are extended substances external to us, he was later prompted by the writings of Desgabets and Foucher to defend the position that they cannot establish this conclusion with certainty; see §1.2.3 (2).

63. See note 58.

64. Descartes mentioned in the *Sixth Meditation* that in the context of a discussion of the teachings of nature, nature itself is nothing other than God (AT VII 80/CSM II 56).

65. Malebranche explained that whereas "we are accustomed to attributing our sensations to objects whenever they act through the motion of invisible particles," we are accustomed to attributing pains and pleasures only to our own body because we typically see the (occasional) causes of these sensations. Thus it is that we feel the heat of the fire as if in the fire but feel the burning sensation that derives from the heat as if only in our own body (RV I.11, OCM I 131–34/LO 54–55).

66. Descartes did not anticipate Malebranche's position that we can refer the light of the torch either to the object alone or also to our own body, depending on the proximity of the torch. Moreover, he did not mention perceptions that are intermediate between perceptions that we refer to our body and perceptions that we refer to other objects.

67. There is some anticipation of this point about extension in *Éclaircissement* X, where Malebranche remarked that "[t]he soul does not contain intelligible extension as one of its manners of being, because this extension is not perceived as a manner of being of the soul, but simply as a being" (OCM III 148/LO 624). In this text, however, he went on to claim that extension cannot be a modification of the soul both because extension is divisible whereas the soul is not and because extension is general whereas the soul's modifications are particular. As Arnauld indicated, both reasons are problematic. Malebranche himself claimed that intelligible extension can be contained in God despite the fact that God is not divisible. Moreover, the fact that the idea of extension is a particular modification does not seem to preclude the fact that it is general in signification (for Arnauld's criticisms along these lines, see VFI, c. 14, OA XXXVIII 253–55/TFI 75–76; *Défense*, OA XXXVIII 393–95). Malebranche's better point is that the idea of extension cannot be a modification of any particular soul because it is the object of knowledge common to all souls.

68. In what follows, I use the term *modification* to refer to a modification in Malebranche's loose sense unless otherwise indicated.

69. There is some anticipation of this point in the *Recherche* itself, where Malebranche emphasized that we know by reasoning rather than by simple perception that weak and languid perceptions are modifications of the soul (RV I.12, OCM I 139/LO 58). I discuss this line of argument in §2.3.1.

70. VFI, c. 23, OA XXXVIII 321–22/TFI 143.

71. VFI, c. 24, OA XXXVIII 324/TFI 146. Cf. *Défense*, OA XXXVIII 616–18.

72. There is a similar remark in *Écl.* XI, OCM III 164/LO 633–34.

73. RV III–2.7, OCM I 450/LO 237; *Écl.* XI, OCM III 164/LO 633.

74. VFI, c. 22, OA XXXVIII 302/TFI 124.

75. VFI, c. 24, OA XXXVIII 323–24/TFI 145; cf. *Défense*, OA XXXVIII 616. Arnauld alluded in both passages to Descartes' distinction in the *Fourth Replies* between adequate and complete knowledge of an object. In response to Arnauld's own objection that we do not have adequate knowledge of mind and thus cannot be certain that it is distinct from body (AT VII 200/CSM II 140–41), Descartes had insisted that while we cannot be certain that we have an adequate knowledge of mind that reveals all its properties, we can be certain that our knowledge that the mind is a substance that excludes extension is complete (AT VII 220–22/CSM II 155–57). In §4.3.1 I consider Descartes' position that our knowledge of mind is complete in this sense.

76. Cf. *Réponse*, c. 23, OCM VI 161.

77. VFI, c. 23, OA XXXVIII 320/TFI 142. Descartes himself had claimed that the proper formation of hypotheses concerning the particular features of bodies requires *expérience*. See his methodological remarks in the *Discourse* (DM IV, AT VI 64–65/CSM I 144) and also the discussion of Descartes' use of the term *expérience* in Clarke, *Descartes' Philosophy of Science*, c. 2.

78. *Critique de Crit.*, 190.

79. *Système*, Meta., II–1.6, I 165.

80. *Système*, Meta., II–1.6, I 165. Regis emphasized here that there is a distinction between the idea of extension and the idea of the human body, one which corresponds to the distinction between the idea of mind (*l'esprit*) and the idea of a soul united to a human body (*l'âme*). He argued against Malebranche that our knowledge of our soul should be compared to our knowledge not of extension but of our own body. In §2.3.2 (3) I consider further Regis' distinction, which he borrowed from Desgabets, between the idea of mind and the idea of the human soul.

81. RV VI–2.8, OCM II /LO 502–9; and *Système*, Phys., VII–2.5, II 580–83. Cf. Descartes' discussion in *PS* I.10, AT XI 334–35/CSM I 331–32.

82. Malebranche stated at one point that the nature and virtues of fire depend on the laws of motion and thus "are but consequences of the general and efficacious will of God, who does everything in all things" (*Écl.* XV, OCM III 212–13/LO 662).

83. In response to Arnauld's objection that God is on Malebranche's view fated to follow the laws of motion (*Réflexions* I.2, OA XXXIX 186), Malebranche claimed that these laws must in some sense be arbitrary given that "God can dispense with following the laws that he has established for conserving [the world], provided that Order permits it" (*Rép. Réf. III*, OCM VIII 752). It is difficult to see how the possibility of miraculous exceptions shows that God's action is arbitrary since, on Malebranche's own view, it seems that God is determined by "Order" to dispense with the laws at certain times. Nonetheless, Malebranche could perhaps say that the mere fact that the laws of motion can have exceptions serves to show that they depend on the divine will and thus are distinct from the absolutely exceptionless eternal truths deriving from clear ideas, which depend only on the divine understanding.

84. McCracken, *Malebranche and British Philosophy*, 78. Cf. the extended defense of such a reading of Malebranche in Dreyfus, *Volonté selon Malebranche*, c. 10.

85. I have mentioned difficulties with the view here that the laws are arbitrary (see note 83), but Malebranche's main point seems to be that we cannot determine a priori the laws that are best suited to God's will. He made a similar point in the *Lois de la communication des mouvemens* (1712), OCM XVII–1 55 (cf. 201 n.11). For more on the evolution of Malebranche's account of motion and the role of his exchanges with Leibniz, see Mouy, *Le développement de la physique cartésienne*, 292–304; and Rodis-Lewis, *Malebranche*, 157–62.

86. For the point that the connection between human volition and bodily motion is not necessary and thus is forged by God, see RV VI–2.3, OCM II 315–16/LO 449–50; and *Écl.* XV, OCM III 224–29/LO 669–71. According to Malebranche, moreover, the human body is capable of certain free movements in virtue of the fact that the human soul can determine its volitions in a certain manner. I discuss his various accounts of this sort of determination in §6.2.4 (2).

87. *Supplément* I.8.v, RD V 201. Cf. *Critique de Crit.*, 197.

88. *Seconde Replique*, 22. Earlier Regis had distinguished in the *Système* between "sentiments or sensations," which are "nothing other than manners of thought that I know through themselves [*par elles-mêmes*], and that represent to me nothing external to me," and "ideas or perceptions," which are "also manners of thought that I know through themselves, but that represent to me things that are outside of me" (Meta., I–1.2, I 72–73).

89. Thus Malebranche spoke to Arnauld of the "*idea*, or *archetype* according to which God has formed" the soul (*Réponse*, c. 19, OCM VI 138). Cf. *TL I*, OCM VII 245; and *Lettre III*, OCM X 921, 956.

90. For Malebranche's view of the idea of extension, see note 6. Jolley supposes that when Malebranche "says we have no idea of our mind, he is talking about the human mind in general" (*Light of the Soul*, 119).

91. In the *Recherche* Malebranche ventured that God has not provided us access to his idea of the soul because contemplation of the idea would diminish the union of our mind to our body (RV III–2.7, OCM I 453/LO 239). In the *Méditations Chrétiennes*, he further explained that this idea would be so intellectually seductive that we would be

tempted to contemplate it all the time and thereby to fail to attend to what is beneficial or harmful to our body (MC IX, OCM X 104). Cf. Réponse, c. 22, OCM VI 156.

92. Critique de Crit., 193.

93. Seconde Replique, 22.

94. There is a similar appeal to divine knowledge even later in Lettre III (1699), at OCM IX 917 and in Prémotion physique (1715), at OCM XVI 29.

95. My reading provides one way of understanding Gueroult's claim that there is "in the spiritual world two radically distinct spheres which do not communicate naturally with one another: the sphere of the idea, where is found the psychic reality in itself and such as God perceives it, . . . and the sphere of sentiment where the soul is manifested to itself in a manner that without radically misleading us about its subject, . . . remains however estranged from its true innermost nature" (Étendue et psychologie, 68). In this passage Gueroult concludes by comparing this distinction to the Kantian distinction between the soul as noumenal and as phenomenal.

96. Luce has documented this influence in considerable detail in his Berkeley and Malebranche.

97. Works of George Berkeley II 241.

98. Principles of Human Knowledge, Pt. I, art. 135, in Works II 103. Whereas Malebranche held that God has an idea of our soul, though one to which we have no access, Berkeley went on to argue in this passage that there can be no idea of spirits since passive ideas cannot resemble active spirits.

99. On Berkeley's distinction between ideas and notions, which first became explicit in his 1734 additions to the Principles and Three Dialogues, see Adams, "Berkeley's 'Notion' of Spiritual Substance."

100. For the reference to divine ideas as archetypes of our sensory ideas, see the Three Dialogues (Works II 248, 254) as well as Berkeley's brief remarks in a letter to Samuel Johnson (24 Mar. 1730, in Works II 292). In the Three Dialogues Berkeley had Philonous emphasize the difference between God's archetypal and eternal ideas and our ectypal and natural ones (Works II 254). However, Philonous' claim earlier in this work that only a sensation or idea can be like another sensation or idea (Works II 206) suggests that these archetypal ideas must be similar in nature to our own ectypal sensory ideas, even given the fact that God does not "sense" his ideas but merely "understands" them. For a discussion of Berkeley's account of divine archetypes, see Winkler, Berkeley, 228–36.

101. Principles, Pt. I, art. 101, in Works II 85.

102. Nicholas Jolley pointed this out to me in correspondence.

103. In Éclaircissement VI Malebranche held that this must be so because the existence of bodies is not necessary but depends on God's volitions (OCM III 60–62/LO 572–73).

104. Cf. the same point in Écl. X, OCM III 150–51/LO 625–26 and later in Pré. phy., sec. VIII, OCM XVI 29.

105. VFI, c. 24, OA XXXVIII 324/TFI 145.

106. "Flavors, Colors, and God," 257–58.

107. "Flavors, Colors, and God," 258.

108. See the related remarks in RV VI–1.4, OCM II 274–75/LO 427.

109. VFI, c. 23, OA XXXVIII 315/TFI 137. For Malebranche's claim that the senses do not judge, see RV I.7, OCM I 96–97/LO 34.

110. OA XXXVIII 316/TFI 138.

111. OA XXXVIII 317/TFI 138; the passage quoted is from *RV* I.13, OCM I 144/ LO 61. Cf. *Défense*, OA XXXVIII 622–23.

112. OA XXXVIII 317/TFI 139. Arnauld was quoting Descartes' remarks in *PP* I.68, AT VIII-1 33/CSM I 215.

113. *VFI*, c. 23, OA XXXVIII 314–15/TFI 137.

114. "Flavors, Colors, and God," 260. Adams is quoting Nagel's remarks in "Pansychism," 194.

115. *View from Nowhere*, 29. Cf. McGinn, "Philosophical Materialism," 164 n.19.

116. Nagel claims that substance dualism is "implausible" and that "there are better alternatives, even if the best hasn't been thought of yet" (*View from Nowhere*, 29). In an article influenced by Nagel's earlier work, McGinn argues that there must be a nonmiraculous, naturalistic explanation of consciousness in terms of properties of the brain, though such an explanation is inaccessible to us due to our cognitive limitations ("Can We Solve the Mind–Body Problem?", 17–18). Cf. Searle's position that, contrary to the Cartesian view, subjective consciousness is a biological feature of the brain and thus is as subject as other such biological features to scientific scrutiny (*Rediscovery of the Mind*, c. 4).

117. The passage is cited in *VFI*, c. 23, OA XXXVIII 310/TFI 132–33. As we have seen, however, Arnauld emphasized Descartes' position that while we do not know what it is for color to exist in a body, we do know the color clearly and distinctly when we regard it merely as a thought or sentiment.

118. This sort of reading is indicated by Wilson's remark that Descartes was concerned to show "the mere subjectivity of much of the sensory image of reality" (*Descartes*, 8).

119. The phrase "and the other weak and languid sensations" was added to the third edition (1678); see OCM I 139h.

120. The phrase "or are not" was added to the fifth edition (1700); see OCM I 452e.

121. For some complications concerning the premise here that minds and bodies are the only kinds of beings, see chapter 4, note 23.

122. Malebranche mentioned this Cartesian argument in his *Méditations Chrétiennes* (1683) and repeated the moral that conclusions regarding the soul "are supported only by the clear idea that you have of body, and not by the idea of the soul" (MC IX, OCM X 106).

123. The passages Arnauld cited, in particular, are from *PP* I.68, 70, AT VIII-1 33, 34–35/CSM I 217, 218.

124. OA XXXVIII 310–11/TFI 133.

125. Rodis-Lewis cites this passage from the *Passions* to illustrate Malebranche's claim that the Cartesians consult the idea of extension in order to show that sensible qualities are modifications of the soul (OCM III 367 n.91), and in the context of considering this claim Alquié takes the same passage to show that "the reasoning of Malebranche is . . . faithfully Cartesian" (*Cartésianisme de Malebranche*, 99). However, it is important to note that the passage itself emphasizes neither sensible qualities nor the idea of extension in the manner that Malebranche's Cartesian argument does in *Éclaircissement XI*. Moreover, the passage from the *Passions* assumes that thought is present in us whereas Malebranche's Cartesian argument is supposed to establish that sensible qualities are in us rather than in bodies external to us. I argue in §4.2.2 that when Malebranche referred in *Éclaircissement XI* to the Cartesian view of sensible qualities, he

in fact had in mind the view in Desgabets and La Forge. For more on the passage from the *Passions*, see chapter 4, note 56.

126. Jolley has noted this problem with Arnauld's remarks; see *Light of the Soul*, 127.

127. After claiming in Book One that we do not know directly that sensations such as light and colors are modifications of our soul, furthermore, Malebranche went on to speak of "light and colors, as well as all the other sensible qualities" (RV I.12, OCM I 141/LO 59).

128. In his account in Book Five of the *Recherche* of the sevenfold sequence of the passions, Malebranche distinguished sentiments that accompany the impulse of the will from sentiments that accompany the flow of the animal spirits in the body (RV V.3, OCM II 142–46/LO 347–49). For a discussion of this account and its difficulties, see Hoffman, "Three Dualist Theories of the Passions," 186–92.

129. Arnauld no doubt had in mind Descartes' claim in the *Third Meditation* that "concerning ideas, if they are considered solely in themselves, and I do not refer them to anything else, they cannot properly be false" (AT VII 37/CSM II 26).

130. Descartes also suggested in the *Principles* that sensory ideas provide matter for error because that they do not clearly reveal the bodily features that they in fact represent (see for instance PP I.68, AT VIII-1 33/CSM I 217). The view that these ideas represent bodily features is in line with his position in this work that our sensations correspond neatly to bodily dispositions (see §2.1.2 [2]).

131. *Alambic* I.66, PL 323–24.

132. OR IX 236.

133. OR IX 242.

134. See her claim to her daughter, Mme de Grinan, that "notre âme *est verte*" (30 June 1677, *Correspondance* II 283); that "Si ce discours ne vient pas d'une âme verte, c'est moins d'une tête verte" (16 July 1677, *Corr.* II 296); and that "Si votre père Descartes le savait, il empêcherait votre âme d'être verte, et vous seriez bien honteuse qu'elle fût noire, ou de quelque autre couleur" (19 July 1677, *Corr.* II 299). There is a brief discussion of these remarks in Deprun, "Madame de Sévigné," 46.

135. The joke caught on in particular with certain critics of Malebranche's view of sensible qualities; see next note.

136. This view was in fact attributed to Malebranche by his critics. Thus in his *Observations sur une lettre de lautheur de la Recherche de la vérité* (1678), Anselme of Paris challenged Malebranche's Cartesian account of light and colors by asking: "[I]s it possible to imagine or to conceive souls modified by a light or by a common color? Of white, red, blue souls, of a white, of a blue, of a red peripatetic?" (OCM XVII-1 665). And later the contentious Pierre-Valentin Faydit, of whom Malebranche had a low opinion (see *EM*, Preface, OCM XII 21–26; *To P. Bernard*, 6 Oct. 1699, OCM XIX 692), ridiculed Malebranche's account of sensible qualities by noting in his *Remarques sur Virgile et sur Homere* (1705) that it is in virtue of the colors of their vestments that the Cardinal has a red soul, the Capuchin a grey soul, and the Jesuit a black soul (390–91).

137. OR IX 234.

138. There is considerable reason to attribute to Desgabets and Malebranche alike an adverbial account of sensation according to which we have, for instance, a sensation of green not by perceiving a green mental object but rather by perceiving greenly.

139. VFI, c. 23, OA XXXVIII 314/TFI 136.

140. In this text Malebranche cited those who doubt that "when one senses carrion,

the soul becomes formally rotten; and that the taste of sugar, or of pepper, of salt, is something that belongs to it" (OCM III 166/LO 634).

141. See his claim that "it cannot be that we do not always experience [*experiamur*] within ourselves that we are thinking" (*Sixth Rep.*, AT VII 427/CSM II 288). Descartes also referred to our *expérience* of *sentimens*; see, for instance, his remarks in the *Meteorology*, one of the *Essays* published with the *Discourse on the Method*, at AT VI 334.

142. See MC IX, OCM X 102; *Rép. Regis*, c. 2, OCM XVII–1 297–98; and *Lettre III*, OCM IX 917.

143. Jackson, "Phenomenal Qualia." Jackson takes introspection to reveal "raw feels, phenomenal features or qualia" (471–72). It is Lewis who, in summarizing Jackson's position, uses the term "phenomenal information"; see "What Experience Teaches."

144. Malebranche therefore must reject the Hypothesis of Phenomenal Information, which Lewis attributes to Jackson, according to which phenomenal information cannot be explicated in terms of any other kind of nonphenomenal information ("What Experience Teaches," 505–7, 511–12).

145. For Malebranche's citation, see OCM III 167/LO 635. Rodis-Lewis makes a point of Malebranche's exclusion of Descartes' examples in her note to this text; see OCM III 367 n.95.

146. *Cartésianisme de Malebranche*, 98.

147. Thus I think that Alquié goes too far in saying that when Malebranche concludes "that we do not have an idea of the soul, he wants to recall only that we do not perceive an idea that God has of our mind before creating it, and, on this point, Descartes would agree with him" (*Cartésianisme de Malebranche*, 100–101). Malebranche wanted to recall not only that we do not perceive an idea in God, but also that our view of our own soul is inferior in kind to our view of body. Descartes could not easily accept this latter point.

148. Descartes did claim in the *Sixth Meditation*, however, that sensations such as pain, hunger, and thirst differ from intellectual thoughts in virtue of the fact that the former derive from "the union and as it were intermixture [*quasi permixtione*] of the mind with the body" (AT VII 81/CSM II 56). His remarks to Elisabeth are naturally read as providing one way of explicating this sort of distinction.

149. See *Sixth Med.*, AT VII 72–73/CSM II 50–51; the remarks on this passage in *Third Obj. and Rep.*, AT VII 178/CSM II 126; and *Fifth Rep.*, AT VII 358–59, 385/CSM II 248, 264.

150. See the discussion of these and related passages in my "Descartes and Malebranche," 287–89.

151. See his *Descartes*, 127–34.

152. *Traité*, c. 13, LF 206–7.

153. Descartes announced to Mersenne at the end of 1640 that he had begun work on the First Part of the *Principles* (31 Dec. 1640, AT III 276/CSMK 167).

154. Descartes did go on to say in this passage that "we experience in ourselves certain other things, which must be referred [*referri*] neither to the mind alone, nor to the body alone, and that ... arise from the close and intimate [*arcta & intima*] union of our minds with the body" (AT VIII–1 23/CSM I 203). He did not indicate clearly, however, that these experienced features must be attributed to a substance that is distinct from mind and body.

155. For one such defense, see my "Descartes and Malebranche," 289–98.

156. VFI, c. 23, OA XXXVIII 317/TFI 139.

157. See his remark in *Descartes à l'alambic* that the soul is best defined as "intellectual substance depending on body" (I.48, PL 322) as well as his suggestion in the *Supplément* that among creatures only angels or pure spirits have thoughts that do not depend on body (I.2.vi, RD V 179).

158. *Supplément* I.6.iii, RD V 193–93. At the Commercy conferences Desgabets distinguished between the passions of the soul, which depend immediately on body as their efficient cause, and its actions, which depend immediately on the will but ultimately on the passions produced by the body (OR IX 233).

159. *Système*, Meta., I–2.1, I 113. Cf. *Usage* I-1.1, 1–2.

160. *Système*, Meta., I–2.1, I 113.

161. In the "Dictionaire" at the end of the first volume of the *Système*, Regis defined the soul in man as "the mind considered as being united to body."

162. *Système*, Meta., I–2.2, I 117. Regis' talk here of "a Formal or Modal distinction" recalls Descartes' remarks in *First Rep.*, AT VII 120–21/CSM II 85–86. Cf. Descartes' corrections to these remarks in *PP* I.62 AT VIII–1 30/CSM I 215.

163. Desgabets spoke of "matter and spiritual substances" as the only substances in the world (*Indéfectibilité*, c. 2, RD II 21), and Regis remarked that the man cannot be a substance, since body and mind "are the only substances that I know" (*Système*, Meta., I–2.1, I 114).

164. *Système*, Meta., II–1.6, I 164–65.

165. *Système*, Meta., I, Avertissement, I 63.

166. In the *Système* Regis warned that since the soul as it exists after death does not have faculties similar to those that it had when it was united to a body, reason cannot reveal how such a soul knows or acts (Meta., III.1, I 267–69). Cf. *Usage* I–2.39, 214–15.

Chapter Three

1. This account of the distinction goes back to the *Rules*, where Descartes claimed that though the power through which the mind attains knowledge "applies itself" (*se applicat*) to the body in sensation and imagination, "when it acts on its own, it is said to understand [*intelligere*]" (RM XII, AT X 415–16/CSM I 42). See *To Mersenne*, 13 Nov. 1639, AT II 598/CSMK 140; the related distinction between corporeal and spiritual memory in *To Regius*, 24 May 1640, AT III 48/CSMK 146; and *To Mersenne*, 6 Aug. 1640, AT III 143/CSMK 151.

2. See *L'Homme*, AT X 176–77/CSM I 106; *Dioptrics*, AT VI 140/CSM I 172; *Second Rep.*, AT VII 160–61/CSM II 113; and *Conversation with Burman*, AT V 162/CSMK 344–45.

3. *Alambic* II.3, PL 324. In his *Supplément*, Desgabets identified "pure intellections" with sensations that allow the perceiver to "know immediately the thing such as it is in itself" (I.3.vi, RD V 186).

4. *Usage* I–2.3, 106–7.

5. Wilson emphasizes this point in *Descartes*, 200–201.

6. In the preface to the *Recherche*, Malebranche quoted Augustine's remark in *De verbis Domini*, "Non a me lumen existens, sed lumen non participans nisi IN TE" (OCM I 24/LO xxviii). Cf. RV III–2.5, OCM I 434/LO 229.

7. See his claim to Mersenne that the eternal truths created by God "are all inborn in our minds [*mentibus nostris ingentiæ*], just as a king would imprint his laws on the heart of his subjects, if he had the power to do so" (15 Apr. 1630, AT I 145/CSMK 23).

In "Platonism and Descartes' View of Immutable Essences," I discuss the connection between Descartes' innatism and his doctrine that God has created the eternal truths. For Malebranche's rejection of this Cartesian doctrine, see §5.3.2.

8. I discuss this distinction futher in "Descartes on Innate Ideas."

9. *Traité*, c. 10, LF 181. La Forge went on to say that these ideas are contained in the mind in the same manner shapes are contained in a piece of wax, with the difference that the power in the wax is passive, whereas the power in the mind is active (*active*).

10. For a similar account of the difficulties with Malebranche's characterization of innatism, see Nadler, *Malebranche and Ideas*, 128–29, and Jolley, *Light of the Soul*, 70, 73–74. Alquié argues that Malebranche provides more than a mere caricature of innate ideas since his point is that no idea can be present in the mind in a merely virtual manner (*Cartésianisme de Malebranche*, 195). However, Malebranche's full argument against virtual presence requires the premise that the mind cannot possess any active power to produce its own perceptions, a premise that plays no role in the critique of innatism in the *Recherche*.

11. This passage was added to the fifth edition (1700). I indicate below that Malebranche came to speak consistently of the efficacy of divine ideas only after 1695.

12. The reference to God's causation of all that is *de physic* in the mind was added to the sixth edition (1712) (see OCM III 145c). I indicate in §6.2.4 (2) that this is a term of art that Malebranche introduced in the context of a discussion of human freedom.

13. Malebranche was considering here the nature of spiritual memory as well as of habits related to the will.

14. *Cartésianisme de Malebranche*, 195.

15. See introduction, note 4.

16. *Système*, Meta., II–1.9, I 171.

17. *Système*, Meta., I–2.4, I 121.

18. *Usage* I–2.6, 21.

19. Jolley, "Intellect and Illumination in Malebranche," 213–15. Jolley claims as well that Malebranche's Augustinian position that the mind is not a light to itself precludes an appeal to a faculty of pure understanding (cf. *Light of the Soul*, 97–98, where he cites a similar claim in Gueroult, *Malebranche* 1:197). I will respond to such a claim shortly.

20. In the *Sixth Meditation* Descartes had emphasized that the different mental faculties are not different parts of the mind "since it is one and the same mind that wills, that senses, that understands" (AT VII 86/CSM II 59). See also *To Mersenne*, May 1637, AT I 366/CSMK 354; *To Mersenne*, 13 Nov. 1639, AT II 598/CSMK 139–40; and *To Regius*, May 1641, AT III 372/CSMK 182. I take these passages to be in some tension with Jolley's claim that Descartes taught that it is the faculty of understanding, rather than the mind itself, that is passive ("Intellect and Illumination," 215).

21. This seems to be the sort of reduction suggested in *Éclaircissement II*. The view in *Éclaircissement VII* that the soul is capable of certain thoughts in virtue of its underlying habits or dispositions (OCM III 68–69/LO 578), however, seems to suggest a reduction of the difference between mental faculties to a difference between kinds of underlying mental dispositions rather than to one between kinds of occurrent thoughts. Yet Malebranche also insisted elsewhere that inner sentiment provides no access to these dispositions (see §6.1.2). On his view, therefore, we can distinguish these faculties by means of inner sentiment only if we identify them with thoughts rather than with dispositions.

22. "Meditations on Knowledge, Truth, and Ideas," in *Philosophical Essays*, 27. Ar-

nauld argued throughout the *Vraies et fausses idées* that since perceptions are both necessary and sufficient for any sort of knowledge of objects, Malebranche's ideas as representative beings distinct from these perceptions are superfluous (see, for instance, VFI, c. 9, OA XXXVIII 220–21/TFI 42–43).

23. For another example of a broader understanding of *perception pur*, see the passage cited in chapter 1, note 31.

24. Such talk is at odds as well with the definition in this text of *entendement pur* as "only the faculty that the mind has to know external objects" by means of intellectual ideas (RV III–1.1, OCM I 381/LO 198).

25. Malebranche, in fact, offered nothing in the way of a systematic account of the soul's second-order reflective thoughts. His theoretical attention was devoted rather to the first-order thoughts that the soul has in virtue of its union with the body or with God.

26. *Système et existence*, 259–62. There is room to quibble with the dating; in a letter that may have been written prior to 1695, Malebranche claimed that "it is precisely what one sees that affects the soul by its efficacy" (OCM XVIII 280). Certainly the doctrine of efficacious ideas is linked to the earlier account in the *Entretiens* of the soul's union with God. Robinet has done a service, however, in showing that the vast majority of the passages from Malebranche's writings that emphasize the efficacy of God's ideas were written subsequent to his exchange with Regis.

27. *Système*, Meta., II–1.14, I 184–85.

28. *Système*, Meta., II–1.14, I 188.

29. See the preface (OCM XII 19) and the *Entretiens sur la mort* (E. mort II, OCM XIII 409), which were published with the third edition (1696) of the *Entretiens sur la Métaphysique*. Cf. the 1699 response to Arnauld in *Lettre III* (OCM IX 958–59), as well as important additions to the fifth edition (1695) of the *Conversations chrétiennes* (C III, OCM IV 67–76) and to the fifth edition (1700) of the *Recherche* (RV III–2.6, OCM I 442).

30. Alquié, *Cartésianisme de Malebranche*, 209–10; and Robinet, *Système et existence*, 259–72.

31. Alquié notes, for instance, that Malebranche never settled the question of whether it is the divine idea or rather the divine will that acts directly on the soul (*Cartésianisme de Malebranche*, 210–11). Cf. the discussion of this difficulty in Gueroult, *Malebranche* 1:178–87, and Jolley, "Intellect and Illumination in Malebranche."

32. *Réponse*, c. 5, OCM VI 53–54.

33. *Malebranche* 1:189–90.

34. Malebranche differed with Descartes, however, over the nature of the relation between intellectual perception and its object. For Descartes "the thing represented by the operation of the intellect" is the object represented insofar as it exists objectively in the intellect (*First Rep.*, AT VII 102–3/CSM II 75). As I have already noted, Malebranche held that the idea that is the object of pure perception exists external to the soul, in God (see §3.2.1). Moreover, he insisted that it is the pure idea, rather than the pure perception itself, that represents objects (see §3.2.2 [3]). What I want to emphasize, though, is merely the basic distinction between a perception as a mere mental operation and that same perception as an operation with a certain sort of intellectual content.

35. See the reference added to the third edition (1678) of the *Recherche* to *sentimens ou sensations* (RV I.4, OCM I 67/LO 17) and the note equating the two that was added to the fourth edition (1711) of the *Entretiens* (EM V, OCM XII 117/D 125 n.1).

36. *Écl.* X, OCM III 157–58/LO 630.

37. Cf. *E. mort II*, OCM XIII 407–9.

38. Cf. the claim in the later addition to the *Conversations* that "it is uniquely through the variety of colors that we see and that we distinguish the diversity of objects" (*C III*, OCM IV 76). Malebranche offered the view that color "particularizes" intelligible extension in earlier texts; see *Écl. X*, OCM III 149/LO 625, and *Réponse*, c. 6, OCM VI 61. For examples of the same view in later works, see *Rép. Regis*, c. 2, OCM XVII-1 282, and *Lettre III*, OCM IX 936.

39. See for instance his talk of the extension "of the pain, that of the heat, that of the cold, that you can sense there [in the hand]" (*EM V*, OCM XII 115–16/D 111). In a later response to Arnauld, Malebranche spoke of seeing the idea of extension through color (*Lettre III*, OCM IX 963–64).

40. In the remarks to Arnauld cited in the previous note, Malebranche emphasized that we see in the divine idea of extension only what we know "clearly and certainly" (*Lettre III*, OCM IX 964). This suggests that we do not see in God what we sense in a confused manner. Cf. his emphasis in other passages on the fact that the idea of extension is intelligible rather than sensible (e.g., in *EM*, Preface, OCM XII 19, and in *To Mairan*, 12 June 1714, OCM XIX 884).

41. For a discussion of this difference between Descartes and Malebranche, see §2.1.3.

42. This passage was added to the sixth edition (1712).

43. See Bréhier's claim that Malebranche's theory of natural judgment forces him "to concede a domain common to sensible optics and geomtery, which is rational" ("Les 'jugements naturels' chez Malebranche," 78). Cf. Robinet, *Système et existence*, 281–83.

44. *RV VI–1.4*, OCM II 262–81/LO 419–30. Cf. Descartes' remark in the 1643 correspondence with Elisabeth that features of extension can be known "by the understanding alone, but much better by the understanding aided by the imagination" (AT III 691/CSMK 227). For other passages from Descartes' writings that indicate the importance of imagination for geometrical understanding, see *RM XIV*, AT X 444/CSM I 60; and *Fifth Med.*, AT VII 63/CSM II 44.

45. This passage differs from the passage from the *Recherche* just cited insofar as the point in the latter is not that the imaginary idea cannot conform exactly to the intelligible idea, but rather that it can be known distinctly only to the extent that it does so conform.

46. At the very least, the character Socrates allows this when he indicates that recollection may be triggered by sensory experience of objects (*Phædo* 74, in *Collected Dialogues*, 56–57).

47. Ariste's claim in the *Entretiens* that vision "does not wholly disguise its object" (*EM V*, OCM XII 119/D 115) even seems to suggest that our sensations have ideas as their objects.

48. See *EM III*, OCM XII 64–65/D 57, 59, and *EM V*, OCM XII 127/D123.

49. I take such a view to be in accord as well with Malebranche's remark that to say that the intelligible idea of extension becomes sensible is simply to say that it brings about in the soul certain sensible perceptions (*To Mairan*, 12 June 1714, OCM XIX 884; cf. *E. mort II*, OCM XIII 408). What is sensible here is not the intelligible idea itself but rather the perceptions.

50. That Descartes took there to be a sensory idea of extension is indicated by his claim in the *Second Meditation* that the senses reveal the "color, shape and size" of the wax (AT VII 30/CSM II 20). There is a complication, however, that derives from his claim in the *Sixth Replies*, discussed in §2.1.3, that the determination of shape and size

is not sensory. He argued that such a determination occurs at a third stage of sense that is intellectual rather than sensory since it is distinct from the second stage that comprises the sensory effects produced in the mind by the body. It is interesting, however, that Descartes admitted in this same text that the second stage includes the perception not only of light and color, but also of "the extension of the color and its boundaries together with its position in relation to the parts of the brain" (AT VII 437/CSM II 295). He therefore consistently indicated that there is some sort of idea of extension that is properly attributed to the senses.

51. This passage was first added to the fifth edition (1700) of the *Recherche*, with the exception of the reference to the efficacy of ideas, which was added to the sixth (1712) edition.

52. Gueroult has urged that in the first edition of the *Recherche*, Malebranche accepted a theory of finite and created ideas and only later adopted the view that ideas are eternal, uncreated, and infinite (*Malebranche* 1:62–81; cf. Robinet, *Système et existence*, 213–14; and Alquié, *Cartésianisme de Malebranche*, 218–20). I am sympathetic, however, to Rodis-Lewis' claim that Malebranche never denied that divine ideas are infinite and uncreated; see her "La connaissance par idée chez Malebranche" as well as her response to Gueroult in the accompanying "Échange de vues." Cf. chapter 2, note 6.

53. *Système*, Meta., II–1.18, I 194.

54. *Quatre lettres . . . au Pere Malebranche*, Lettre III, OA XL 88–89. In the *Système* Regis had argued that while the idea of God is finite "according to its formal being," it is infinite in that it represents the perfections of its object (Meta., II–1.18, I 194). It was Malebranche who, in his response to Regis, introduced the *in essendo/in repræsentando* distinction (*Rép. Regis*, c. 2, OCM XVII–1 302).

55. Cf. the related remarks added to the fifth edition (1700) of the *Recherche* (RV IV.11, OCM II 100–101/LO 321) and to the sixth edition (1702) of the *Conversations chrétiennes* (C III, OCM IV 74).

56. For somewhat different perspectives on Malebranche's response to Arnauld, see Radner, *Malebranche*, 107–18, and Nadler, *Malebranche and Ideas*, 40–44.

57. This distinction is related to Descartes' claim to Arnauld that while we are always conscious of our mental acts, we are only potenially conscious of our mental faculties and potentialities (*Fourth Rep.*, AT VII 246–47/CSM II 172).

58. I take this sort of response to create some difficulty for Arnauld's argument against Malebranche that Descartes and other Cartesians can simply identify ideas with perceptions.

59. As Wilson has shown, however, Descartes himself was not always careful to distinguish these two different accounts of our knowledge of innate ideas (*Descartes*, 155–65).

60. Cf. RV III–2.8, OCM I 456–57/LO 241.

61. Cf. the remark in the *Entretiens sur la mort* (1696) that "it is by the impression that this idea [of extension] makes on the mind of the Geometers as a result of their attention, that they constantly acquire new thoughts" (*E. mort II*, OCM XIII 409).

62. In a letter to Arnauld Malebranche himself spoke of perceptions that "contain" (*contient*) infinite representative reality (*TL I*, OCM VI 217). The "as it were" is appropriate, though, given that he went on to deny in this letter that the fact that a perception contains the idea reveals that the idea is itself a modification of the soul (OCM VI 217–18). Talk of the perception's containing an infinite idea indicates not that the idea is literally contained in the perception but that the perception is intentionally directed toward that idea.

63. *Critique*, 46. Foucher was concerned to argue that these modifications can no more represent external objects than sensory modifications can. For a discussion of this argument, see Watson, *The Breakdown of Cartesian Metaphysics*, c. 5.

64. Malebranche no doubt was playing on the title of Foucher's work, *Critique de la Recherche de la vérité*.

65. *VFI*, c. 3, OA XXXVIII 187/TFI 9.

66. See the discussion of this distinction in §2.1.3.

67. Cf. *EM I*, OCM XII 46/D 39; *E. mort II*, OCM XIII 407–9. This sort of position is anticipated in the first edition of the *Recherche*; see RV I.18, OCM I 177/LO 79.

68. Malebranche began the section that contains his discussion of the difference between sensation and pure perception by comparing the two main faculties of mind, (viz. understanding and will) to the two main faculties of matter (viz. the faculty for receiving different shapes and the faculty for receiving different motions) (RV I.1, OCM I 41/LO 2).

69. Malebranche argued explicitly, of course, that the clear and distinct ideas that we have of objects are external to our soul. On my reading, he also held that confused sensory ideas are wholly internal to it.

70. Cf. the distinction between two species of bodily modes in *Écl. XII*, OCM III 174/LO 639–40. There is a discussion of this sort of distinction in a different context in §2.2.1 (1).

71. The implication derives from his claim that external shape is an internal modification of body and that pure perception is akin to external shape. Malebranche's claim in the *Recherche* that sensations must be internal modifications since they "contain no necessary relation to the bodies that seem to cause them" (OCM I 42/LO 3), however, indicates that he took sensations and pure perceptions to be modifications that are internal in virtue of the fact that they bear no essential relation to *body*.

72. See, for instance, *Réponse*, c. 13, OCM VI 98–99; *C III*, OCM IV 69 (add. to sixth ed. [1702]).

73. In "Platonism and Descartes' View of Immutable Essences," I argue that Descartes took these natures to be ontologically distinct from our mind and its modifications. Descartes differed from Malebranche, however, in holding that these natures are determined by the divine will (see §5.3.2).

74. Malebranche thus argued that the Cartesian identification of ideas with perceptions leads to Pyrrhonism since it supports the view that truth is merely subjective, depending only on our mind, rather than something objective that depends on necessary and objective features of reality; see *Écl. X*, OCM III 140/LO 620; *Lettre III*, 925–26; *C III*, OCM IV 70–72 (add. to sixth ed. [1702]). It is open to the Cartesian to respond, however, that the truths we perceive remain objective and necessary since they depend not on our mind but on external immutable natures.

75. See the reference to these rules that was added to the sixth edition (1702) of the *Conversations chrétiennes* at C III, OCM IV 76, as well as the related remarks in the addition to the sixth edition (1712) of the *Recherche* at RV I.9, OCM I 120/LO 46–47, and in a final *Éclaircissement* on optics, which was published with this edition, at OCM III 327/LO 733–34.

76. This is Malebranche's concession to Arnauld's claim that "all our perceptions are modalities that are essentially representative" (*VFI*, c. 5, OA XXXVIII 199/TFI 20). Cf. *Lettre III*, OCM IX 905, 945–50.

77. *Malebranche* 1:190.

78. Cf. *C III*, OCM IV 71 (add. to sixth ed. [1702]).

79. VFI, c. 6, OA XXXVIII 204/TFI 25. Arnauld contrasted the immediate reflection on thought, or virtual reflection, with the perception of one thought by another through explicit reflection. Malebranche's response is concerned only with virtual reflection, which is essential to perception as such.

80. Alquié takes Malebranche's remarks to suggest a distinction between *l'esprit comme subjet* and *l'esprit comme substance*; see *Cartésianisme de Malebranche*, 110–11; "Sources cartésiennes de Malebranche," 440–43.

81. Malebranche did allow that we can know a priori that the soul is spiritual and immortal, but he held that our knowledge of these properties cannot derive simply from reflection on the nature of thought since such knowledge must depend as well on the clear idea of extension. See chapters 4 and 5.

82. See this distinction in *Third Med.*, AT VII 40–41/CSM II 28–29. In response to Arnauld's claim that Descartes himself had identified ideas with perceptions, Malebranche put great emphasis on the distinction between ideas as *realité objective* and perceptions as *modalitez de l'ame* (*Réponse*, c. 24, OCM VI 172; *TL I*, OCM VI 217). At one point Malebranche even suggested that Descartes would have endorsed the view that ideas are distinct from perceptions (OCM VI 172), though he in effect conceded that he was going beyond Descartes' own view when he told Arnauld in a different work that "this great Philosopher has not examined to the bottom in what consists the nature of ideas" (*TL I*, OCM VI 214). Cf. introduction, note 6.

83. Malebranche claimed, in a previously cited passage, that just as we cannot comprehend all of the modifications of which extension is capable, so we cannot comprehend all of the modifications of which the soul is capable (RV III-1.1, OCM I 385/LO 200). Thus his argument that the clear idea of extension must be external to our soul since we cannot take its measure would apply equally to the clear idea of the soul.

84. *Malebranche* 1:197.

85. *Light of the Soul*, 98. Cf. Jolley's "Intellect and Illumination in Malebranche."

Chapter Four

1. VFI, c. 24, OA XXXVIII 326/TFI 148.

2. Cf. RV, Preface, OCM I 20–21/LO xxvi.

3. Malebranche may well have been thinking of Montaigne, who composed the *Essais* over a twenty year period, when he wrote in the *Recherche* that one must have compassion for those who "have been consumed for a number of years only to learn this false proposition that is the enemy of all knowledge and of all truth, *That one can know nothing*" (RV I.3, OCM I 59/LO 13).

4. Pollnow nonetheless urges that Montaigne's "conception of a concrete psychology," which emphasizes the role of *expérience*, anticipates Malebranche's own work in psychology. According to Pollnow, the main difference is that whereas Montaigne offered an *expérience psychologique* that does not go beyond observation, Malebranche offered a *psychologie empirique* that attempts to uncover the structure of the phenomena ("Réflexions sur les fondements de la psychologie chez Malebranche," 194–99).

5. Elsewhere Malebranche attempted to explain this malady by noting that Academic skepticism springs "from passion and from stupidity, from blindness and from malice, or simply from caprice and because one wants to doubt" (RV I.20, OCM I 188/LO 86).

6. In general Malebranche criticized the *Essais* for enticing the reader to accept unsupported conclusions by means of a rhetorical style pleasing to the imagination. It is

not surprising, then, the section on Montaigne is from Book Two of the *Recherche*, which is devoted to the errors of the imagination.

7. On a more staightforward reading, Montaigne cited the various ancient opinions not to support a positive account of the soul but to illustrate the inability of human reason to establish any such account.

8. In the version of this passage in the first two editions, Malebranche held that just as we know matter through a distinct idea of extension, so we know our soul through a distinct idea of thought (OCM I 389a). No doubt he changed these remarks because they are in some tension with the official doctrine of the *Recherche* that inner sentiment yields knowledge that is radically inferior to the knowledge provided by the clear idea of extension. Cf. the related changes to the *Recherche* cited in the introduction, note 22.

9. Earlier in the *Recherche* Malebranche had claimed in a passage added to the fifth edition (1700) that "it is not necessary to attribute to the soul any property different from its diverse thoughts" since the soul itself "is the substance in which are found all the modifications of which I have an inner sentiment" (RV I.10, OCM I 123/LO 49). In light of such a claim, the remark that inner sentiment reveals "the nature of the soul" says only that this sentiment reveals the thoughts that are modifications of it.

10. Such an interpretation is supported by the immediately following claim, which was added to the sixth edition (1712) of the *Recherche*, that it is the idea of body that allows us to know that the soul is not in fact a body (OCM I 453/LO 239).

11. Indeed, Descartes' reading is even less plausible since Gassendi himself offered arguments for the incorporeality of the rational soul. See Osler, "Baptizing Epicurean Atomism."

12. See the strikingly similar claim in Aquinas that since knowledge of the nature of the human mind or intellect requires "diligent inquiry," many "are ignorant of the nature of the soul, and many also in error with respect to its nature" (*Summa Theologiæ* Ia, Q. 87, art. 1). Aquinas' view here seems to conflict with Descartes' official position that the nature of the soul is the best known of all, but Malebranche can be seen as claiming in *Éclaircissement* XI that Cartesians must concede much to such a view.

13. As I indicated in §2.3.2 (1), Malebranche could allow that consciousness reveals the disposition of the soul to have certain feelings. What he came to deny is that it allows us to know the nondispositional features of the soul that ground these dispositions.

14. Thus Theodore emphasizes that all modifications of body "consist only in relations of distance" and that "these relations are not perceptions, reasonings, pleasures, desires, sensations; in a word, thoughts" (*EM I*, OCM XII 32–33/D 25). I will shortly consider why Malebranche took it to be evident that relations of distance cannot be thoughts.

15. Cf. the related addition to this final edition at RV I.10, OCM I 122–23/LO 49.

16. RV I.6–9, OCM I 79–120/LO 25–47. Malebranche was concerned in these chapters to emphasize the deceptiveness of sensations of extension, shape, and motion.

17. Lelong sent Malebranche's *Entretiens* to Leibniz in 1712, and Leibniz's own *Entretiens* is based on his notes to that work; see Robinet, *Malebranche et Leibniz*, 427–33.

18. *Philosophical Essays*, 263.

19. For a discussion of this sort of objection to the argument in Leibniz's *Entretiens*, see Wilson, "Leibniz and Materialism," 502–6.

20. Ayers uses this phrase to explain the position of Ralph Cudworth in his *True Intellectual System of the Universe* (1678) that sensations are attributes of an incorporeal substance ("Mechanism, Superaddition, and the Proof of God's Existence," 236–37).

21. Malebranche was defending here the Cartesian view that animals cannot have sensations since they lack immaterial souls. See the discussion of this defense in §5.2.1.

22. See, for instance, Nagel, *View from Nowhere*, c. 1–3; Jackson, "Epiphenomenal Qualia"; and McGinn, "Can We Solve the Mind–Body Problem." Each of these three nonetheless conclude, contrary to Malebranche, that states of consciousness are properties of matter. For an argument that is more sympathetic to Malebranche's dualism, see Adams, "Flavors, Colors, and God."

23. It is interesting that Malebranche himself cast doubt on the premise of this argument that "there are only two different kinds of beings, minds and bodies" (*Écl.* XI OCM III 165/LO 634), when he claimed in the *Recherche* that "we should not claim . . . that all that exists are minds and bodies, thinking beings and extended beings" since "speaking absolutely" it is possible that God creates beings of a completely different kind but "has reasons we do not know for concealing them from us" (RV III–2.9, OCM I 471–72/LO 250). He had emphasized in an earlier passage, however, that there also is no good reason to believe that there is any sort of created substance besides mind and body (RV III–2.7, OCM I 455/LO 240).

24. *Sentimens*, Pt. I, c. 4, pp. 74–75.

25. La Ville cited in particular the Council's determination in 1551 that the Transubstantiation of the substance of the bread into Christ's body and the substance of the wine into his blood occurs "while the species [*speciebus*] of bread and wine alone remain" (*Sentimens*, Pt. II, c. 1, pp. 102–3). For a discussion of the different scholastic accounts of the Eucharist, see Armogathe, *Theologia Cartesiana*, sec. 1.

26. Thus, in the title of his work La Ville charged that the sentiments of Descartes concerning the essence of matter *opposez a la doctrine de l'Eglise, et conformes aux erreurs de Calvin, sur le sujet de l'eucharistie.*

27. See McLaughlin, "Censorship and Defenders of the Cartesian Faith," and Nadler, "Arnauld, Descartes, and Transubstantiation."

28. Malebranche noted that La Ville has not shown that the Cartesian account of matter is contrary to the doctrine of Transubstantiation and, moreover, has not combatted his own account of this doctrine (OCM XVII–1 528). In the pre–1680 editions of the *Recherche*, however, Malebranche restricted himself to the comment that the Calvinist fails to recognize the weakness of the human mind when he concludes that Christ's body cannot be in the host simply because he cannot conceive how it can be present there at the same time that it is present in heaven (RV III–1.2, OCM I 394–95/LO 205). Malebranche also restricted himself to the remark that since the doctrine of Transubstantiation is an "incomprehensible mystery," he can be excused from entering into disputes about it (RV III–2.8, OCM I 464–66/LO 246–47; La Ville cites this passage in *Sentimens*, Pt. II, c. 3, pp. 115, 137). There are three anonymous responses to La Ville written about 1680, perhaps from the hand of Malebranche, that address more directly the issue of the Eucharist: *Reponse de Mxxx a une Lettre de ses Amis* (OCM XVII–1 477–90); *Memoire Pour expliquer la possiblité de la Transsubstantiation* (OCM XVII–1 491–95); and *Demonstration de la possibilité de la présence réelle* (OCM XVII–1 497–505) (see the discussion of these responses in OCM XVII–1 447–76; and in Gouhier, "Philosophie chrétienne et théologie," 136–40). The positive view suggested in these works is that Transubstantiation involves the conversion of a particular extended substance into a different extended substance with the same quantity that is united to the soul of Christ (*Memoire*, OCM XVII–1 493–95; *Demonstration*, OCM XVII–1 502–5). Cf. Descartes' similar account of the Eucharist in *Fourth Rep.*, AT VII 248–56/CSM II 173–78.

29. Cf. *EM III*, OCM XII 73/D 65, 67.

30. Cf. RV III–2.8, OCM I 466/LO 247 (add. to sixth ed. [1712]).
31. *Essay* IV.iii.6.
32. *Essay* II.xxiii.23.
33. *Mr. Locke's Reply to the Right Reverend the Lord Bishop of Worcester's Answer to his Second Letter* (hereafter, *Reply to Second Letter*), in *Works of Locke* IV 466. This passage from Locke's 1699 letter is a response to the objection of the Bishop Edward Stillingfleet that the suggestion in the *Essay* that matter might think confuses the ideas of matter and spirit.
34. *Reply to Second Letter*, in *Works* IV 469.
35. Locke of course also rejected the more specific Cartesian doctrine that the nature of matter consists in extension on the grounds that the extension of body depends on solidity and thus differs from the extension of space; see *Essay* II.iv.5.
36. There are references to Locke in Malebranche's later writings, where the views of the former are linked to the dangerous position of Hobbes; see the *Entretien d'un philosophe chrétien et d'un philosophe chinois* (1708) (OCM XV 51–52) and the *Réflexions sur la prémotion physique* (1715) (OCM XVI 98). However, though Coste's French translation of Locke's *Essay* was published in 1700, one correspondent suggested to Leibniz in a 1714 letter that Malebranche had not yet read the work (see OCM XIX 868). It is at the very least unclear whether Malebranche had first-hand knowledge of Locke's suggestion in the *Essay* of the possibility of thinking matter, or whether he followed the early coverage in the French journals of Locke's exchange with Stillingfleet concerning that suggestion (on this coverage, see Yolton, *Thinking Matter*, 11–12; and *Locke and French Materialism*, 1–2, 57).
37. Hobbes had recommended such a position to Descartes at *Third Obj. and Rep.*, AT VII 173–74/CSM II 122–23.
38. Another point made by Descartes is that Arnauld's analogy is odd insofar as it suggests that body is a property of some other substance, rather than a substance in its own right (AT VII 224–25/CSM II 158–59). This analogy thus conflicts with the Hobbesian position broached by Arnauld, according to which thought is a property of bodily substance.
39. June 1648, AT V 188/TFI 185. Arnauld did go on in this letter, though, to object to Descartes' claim that the soul is always thinking (AT V 188/TFI 185–86).
40. VFI, c. 24, OA XXXVIII 324/TFI 146. This is the last of four prejudices mentioned by Arnauld, the other three being: (1) that a clear idea of an object must allow us to know clearly all the modifications of which that object is capable; (2) that we cannot know two objects through a clear idea unless we know their relations; and (3) that we know through a clear idea only what we discover by a "simple vision" (OA XXXVIII 323–24/TFI 145–46). I claimed in §2.2.1 (1), and argue again presently, that Arnauld's objection to prejudice (3) is on target. I also have indicated, however, that his objections to prejudices (1) and (2) miss the mark. Arnauld protested that prejudice (1) confuses a clear idea of an object with a comprehensive one that provides us with complete knowledge of that object, and that prejudice (2) confronts two objections, the first that we have clear ideas of circles and squares even though we do not know their relations, and the second that objects without quantities have no relations. However, the objection to prejudice (1) is deflected by Malebranche's admission that a clear idea of an object need not reveal all its modifications to us at once (see §2.2.1 [2]). Moreover, the first objection to prejudice (2) is parried by Malebranche's claim that circles and squares have determinate but infinitely complex relations that our finite minds cannot grasp, and the second

objection is blocked by his view that even modifications of an object that lacks extension have determinate relations that are grounded in features that can be clearly perceived only through a clear idea (see §2.2.2 [2]).

41. OA XXXVIII 324/TFI 146. Cf. §1.3.2 (2).

42. OA XXXVIII 329/TFI 150.

43. VFI, c. 23, OA XXXVIII 321/TFI 142–43. In this passage Arnauld equated the perception of a demonstrated property with a clear idea of it, thus contravening Malebranche's official doctrine that ideas are distinct from our perceptions. Arnauld himself was of course fully aware that he was departing from Malebranche's own view on this point.

44. VFI, c. 23, OA XXXVIII 322/TFI 143.

45. Cf. §§1.2.1 (1) and 2.2.1 (1).

46. VFI, c. 23, OA XXXVIII 309/TFI 132. See §2.3.1 (1).

47. This is the hypothesis that Rodis-Lewis has offered in her editorial notes to *Éclaircissement XI*, at OCM III 367 n.89.

48. *Alambic* I.66, PL 323. In the preface to the *Recherche*, Malebranche had earlier made the strikingly similar remark, which I have just quoted, that "it can be said with some assurance that the difference between the mind and the body has been known with sufficient clarity only for a few years," particularly since the realization that sensible qualities "are not clearly contained in the idea we have of matter" (OCM I 20/LO xxvi).

49. *Supplément* I.1.i, RD V 164.

50. *Supplément* I.8.i, RD V 197. Later in this work Desgabets noted explicitly that it is "the immediate consequence" (*la suite immédiate*) of Descartes' identification of matter with extension that "the pretended sensible qualities of light, color, sound, odor, taste, heat, cold etc., are our own sentiments" (I.13.v, RD VI 276).

51. *Alambic* I.66, PL 323–24.

52. See Desgabets' conclusion that "one knows intuitively the nature of the soul, as also of external things when the senses make us think of them" (*Critique de Crit.*, 189).

53. See introduction, note 21.

54. *Traité*, c. 3, LF 114–15.

55. See, e.g., *Sixth Med.*, AT VII 80/CSM II 55; *Sixth Rep.*, AT VII 440/CSM II 297.

56. In *Malebranche*, 182–83, Rodis-Lewis claims that Malebranche's indirect argument for the soul's spirituality is anticipated by Descartes' remark in the *Passions of the Soul* that "because we cannot conceive that body thinks in any manner, we have reason to believe that all sorts of thoughts that are in us belong to the soul" (*PS* I.4, AT XI 329/CSM I 329). I think that Rodis-Lewis' claim here is more plausible than her claim that this passage anticipates Malebranche's argument for the conclusion that sensible qualities belong to the soul (see chapter 2, note 125). Nonetheless, the passage from the *Passions* concerns "all sorts of thoughts" rather than just sensible qualities, and in this text Descartes relied on an enumeration of the mechanistic functions of the human body, rather than on the point that bodily modifications consist only in relations of distance, in order to show that body cannot think (see *PS* I.17, AT XI 343/CSM I 335. Cf. *DM* V, AT VI 55–60/CSM I 139–41). In §4.3.2 I cite one passage in which Descartes did argue for the difference between soul and body by appealing to the difference between sensations and modifications of extension, though I also indicate that his argument there does not correspond exactly to Malebranche's Cartesian argument.

57. Descartes admitted to certain correspondents that minds are extended in the sense that they are coextensive with bodies in virtue of their power to act on these bodies,

but he was careful to distinguish this sort of extension from the extension in space that pertains to body. See *To Hyperaspistes*, Aug. 1641, AT III 434/CSMK 197; *To Elisabeth*, 28 June 1643, AT III 694–95/CSMK 228; *To More*, 5 Feb. 1649, AT V 269–70/CSMK 361.

58. In the *Fourth Replies* Descartes spoke of conceiving of the mind as a substance without conceiving of it as possessing bodily attributes, thus stressing the conceptual independence of mind from those attributes. In the 1644 letter to Mesland, on the other hand, he spoke of conceiving of the mind as a substance that can exist without bodily attributes, thus stressing the existential independence of mind from those attributes. The difference is explained by the fact that in the *Fourth Replies* he was referring to the conception of the nature of mind in general, whereas in the 1644 letter he was referring to the conception of his particular mind. Descartes' own view is that universals considered in the abstract are mere "modes of thought" that cannot exist in reality in the way that particulars can (*PP* I.58, AT VIII-1 27/CSM I 212). Thus, a particular mind, but not the nature of mind in general, can be conceived to exist in reality. Nonetheless, the fact that Descartes moved freely between talk of conceptual independence and talk of existential independence indicates that he took the two to be interconnected in some way. One way to make sense of this movement is to attribute to him the view that one can distinctly perceive that mind in general is conceptually independent of bodily attributes just in case one can distinctly perceive that a particular mind is existentially independent of those attributes. While I attempt to observe the difference between these two kinds of distinct perception, I also assume that Descartes took them to be interconnected in the manner just indicated.

59. *Descartes*, 180–81. As Wilson's remarks suggest, this difference stems from the fact that Descartes attempted to establish that mind can exist without body whereas the more contemporary Cartesian dualist claims merely that conscious experiences are not identical to any bodily event. For an example of the more contemporary form of dualism, see Kripke, *Naming and Necessity*, 144–55.

60. In note 38 I cited one deficiency of Arnauld's analogy. Descartes drew attention to another when he indicated that though we cannot distinctly understand a triangle to possess the Pythagorean property without understanding it to be right triangle, we can distinctly understand body to be an extended thing without understanding it to think (AT VII 224–25/CSM II 158). Nonetheless, in order to parry the main thrust of Arnauld's objection, Descartes requires the premise that we can distinctly understand mind to be a thinking thing without understanding it to be extended. This is the very premise, however, with which the Hobbesian materialist takes issue.

61. Hobbes argued in particular that sensory appearances produced in us by motions in external objects must themselves be motions, since "motion produceth nothing but motion" (*Leviathan*, Pt. I, c. 1, pp. 21–22). For a discussion of Hobbes' reductionist account of sensory thought and its attendant difficulties, see Sorell, *Hobbes*, c. 6.

62. *Défense*, OA XXXVIII 614.

63. The objection is to the remarks in *DM* IV, AT VI 32–33/CSM I 127.

64. *Disquisitio*, Med. II, Dub. IV, in *Opera Omnia* III 300. Gassendi was developing his earlier objection that in the *Second Meditation* Descartes was not entitled to the supposition that he is a thinking thing rather than some bodily element (*Fifth Obj.*, AT VII 264–65/CSM II 184–85).

65. *Second Rep.*, AT VII 131–32/CSM II 94–95; *Fifth Rep.*, AT VII 357/CSM II 247.

66. As Descartes himself acknowledged in a parenthetical remark in *Second Rep.*, AT VII 170/CSM II 119.

67. What is controversial in the context of modern thought, however, is Descartes'

realist assumption that bodies can be conceived to exist apart from any human perception. Despite differences in their specific arguments and conclusions, Berkeley, Leibniz, and Kant agreed on the broadly idealistic point that the physical world is in some sense dependent on human perceivers.

68. This resemblance is ironic in light of the fact that Arnauld, in his role of surrogate for Descartes, took issue with Malebranche's position (VFI, c. 23, OA XXXVIII 308–9/TFI 131–32). It is likely that Arnauld overlooked the connection between this position and Descartes' remarks in the Fourth Replies because he focused on Malebranche's admittedly implausible suggestion that no discursive argument is needed to see that thought cannot be a modification of extension.

69. Notice that this symmetry differs from the symmetry indicated by the Real Distinction Argument. This argument suggests that just as a consideration of the nature of mind suffices for the distinct perception that this nature excludes extension, so a consideration of the nature of body suffices for the distinct perception that that nature excludes thought. Both symmetries indicate, however, that knowledge of mind and knowledge of body have an equal footing.

70. *Sentimens*, Pt. I, c. 4, p. 61. The Minim of Toulouse, E. Maignan, had argued in 1653 that atomism is supported by the (somewhat obscure) consideration that the divine act of creation must have a determinate and simple substance as its object (see Prost, *Essai sur l'atomisme*, 59–60). Cordemoy argued more clearly in his 1666 *Discernement du corps et de l'ame* that atomism is required in order to attribute a fixed shape to body and to allow for the conceivability of a distinction among different bodies that are at rest relative to each other (see Battail, *L'avocat philosophe*, c. 4).

71. As indicated in §4.2.2, Desgabets claimed that Descartes' "grand discovery" that the corporeal world is nothing other than extension provides the "fundamental proof of the distinction between the soul and the body." For the related position in Regis, see *Usage* I–2.6, 119–20.

72. Yolton has argued that the move toward materialism in the eighteenth century in general was accompanied by a rethinking of the concept of matter. See in particular his discussion of Joseph Priestly in *Thinking Matter*, c. 6, and of Denis Diderot in *Locke and French Materialism*, 183–194.

73. *Étendue et psychologie*, 45.

74. *Critique of Pure Reason*, A 343/B 401, p. 330 (translation from Kemp Smith ed.).

75. McCracken, *Malebranche and British Philosophy*, 80; cited with approval in Jolley, *Light of the Soul*, 130.

Chapter Five

1. In 1513 the Lateran Council had condemned the Averroist doctrine that only an intellect common to all human souls is immortal, and had declared the immortality of the individual human soul to be a dogma of the Church. For discussion of the background to this decree, see Kristeller, "The Immortality of the Soul."

2. It is significant that Descartes had left to Mersenne the "power to baptise" his work by making the final determination as to its title (*To Mersenne*, 11 Nov. 1640, AT III 239/CSMK 158; cf. *To Mersenne*, 31 Mar. 1641, AT III 350/CSMK 177).

3. The notion of God's absolute power became prominent in discussions of Aristotelian natural philosophy in response to the Condemnation of 1277, a criticism of 219 articles on theology and natural philosophy by the bishop of Paris, Étienne Tempier. Especially relevant here is the condemnation of article 147, which asserts "that the ab-

solutely impossible cannot be done by God or another agent," where "impossible is understood according to nature" (cited in Grant, *Much Ado about Nothing*, 108). As Grant has noted, after 1277 scholastics in Paris felt obliged to hold that God can do what is naturally impossible, such as creating several worlds or a void in nature, by means of his absolute power (*Much Ado about Nothing*, 108–10, 127–34).

4. On the traditional view in Aquinas, a name of a property can be predicated of two or more subjects univocally only if the subjects have the same sort of property; see *Summa Theologiæ* Ia, Q. 13, art. 6.

5. See *Third Med.*, AT VII 48–49/CSM II 33; *First Rep.*, AT VII 111/CSM II 80.

6. Descartes admitted earlier in this letter that the surface of the body could survive a change in its parts, and that for this reason "we can say that the Loire is the same river it was ten years ago, although it no longer has the same water, and although there may no longer be any part of the same earth that surrounded the water" (AT IV 165/CSMK 242). What his remarks in this letter commit him to denying, however, is that the Loire qua determinate part of matter is the same river as ten years ago.

7. See, for instance, (Rodis-) Lewis, *L'Individualité selon Descartes*, 39–41.

8. See his claim in a 1631 letter that "there is only one material substance" (*To Villebressieu*, Summer 1631, AT I 216/CSMK 33) as well as his talk in the 1644 *Principles* of a single matter as occupying all places (PP II.23, AT VIII-1 52/CSM I 232).

9. *Rationalisme de Descartes*, 187–88.

10. One could perhaps draw on Descartes' account of space. He noted in the *Principles* that while space does not differ in reality from the body that occupies it, nonetheless there is a difference between conceiving of body as a concrete individual that can move with its extension and conceiving of it as a generic space that can be occupied by different concrete individuals (PP II.12, AT VIII-1 46–47/CSM I 228). It may be that while the concrete individual can be destroyed, the space conceived generically cannot. Descartes did not avail himself of this position, however, and even suggested in the section of the *Principles* just cited that body conceived as generic space can cease to exist if it does not retain the same position relative to external bodies.

11. Descartes' claim in the letter to Mesland that the unity of this body derives from its union with the human soul may seem to conflict with his claim in the *Passions* that the human body is one "due to the disposition of its organs" (PS I.30, AT XI 351/CSM I 339), as well as with his view in the *Synopsis* that the identity of a human body depends essentially on the shape of certain of its parts. I think that there need be no conflict, however. Descartes in fact suggested in his letter to Mesland that the union with the human soul presupposes that the body has a certain set of dispositions. So once the body loses those dispositions, presumably through a change in the shape of certain of its parts, it must become disengaged from the human soul and so cease to exist as a human body.

12. The priority of the conception of the soul as indivisible is indicated by Descartes' comment in the *Sixth Meditation* that the indivisibility argument "would suffice to teach me that mind is completely different from body, even if I did not already know this from other things" (AT VII 86/CSM II 59).

13. See Cicero's argument in the *Tusculan Disputations* that since the mind has no material parts, "it is certain that it cannot be severed or divided or disrupted or torn apart, and therefore cannot be destroyed either, for destruction is as a separation and severance and disruption of the parts, which before the destruction were held together in some kind of union" (Bk. I, sec. 29, pp. 82–85).

14. For Russier's discussion of the distinction between *immortalité de nature* and *immortalité de fait*, see *Sagesse cartésienne et religion*, 43–70.

15. *To Molanus (?)*, c. 1679, in *Philosophical Essays*, 243.

16. Descartes' first rule of method in the *Discourse* is "to include nothing more in my judgments than what presented itself to my mind so clearly and so distinctly that I had no occasion to doubt it" (*DM II*, AT VI 18/CSM I 120). Cf. RM V–VI, AT X 379–87/ CSM I 20–24.

17. The author of this claim is the Jesuit Gabriel Daniel, and the claim itself is found in his 1693 *Nouvelles difficultez . . . Touchant la connoissance des bestes*, 5–6.

18. Cf. RV VI–2.7, OCM II 392/LO 493–94, and *Écl.* XV, OCM III 236–37/LO 675–76. In the former passage Malebranche characteristically downplayed the differences between Augustine and Descartes, noting that Augustine himself did not seriously consider the implications of attributing immaterial souls to animals. In the latter passage, moreover, he cited the claim of André Martin (pseud. Ambrosius Victor) in *De anima bestiarum*, the separately published sixth volume added to the second edition (1671) of the *Philosophia christiana*, that Augustinian principles in fact support the rejection of animal souls. For more on *De anima bestiarum*, see Gouhier, *Cartésianisme et augustinisme*, 96–98, 154–55.

19. Cf. the remarks in the 1633 *L'Homme* (which Clerselier and La Forge published in 1664) at AT XI 200–2/CSM I 107–8.

20. In the *Discourse* Descartes had distinguished between "moral certainty," which we have when "we cannot doubt" without "being extravagent," and "metaphysical certainty," which precludes even extravagent reasons for doubt (*DM IV*, AT VI 37–38/CSM I 130). If we can be only morally certain about what is morally impossible, then the implication in this text (which Descartes did not explore) is that we cannot be metaphysically certain that other humans are more than mere machines. Conversely, Descartes clearly held that we can be metaphysically certain that we ourselves have rational thoughts and thus are not mere machines.

21. For Descartes' response, see *To Plempius for Fromondus*, 3 Oct. 1637, AT I 414–16/CSMK 62–63. Cf. Descartes' defense of his remarks in the *Discourse* in *To Newcastle*, 23 Nov. 1646, AT IV 573–76/CSMK 302–4; and *To Reneri for Pollot*, Apr. or May 1638, AT II 39–41/CSMK 99–100.

22. *Discours*, 99. In this work Pardies went on to offer several responses to this line of objection on Descartes' behalf. In fact, his fellow Jesuit, Gabriel Daniel, noted that Pardies' defense of Descartes was so vigorous that his *Discours* "a fait passer son auteur parmi les Péripatéticiens pour un prévaricateur qui étoit Cartésien dans l'âme" (*Nouvelles difficultez*, 14). However, this does not seem to be a fair judgment, given Pardies' insistence toward the end of his work that beasts have *connoissances sensibles* that are *simples perceptions* (*Discours*, 150–51). For the role of Pardies' text in the early modern dispute over the Cartesian doctrine of the beast machine, see Rosenfield's introduction to the reprint of the *Discours*; for a general discussion of the dispute itself, see her *From Beast-Machine to Man-Machine*, as well as Gouhier's *Cartésianisme et augustinisme*, 147–56.

23. Cf. Daniel's challenge to the Cartesians: "[W]hy it is that you, a Cartesian (who I would like to assume is not an automaton) make an exception from the general rule for just one species of beings, of which all that you can see is a machine just like the bodies of other animals?" (*Nouvelles difficultez*, 100).

24. Malebranche cited in particular the criticism in the *Essais* of one who "sorts and separates himself from the throng of other creatures," creatures that are in fact "our

fellow bretheren and companions" (see *Essais*, Bk. II, c. 12, II 239). Descartes had earlier rejected Montaigne's view that beasts have souls with understanding and thought, alluding to his position in the *Discourse* that there is sufficient reason to conclude that beasts are mere machines (*To Newcastle*, 23 Nov. 1646, AT IV 573–76/CSMK 302–4).

25. Cf. RV V.3, OCM II 150–52/LO 351–53.

26. Descartes at times spoke of the blood of beasts as their soul; see *To Plempius for Fromondus*, 3 Oct. 1637, AT I 414–16/CSMK 62–63; *To Buitendijck*, 1643 (?), AT IV 65/CSMK 230; *To More*, 5 Feb. 1649, AT V 276/CSMK 365.

27. Pardies had granted, for instance, that it is not necessary that the principle that makes beasts sense "is indivisible; it may be spread out [*repandu*] throughout the body, and even can somehow be divided when one cuts the animal into pieces, in the same manner in which the principle that gives life to plants can be divided when one extracts an offshoot of a tree and transplants it" (*Discours*, 179).

28. Some have even taken two later letters from Descartes (*To Newcastle*, 23 Nov. 1646, AT IV 573–74/CSMK 303; *To More*, 278–79/CSMK 366) to provide evidence that he did not consistently deny that animals have sensations and passions; see for instance Cottingham, "A Brute to the Brutes?" and Grene, *Descartes*, 49–52. In these letters, however, Descartes granted only that animals have passions that "do not depend on thought" (AT IV 574/CSMK 303), and that they have sensations that consist "simply in the heat of the heart" (AT V 278/CSMK 366). I think that these letters are best read as claiming, in line with Descartes' official position, that animals without rational souls have sensations and passions only in the sense that they have something similar to the physical correlates in the human body of the sensations and passions of the human soul.

29. The difference here between Descartes and Malebranche seems to be one of emphasis rather than one of substance. Malebranche himself concluded at one point that "in the animals there is neither intelligence nor soul, as one ordinarily understands it" (RV VI-2.7, OCM II 394/LO 494), after all, while Descartes allowed that beasts without rational souls do not have sensory thoughts (see note 28).

30. *Entretien II*, in *Jacques Rohault*, 145. There is something of an anticipation of this sort of argument in Descartes' remark in a letter to Regius that the acceptance of substantial forms "allows the easiest slide to those who maintain that the human soul is corporeal and mortal" (Jan. 1642, AT III 503/CSMK 207).

31. This book is listed as item number 454 in Lelong's inventory of Malebranche's library (OCM XX 245, 277).

32. Malebranche offered a more elaborate version of this argument in the 1696 *Entretiens sur la mort* (E. mort I, OCM XIII 373–78).

33. Just prior to this passage, Malebranche had referred in the first edition to a distinct perception of ideas "as clear as those of thought and extension" (OCM II 25h). While in subsequent editions he left in the problematic reference to a distinct perception of an idea of thought, he removed the claim that this idea is "as clear as" the idea of extension. In any case, from the first edition on he emphasized that it is the clear and distinct idea of extension that reveals that extension cannot be related to thought.

34. In *Éclaircissement* XV Malebranche explicitly criticized the scholastic position that God conserves the world by means of his concourse (*concours*) with the action of secondary causes (OCM III 216–18/LO 664–65).

35. Cf. Callot's objection that since Malebranche has not precluded the possibility that our mind is only a mode of thinking substance, "nothing is guarenteed to us concerning personal survival and we are even certain that after death these modalities will

evaporate as 'what is flesh will turn into earth, vapor and all that you please'" (*Problèmes du cartésianisme*, 202; the quoted passage is from RV IV.2, OCM II 24/LO 273).

36. Wilson has drawn attention to the fact that Leibniz himself took an order rooted in God's goodness to ensure that memory will survive death ("Leibniz: Self-Consciousness and Immortality," 342–44). As I indicate in §5.2.3, Malebranche took the nature of the divine order to show that God does not annihilate the soul by means of his absolute power.

37. Cf. the discussion of this passage in §3.2.2 (1).

38. See also *Rép. Diss.*, c. 7, OCM VII 514. The conclusion in these texts is linked to Malebranche's argument in the *Entretiens* that nothingness cannot be the object of the divine volition since God wills only what is lovable and since nothingness is not lovable (*EM VII*, OCM XII 158/D 155).

39. Cf. Malebranche's claim in the *Traité de la Nature et de la Grâce* that "the annihilation of substances is a mark of inconstancy in that which produces them; they thus will never come to an end" (*TNG* I.iv, OCM V 19).

40. This view is central to his solution to the problem of evil; see *TNG* I.xiii–xiv, OCM V 28–29.

41. Malebranche was arguing in this section against Descartes' view in the *Principles* that rest in bodies involves a positive force to remain at rest (see *PP* II.43, AT VIII–1 66–67/CSM I 243–44).

42. The example of the hand is from *Fourth Rep.*, AT VII 222/CSM II 157, and the example of the clothes from *Notes*, AT VIII–2 351/CSM I 299.

43. See the title to *Principles* I.52: "The term substance applies univocally to mind and to body" (AT VIII–1 24/CSM I 210).

44. See RV III–2.8, OCM I 461–62/LO 244; VI–2.9, OCM II 425/LO 513.

45. Malebranche was responding here to the objection of his former student, Jean-Jacques Dortous de Mairan, that he is committed to the view that bodies are merely modifications of a single Spinozistic substance. The correspondence between the two consisted of an exchange of four letters between 1713 and 1714 (the original collection of which is now lost). For a discussion of this correspondence that defends Malebranche against de Mairan's charge of Spinozism, see Moreau, "Malebranche et le spinozisme."

46. Malebranche's talk of the "substance of" bodies has some precedent in Descartes; see the claim in the French edition of the *Principles*, which has no counterpart in the original Latin edition, that matter is "la substance des choses materielles" (*PP* II.1, AT IX–2 64).

47. See RV IV.2, OCM II 24/LO 274; *Déf. La Ville*, OCM XVII–1 521–22; *Réponse*, c. 23, OCM VI 163; and *E. mort I*, OCM XIII 369.

48. *Étendue et psychologie*, 52–53.

49. This idea thus reveals that the soul qua indivisible substance differs in nature from matter and, at the same time, that the soul qua indestructible substance is essentially similar to matter. Gueroult discusses this dual role for the idea of matter, though without mentioning the particular issue of the indivisibility and indestructibility of the soul, in *Étendue et psychologie*, 52–55.

50. Malebranche admittedly did not emphasize the lack of access to a clear idea of the soul, noting instead that the comparison to matter is required since the ideas of mental faculties are "abstract" and thus not as easy to imagine as the faculties of matter. However, he did say that it is difficult to attach precise notions to the terms *entendement* and *volonté* since "the notions or ideas that one has of these two faculties are neither clear nor distinct enough" (OCM I 41/LO 2).

51. *Third Med.*, AT VII 48–49/CSM II 33–34; *First Rep.*, AT VII 111/CSM II 80; *Second Rep.*, AT VII 165/CSM II 116.

52. In *Éclaircissement* VI Malebranche argued along similar lines that the existence of bodies cannot be "parfaitement démonstrée . . . en riguer géométrique" (OCM III 60/ LO 572). In §2.2.1 (2), moreover, I attributed to Malebranche the position that the idea of extension does not suffice to demonstrate that bodies have those properties that derive from laws that depend on God's will.

53. See *Réponse*, c. 26, OCM VI 183. Malebranche here was replying to Arnauld's arguments for the existence of bodies (offered in *VFI*, c. 28, OA XXXVIII 354–58, TFI 176–80), which he called *bonnes preuves* but *fort méchantes démonstrations*.

54. See, for instance, his claim there that since "God always acts as God [*en Dieu*], it is necessary that we exist eternally" (OCM XIX 605). Malebranche's suggestion is that the argument for the soul's immortality is a proof rather than a demonstration since its conclusion is established by means of a consideration of the nature of the divine will rather than of the nature of the soul.

55. One therefore cannot accept without qualification Callot's view that for Malebranche immortality "is not even assured to us [since] creatures and the laws of creatures exist and persist only through the free will of God" (*Problèmes du cartésianisme*, 202).

56. *Défense*, OA XXXVIII 613.

57. Descartes was here reflecting on his comment in the *Fourth Meditation* that "there is considerable rashness in thinking myself capable of investigating the purposes of God" (AT VII 55/CSM II 39).

58. In the *Principles* Descartes attempted to derive the law of the conservation of the quantity of motion from the divine attribute of immutability, though, as I note in §6.2.3 (1), he also allowed for exceptions to this law pertaining to changes "that evident experience [*experientia*] or divine revelation renders certain" (PP II.36, AT VIII-1 61/ CSM I 240). At the very start of his work Malebranche indicated his concern to provide a critique of Descartes' account of motion (OCM XVII-1 53).

59. This position reflects a change in Malebranche's thought initiated by Leibniz's earlier criticisms of his account of the laws of motion; see chapter 2, note 85.

60. Malebranche was addressing a position that he attributed to François Lamy (or Lami) but that is perhaps most clearly expressed in the 1697 *Explication des Maximes des Saintes* of François Fénelon: the just who have the purest love of God would willingly accept even damnation (see the passage from Fénelon's text cited in the first of Malebranche's *Lettres au Lamy*, OCM XIV 37–38, 246 n.230). Malebranche conceded something to this position when he admitted that these individuals can accept their annihilation by God, given that "being precisely as such, without a good and bad being that is actual or future, appears strongly indifferent to the will" (OCM XIV 25). However, he insisted that the true God could not will the damnation of the just and that even if he could, it would be psychologically impossible for the just to accept a damnation that is contrary to their happiness (OCM XIV 25; cf. *To Berrand*, 10 Nov. 1699, OCM XIX 699). For a discussion of this response in Malebranche, see Montcheuil, *Malebranche et le quiétisme*, c. 7; for a discussion of the position in Fénelon to which Malebranche most likely was responding, see Gouhier, *Fénelon philosophe*, c. 2. Cf. chapter 6, note 30.

61. In the 1698 letter Malebranche emphasized that it is through the Incarnation of Christ that the universe (and thus the human soul) has been "sanctified" and "rendered worthy of [God's] infinite Magesty" (OCM XIX 606; cf. *EM* IX, OCM XII 204–5/ D 203, 205). This consideration clearly takes us beyond the realm of reason, invoking as it does an article of faith.

62. Malebranche could perhaps claim at this point that the human soul is also more noble than matter itself. Given that this matter is indestructible, it would follow that the soul must be indestructible as well. What is required here, however, is a proof from reason that God will not exercise his power to annihilate matter.

63. In the seventeenth century the French term *indéfectibilité* was used primarily to indicate the indestructability of the Church and the faultlessness of its official doctrines; see Dublanchy, "Église," 2145–50. In using this term Desgabets no doubt wanted to indicate not only the indestructability of substance but also its resistance to any sort of corruption.

64. This passage from Desgabets' 3 March 1674 letter to the Cartesian Oratorian, Nicolas Poisson, is quoted in Beaude, "Desgabets et son œuvre," 11.

65. This is the title of the last (the so-called E) version of this text; earlier (the so-called A, B, C and D) versions bear title, *Traité de l'indéfectibilité des substances*. Beaude notes other differences among the various versions in "Desgabets et son œuvre," 8–9.

66. *Indéfectibilité*, c. 4, RD II 29. Desgabets' talk here of "the least atom of substance" is somewhat misleading given his explicit rejection of the doctrine, central to atomism, of the indivisibility of atoms (see note 69). For him an atom is simply a divisible parcel of matter.

67. Cousin, *Fragments de philosophie cartésienne*, 104; cf. Armogathe, *Theologia cartesiana*, 87. This reading of Desgabets is perhaps supported most directly by his rejection of a pure intellect distinct from the senses (see §§2.3.2 [3] and 3.1.1 [1]). Whereas Gassendi identified the sensations of animals and humans alike with corporeal images, Desgabets followed the Cartesian line that animals cannot have sensations since these modifications belong to an immaterial soul.

68. RD II 29–30. Gassendi held that he meant by imaginary spaces nothing more than the "majority of sacred doctors" who concede that "it is nothing positive, neither a substance nor an accident, under which heading all things created by God are subsumed" (*Opera Omnia* I 183–84). For a discussion of this position in Gassendi and the precursors to it in the writings of the scholastics, see Grant, *Much Ado about Nothing*; 157–81, 199–221.

69. RD II 28. Cf. Descartes' claim in the *Principles* that "there is no real difference between space and corporeal substance" (*PP* II.11, AT VIII-1 46/CSM I 227). Desgabets' distaste for Gassendi's natural philosophy is confirmed by his complaint in a letter to Clerselier that the atomism in the recently published *Discernement* of Geraud de Cordemoy constitutes a "schism" that is "all the more serious since it all of a sudden removes from the true philosophy one of its strongest columns and notably strengthens the camp of Gassendi, which already seems only too likely to support itself and overcome that of Descartes" (quoted in Prost, *Essai sur l'atomisme*, 158).

70. RD II 29.

71. Cf. *Supplément* II.6.v, RD VI 232–33.

72. See the detailed discussion of Descartes' rejection of the vacuum in Garber, *Descartes' Metaphysical Physics*, 127–54.

73. RD II 28.

74. It seems that continuity would not be broken if a new portion of space immediately took the place of the annihilated portion. Desgabets sidestepped such a possibility when he spoke in his *Traité* of "there being a void in nature and each body rightly filling its place."

75. *Supplément* II.7.vi, RD VI 240–42; II.12.vii, RD VII 271–72.

76. RD II 36.

77. *Indéfectibilité*, c. 5, RD II 35. Cf. *Supplément* II.9.vi, RD VI 212.
78. *Usage* I–2.8–9, 123–27.
79. *Usage* I–2.19, 156.
80. *Usage* I–2.20, 158–60. In his discussion of simple and divisible substance, Regis focused primarily on the distinction between "body in itself," which is indivisible, and its quantity, which is infinitely divisible (*Usage* I–2.13–14, 135–42). This distinction between indivisible body and its divisible quantity is anticipated in Desgabets; see *Indéfectibilité*, c. 6, RD II 37.
81. *Alambic* I.21, PL 322. Cf. *Third Med.*, AT VII 48–49/CSM II 33.
82. PL 322. Cf. *Supplément* II.12.vii, RD VII 271.
83. *Alambic* II.36, PL 324–25.
84. *Usage* I–2.10, 127–29; I-2.21, 164. Cf. the discussion of the distinction between divine creation and generation in *Système*, Meta., I–1.12, I 100–1.
85. OR IX 296–306. Retz was speaking here specifically of spiritual substance, arguing that we can conceive the duration of this substance apart from bodily motion.
86. There is a complication introduced by Malebranche's distinction in the *Recherche* between two kinds of bodily modes: internal relations between the parts of a body, modes of that body in a strict sense, and external relations among different bodies, modes of any one of the bodies only in a loose sense (see §§2.2.1 [1] and 3.2.2 [1]). The claim that a mode is only the substance itself in a certain way applies more clearly to modes in a strict sense than it does to modes in a loose sense. This complication does not affect the case of matter as a whole, however, since it can bear no external relation to other bodies.
87. Desgabets cited this concession in *Supplément* I.9.i, RD VI 208–9. In the *Traité* he made the interesting but questionable suggestion that while Descartes recognized that substance is indefectible, he offered such a concession simply because "he did not wish to engage in new quarrels, already having his arms full with other things that would hinder the publication of his philosophy" (*Indéfectibilité*, c. 4, RD II 29).
88. OR IX 326.
89. The ninth proposition on OR IX 329.
90. *Indéfectibilité*, c. 5, RD II 32.
91. RD II 34.
92. Following his summary of this doctrine, Desgabets' claimed that "I have only spoken for Descartes" (RD II 34). Regis accepted Descartes' doctrine as well; see *Usage* I–2.12, 132–35; *Système*, Meta., I–1.13, I 102–5. Desgabets and Regis were part of a small group of Cartesians committed to the doctrine of the creation of the eternal truths. For a discussion of the reception of Descartes' account of the eternal truths among Cartesian sympathizers and critics, see Rodis-Lewis, "Polémique sur la création des possibles."
93. See RD II 33, which is just one of many passages in which Desgabets cited the maxim from Augustine, "Uniuscujusque rei natura voluntas Dei est" ("The nature of a thing and God's will are one and the same"). Cf. *To Mesland*, 2 May 1644, AT IV 119/CSMK 235, where Descartes cited Augustine's remark, "Quia vides [Domine] ea sunt" ("What you see [God] is so").
94. RD II 34. Cf. *To Mersenne*, 15 Apr. 1630, AT I 145/CSMK 23; 27 May 1630, AT I 151–52/CSMK 25.
95. OR IX 326.
96. RD II 34. Likewise, Regis spoke of the indefectibility of substances as "an indefectibility participated and dependent on the will of God" (*Usage* I–2.20, 160).
97 RD II 35. While some have taken Descartes to hold that the eternal truths are

in fact contingent, I have argued, in line with Desgabets' remarks here, that he took them to have a necessity dependent on the divine will; see my "Platonism and Descartes' View of Immutable Essences," 152–54.

98. Retz himself admitted at one point that if Desgabets "understands by the indefectibility of substance the immutability of the will of God, everyone agrees, although under different terms" (OR IX 331). He went on to say, however, that he still could not accept Desgabets' position that substance has an indivisible being that renders it eternal.

99. RD II 35.

100. Desgabets' appeal to the principle of the conservation of motion in support of the indefectibility of substance (see *Indéfectibilité*, c. 17, RD III 91–98; *Supplément* I.9.v, RD VI 210–12), moreover, is connected to Descartes' suggestion that eternal truths are akin to natural laws that are immutable because they derive from God's immutable will. For more on this suggestion, see my "Platonism and Descartes' View of Immutable Essences," 136–45.

101. July 1648, AT V 215/TFI 192. Arnauld was returning to his objection in an earlier letter to Descartes that the claim that there cannot be a vacuum in nature "certainly seems to take away from divine omnipotence" (3 June 1648, AT V 190/TFI 188). Henry More raised a similar objection in his correspondence with Descartes (*More to Descartes*, Dec. 1648, AT V 240–41).

102. More accurately, Descartes claimed in the *Sixth Replies* that it is because "God willed that the three angles of a triangle necessarily equal two right angles that this is now true, and cannot be otherwise" (AT VII 432/CSM II 29). Given his claim in this text that every reason for anything's being true depends on God (AT VII 435/CSM II 293–94), this point can be extended to other mathematical truths, including the truth that one and two necessarily equal three.

103. The impossibility of annihilation would not follow if, as Arnauld suggested to Descartes in the passage previously cited, God immediately fills the space of the annihilated body with a different body that has the same quantity. Desgabets discounted this possibility, but Descartes himself did not reject it in his response to Arnauld. Perhaps Desgabets could draw, however, on Descartes' argument in the *Principles* that "one and the same matter" must occupy all possible space (PP II.22, AT VIII-1 52/CSM I 232). If the matter with the added body could be said to differ from the original matter, this line of argument would preclude the possibility suggested by Arnauld.

104. *Indéfectibilité*, c. 5, RD II 34–35.

105. It is interesting that Descartes had announced to Mersenne in 1630 that he would discuss the doctrine of the creation of the eternal truths in a treatise on physics (15 Apr. 1630, AT I 145/CSMK 22–23). Garber has recently appealed to this fact in support of the hypothesis that Descartes originally formulated the doctrine in order to render the impossibility of a void consistent with divine omnipotence (*Descartes' Metaphysical Physics*, 153–54).

106. *Critique de Crit.*, 69. In the first edition of the *Recherche*, Malebranche referred at one point to "necessary truths, immutable by their nature and because they have been determined by the will of God, which is not subject to change" (RV I.3, OCM I 63a). Foucher had read this passage as endorsing the doctrine that eternal truths depend on the divine will (*Critique*, 27). Desgabets no doubt read the passage in a similar manner.

107. In his *Philosophia christiana*, which was the source for Malebranche's reading of Augustine (see chapter 2, note 1), André Martin (pseud. Ambrosius Victor) emphasized the Augustinian doctrine of the vision of eternal truths in God but did not mention the view that these truths are freely created by God.

108. See *Écl.* VIII, OCM III 84–87/LO 586–88, and *Écl.* X, OCM III 136–37/LO 617–18; in both passages Malebranche attributed the position that eternal truths derive from God's will to Descartes. Robinet has cited the passage from the *Recherche* that Foucher emphasized (see note 106) in support of the view that Malebranche came to reject such a position only after the "crise de 1677" (*Système et existence*, 233–35). In his 1675 response to Foucher, however, Malebranche distinguished between truths that are immutable "through their nature or through themselves" and truths that "have been determined by the will of God," even though he also admitted that he was not "explicit enough" on this distinction in the *Recherche* ("Préface," OCM II 488–89; cf. the correction at RV I.3, OCM I 63a). I believe that there is, in fact, no convincing evidence that Malebranche was ever attracted to Descartes' view, indicated in his 1630 letter to Mersenne, that God must be the cause of eternal truths given that there is no distinction in him between intellect and will (6 May 1630, AT I 149–50/CSMK 24–25). For a defense of this claim, see Rodis-Lewis, "Les limites initiales," 244–49, and "La connaissance par idée chez Malebranche," 119–20.

109. *Alambic* II.21, PL 324.

110. *Système*, Meta., III.1, I 266–67.

111. *Supplément* II.7.ii, RD VI 236.

Chapter Six

1. Alquié has claimed, however, that there are two different accounts of freedom in Descartes, the first of which allows for free actions that are determined, and the second of which requires that free actions be undetermined (*Cartésianisme de Malebranche*, 376–77). In §6.2.2 (1) I consider the relation between these two different accounts of freedom in Descartes.

2. RV V.1, OCM II 128/LO 338. For a discussion of Malebranche's account of the passions in the context of Descartes' own account, see Hoffman, "Three Dualist Theories of the Passions," 182–94.

3. In addition to the primary natural inclination toward God, Malebranche held that we have secondary natural inclinations for the preservation of our own being and for the preservation of others (RV IV.1, OCM II 11–12, LO 267–68). Nonetheless, he held that God is the final end even of these secondary natural inclinations since the inclinations dispose us to love self and others insofar as they are related to God (see RV IV.5, OCM II 45–46/LO 287; IV.13, OCM II 113–14/LO 330–31).

4. *Cartésianisme de Malebranche*, 325. Cf. Montcheuil, *Malebranche et le quiétisme*, 330–31.

5. In this letter Descartes distinguished between rational love, which includes a movement of the will that accompanies the knowledge that a good is present, and sensuous love, which is simply a confused feeling of heat around the heart (AT IV 602–3/CSMK 306–7).

6. Descartes much preferred to speak of the will as involving an action of the soul; see, for instance, PS I.18, AT XI 343/CSM I 335.

7. Malebranche's claim in the *Recherche* that all minds will to possess the sovereign good "by the necessity of their nature" (RV III–1.4, OCM I 405/LO 212) may seem to suggest that the will is essential to the soul. As the context reveals, however, the main point here is not that will is essential to mind, but that there is a feature of the will that is a necessary consequence of the laws that govern its nature and thus that does not issue from free choice.

8. Malebranche spoke in Book Three of the conception of *a* mind (*une esprit*) that has neither sensation nor imagination nor will (RV III–1.1, OCM I 382/LO 198). He evidently assumed that differences in intellectual thought suffice to distinguish one particular mind from others.

9. Malebranche extended the analogy between the will and bodily motion even further in *Éclaircissement I*, when he claimed that God "always conserves in our soul an equal capacity for willing, or the same will, as he conserves in all matter taken as a whole an equal amount of force or movement in the same direction [*de même part*]" (OCM III 23/LO 550).

10. This section focuses almost exclusively on the way in which the case of sensation supports such a thesis.

11. For more on the animal spirits, see the texts cited in chapter 2, note 81.

12. Cf. Descartes' similar account of memory in *To Meyssonnier*, 29 Jan. 1640, AT III 20–21/CSMK 143–44; and *To Mersenne*, 11 Mar. 1640, AT III 48/CSMK 145–46.

13. He held in this passage that memory is distinguished from other habits by the perceptions that it brings about, and that "if there were no perceptions attached either to the course of the animal spirits, or to these traces [in which memory consists], there would be no difference between memory and other habits" (OCM I 228–29/LO 108).

14. It is devoted in particular to a discussion of the errors that derive from this mental faculty. See the outline of the general plan of the *Recherche* in chapter 1, note 6.

15. There is an anticipation of this point in the 1683 *Meditations Chrétiennes* (MC XVI, OCM X 184–85).

16. Cf. MC XVI, OCM X 182.

17. See for instance his claim in *Éclaircissement XI* that our hesitation over whether the soul has habits "is a certain sign that we are not as enlightened as we might say, for doubt does not agree with evidence and clear ideas" (OCM III 170/LO 637).

18. Cf. his comment in the *Meditations Chrétiennes* that "as a man has no distinct idea of the soul, it is not possible for him to indicate distinctly in what consists the nature of his habits" (MC XVI, OCM X 181–82).

19. See Malebranche's remark to Arnauld that "man does not know these inner dispositions if they are not actually excited; and even when they are, one knows them only in a very imperfect manner" (*Deux lettres I*, OCM VIII 796).

20. There is nothing in Descartes, for instance, that corresponds to Malebranche's discussion of the habits formed by the grace of reason (*grâce de lumière*) and the grace of sentiment (*grâce de sentiment*). For one such discussion, see TNG II.xxx–xxxv, OCM V 97–101.

21. In this work Malebranche asserted as the first "fundamental truth" that "the acts [of the soul] produce [its] habits, and the habits the acts" (*Mor.* I.4, OCM XI 51).

22. *Second Rep.*, AT VII 160/CSM II 113.

23. *Réflexions III*, Preface, OA XXXIX 648.

24. Malebranche's suggestion in this passage that we can know our dispositions when they are excited, which is strengthened by several other texts, may seem to be at odds with his official view that inner sentiment reveals only the acts of the soul and not its habitual dispositions. He could perhaps hold that the acts and actual motions of our soul to which we have direct access provide an indirect sort of access to the dispositions that produce and are strengthened by these elements. As I indicate in §6.1.2 (2), however, Malebranche emphasized that this sort of access is in no way certain.

25. *Descartes*, 150.

26. Wilson herself focuses on problems for this doctrine deriving from Descartes' treatment of the innate intellectual ideas; see *Descartes*, 156–65.

27. The distinction between free and natural inclinations derives from the *Recherche*; see, for instance, RV I.1, OCM I 47/LO 5. What is not anticipated in this text, as far as I know, is the distinction in the *Traité de Morale* between free and natural habitual dispositions.

28. There is also an immutable order that explicates *rapports de grandeur*, the primary examples of which are mathematical relations (see *Mor.* I.1, 17–19).

29. *Mor.* I.1, OCM XI 19–22.

30. Malebranche thus distinguished *l'amour pour l'Ordre* directed primarily toward God from *l'amour propre* directed primarily toward the self (*Mor.* I.3, OCM XI 44–45). In the third volume of his *Connoissance de soinmesme*, François Lamy had taken Malebranche's remarks in the 1677 *Conversations chrétiennes* to support his own view that the love of God or Order involves no concern for the self and its happiness (see the extract from this volume in OCM XIV 127–28; cf. C VIII, OCM IV 179–80). Though this reading is at odds with the view in Malebranche's text that the just can love only that which makes them happy (C VIII, OCM IV 170–71), it is encouraged to some extent by the suggestion there that love of God and love of self are mutually exclusive. In his dispute with Lamy, however, Malebranche introduced a distinction between two kinds of love of self, the first a "free and disordered love of complaisance" (*libre et déréglé amour de complaissance*), which is directed primarily toward the self, and a natural and ordered "love of benevolence" (*amour de bienveillance*), which is directed primarily toward God (see *Lettres au Lamy* I, OCM XIV 40–42; *Réponse générale*, OCM XIV 176). While Malebranche expressed this distinction in different ways in different works, Montcheuil has concluded that "les différentes notions d'amour restent dans son esprit parfaitement nettes" (*Malebranche et le quiétisme*, 136). For discussions that emphasize more complications deriving from differences among Malebranche's various notions, see Dreyfus, *Volonté de Malebranche*, 300–351; and Gueroult, *Malebranche* 3:260–85. Cf. chapter 5, note 60.

31. Malebranche cited in particular the remark in the Latin edition of the first of Paul's letters to the Corinthians that "I do not judge myself" since although "I am conscious [*conscius*] of nothing in me, I am not justified in this; it is God who judges me" (OCM III 170/LO 637).

32. VFI, c. 23, OA XXXVIII 320/TFI 141.

33. Indeed, he insisted on the prevalance of such error in *Mor.* I.5, OCM XI 67–69.

34. VFI, c. 23, OA XXXVIII 321/TFI 142.

35. See note 24.

36. See, for instance, MC XVI, OCM X 182.

37. See chapter 4, note 75.

38. "Essais," Pt. I, sec. 50, *Phil. Schriften* VI 130/*Theodicy*, 150–51.

39. See Wilson's comment that such talk in Leibniz "seems to go beyond Descartes' relatively bland characterizations of the apprehension of freedom" ("Leibniz and Materialism," 478 n.5).

40. The merely subsidiary nature of this argument from reason is revealed by Malebranche's remark to Arnauld that "it is useless to search for proofs of freedom stronger than those that the inner sentiment that one has of oneself supplies" (OCM VI 164).

41. Cf. *Écl.* I, OCM III 27–28/LO 552–53. Malebranche held that our freedom is also revealed by faith since freedom is required for the system of rewards and punishments

that the Scriptures portend; see *Écl. I*, OCM III 28/LO 554; *Écl.* XV, OCM III 225/ LO 669.

42. See Kenny, "Descartes on the Will," 2–7.

43. *PP* I.36, AT VIII–1 18/CSM I 205.

44. Though Descartes only hinted at this point about the will in *Principles* (see *PP* I.35, AT VIII–1 18/CSM I 204; I.37, AT VIII–1 18–19/CSM I 205), in the *Fourth Meditation* he emphasized explicitly that it is in virtue of the infinity of our will that we "bear in some way the image and likeness of God" (AT VII 57/CSM II 40).

45. In the *First Meditation* Descartes distinguished between action and acquisition of knowledge (AT VII 22/CSM II 15), and he noted in the *Second Replies* that with respect to action, it is not blameworthy to assent to something that is not clearly and distinctly perceived, since "from time to time we must choose one of many alternatives about which we are wholly ignorant" (AT VII 149/CSM II 106. Cf. AT VI 24–25/CSM I 123).

46. Descartes suggested an account of free action in accord with the theory of agent causation when he held that we are the cause of such action. Sometimes he spoke of our faculty of will as the cause, but he indicated that the action of this faculty is simply the action of the mind that has the faculty; see *Sixth Med.*, AT VII 86/CSM II 59; *Third Obj. and Rep.*, AT VII 174/CSM II 123; *To Regius*, May 1641, AT III 372/CSMK 182. For Malebranche's similar view, see *Écl. II*, OCM III 40–41/LO 560.

47. This emphasis on mere spontaneity is reflected in the claim in the *Sixth Replies* that "indifference does not belong to the essence of human freedom, since we are free not only when ignorance of what is right makes us indifferent, but most also when a clear perception impels us to pursue something" (AT VII 433/CSM II 292). Cf. *Second Rep.*, AT VII 166/CSM II 117.

48. For a discussion of the critique of the Jesuits in Gibieuf's work, see Gilson, *Liberté chez Descartes*, 286–316, and Ferrier, *Giullaume Gibieuf et sa philosophie de la liberté*.

49. Other commentators have appealed to these features of the *Principles* in support of the position that the account of human freedom in this text is compatible with the account in the *Fourth Meditation*. See Kenny, "Descartes on the Will," 20–21, and Cottingham, "The Intellect, the Will, and the Passions," 250–52.

50. See the argument for consistency in Kenny, "Descartes on the Will," and in Laporte, "La liberté selon Descartes."

51. *Découverte métaphysique*, 289–90.

52. For a discussion of problems in identifying the date and recipient of the letter, see Kenny, "Descartes on the Will," 24–26.

53. "The Intellect, the Will, and the Passions," 254.

54. OA I 671.

55. For the historical background to the heated dispute between the Jansenists and the Jesuits, see Abercrombie, *Origins of Jansenism*, 161–313, and Gilson, *Liberté chez Descartes*, 337–68. As these works show, the Jansenists often accused their Jesuit opponents of the heresy of Pelagianism while the Jesuits answered that their Jansenist critics had fallen into the error of Calvinism. There is a comprehensive discussion of the issues involved in the dispute between these parties in Carreyre, "Jansenisme."

56. When Mersenne offered as a counterexample to the principle that the cause contains at least as much perfection as the effect that the sun and rain are not as perfect as the animals they generate, Descartes responded that this principle concerns only the

"total and efficient cause" of these effects (*To Mersenne*, 31 Dec. 1640, AT III 274/CSMK 166. Cf. *Second Rep.*, AT VII 134/CSM II 96). The implication here is that sun and rain are causes, though not total and efficient causes, of the animals.

57. Cf. Leibniz's objection in the *Theodicée* that Descartes cannot simply state that the claim that our actions are free seems to conflict with the undeniable fact that they are determined by God's power and leave it at that ("Discours preliminaire," sec. 68–69, *Phil. Schriften* VI 88–90/*Theodicy*, 111–12).

58. "Essais," Pt. I, sec. 60, *Phil. Schriften* VI 135–36/*Theodicy* 156. For similar accounts of Descartes' position, see Leibniz's 1696 response to Foucher's objections to his first published writing, the "New System," in *Phil. Schriften* IV 497–98, as well as his remarks in the 1714 *Monadology*, sec. 80, *Phil. Schriften* VI 620–21/*Phil. Essays*, 223. In a passage from the 1695 "New System" (see chapter 2, note 16) however, Leibniz expressed the different position that Descartes "had given up the game" of providing a solution to the problem of mind–body interaction.

59. As documented by Garber in *Descartes' Metaphysical Physics*, 188–93.

60. *To Mersenne*, 4 March 1641, AT III 324. Hobbes' position, which anticipates Newton's, is that motion is per se directional. For a discussion of the exchange between Hobbes and Descartes on determination, see Knudsen and Pedersen, "The Link between 'Determination' and Conservation."

61. Descartes wrote that his third law governing the impact of bodies, which he took to follow from his conservation law, governs all changes in bodies "at least insofar as they are corporeal; for we are not inquiring now into whether or how the minds of humans or angels have the power to move bodies ..." (PP I.40, AT VIII–1 65/CSM I 242).

62. There is a defense of Leibniz's reading in Gabbey, "The Mechanical Philosophy and its Problems," and in McLaughlin, "Descartes on Mind–Body Interaction." To my mind, however, these works overlook the significance of the escape clause in the *Principles*.

63. After Descartes' death Clerselier inherited his manuscripts from his father-in-law, the French diplomat Hector-Pierre Chanut. Clerselier allowed Leibniz to examine some of these manuscripts when the latter visited Paris in the 1670s.

64. *Clerselier to La Forge*, 4 Dec. 1660, *Lettres de Descartes* III 640–46. Cf. the discussion of this letter in Gabbey, "The Mechanical Philosophy," 23–25.

65. *Lettres de Descartes* III 641.

66. Descartes allowed that only infinite substance can create or conserve a finite substance when he wrote in the *First Replies* that a cause "in which there is such great power that it conserves a thing situated outside itself, has such great power to conserve itself by its own power, and hence exists *a se*." He went on to note that only God could have the superabundance of power required to derive his existence from himself (AT VII 111–12/CSM II 80). Although this claim that only God could create something outside himself does not explicitly exclude the creation of modes, Descartes suggested the need for such an exclusion when he noted in the *Second Replies* that "it is a greater thing to create or to preserve substance than to create or preserve the attributes or properties of substance" (AT VII 166/CSM II 117).

67. *Lettres de Descartes* III 641–42.

68. *Lettres de Descartes* III 642–43.

69. *Lettres de Descartes* III 646. Cf. Descartes' remark to Elisabeth, discussed in §2.3.2 (2), that "those things which pertain to the union of the soul and the body," including the soul's power to move the body, are "known only obscurely by the intellect

alone" though they are "known very clearly by the senses" (28 June 1643, AT III 691–92/CSMK 227).

70. *Lettres de Descartes* III 645.

71. The edition of this conversation, which was recopied by an unknown scribe, is now known as the *Conversation with Burman*.

72. Leibniz to Thomasius, 20/30 Apr. 1669, *Phil. Schriften* I 16. Clerselier is one of the "other Cartesians" mentioned by Leibniz in this letter.

73. The first edition of Clauberg's text was published in 1664, and the fourth and final edition published posthumously in his 1691 *Opera Omnia Philosophica*.

74. *Opera Omnia* I 221. Clauberg cited theses concerning motion found in *Physica Contracta*, sec. 146–47, in *Opera Omnia* I 7. Cf. his more complete account of motion in *Disputatio Physica*, c. 18, in *Opera Omnia* I 97–103.

75. *Opera Omnia* I 221.

76. For a standard scholastic account of this distinction, see Aquinas, *Summa Theologiæ* Ia, Q. 104, art. 1.

77. Cf. MC V, OCM X 49–52.

78. There is one objection open to Descartes, which R. C. Sleigh has offered on Leibniz's behalf, that even if it is granted that we cannot act against God, it does not seem to follow that we cannot act with God's concurrence (see "Leibniz on Malebranche on Causality," 191 n.27). Though Malebranche attempted to establish that the traditional notion of divine concurrence is unintelligible, his main argument for unintelligibility relies on the fact that we cannot move a body in a way that is contrary to the way in which God moves it (besides the remarks in the *Entretiens* and *Conversations*, see RV VI–2.3, OCM II 316–17/LO 450). Nonetheless, I think that Malebranche at least hinted at the argument that since God's conservation of a body determines the position of that body prior to any act of ours, subsequent to that act there is nothing for us to causally determine. According to this argument, the central contention against Descartes is that God cannot cause the existence of a body without at the same time causally determining every feature of that body.

79. Malebranche did emphasize in the *Recherche*, however, that the assent of the will must be distinguished from its consent to love of a good, insofar as "there is but one action of the will with regard to the truth, which is its acquiescence or its consent to the representation of the relation which is between things; and there are two with regard to goodness, which are its acquiescence or consent to the relation of agreement between the thing and us, and its love or impulse toward that thing . . ." (RV I.2, OCM I 53/LO 9).

80. *Défense*, OA XXXVII 648–49. Note that whereas Malebranche's discussion of human freedom focuses on our free consent to falsehood, Arnauld emphasized that God acts in us when we consent to truth. Arnauld himself could not have straightforwardly endorsed the view that God acts in us when we consent to falsehood, for such a view seems to indicate as well that God acts in us when we consent to a false good and, thus, that he is, at least in part, a cause of sin. Arnauld wanted to hold that God permits our sin but does not bring it about by acting in us. Even so, he seems to be committed to denying Malebranche's claim that we have freedom of indifference with respect to our consent to sin, given his view that the very fact that God does not provide us with the efficacious grace that necessitates resistance to sin (in Jansenist terms, the grace *adiutorium quo*) makes it impossible for us to withhold from consenting to sin. Any full discussion of Arnauld's position, however, must take into account his desire to deny the

proposition, declared heretical by Pope Innocent X in 1653, that "there are just men for whom some of God's commandments are impossible, even though they want to fulfill them and try to do so with their existing powers; and the grace that would make them possible is also lacking." For more on Arnauld's attempt to accommodate this declaration, see Carreyre, "Jansenisme," 479–84.

81. Malebranche denied the charge of Pelagianism in his brief remarks on the nature of grace in *Éclaircissement I* (OCM III 32–33/LO 555). He provided a more detailed discussion of his views on grace as a response to Arnauld's remarks in Lettres 5–7 of the *Quatre Lettres de Monsieur Arnauld au Pere Malebranche* (in OA XL 69–110), in the second of his *Trois Lettres de l'auteur De la Recherche de la Verité* (OCM VII 275–98), and also in his *Lettres de Pere Malebranche* (OCM VII 345–467). Malebranche's last published work, the *Réflexions sur la prémotion physique*, is primarily a consideration of the relation between divine grace and our freedom (see §6.2.4 [2]). Incidentally, the fact that Malebranche was willing to discuss the issue of grace while Descartes was not may well explain why Arnauld was more worried by the Pelagianism he perceived in Malebranche's account of freedom than he was by the same feature he perceived in Descartes' account.

82. *Mor.* I.4, OCM XI 56. For a discussion of the view that it is the dominant free disposition that renders us morally worthy, see §6.1.2 (2).

83. For Arnauld's position, see VFI, c. 27, OA XXXVIII 342–46/TFI 164–68; and *Dissertation de Arnauld*, in OA XXXVIII 686–89. In these texts Arnauld was concerned to defend our power to determine our volitions against threats to that power which he took to derive from Malebranche's system. Nonetheless, he insisted that Malebranche's claim that such a power is not determined by God is unacceptable because of its Pelagian overtones. For this objection see, in addition to Arnauld's texts cited in note 81, his *Réflexions* I.9, in OA XXXIX 479–84.

84. One possible counterexample to the claim that Malebranche differs from Descartes on this point is his remark in the *Recherche*, which seems to be in line with Descartes' view in the *Principles*, that a person who fails "to reflect sufficiently on the weakness of his mind" will imagine "that he can penetrate the means that God has to reconcile his decrees with our freedom" (RV III-1.2, OCM I 394/LO 205). Nonetheless, Malebranche went on to say that human reason does not reveal "how it can be that man is free, although God knows from all eternity what he will do" (OCM I 395/LO 206), thus indicating that the problem here concerns the reconciliation of our freedom with God's knowledge rather than with his power. In §6.2.4 (3) I consider his view that we cannot solve the problem concerning divine knowledge because we do not have access to a clear idea of our soul.

85. Cf. RV IV.1, OCM II 12–13/LO 267. Malebranche's language in these passages indicates that he followed Descartes in adopting the position, in line with the theory of agent causation, that we (i.e., our souls) are the cause of our free actions (see note 46).

86. See chapter 2, note 36.

87. *Mor.* I.3, OCM XI 49. See the similar distinction in the 1697 *Traité de l'amour de Dieu*, at OCM XIV 13.

88. Malebranche therefore must deny the possibility of the lowest grade of freedom mentioned in the *Fourth Meditation*, which can be present only when no reason pushes more in one direction than in another (AT VII 58/CSM II 40).

89. Cf. OCM III 24–25/LO 550–51.

90. For a similar reading of the account of consent in *Éclaircissement I*, see Hoffman, "Three Dualistic Theories," 184, and Dreyfus, *Volonté selon Malebranche*, 272–83.

91. Cf. the replacement of the original comment that consent "is only a repose" with the later remark that "this immanent act of my will is only a repose" (OCM VII 567a).

92. In some of the passages I cite, Malebranche spoke as if ideas are perceptual modifications of our soul. On his official view, though, ideas cannot be identified with any modification of finite souls since they can exist only in the divine mind. For more on the official view, see §3.2.1 (2).

93. There are anticipations of this view in passages from the first edition (1678) of *Éclaircissement I* (OCM III 26/LO 551) and also from the fourth edition (1700) of this text (OCM III 22/LO 549–50).

94. For Malebranche's argument against Descartes' view that rest as well as motion has force (e.g., in PP II.43, AT VIII–1 66–67/CSM I 243–44), see RV VI-2.9, OCM II 427–49/LO 514–26.

95. The full title of Boursier's work is *De l'action de Dieu sur les créatures: traité dans lequel on prouve la prémotion physique par le raisonnement. Et où l'on examine plusieurs questions qui ont rapport à la nature des esprits et à la grâce.* For background to this work and to Malebranche's response, see OCM XVI i–xx.

96. Extracts from *De l'action de Dieu* are provided in several of the notes in OCM XVI 199–212. For Boursier's acceptance of Malebranche's conclusion, see OCM XVI 203–4, n.33; for his rejection of Malebranche's account of consent, see OCM XVI 199–200 n.3, and 207 nn.54–55.

97. The implication that the quantity of motion is a modification of body in a strict sense seems to conflict with Malebranche's insistence in the *Recherche* that motion itself involves external relations and thus is a modification of body only in a loose sense (cf. *Écl. XII*, OCM III 174/LO 639–40). Malebranche could perhaps respond by drawing on his own Cartesian view that the quantity of motion in a body is the product of the "mass" (i.e., the size) of that body and the speed of its motion (RV VI–1.4, OCM II 273/LO 426; cf. Descartes' view in PP II.36, AT VIII–1 61/CSM I 240). Since the mass or size of the body is a modification of it in a strict sense, consisting as it does in certain of its internal relations, quantity of motion cannot consist entirely in external relations. Thus, while quantity of motion depends on external relations to some extent, and therefore must be distinguished from shape more than the remarks in the *Prémotion physique* indicate, it can still be distinguished from the direction of motion since it is constituted at least in part by internal relations.

98. In the *Prémotion physique*, however, Malebranche claimed that the "particular and unconsidered determinations" of the motion of the soul are among the *motifs physics* produced by God (Pré. phy., sec. X, OCM XVI 42). Such a claim seems to indicate that certain determinations are physical rather than moral features of the soul, but Malebranche also noted in the same passage that these determinations follow simply from God's creation both of motion toward the good in general and of interesting perceptions. The suggestion is that God is the physical cause of the determinations in the sense that he is the cause of those physical elements that make such determinations inevitable (though not irresistable).

99. In the last of his *Trois Lettres au P. Lamy*, first published in 1699, Malebranche had distinguished between *motifs* such as the desire for happiness that move the soul "invincibly and physically" since one must consent to them, on the one hand, and freely chosen *motifs* that move the soul only morally since one can refuse to consent to them, on the other (OCM XIV 99, 116). Here he was drawing on a rather traditional distinction between moral and physical causes (see the references to this distinction in Garrigou-

Lagrange, "Premotion physique," 58, 65). What is not clearly anticipated in this letter, however, is the more Claubergian distinction between these causes in the *Prémotion physique*.

100. See note 97. Descartes himself held (e.g., in *PP* II.25, AT VIII–1 53–54/CSM I 233) that motion consists merely in changes of relations of distance among bodies.

101. For a similar reading, see Gueroult, *Malebranche* 3:184–87.

102. Cf. the remark in the second edition of the *Réponse* that in suspending consent "I only follow by my act the natural movment that God impresses in me in order to carry me to him" (OCM VII 567).

103. See the passage from Boursier's text in OCM XVI 202 n.17.

104. For a helpful summary of different medieval attempts to address this problem, see Normore, "Future Contingents."

105. Aquinas had insisted that God moves our will to action (see *Summa Theologiæ* Ia, Q. 105, art. 4). Later Thomists spoke more precisely of God's "predetermining physical premotion" of our will. On their view, God's contribution is a "premotion" in the sense that it prepares for the motion of the will, it is "physical" as opposed to "moral" because it is an efficient rather than a final cause of that motion, and it is "predetermining" in the sense that it brings about the very motion that God intends. The use of this technical terminology is explained by the desire on the part of the Thomists to distinguish themselves sharply from the Molinists, who held that God concurs in our action by means of a simultaneous concourse that brings about the effects that God intends only by means of our cooperation. For a discussion of this dispute that is sympathetic to the view of the Thomists, see Garrigou-Lagrange, "Premotion physique." For a discussion of it sympathetic to the view of the Molinists, see Freddoso's introduction to his translation of Molina, *On Divine Foreknowledge*, 1–81.

106. For more on the distinction among these three kinds of knowledge, see Vansteenberghe, "Molinisme," 2119–2122, 2140–41, and especially Freddoso, *On Divine Foreknowledge*, 9–29.

107. *Défense*, OA XXXVIII 376–77.

108. Claims such as these provide some support for the view in the French literature that Malebranche was closer to the view of the Jansenists than he was to that of Molina; see the literature cited in Rodis-Lewis, *Malebranche*, 228 n.3.

109. *On Divine Foreknowledge*, Disp. 52, sec. xi, p. 171.

110. "Divine Omniscience, Omnipotence, and Future Contingents," 15–16.

111. *Rép. Réf. III*, OCM VIII 752–53.

112. Nagel, *View from Nowhere*, 113–20.

113. Nagel, *View from Nowhere*, 117.

114. See note 78.

Bibliography

Citations in the text and endnotes of this book are by abbreviation or short name and title, keyed to this bibliography. I cite primary sources and recent editions and translations containing more than one volume by volume number (roman numeral) and page (arabic numeral), whereas secondary sources containing more than one volume are cited by volume and page (both arabic numerals). Wherever possible I have cited published English translations of passages from Malebranche's writings and other foreign-language historical sources. Unless otherwise indicated, I have provided my own translations from the French or Latin in cases where I cite the original text of these passages. Where I cite only an English translation, I follow the translation in that text. I have provided my own translations of all passages from French secondary sources.

The listing of titles or early-modern writings was no straightforward matter, given the considerable variation in the spelling and capitalization of French and Latin words and the erratic use of French accents in the seventeenth and early eighteenth centuries. I list individuals works by Malebranche according to their titles as they appear in OCM. Unless otherwise indicated, I cite passages from the final editions of those works that have more than one edition. Other early-modern editions are listed by the titles that appear in those editions, many of which are provided in *The National Union Catalog Pre-1956 Imprints*.

I. Works by Malebranche

	C	*Conversations chrétiennes* (1677–1702), in OCM IV.
	D	*Entretiens sur la Métaphysique/Dialogues on Metaphysics*. Trans. W. Doney. New York: Abaris Books, 1980.
Déf. La Ville		*Défense de l'auteur de la Recherche de la vérité Contre l'Accusation de Mons. de la Ville* (1682), in OCM XVII-1 509–31.
Deux Lettres		*Deux Lettres du P. Malebranche Touchant le II. et le III. Volumes des Réflexions Philosophiques et Théologiques de Mr. Arnauld* (1687–1709), in OCM VIII 791–894.

E. mort	*Entretiens sur la mort* (1696–1711), in OCM XIII.
Écl.	*Éclaircissements sur la Recherche de la Vérité* (1678–1712), in OCM III.
EM	*Entretiens sur la Métaphysique et sur la Religion* (1688–1711), in OCM XII.
Lettres au Lamy	*Trois Lettres au P. Lamy* (1698–1707), in OCM XIV 33–121.
Lettre III	*Réponse du Pere Malebranche a la Troisième Lettre de M. Arnauld* (1703–9), in OCM IX 899–989.
LO	*The Search After Truth.* Trans. T. M. Lennon. *Elucidations of the Search After Truth.* Trans. T. M. Lennon and P. J. Olscamp. Columbus: Ohio State University Press, 1980.
MC	*Meditations Chrétiennes et Métaphysiques* (1683–1707), in OCM X.
Mor.	*Traité de Morale* (1684–1707), in OCM XI. Cited by Part and chapter.
OCM	*Œuvres complètes de Malebranche*. 20 vols. Ed. A. Robinet. Paris: Vrin, 1958–78. Cited by volume and page.
Pré. phy.	*Réflexions sur la prémotion physique* (1715), in OCM XVI 33–121.
Quatre Lettres	*Lettres du Pere Malebranche touchant celles de Mr. Arnauld* (1687–1709), in OCM VII 343–467.
Réponse	*Réponse de l'Auteur de la Recherche de la Verité au Livre de Mr. Arnauld* (1684–1709), in OCM VI 3–189.
Rép. Diss	*Réponse à une Dissertation de Mr. Arnauld contre un Éclaircissement du Traité de la Nature et de la Grace* (1685–1709), in OCM VII 471–615.
Rép. Réf.	*Réponse au Livre I des Réflexions Philosophiques et Théologiques de Mr. Arnauld* (1686–1709), in OCM VIII 621–787. Cited by *Lettre*.
Rép. Regis	*Réponse à Regis* (1693–1712), in OCM XVII-1 263–318.
RV	*Recherche de la Vérité, où l'on traite de la nature de l'esprit de l'homme et de l'usage qu'il en droit faire pour éviter l'erreur dans le sciences* (1674–1712), in OCM I–II. Cited by Book or Book-part and chapter.
TL	*Trois Lettres de l'auteur De la Recherche de la Verité touchant La Défense de Mr. Arnauld contre La Réponse au Livre des vrayes et fausses Idées* (1685–1709), in OCM VI 192–339.
TNG	*Traité de la Nature et de la Grâce* (1680–1712), in OCM V. Cited by Discourse and section.

2. Other Historical Sources

Arnauld

Art de penser — *La Logique, ou l'Art de penser*, coauthored with Nicole (1662–83), in OA XLI. Cited by Part and chapter.

Défense — *Défense de M. Arnauld, Contre La Réponse au Livres des vraies et des fausses Idées* (1684), in OA XXXVIII.

OA — *Œuvres de Messire Antoine Arnauld, Docteur de la Maison et Société de Sorbonne.* 43 vols. 1775–83. Rpt. Brussels: Culture et Civilisation, 1967. Cited by volume and page.

Réflexions — *Réflexions Philosophiques et Théologiques sur la nouveau Système de la nature et de la Grace* (1685–86), in OA XXXIX. Cited by Book and chapter.

TFI — *On True and False Ideas, New Objections to Descartes' Meditations, and Descartes' Replies.* Trans. E. J. Kremer. Lewiston: The Edwin Mellen Press, 1990.

VFI — *Des Vraies et des Fausses Idées* (1683), in OA XXXVIII.

Descartes

AT — *Œuvres de Descartes.* 12 vols. Ed. C. Adam and P. Tannery. 1897–1913. Rpt. Paris: J. Vrin, 1964–1975. Cited by volume and page.

CSM — *The Philosophical Writings of Descartes.* 2 vols. Trans. J. Cottingham, R. Stoothoff, and D. Murdoch. Cambridge: Cambridge University Press, 1984–85. Cited by volume and page.

CSMK — *The Philosophical Writings of Descartes.* Vol. III, *The Correspondence.* Trans. J. Cottingham, R. Stoothoff, D. Murdoch, and A. Kenny. Cambridge: Cambridge University Press, 1991.

DM — *Discourse on the Method* (1637), in AT VI. Cited by Part.

H — *Treatise of Man.* Trans. T. S. Hall. Cambridge: Harvard University Press, 1972.

Med. — *Meditations on First Philosophy* (1641–42), in AT VII (1647 French trans. in AT IX–1). Unless otherwise indicated, passages are cited from the second Latin edition (1642).

Notes — *Notes on a Certain Programme* (1647), in AT VIII–2.

Obj. and Rep. — *Objections* and *Replies to Objections*, published with the *Meditations.*

RM — *Rules for the Direction of the Mind* (c. 1628; pub. 1701), in AT X.

PP	*Principles of Philosophy* (1644), in AT VIII–1 (1647 French trans. in AT IX–2). Cited by Part and article. Unless otherwise indicated, passages are cited from the 1644 Latin edition.
PS	*Passions of the Soul* (1649), in AT XI. Cited by Part and article.

Desgabets

Alambic	*Descartes à l'alambic* (c. 1677), in PL 320–25. Cited by Part and article.
Critique de Crit.	*Critique de la Critique de la recherche de la vérité, où l'on découvre le chemin qui conduit aux connoissances solides. Pour servir de reponse à la lettre d'un academicien*. Paris: J. Du Puis, 1675.
Indéfectibilité	*Traité de l'indéfectibilité des créatures* (c. 1654–62), in RD II–III.
PL	Paul Lemaire, *Le cartésianisme chez les bénédictins. Dom Robert Desgabets, son système, son influence et son école, d'après plusieurs manuscrits et des documents rares ou inédits*. Paris: Alcan, 1901.
OR IX	*Œuvres de cardinal de Retz*, vol. IX. Ed. M. R. Chantelauze. Paris: Hachette, 1887. "Dissertation sur le cartésianisme, par le cardinal de Retz et le bénédictin Dom Robert Des Gabets" (c. 1677), 209–360.
RD	*Œuvres philosophiques inédites*. Analecta Cartesiana. 7 vols. Ed. J. Beaude. Amsterdam: Quadratures, 1983–85. Cited by volume and page.
Supplément	*Supplément à la philosophie de Monsieur Descartes* (1675), in RD V–VII. Cited by Part, chapter, and section.

La Forge

LF	*Louis de la Forge: Œuvres philosophiques*. Ed. P. Clair. Paris: Presses Universitaires de France, 1974.
Traité	*Traité de l'esprit de l'homme* (1666), in LF.

Locke

Essay	*An Essay concerning Human Understanding*. Ed. P. H. Nidditch. Oxford: Clarendon Press, 1975. Cited by Book, chapter, and section.

Regis

Réponse au livre	*Réponse au livre qui a pour titre, P. Danielis Huetii, ... Censura philosophiae cartésianae. Servant d'éclaircissement à toutes les parties de la philosophie, surtout à la métaphysique.* Paris: J. Cusson, 1691.
Système	*Système de philosophie, contenant la logique, la métaphysique, la physique et la morale.* 3 vols. Paris: D. Thierry, 1690. Cited by Subject, Book-part, chapter, volume, and page. Though I cite this work by the title of the 1690 edition, which Malebranche read, the particular passages I cite are from the 1691 edition, *Cours entier de philosophie, ou Systeme general selon les principes de M. Descartes contenant la logique, la metaphysique, la physique, et la morale.* 3 vols. 1691. Rpt. Ed. R. A. Watson. New York: Johnson Reprint, 1970.
Usage	*L'usage de la raison et de la foy, ou L'accord de la foy et de la raison, contenant la Réfutation de l'opinion de Spinoza touchant l'existence et la nature de Dieu.* Paris: J. Cusson, 1704. Cited by Book-part, chapter, and page.

Aquinas, Thomas. *Summa Theologiæ.* 60 vols. Ed. and trans. Blackfriars. New York: McGraw-Hill, 1964.

Berkeley, George. *The Works of George Berkeley, Bishop of Cloyne.* 9 vols. Ed. A. A. Luce and T. E. Jessop. Edinburgh: T. Nelson, 1948–57.

Boursier, Laurent-François. *De l'action de Dieu sur les créatures, traité dans lequel on prouve la prémotion physique par le raisonnement des esprits et à la grâce.* 6 vols. Paris: P. Babuty, 1713.

Cicero, Marcus Tullius. *Tusculan Disputations.* Trans. J. E. King. The Loeb Classical Library. New York: G. P. Putnam's Sons, 1927.

Clauberg, Johann. *Opera Omnia Philosophica.* 2 vols. Amsterdam, 1690. Rpt. Hildesheim: Georg Olms, 1968.

Clerselier, Claude, ed. *Lettres de Mr Descartes.* Vol. I, *Lettres de Mr Descartes où sont traitées plusier belles questions touchant la morale, physique, medicine, et les mathematiques.* Paris: Charles Angot, 1667.[New edition of *Lettres de Mr Descartes où sont traitées les plus belles questions de la morale, physique, medicine, etdes mathematiques.* Paris: H. Le Gras, 1657].

———. *Lettres de Mr Descartes.* Vol. II, *Lettres de Mr Descartes où sont expliquées plusieurs difficultez touchant ses autres ouvrages.* Paris: Charles Angot, 1666. [New edition of *Lettres . . . où sont expliquées plusieurs belles difficultez touchant sesautres ouvrages. Tome II.* Paris: H. Le Gras, 1659].

———. *Lettres de Mr Descartes.* Vol. III, *Lettres de Mr Descartes où il répond à plusieurs difficultez sur la dioptrique, la geometrie, et sur plusieurs autres sujets.* Paris: Charles Angot, 1667.

Cordemoy, Geraud de. *Œuvres philosophiques.* Ed. P. Clair and F. Girbal. Paris: Presses Universitaires de France, 1968.

Cousin, Victor. "Procès-verbal de quelques séances d'une société cartésienne qui s'était formée à Paris dans la seconde moitié du XVIIe siècle." *Journal des savants* (février 1842): 97–116.

———. "Le cardinal de Retz cartésien." Parts 1, 2, and 3. *Journal des savants* (mars 1842): 129–44; (avril 1842): 193–210; (mai 1842): 288–315.

———. *Fragments de philosophie cartésienne*. Paris: Didier, 1855.

———. *Fragments philosophiques*. Vol. III, *Philosophie moderne*, pt. 1. Paris: Didier, 1866.

Daniel, Gabriel. *Nouvelles difficultez proposées par un peripateticien a l'autheur de voyage du monde de Descartes. Touchant la connaissance des bestes. Avec la réfutation de deux défenses du systéme général du monde de Descartes*. Paris: V. de S. Benard, 1963.

Descartes, René. *The Passions of the Soul*. Trans. S.H. Voss. Indianapolis: Hackett, 1989.

Faydit, Pierre-Valentin. *Remarques sur Virgile et sur Homere, et sur le stile poetique de l'Ecriture-Sainte, où l'on refute les inductions pernicieuses que Spinoza, Grotius et m^r Le Clerc en ont tirées et quelques opinions particulieres du pere Mallebranche, du sieur l'Elevel & de monsieur Simon*. Paris: Jean and Pierre Cot, 1705.

Fénelon, François de Salignac de la Motte. *Explication des Maximes des Saints sur la vie intérieure*. Paris: Aubouin, 1697.

Foucher, Simon. *Critique de la Recherche de la vérité; oú l'on examine en même-tems une partie des principes de Mr Descartes. Lettre par une academicien*. 1675. Rpt. Ed. R. A. Watson. New York: Johnson Reprint, 1969.

Furetière, Antoine. *Dictionaire universel, contenant generalement tous les mots françois tant vieux modernes, et les termes de toutes les sciences & des arts . . . Seconde ed. rev., corr. et augm. Basgne de Beauval*. 3 vol. La Haye: Arnoud and Reinier Leers, 1701.

Gassendi, Pierre. *Opera Omnia*. 6 vols. Paris: L. Annison and I. B. Devenet, 1658.

Gibieuf, Guilluame. *De libertate dei et creaturae*. Paris: J. Cottereau, 1630.

Hennequin, Amédée. "Les œuvres philosophiques de cardinal de Retz publiées sur un manuscrit d'Epinal." *La France littéraire* 1842, 1 mai: 93–108; 1 juin: 189–200; 15 juin: 232–49.

Hobbes, Thomas. *Leviathan, or the Matter, Forme and Power of a Commonwealth, Ecclesiastical and Civil*. Ed. M. Oakeshott. New York: Macmillan, 1962.

Huet, Pierre-Daniel. *Censura philosophiae cartesianae* [1689]. 4th edn. Paris: J. Anisson, 1694.

Kant, Immanuel. *Critique of Pure Reason*. Trans. N. Kemp Smith. New York: St. Martin's Press, 1929.

La Forge, Louis de. *L'Homme de René Descartes et une traité de la formation du fœtus de mesme autheur, avec les remarques de Louis de la Forge, docteur en medicine, demeurant à la Fleche, sur le traitté de l'homme de René Descartes, & sur les figures par luy inventées*. Paris: Jacques le Gras, 1664.

Lamy, François. *De la Connaissance de soi-mesme*. 4 vols. Paris: A Pralard, 1694–98.

Leibniz, Gottfried Wilhelm. *Die Philosophischen Schriften von Gottfried Wilhelm Leibniz*. 7 vols. Ed. C. I. Gerhardt. Hildesheim: Olms Verlagsbuchhandlung, 1960–61.

———. *New Essays on Human Understanding*. Trans. P. Remnant and J. Bennett. Cambridge: Cambridge University Press, 1981.

———. *Theodicy: Essays on the Goodness of God, the Freedom of Man, and the Origin of Evil*. Ed. A. Farrer. La Salle: Open Court, 1985.

———. *G. W. Leibniz: Philosophical Essays*. Trans. and ed. R. Ariew and D. Garber. Indianapolis: Hackett, 1989.

Le Valois, Louis (pseud. Louis de la Ville). *Sentiments de M. Descartes touchant l'essence et les propriétés des corps, opposés à la doctrine de l'Eglise et conformes aux erreurs de Calvin sur le sujet de l'Eucharistie*. Paris: Michallet, 1680.

Locke, John. *The Works of John Locke*. 10 vols. London: T. Tegg et al., 1823.
Martin, André (pseud. Ambrosius Victor), ed. *Philosophia christiana*. 5 vols. Paris: P. Promé, 1667.
———. *Philosophia christiana, Volumen sextum seu Sanctus Augustinus de anima bestiarum*. Saumur: F. Ernou, 1671.
Molina, Luis de. *On Divine Foreknowledge: Part IV of the Concordia*. Trans. A. J. Freddoso. Ithaca: Cornell University Press, 1988.
Montaigne, Michel Eyquem de. *Les Essais de Michel de Montaigne*. 3 vols. Ed. P. Villey. Paris: Alcan, 1930–31.
Pardies, Ignace-Gaston. *Discours de la connaissance des bestes*. Paris: S. Mabre-Cramoisy, 1672. Rpt. Ed. L. C. Rosenfield. New York: Johson Reprint, 1972.
Plato. *The Collected Dialogues of Plato*. Ed. E. Hamilton and H. Cairns. Princeton: Princeton University Press, 1961.
Poisson, Nicolas-Joseph. *Commentaire ou remarques sur la méthode de Mr Descartes*. Paris: Thiboust, 1671.
Regis, Pierre-Sylvain. *Première Réplique de Mr Regis à la Réponse du R. P. Malebranche, prestre de l'Oratorie, touchant la raison physique de diverses apparences de grandeur du soleil et de la lune dans la horison et dans le meridien (1–16), Seconde Réplique ... touchant la manière dont nous voyons les objets qui nous environment (17–27)*, and *Troisième Réplique (27–28)*. Paris: J. Cusson, 1694.
Rohault, Jacques. *Traité de physique*. 2 vols. Paris: Juré, 1671.
———. *Jacques Rohault (1618–1672): bio-bibliographie*, Ed. P. Clair. Paris: Centre National de la Recherche Scientifique, 1978.
Sévigné, Marie (de Rabutin-Chantal), marquise de. *Correspondance*. Ed. R. Duchêne. 3 vols. Paris: Gallimard, 1972–78.

3. Secondary Sources

Abercrombie, Nigel. *The Origins of Jansenism*. Oxford: Oxford University Press, 1936.
Adams, Robert M. "Berkeley's 'Notion' of Spiritual Substance." *Archiv für Geschichte der Philosophie* 55 (1973): 47–69.
———. *The Virtues of Faith and Other Essays in Philosophical Theology*. Oxford: Oxford University Press, 1987.
———. "Flavors, Colors, and God." In Adams, *The Virtues of Faith*, 243–62.
Alquié, Ferdinand. *Le cartésianisme de Malebranche*. Paris: J. Vrin, 1974.
———. "Sources de la philosophie de Malebranche. Le cartésianisme implicite: influence, sur Malebranche, de la conception substantialiste du sujet pensant." *Etudes philosophiques* 29 (1974): 437–48.
———. *La découverte métaphysique de l'homme chez Descartes*. Paris: Presses Universitaires de France, 1950.
Armogathe, Jean-Roberts. *Theologica Cartesiana: L'explication physique de l'eucharistie chez Descartes et Dom Desgabets*. International Archives of the History of Ideas, no. 84. The Hague: M. Nijhoff, 1977.
Ayers, Michael R. "Mechanism, Superaddition, and the Proof of God's Existence in Locke's Essay." *Philosophical Review* 90 (1981): 210–51.
Bastide, G., ed. *Malebranche: L'Homme et l'œuvre, 1638–1715*. Centre Internationale de Synthèse. Paris: Vrin, 1957.
Battail, Jean-François, *L'avocat philosophe Géraud de Cordemoy (1626–1684)*. The Hague: Martinus Nijhoff, 1973.

Beaude, Joseph. "Desgabets et son œuvre. Equisse d'un portrait de Desgabets par lui-même." *Revue de synthèse* 74 (1974): 7–17.
Biéma, E. Van. "Comment Malebranche conçoit la psychologie." *Revue de métaphysique et de morale* 23 (1916): 127–46.
Blondel, Maurice. *Dialogues avec les philosophes: Descartes, Spinoza, Malebranche, Pascal, Saint Augustine*. Paris: Aubier-Montaigne, 1966.
———. "L'Anticartésianisme de Malebranche." In Blondel, *Dialogues avec les philosophes*, 61–89.
Boas, G. *Dominant Themes of Modern Philosophy*. New York: Ronald Press, 1957.
Bouillier, Francisque. *Histoire de la philosophie cartésienne*. 3rd. ed. 2 vols. Paris: Delagrave, 1868.
Bréhier, Emile. *Études de philosophie moderne*. Paris: Presses Universitaires de France, 1965.
———. "Les 'jugements naturels' chez Malebranche." In Bréhier, *Études de philosophie moderne*, 72–78.
Broughton, Janet. "Adequate Causes and Natural Change in Descartes' Philosophy." In *Human Nature and Natural Knowledge*, ed. Donagan et al., 107–27.
Callot, Emile. *Problèmes du cartésianisme: Descartes, Malebranche, Spinoza*. Annecy: Gardet, 1956.
Carreyre, J. "Jansenism." In *Dictionnaire de théologie catholique*, ed. Vacant et al. Vol. 8, pt. 1, 318–529.
Clair, Pierre. "Louis de la Forge et les origines de l'occasionalisme." *Recherches sur la xviie siècle* 1 (1976): 63–72.
Clarke, Desmond. *Descartes' Philosophy of Science*. University Park: Pennsylvania State University Press, 1982.
Connell, Desmond. *The Vision in God: Malebranche's Scholastic Sources*. Paris and Louvain: Nauwelaerts, 1967.
———. "Gassendi and the Genesis of Malebranche's Philosophy." In *Storia della filosophia moderna e contemporanea*. Douzième congrès international de philosophie. Florence: Sansoni, 1961. 109–13.
———. "La passivité de l'entendement selon Malebranche." *Revue philosophique de Louvain* 53 (1955): 542–65.
Coppleston, Frederick. *A History of Philosophy*, vol. IV, *Descartes to Leibniz*. London: Burns Oats & Washburn, 1958.
Cottingham, John. "A Brute to the Brutes? Descartes' treatment of animals." *Philosophy* 3 (1978): 551–59.
———. *Descartes*. Oxford: Basil Blackwell, 1986.
———. "The Intellect, the Will, and the Passions: Spinoza's Critique of Descartes." *Journal of the History of Philosophy* 26 (1988): 239–57.
Cover, J. A., and Mark Kulstad, eds. *Central Themes in Early Modern Philosophy: Essays Presented to Jonathan Bennett*. Indianapolis: Hackett, 1990.
Cummins, Phillip, and Guenter Zoeller, eds. *Minds, Ideas and Objects: Essays on the Theory of Representation in Modern Philosophy*. North American Kant Society Studies in Philosophy, vol. 2. Atascadero, Ca.: Ridgeview, 1992.
Curley, E. M. *Descartes against the Skeptics*. Harvard: Harvard University Press, 1978.
Davies, Catherine Glynn. *Conscience as consciousness*. Studies on Voltaire and the eighteenth century, vol. 272. Oxford: The Voltaire Foundation, 1990.
Delon, Jacques. "Les conférences de Retz sur le cartésianisme." *XVIIème siècle* 124 (1979): 265–76.

Deprun, Jean. "Madame de Sévigné et les controverses post-cartésiennes: des 'Animaux-Machines' aux 'Ames Vertes.' " *Revue Marseille* 95 (1973): 43–52.
Donagan, Alan; A. N. Perovich, Jr.; and M. V. Wedin, eds. *Human Nature and Natural Knowledge: Essays Presented to Marjorie Grene*. Dordrecht: Reidel, 1986.
Dreyfus, Ginette. *La volonté selon Malebranche*. Paris: J. Vrin, 1958.
Dublanchy, E. "Église." In *Dictionnaire de théologie catholique*, ed. Vacant et al. Vol. 4, pt. 2, 2108–2224.
Ferrier, Francis. *Un oratorien ami de Descartes: Guillaume Gibieuf et sa philosophe de la liberté*. Paris: J. Vrin, 1980.
Flanagan, Owen. *The Science of the Mind*. 2nd ed. Cambridge: The MIT Press, 1984.
Gabbey, Alan. "Force and Inertia in Seventeenth-Century Philosophy: Descartes and Newton." In *Descartes: Philosophy, Mathematics, and Physics*, ed. Gaukroger, 230–320.
———. "The Mechanical Philosophy and Its Problems: Mechanical Explanations, Impenetrability, and Perpetual Motion." In *Change and Progress in Modern Science*, ed. Pitt, 9–84.
Garber, Daniel. *Descartes' Metaphysical Physics*. Chicago: University of Chicago Press, 1992.
Garrigou-Lagrange, R. "Prémotion physique." In *Dictionnaire de théologie catholique*, ed. Vacant et al. Vol. 13, pt. 1, 31–77.
Gaukroger, Stephen, ed. *Descartes: Philosophy, Mathematics, and Physics*. Sussex: Harvester Press, 1980.
Gilson, Étienne. *La liberté chez Descartes et la théologie*. Paris: F. Alcan, 1913.
———. *The Christian Philosophy of St. Augustine*. New York: Random House, 1967.
Gouhier, Henri. *La vocation de Malebranche*. Paris: J. Vrin, 1926.
———. *La philosophie de Malebranche et son expérience religieuse*. 2nd edition. Paris: J. Vrin, 1948.
———. *Études d'histoire de la philosophie française*. Hildesheim: Georg Olms Verlag, 1976.
———. "La première polémique de Malebranche." In Gouhier, *Études d'histoire de la philosophie française*, 64–113.
———. "Philosophie chrétienne et théologie. A propos de la seconde polémique de Malebranche." In Gouhier, *Études d'histoire de la philosophie française*, 114–56.
———. *Fénelon philosophe*. Paris: J. Vrin, 1977.
———. *Cartésianisme et augustinisme au XVIIe siècle*. Paris: J. Vrin, 1978.
Grant, Edward. *Much Ado about Nothing: Theories of Space and Vacuum from the Middle Ages to the Scientific Revolution*. Cambridge: Cambridge University Press, 1981.
Grene, Marjorie. *Descartes*. Philosophers in Context. Minneapolis: University of Minnesota Press, 1985.
Gueroult, Martial. *Etendue et psychologie chez Malebranche*. Publications de la faculté des lettres de l'Université de Strasborg, no. 91. Paris: Les belles lettres, 1939.
———. *Malebranche*. Vol. I, *La Vision en Dieu*. Paris: Aubier, 1955.
———. *Malebranche*. Vol. 2, *Les cinq abîmes de la providence: l'Ordre et l'Occasionalisme*. Paris: Aubier, 1959.
———. *Malebranche*. Vol. 3. *Les cinq abîmes de la providence; la Nature et la Grâce*. Paris: Aubier, 1959.
———. "The Metaphysics and Physics of Force in Descartes." In *Descartes: Philosophy, Mathematics, and Physics*, ed. Gaukroger, 196–229.

Hatfield, Gary. "Force (God) in Descartes' Physics." *Studies in the History and Philosophy of Science* 10 (1979): 113–40.
Hessen, Johannes. "Malebranches Verhältnis zu Augustin." *Philosophisches Jahrbuch* 33 (1920): 52–62.
Hoffman, Paul. "Three Dualist Theories of the Passions." *Philosophical Topics* 19 (1991): 153–200.
Hooker, Michael, ed. *Descartes: Critical and Interpretive Essays.* Baltimore: Johns Hopkins University Press, 1978.
Jackson, Frank, "Epiphenomenal Qualia." In *Mind and Cognition*, ed. Lycan, 469–77.
Jolley, Nicholas. *The Light of the Soul: Theories of Ideas in Leibniz, Malebranche, and Descartes.* Oxford: Clarendon Press, 1990.
———. "Intellect and Illumination in Malebranche." *Journal of the History of Philosophy* 32 (1994): 209–24.
Kenny, Anthony. "Descartes on the Will." In *Cartesian Studies*, ed. Butler, 1–31.
Knudson, Ole, and Kurt M. Petersen. "The Link between 'Determination' and Conservation of Motion in Descartes' Dynamics." *Centaurus* 13 (1968–69): 183–86.
Kretzmann, Norman, Anthony Kenny, and Jan Pinborg, eds. *The Cambridge History of Later Medieval Philosophy: From the Redscovery of Aristotle to the Disintegration of Scholasticism, 1100–1600.* Cambridge: Cambridge University Press, 1982.
Kripke, Saul A. *Naming and Necessity.* Cambridge: Harvard University Press, 1980.
Kristeller, Paul O. *Renaissance Concepts of Man and Other Essays.* New York: Harper and Row, 1972.
———. "The Immortality of the Soul." In Kristeller, *Renaissance Concepts of Man and Other Essays*, 22–42.
Laporte, Jean. *Le rationalisme de Descartes.* Paris: Presses Universitaires de France, 1950.
———. *Etudes d'histoire de la philosophie française au XVIIe siècle.* Paris: J. Vrin, 1951.
———. "La liberté selon Descartes." In Laporte, *Etudes d'histoire de la philosophie française au XVIIe siècle*, 37–87.
Lennon, T. M. "Philosophical Commentary." In N. Malebranche, *The Search After Truth*, 755–848.
Lewis, David. "What Experience Teaches." In *Mind and Cognition*, ed. Lycan, 499–519.
Loeb, Louis. *From Descartes to Hume: Continental Metaphysics and the Development of Modern Philosophy.* Ithaca: Cornell University Press, 1981.
Luce, A. A. *Berkeley and Malebranche.* Oxford: Oxford University Press, 1934.
Lycan, William G., ed. *Mind and Cognition: A Reader.* London: Basil Blackwell, 1990.
McCracken, Charles. *Malebranche and British Philosophy.* Oxford: Clarendon Press, 1983.
McGinn, Colin. *The Problem of Consciousness: Essays toward a Resolution.* London: Basil Blackwell, 1991.
———. "Can We Solve the Mind-Body Problem?" In McGinn, *The Problem of Consciousness*, 1–22.
McLaughlin, Peter. "Descartes on Mind-Body Interaction and the Conservation of Motion." *Philosophical Review* 102 (1993): 155–82.
McLaughlin, Trevor. "Censorship and the Defenders of the Cartesian Faith in Mid-Seventeenth Century France." *Journal of the History of Ideas* 40 (1979): 563–81.
Marion, Jean-Luc, and Jean Deprun, eds. *La passion de la raison: hommage à Ferdinand Alquié.* Paris: Presses Universitaires de France, 1983.
Montcheuil, Yves de. *Malebranche et le quiétisme.* Paris: Aubier, 1946.

Moreau, Joseph. "Malebranche et le spinozisme." In *Correspondance avec J.-J. Dortous de Mairan*, ed. Moreau, 1–98.

———, ed. *Correspondance avec J.-J. Dortous de Mairan*. Paris: J. Vrin, 1947.

Mouy, Paul. *Le développement de la physique cartésienne: 1646–1712*. Paris: J. Vrin, 1934.

Nadler, Steven. "Arnauld, Descartes, and Transubstantiation: Reconciling Cartesian Metaphysics and the Real Presence." *Journal of the History of Ideas* 59 (1988): 229–46.

———. *Arnauld and the Cartesian Philosophy of Ideas*. Studies in Intellectual History and the History of Philosophy. Princeton: Princeton University Press, 1989.

———. *Malebranche and Ideas*. New York: Oxford University Press, 1992.

———. "The Occasionalism of Louis de la Forge." In *Causation in Early Modern Philosophy*, ed. Nadler, 57–74.

———, ed. *Causation in Early Modern Philosophy: Cartesianism, Occasionalism, and Pre-established Harmony*. University Park: Pennsylvania State University Press, 1993.

Nagel, Thomas. *Mortal Questions*. Cambridge: Cambridge University Press, 1979.

———. "Pansychism." In Nagel, *Mortal Questions*, 181–95.

———. *The View from Nowhere*. Oxford: Oxford University Press, 1986.

Normore, Calvin. "Future Contingents." In *The Cambridge History of Later Medieval Philosophy*, ed. Kretzmann et al, 358–81.

———. "Divine Omniscience, Omnipotence and Future Contingents: An Overview." In *Divine Omniscience and Omnipotence in Medieval Philosophy*, ed. Rudavsky, 3–22.

Osler, Margaret J. "Baptizing Epicurean Atomism: Pierre Gassendi on the Immortality of the Soul." In *Religion, Science, and Worldview*, ed. Osler and Farber, 163–84.

Osler, Margaret, and Paul Lawrence Farber, eds. *Religion, science, and worldview: essays in honor of Richard S. Westfall*. Cambridge: Cambridge University Press, 1985.

Pitt, J. C., ed. *Change and Progress in Modern Science*. Dordrecht: D. Reidel, 1985.

Plaisance, D. "Corbinelli auteur de comptes rendus de séances cartésiennes?." *Travaux de linguistique et de littérature* 19 (1981): 39–52.

Pollnow, Hans. "Réflexions sur les fondements de la psychologie chez Malebranche." *Revue philosophique de la France et de l'étranger* 125 (1938): 194–214.

Prost, Joseph. *Essai sur l'atomisme et l'occasionalisme dans l'école cartésienne*. Paris: Paulin, 1907.

Radner, Daisie. *Malebranche: A Study of a Cartesian System*. Assen: Van Gorcum, 1978.

———. "Is There a Problem of Cartesian Interaction?." *Journal of the History of Philosophy* 23 (1985): 35–49.

———. "Rejoinder to Professors Loeb and Richardson." *Journal of the History of Philosophy* 23 (1985): 232–36.

Richardson, Robert C, and Louis Loeb. "Replies to Daisie Radner's 'Is There a Problem of Cartesian Interaction?'" *Journal of the History of Philosophy* 23 (1985): 221–31.

Robinet, André. *Système et existence dans l'œuvre de Malebranche*. Paris: J. Vrin, 1965.

———. "Dom Robert Desgabets: le conflit philosophique avec Malebranche et l'œuvre métaphysique." *Revue de synthèse* 74 (1974): 65–83.

———, ed. *Malebranche et Leibniz: relations personnelles*. Paris: J. Vrin, 1955.

[Rodis-] Lewis, Geneviève. *Le problème de l'inconscient et le cartésianisme*. Paris: Presses Universitaires de France, 1950.

———. *L'individualité selon Descartes*. Paris: J. Vrin, 1950.

Rodis-Lewis, Geneviève. *Nicolas Malebranche*. Paris: Presses Universitaires de France, 1963.

———. "La connaissance par idée chez Malebranche" and "Échange de vues." In *Malebranche*, ed. Bastide, 111–36 and 137–52, respectively.

———. "Polémiques sur la création des possibles et sur l'impossible dans l'école cartésienne." *Studia cartesiana* 2 (1981): 105–23.

———. "Les diverses éditions des discussions entre Desgabets et le cardinal de Retz (corrections d'après un manuscrit inédit)." *Studia cartesiana* 2 (1981): 155–64.

———. "Les limites initiales de cartésianisme de Malebranche." In *La Passion de la raison*, ed. Marion and Deprun, 231–53.

———. *L'anthropologie cartésienne*. Paris: Presses Universitaires de France, 1990.

———. "L'âme et la durée d'après une controverse cartésienne." In Rodis-Lewis, *L'anthropologie cartésienne*, 181–200.

Rorty, Richard. *Philosophy and the Mirror of Nature*. Princeton: Princeton University Press, 1979.

Rosenfield, Leonora Cohen. *From Beast-Machine to Man-Machine: Animal Soul in French Letters from Descartes to La Mettrie*. 2nd edn. New York: Oxford University Press, 1968.

Rudavsky, T., ed. *Divine Omniscience and Omnipotence in Medieval Philosophy*. Dordrecht: D. Reidel, 1985.

Russier, Jeanne. *Sagesse cartésienne et religion: essai sur la connaissance de l'immortalité de l'âme selon Descartes*. Paris: Presses Universitaires de France, 1958.

Schmaltz, Tad M. "Platonism and Descartes' View of Immutable Essences." *Archiv für Geschichte der Philosophie* 73 (1991): 129–70.

———. "Descartes and Malebranche on Mind and Mind–Body Union." *Philosophical Review* 101 (1992): 281–325.

———. "Sensation, Occasionalism, and Descartes' Causal Principles." In *Minds, Ideas, and Objects*, ed. Cummins and Zoeller, 37–55.

———. "Malebranche on Descartes on Mind–Body Distinctness." *Journal of the History of Philosophy* 32 (1994): 49–79.

———. "Human Freedom and Divine Creation in Malebranche, Descartes and the Cartesians." *British Journal for the History of Philosophy* 2 (1994): 3–50.

———. "Malebranche's Cartesianism and Lockean Colors." *History of Philosophy Quarterly* 12 (1995): 387–403.

———. "Descartes on Innate Ideas, Sensation, and Scholasticism: The Response to Regius." Forthcoming in *Studies in Seventeenth-Century European Philosophy*, ed. Stewart.

Searle, John. *The Rediscovery of the Mind*. Cambridge: The MIT Press, 1992.

Sleigh, R. C., Jr. "Leibniz on Malebranche on Causality." In *Central Themes in Early Modern Philosophy*, ed. Cover and Kulstad, 161–94.

Sorell, Tom. *Hobbes*. The Arguments of the Philosophers. London: Routledge and Kegan Paul, 1986.

Specht, Rainer. *Commercium mentis et corporis: Über Kausalvorstellungen im Cartesianismus*. Stuttgart-Bad: Friedrich Frommann, 1966.

Stewart, M. A., ed. *Studies in Seventeenth-Century European Philosophy*. Oxford Studies in the History of Philosophy. Vol. 2. Oxford: Oxford University Press, forthcoming.

Vacant, A., E. Mangenot, and E. Amann, eds. *Dictionnaire de théologie catholique contenant l'exposé des doctrines de la théologie catholique, leurs preuves et leur histoire*. 15 vols. Paris: Letouzey and Ané, 1931–72.

Vansteenberghe, E. "Molinisme." In *Dictionnaire de théologie catholique*, ed. Vacant et al. Vol. 10, pt. 2, 2094–187.

Watson, Richard. *The Breakdown of Cartesian Metaphysics*. Atlantic Highlands: Humanities Press, 1987.
Wilson, Margaret. "Leibniz and Materialism." *Canadian Journal of Philosophy* 3 (1974): 495–513.
———. "Leibniz: Self-Consciousness and Immortality in the Paris Notes and After." *Archiv für Geschichte der Philosophie* 58 (1976): 335–52.
———. *Descartes*. Arguments of the Philosophers. London: Routledge and Kegan Paul, 1978.
Winkler, Kenneth. *Berkeley: An Interpretation*. Oxford: Clarendon Press, 1989.
Yolton, John W. *Thinking Matter: Materialism in Eighteenth-Century Britain*. Minneapolis: University of Minnesota Press, 1983.
———. *Perceptual Acquaintance from Descartes to Reid*. Minneapolis: University of Minnesota Press, 1984.
———. *Locke and French Materialism*. Oxford: Clarendon Press, 1991.

INDEX

Abercrombie, N., 283
Adam, C., 242
Adams, R., 75, 76, 255, 256, 267
Alquié, F., 6, 49, 86, 100, 194, 209, 236, 239, 242, 252, 256, 258, 260, 261, 263, 265, 280
animal spirits, 68, 197, 254, 257, 281
annihilation
  of body, 176–80, 185–87, 279
  of soul, 165, 173–74, 180–84, 276
  substance, 180–84, 275
  See also indestructibility or indefectibility
Anselme of Paris, 257
Aquinas, T., 266, 272, 285, 288
Armogathe, J., 267, 277
Arnauld, A., 4, 7, 8, 10, 11, 16, 21, 27–28, 35–36, 39–40, 41–42, 44, 45, 46–48, 49, 53, 56, 64–68, 71, 73, 74–77, 79–80, 81, 83, 88, 90, 101–2, 110, 111, 114, 117–20, 121, 128, 142–46, 149, 150–51, 153–55, 157, 158, 175, 180, 181, 182, 184, 188, 191, 192, 193, 199–200, 202–5, 206, 209–10, 213, 215, 216, 219–20, 222, 226–28, 229, 231, 233, 235–36, 237, 238, 240, 242, 244, 245, 246, 248, 250, 253, 254, 256, 257, 260–61, 262, 263, 264, 265, 268, 269, 270, 271, 276, 279, 281, 282, 285, 286
atomism and atomists, 238, 271, 277
Augustine, Saint, 4, 40, 44, 45–49, 65, 76, 93, 96, 98, 101–2, 124, 143, 161, 171, 187–88, 189, 194, 199–200, 229, 235–236, 240, 247–48, 249, 259, 273, 278, 279. *See also* color, Augustine on; eternal truths, Augustine on; will, Augustine on
Ayers, M., 138, 266

Bañez, D., 229
Battail, J., 249, 271

beast-machine. *See* soul(s), animal
Beaude, J., 277
Berkeley, G., 72, 77, 255, 271
Biéma, E., 235
Boas, G., 248
Blondel, M., 236, 247
body
  in general, 166–168, 176, 187, 272
  as cause of sensation, 31, 38–39, 44, 49–55, 57–58, 249
  divisibility of, 169, 174, 278
  inner structure of, 38–39, 250–51
  modifications of
    intrinsic vs. extrinsic, 185–86
    senses of, strict vs. loose, 64–65, 116–17, 225–26, 253, 278, 287
  nature or essence of, as extended thing, 3–4, 16–17, 40, 48–49, 53–54, 64–69, 73–74, 91, 128, 139, 141, 147–49, 151–52, 161–62, 184, 189–91, 238, 248, 268
  and space, 167–68, 184–85, 189–91, 269, 270, 272, 277
  See also annihilation, of body; extension; faculties, of body, comparison to soul; knowledge, of body; indestructibility or indefectibility, of body; motion
Bouillier, F., 249
Boursier, L., 224–25, 228–29, 287
Bréhier, E., 252, 262
Broughton, J., 249

Callot, E., 247, 274, 276
Calvinism, 267, 283
Carreyre, J., 283, 286
Cartesian circle, 25, 246. *See also* malicious demon; skepticism, in Descartes and Malebranche

Cartesian dualism, 3, 89–90, 91, 152, 162, 267, 270. *See also* Cartesian trialism; real distinction argument, in Descartes
Cartesian trialism, 88–89, 91. *See also* Cartesian dualism; union, of soul with body
Cartesianism
  content, 22–23, 76, 241
  process, 22–23, 200, 241
  revisionary 10, 233
  simple, 22–23, 241
cause(s)
  of agents, 283, 286
  moral vs. physical, 216–17, 226–27, 287–88
  occasional, 52–53, 228, 249, 251
  secundum esse vs. *secundum fieri*, 217–18
  total, 210–21, 213, 220, 283–84
  univocal vs. equivocal, 250
  See also body, as cause of sensation; God, as cause of bodily motion; occasionalism; will, as cause of bodily motion
certainty, moral vs. metaphysical, in Descartes, 171, 273
Cerquand, 238
Chanut, H.-P., 284
Cicero, M., 169, 272
Clair, P., 249
Clarke, D., 253
Clauberg, J., 193, 207, 215–16, 217–18, 226, 233, 238, 285, 288
Clerselier, C. de, 7, 18, 53, 155, 156, 193, 207, 215, 216–18, 221, 226, 232, 233, 242, 250, 273, 284, 285
cogito argument
  and general principles, 26–28, 242
  infinite regress in, 240
  and memory and reasoning, 23–26, 242
  and personal identity, 29, 243
  See also inner sentiment, and the cogito
color, 53–59, 77, 80, 82–84, 105, 146, 248, 256, 257
  Augustine on, 4, 44, 46–47, 64–65, 248
  relation to extension, 46–49, 105, 137, 262
  See also sensation(s); sensible qualities
Commercy conferences, 9, 30–31, 146, 186–87, 238, 243, 244, 249, 259
compatibilism, 233
Condemnation of 1277, 271–72
Connell, D., 236
consciousness, 162
  direct vs. reflective, 13–19, 21–22, 42, 82–83, 121, 215, 240, 265
  incorrigibility or indubitability of, 19–23, 200–201, 240
  and inner sentiment, 239–40
  relation to thought, 15, 17–19, 40, 176, 199–201, 203, 240, 263
  senses of, moral vs. psychological, 18, 240
  See also expérience, of soul; inner sentiment

Coppelston, F., 248
Corbinelli, J. de, 9, 30, 238, 243
Cordemoy, G. de, 52–53, 161, 238, 249, 271, 277
Coste, P., 268
Cottingham, J., 88, 209, 274, 283
Cousin, V., 238, 277
Cudworth, R., 266
Curley, E., 241

Daniel, G., 240, 273
Davies, C., 240
Delon, J., 238
Deprun, J., 257
Desgabets, R., 7, 8–10, 15, 29–34, 36, 44, 45, 50, 53, 55, 67, 69, 70, 77, 78, 82–83, 90–92, 95, 98, 101, 139, 146–49, 161, 162, 164, 170, 183–91, 209, 233, 237–38, 239, 243, 244, 245, 249–50, 251, 252, 253, 257, 259, 269, 271, 277, 278–79
Diderot, D., 271
dispositions
  of body, 39, 168, 197, 198, 250–51
  habits vs. memory, 197, 260, 281
  of soul, 6, 85, 98, 192–93, 196–201, 202–4, 233, 260, 266, 281
  inner sentiment of, 198, 281
Dreyfus, G., 254, 282, 286
Dublanchy, E., 277
duration
  and eternity, 185–87, 190
  infinity divisibility of, 24
  and bodily motion, 30–33, 185–87, 244, 245, 278

Éclaircissement XI, 6, 35–36, 64–65, 71, 75, 76, 78–80, 81, 82, 84, 85–86, 122, 127, 133, 134, 135–39, 140, 142, 143, 144–46, 148, 152, 157, 158–59, 196, 197–98, 201–4. *See also Recherche* III-2.7
Elisabeth, Princess Palatine, 51, 52, 53, 55, 78, 86, 87, 88, 89, 90, 91, 92, 96, 149, 210, 211, 212, 213, 220, 244, 249, 250, 258, 262, 270, 284
eternal truths, 45–46, 49, 244, 247, 259–60
  Augustine on, 187–88, 278, 279
  God's creation of, 96, 183, 187–89, 264, 278–80
  and the vacuum, 188–89, 279
eternity. *See* duration, and eternity
Eucharist, 139–40, 267
expérience
  of body, 67–69, 202, 253. *See also* knowledge, of body, empirical or experimental
  of soul, 19, 35, 45, 84–92, 135, 196, 258, 265
extension
  idea(s) of, clear, 11–12, 36, 40, 44–45, 48–49, 63, 64–69, 73–74, 77, 78, 84–85, 93, 98, 101, 108, 109, 113, 118, 136–39, 140, 142, 144–

extension (*continued*)
  46, 147–48, 159–62, 174–75, 177, 191, 230, 253, 263, 265, 266, 268–69, 274. *See also* knowledge, of soul, through clear idea of extension
  ideas of, sensory vs. intellectual, 109–11, 262–63
  sensation of, 104–8, 262
  See also body; knowledge, of body

faculties
  of body, comparison to soul, 179–80, 193–96, 264, 275
  of soul, 94–96, 98–99, 179–80, 193–96, 199, 218–19, 259, 260, 264, 275, 283. *See also* imagination; understanding; will
Faydit, P.-V., 257
Fénelon, F., 276
Ferrier, F., 283
Flanagan, O., 22, 76, 241
Foucher, S., 8, 34, 114, 139, 189, 237–38, 252, 264, 279, 280, 284
Freddoso, A., 288
freedom
  and God's knowledge, 193, 212–13, 228–33, 286
  and God's power or preordination, 193, 206–7, 210–13, 218–28, 286
  grades of, 286
  proof of, 3, 11–12, 127, 162, 204–7, 282–83.
  See also knowledge, of soul, properties of
  See also will, consent of; will, indifference of
Furetiére, A., 127, 246

Gabbey, A., 250, 284
Garber, D., 250, 277, 279, 284
Garrigou-Lagrange, R., 287–88
Gassendi, P., 5, 6, 35–40, 95, 129, 131–33, 135, 137, 142, 154–56, 184, 199, 236, 246, 266, 270, 277. *See also* materialism, in Gassendi; skepticism, in Gassendi
Gibieuf, G., 48, 151, 156, 208, 209, 283
Gilson, É., 247, 283
God
  attributes of, 163, 182–83, 189
  as cause of bodily motion, 53–55, 68–69, 178, 213–19, 220–21, 225–27, 233, 250, 254
  as light of soul, 101–3, 124, 259, 260. *See also* idea(s), in God; union, of soul with God
  love of, 276, 282
  and miracles, 254
  power of, 177–78
    absolute vs. ordinary, 163, 165, 167, 170, 181–83, 187, 271–72
    in creation and conservation, 54–55, 186–87, 213–14, 215, 216, 218–19, 226, 227, 233, 271, 284, 285, 288
    ordinary vs. extraordinary, 166–167

  See also eternal truths, God's creation of; freedom, and God's knowledge; freedom, and God's power or preordination; idea(s), in God; knowledge, of God; union
Gouhier, H., 28, 237–38, 243, 247, 249, 273, 276
grace, 7, 198–99, 210, 220, 229, 281, 286
Grant, E., 272, 277
Grene, M., 274
Gueroult, M., 11, 15, 28, 35, 102, 119, 120, 123, 161, 179, 235, 236, 239, 242, 245–46, 250, 252, 255, 260, 263, 275, 282, 288

habtis. *See* dispositions
Hatfield, G., 250
Hardin, C., 251
Hennequin, A., 238
Hessen, J., 247
Hobbes, T., 142, 153–54, 158, 159, 214, 268, 270, 284. *See also* materialism, in Hobbes
Hoffman, P., 257, 280, 286
Huet, P.-D., 240, 241, 242

idea(s)
  clear
    vs. *expérience*, 81–86
    vs. inner sentiment, 36, 42, 63–64, 69–74, 78, 120–24, 142, 143–46, 201–5, 232, 246, 255, 266
    See also extension, idea(s) of, clear; extention, ideas of, sensory vs. intellectual; soul(s), clear idea of
  clear and distinct, 37, 75–76
  efficacious, 97, 99, 100–1, 103–8, 113–114, 115, 118, 121, 261
  equivocal nature of, 70–71, 114–15
  in God, 3–4, 44, 45–46, 70–74, 93, 96–103, 122, 245–45. *See also* God, as light of soul; union, of soul with God
  infinity of, 108, 111–14, 248, 263
  influence of Augustine, 4, 10, 44–46, 96, 98, 101–2, 124, 235–36, 247–48
  innate, 96–99, 112–13, 199, 260, 282. *See also* occasionalism, and innateness
  See also perception(s), as modifications, vs. ideas; pure perception(s), vs. ideas; soul(s), idea(s) of
imagination, 37, 94–96, 106–7, 262, 265–62
immateriality. *See* immortality, and immateriality
  real distinction argument, in Descartes; spirituality; sufficiency thesis, in Descartes
immortality
  de nature vs. *de fait*, 170, 273
  and immateriality, 173
  indirect argument for, 174–75, 178, 190–91
  and indivisibility, 175–76, 179–80, 272
  and personal identity, 170, 176, 190, 274–75
  See also knowledge, of soul, properties of; indestructibility or indefectibility, of soul

indestructibility or indefectibility, 277
  of body, 164, 166–68, 170, 173–74, 176–80, 183–91, 277
  of soul, 163, 174–76, 190–91, 275, 277. *See also* immortality
  of substance, 163–64, 165, 166, 175–76, 178–79, 188–89, 278, 279
  See also annihilation
inner sentiment
  and the cogito, 15, 17, 19, 42–43, 232
  confusion of, 5, 10–11, 15, 36, 42–43, 69, 74, 94, 121–24, 127, 134–36, 142, 162, 195, 201–4, 228, 233–34, 266
  of freedom, 11, 127, 162, 193, 196, 204–7, 211, 228, 231–32
  of pure perception, 94, 108, 120–24
  of sensation, 19–23, 63, 71–78
  of will, 196–98, 200
  See also consciousness; dispositions, of soul, inner sentiment of; *expérience*, of soul; idea(s), clear; knowledge, of soul; pure perception(s), of thought
Innocent X, 286
intellectual perception. *See* pure perception(s); understanding, pure
intelligible extension. *See* extension, idea(s) of clear

Jackson, F., 258, 267
Jansenism and Jansenists, 7, 210, 283, 285–86, 288
Jesuits, 171–72, 173, 209, 273, 283
Johnson, S., 255
Jolley, N., 43, 123, 235, 240, 247, 254, 255, 257, 260, 265, 271
judgment
  natural vs. free, 61–63, 106–7, 252, 262
  and sensation, 60–63, 252. *See also* sensation(s), grades of
  vs. simple perception and reasoning, 23–24, 241. *See also* view, simple, vs. reasoning
  and will, 60–62, 207, 219, 241. *See also* sensation(s), grades of

Kant, I., 27, 29, 161–62, 242, 243, 245, 255, 271
Kenny, A., 283
knowledge
  of body
    a priori, 66–69, 73, 74, 84–85, 123, 145, 251
    empirical or experimental, 66–69, 123, 202, 253
    existence of, 5, 8, 10, 33–34, 35–37, 40, 251–52, 276
    modifications of, 5 16–17, 36, 39–43, 63, 66–69, 78, 91–92, 118, 122–23, 143–45, 180, 233, 265
    nature or essence of, 3, 5, 35–39, 118, 122–23, 128, 136, 139–40, 142–46, 156–62
    See also body; extension
  of God
    existence of, 242
    purposes of, 182–83, 276
    See also God
  of motion, 69, 182–83. *See also* motion
  of soul
    existence of, 3, 5, 6, 8, 10, 15, 16–17, 33–34, 40, 42–43, 205–6, 237, 245
    through clear idea of extension, 45, 77, 78–84, 128, 136–39, 143–46, 174–75, 178–80, 190–91, 196, 256, 265. *See also* faculties, of body, comparison to soul; will, comparison to bodily motion
    modifications of, 5, 10, 35–43, 63, 77–78, 86–92, 122–23, 135–36, 179–80, 205–6, 265
    nature or essence of, 3, 5–7, 10, 35–43, 86–92, 122–23, 128, 139, 142–46, 150–53, 159–62
    properties of, 3, 11–12, 127–28, 133–34, 162, 192, 233, 246, 265. *See also* freedom, proof of; immortality, indirect argument for; spirituality, indirect argument for
    See also soul
  of substance 23–29, 35–40, 182, 242–43. *See also* substance
Knudson, O., 284
Kripke, S., 270
Kristeller, P., 271

La Forge, L. de, 7–8, 9–10, 15, 16–19, 21, 36, 50–55, 89, 97, 146–49, 176, 215–16, 221, 232, 233, 237, 238, 239, 240, 246, 249, 250, 257, 260, 273, 284
La Ville, L. de. *See* Le Valois
Le Valois, L. (pseud. Louis de la Ville), 140, 141, 161, 173, 175, 267, 275
Lamy (or Lami), F., 276, 282, 287
Laporte, J., 167, 249, 283
Lateran Council, 164, 173, 271
laws
  of motion, 68–69, 123, 213–15, 236–37, 251, 254, 276. *See also* motion
  simplicity of, 177–78
  of soul-body union, 99–101, 113–14, 119. *See also* union, of soul with body
  of soul's union with God, 99–101, 113–14, 119. *See also* union, of soul with God
Leibniz, G., 27, 29, 50, 68, 99, 138, 170, 176, 205, 213–17, 237, 242, 254, 266, 268, 271, 275, 276, 282, 284, 285
Lelong, J., 237, 250, 266
Lennon, T., 248, 249
Lewis, D., 258
Locke, J., 29, 56–58, 141, 170, 243, 251, 268,

Locke, (*continued*)
271. *See also* materialism, in Locke; skepticism, in Locke
Loeb, L., 248, 249
Luce, A., 255

Maignan, E., 61, 271
Mairan, J.-J., 275
malicious genius, 23, 25. *See also* Cartesian circle; skepticism, in Descartes and Malebranche
Martin, A. ((pseud.)Ambrosius Victor), 247, 273, 279
materialism, 133, 271
  concession to, in Descartes, 131–32, 153–56, 159–60, 169
  dogmatic refutation of, in Malebranche, 128, 129–34, 140, 174
  eliminativist and reductive forms of, 76–77, 138, 153–54, 233–34
  in Gassendi, 132, 154
  in Hobbes, 142, 153–54, 158, 270
  in Locke, 141, 268
  in Montaigne, 129–33
matter. *See* annihilation, of body; body; extension; faculties, of body, comparison to soul; indestructibility or indefectibility, of body; knowledge, of body
McCracken, C., 248, 249, 254, 271
McGinn, C., 256, 267
McLaughlin, P., 284
McLaughlin, T., 267
Mersenne, M., 149–50, 164–65, 208, 214, 258, 259, 271, 279, 283
Mesland, D., 150, 155, 156, 209, 272
middle knowledge. *See* Molina
mind
  better known than body, doctrine in Descartes, 3, 5, 6, 8–10, 16, 33, 35–43, 129, 142, 180, 238
  or soul, 3, 235
  See also knowledge, of soul; soul
modification(s)
  moral vs. physical, 97–98, 222–26, 260, 287. *See also* cause(s), moral vs. physical
  and substance, 28–29, 30, 48, 178, 186–87, 190, 284
  See also body, modifications of; knowledge, body of, modifications of; knowledge, of soul, modifications of; perception(s), as modifications, vs. ideas
Molina, L. de, 229–30, 288
Montaigne, M. E. de, 129–32, 140–41, 172, 236, 265, 266, 274. *See also* materialism, in Montaigne; skepticism, in Montaigne
Montcheuil, Y., 276, 280, 282
Moreau, J., 275

motion
  determination or direction of, 214–18, 225–27, 284, 287
  nature of, 69, 213–15, 288
  quantity of, 5, 182–83, 214–18, 225, 227, 276, 287
  See also God, as cause of bodily motion; laws, of motion; occasionalism, and bodily motion; will, as cause of bodily motion; will, comparison to bodily motion
Mouy, P., 254

Nadler, S., 235, 238, 248, 249, 250, 260, 263, 267
Nagel, T., 41–42, 76, 232, 247, 256, 267, 288
Normore, C., 229, 230, 288

occasionalism
  and bodily motion, 54–55, 213–18. *See also* God, as cause of bodily motion
  Cartesian rejection of, 50, 53, 175–76, 198, 214–15, 217–18, 249
  and innateness, 97–98, 118. *See also* ideas(s), innate
  and pure perception, 97–98, 113
  and sensation, 50–55, 57–58, 249
  See also cause(s), occasional; God, power of; union
Oratory and Oratorians, 7, 83, 237, 242
Osler, M., 266

Pardies, I.-G., 171, 273, 274
Paris conference, 9, 29–33, 147, 243, 244
Paul, Saint, 201–2, 282
Pelagianism, 209–10, 220, 283, 286
perception(s),
  content of, 263
  as modifications, vs. ideas, 8, 110–14, 236, 238, 245, 260–61, 263, 264, 269, 287
  objective vs. subjective, 108, 117–20, 121–24
  objective reality of, 102–3, 123, 236, 261, 265
  vs. representation, 120–21
  See also consciousness; inner sentiment; pure perception(s); sensation(s)
Peter, Saint, 202, 203
Petersen, K., 283
Plaisance, D., 238, 243
Plato, 107, 260, 264, 279
Poisson, N.-J., 242, 277
Pollnow, H., 265
premotion, physical, 288, 224–26, 229, 288
Priestly, J., 271
primitive notions, in Descartes, 87–90, 249
Prost, J., 239, 249, 277
psychology, 3–4, 265
  Cartesian, 161–62, 233–34
  rational, 11–12, 161–62

pure perception(s)
  vs. ideas, 99–101, 108, 114
  vs. sensation, 9, 11, 43, 92, 99, 102–3, 108, 114–20, 122–23, 241–42, 254, 264
  See also inner sentiment, of pure perception; occasionalism, and pure perception; understanding, pure

qualia, 45, 75–77, 85, 138, 152, 258

Radner, D., 248, 263
real distinction argument, in Descartes, 146, 151–53, 156–60, 169, 271
  See also sufficiency thesis, in Descartes
reasoning. *See* cogito argument, and memory and reasoning; judgment, vs. simple perception and reasoning; view, simple, vs. reasoning
Recherche III-2.7, 3, 4–5, 21, 22, 33, 35, 41, 42, 67, 69–70, 78, 84, 127, 129, 136, 138, 162, 177, 196. *See also Éclaircissement XI*
Regis, P.-S., 9, 10, 33–34, 44–45, 50, 55, 67–69, 70–71, 78, 90–92, 95, 98, 100, 101, 111, 121, 134–35, 146, 161, 176, 186–87, 190, 233, 238, 240, 241, 242, 245, 250, 251, 253, 254, 258, 259, 261, 262, 263, 271, 278
Regius, H., 52, 88, 274
Retz, Cardinal de, 9, 30, 32–33, 82, 186, 187–88, 238, 239, 243, 244, 279
Richardson, R., 249
Robinet, A., 26, 100, 238, 242, 243, 252, 261, 263, 280
Rodis-Lewis, G., 18, 236, 239, 240, 243, 244, 254, 255–56, 258, 263, 269, 278, 280, 288
Rohault, J., 41, 56–59, 172, 238, 241, 251, 274
Rorty, R., 240
Rosenfield, L., 273
Russier, J., 170, 273

scholastics and scholasticism, 47–48, 172–73, 165, 166–67, 172, 248, 250, 285.
Searle, J., 256
sensation(s)
  actual vs. apparent, 20, 34
  adverbial account of, 257
  compound, 61
  confused relations among, 74–78, 102
  grades of, 60–61, 263
  indefinability of, 40–41, 46, 119, 135, 236, 245
  influence of Descartes, 4, 47–49, 59–63, 124
  material falsity of, 81, 160, 257
  strong, weak, and intermediate, 62–63, 15, 117, 232; *see also* sensible qualities, strong, weak, and intermediate
  and teachings of nature, 44, 59–63, 83, 252
  unreliability of 62–63, 115, 117, 248, 266
  See also body, as cause of sensation; extension, ideas of, sensible vs. intellectual; extension,

sensation of; inner sentiment, of sensation; judgment, and sensation; occasionalism, and sensation; pure perception(s), vs. sensation; sensible qualities; spirituality, and sensations or sensible qualities union, of soul with body
sensible qualities
  equivocal nature of 56–59, 251
  as modifications of soul, 4, 45, 56–59, 78–84, 134, 136, 138–39, 146–47
  relations to bodies, 39, 44, 46–49, 56–59, 75, 77, 79–82, 137–39, 147–49, 157–58, 241, 251, 269
  and sensations, 56–59, 79–84, 149, 157–58, 248, 251, 257, 269
  strong, weak, and intermediate, 80–81, 84, 85, 134; *see also* sensation(s), strong, weak, and intermediate
  See also sensation(s); spirituality and sensations or sensible qualities
sentiment. *See* inner sentiment; sensation(s)
Sévigné, marquise de, 82, 239, 243, 257
simple perception. *See* judgment, vs. simple perception and reasoning; view, simple, vs. reasoning
skeptical turn, in Malebranche, 133–36, 140–42
skepticism,
  in Descartes and Malebranche, 245–46, 264
  in Gassendi, 5, 37–38, 131–33, 137, 154–55, 236
  in Locke, 141, 268
  in Montaigne, 129–33, 140–42, 265–66
  See also malicious genius; skeptical turn, in Malebranche
Sleigh, R., 285
Socrates, 262
soul(s)
  abstraction vs. exclusion of body from, 32, 150–52, 154–56, 270; *see also* real distinction argument, in Descartes; sufficiency thesis, in Descartes
  animal, 163, 171–73, 248, 267, 273–74
  clear idea of
    in God, 70–74, 122, 229–30, 255, 258
    no access to, 4–5, 7, 11–12, 40–41, 44–45, 55, 69–70, 78–79, 84–85, 93, 94, 122, 123, 128, 138–39, 144, 156, 175, 178–80, 182, 193, 196, 197, 201–4, 228, 230–31, 237, 254–55, 258
  ectoplasm of, 76, 123, 198
  idea(s) of
    general vs. particular, 70, 230, 254
    in soul, 70–71, 121
  indivisibility of, 163, 168–70, 173–76, 179–80, 272, 275
  inner structure of, 5–6, 38–39, 199–201. *See also* body, inner structure of
  nature or essence of, as thinking thing, 3, 31–33, 34, 39, 139, 161

Soul(s) (*continued*)
  painted, 77, 79, 82–84, 146, 257
  passions of, 17–18, 20, 60, 80, 194, 239, 240–41, 257, 259, 274, 280
  vs. pure mind, 30–31, 33–34, 90–91, 95
  See also annihilation, of soul; cogito argument; dispositions, of soul; *expérience*, of soul; faculties, of soul; freedom; God, as light of soul; immortality; indestructibility or indefectibility, of soul; knowledge, of soul; psychology; spirituality; union; will, as inessential to soul
Specht, R., 249
species, intentional, 47–48.
spirituality
  indirect argument for, 128, 135–36, 140–42, 145–46, 147–49, 154, 159–60, 256–57, 269
  vs. real distinction from body, 127, 139, 149–50
  and sensations or sensible qualities, 134, 136–39, 146–49, 152, 160, 256–57, 269
  See also knowledge, of soul, properties of; real distinction argument, in Descartes; sufficiency thesis, in Descartes
Stillingfleet, E., 268
substance,
  definition of, in Descartes 166, 178
  of God and creatures, 178, 275
  pure, 165, 168
  See also annihilation, of substance; indestructibility or indefectibility, of substance; knowledge, of substance; modification(s), and substance
sufficiency thesis, in Descartes, 150–53, 156, 158, 169, 174. *See also* real distinction argument, in Descartes

Tannery, P., 242
Tempier, É., 271
thought. *See* consciousness; dispositions, of soul; *expérience*, of soul; faculties, of soul; inner sentiment; knowledge, of soul, nature or essence of; perception(s); pure perception(s); sensation(s); soul(s), nature or essence of, as thinking thing; soul(s), passions of; soul(s), vs. pure mind; understanding; will
Transubstantiation. *See* Eucharist
Trent, Council of, 139, 267

understanding
  broad sense, 94, 98–99
  pure, 87, 90, 94–96, 98–99, 124, 277, 281. *See also* pure perception(s)
  See also will, vs. understanding

union
  of soul with body, 7, 30–33, 45, 51–52, 86–92, 93, 101, 103–8, 115, 118–20, 148–49, 194, 244, 246, 249, 251, 254, 258, 259, 272, 284–85. *See also* laws, of soul-body union; occasionalism, and sensation
  of soul with God, 92, 93, 96, 99–103, 106–8, 115, 118–20, 194, 246, 261. *See also* God, as light of soul; laws, of soul's union with God; occasionalism, and pure perception

vacuum, Cartesian argument against, 184–85, 188–90, 277. *See also* eternal truths, and the vacuum
Vansteenberghe, E., 288
Victor, A. *See* Martin
view
  objective vs. subjective, 10, 41–43, 44–45, 72–74, 76–77, 85, 108, 117–18, 122–24, 135, 138, 161–62, 196, 232–33. *See also* idea(s), clear
  simple, vs. reasoning, 23–26, 65–66, 71, 78, 84–85, 144, 253. *See also* judgment, vs. simple perception and reasoning
vision in God. *See* God, as light of soul; idea(s), in God; union, of soul with God
Voss, S., 240

wax example, 34, 36–37, 86, 108, 109–10, 112, 177
Watson, R., 238, 264
will
  Augustine on, 194, 199–200, 229
  as cause of bodily motion, 207, 213–18, 250, 284
  comparison to bodily motion, 193–96, 218–19, 220–21, 223–24, 225–27, 230–31, 281; *See also* faculties, of body, comparison to soul
  consent of, 219–33, 285–86, 288; *see also* freedom
  indifference of, 205, 207–8, 219, 222
  as inessential to soul, 194–95, 280
  and love, 194, 201, 206, 219, 221–22, 280
  natural vs. free, 221–22, 227, 280, 282; *see also* God, love of
  moral worth of, 197–98, 201–4, 286
  vs. understanding, 60, 94, 98, 194–95, 207, 252, 259. *See also* faculties, of soul
  See also dispositions, of soul; inner sentiment, of will; judgment, and will; sensation(s), grades of
Wilson, M., 38, 152, 200, 256, 259, 263, 266, 270, 275, 282
Winkler, K., 255

Yolton, J., 235, 249, 268, 271